ADVANCED GUNSMITHING

ISBN-10: 1-940849-55-1

ISBN-13: 978-1-940849-55-3

ADVANCED

GUNSMITHING

Manual of Instruction in the Manufacture, Alteration and Repair
of Firearms in-so-far as the Necessary Metal Work with Hand and
Machine Tools Is Concerned

With Chapters on the Boring, Rifling and Chambering of Barrels

For Amateur and Professional Gunsmiths

W. F. VICKERY

WITH ORIGINAL ILLUSTRATIONS BY OLIVER B.
HAMILTON

REPRINTED BY MURINE PRESS

WOODLAND, CALIFORNIA

Contents

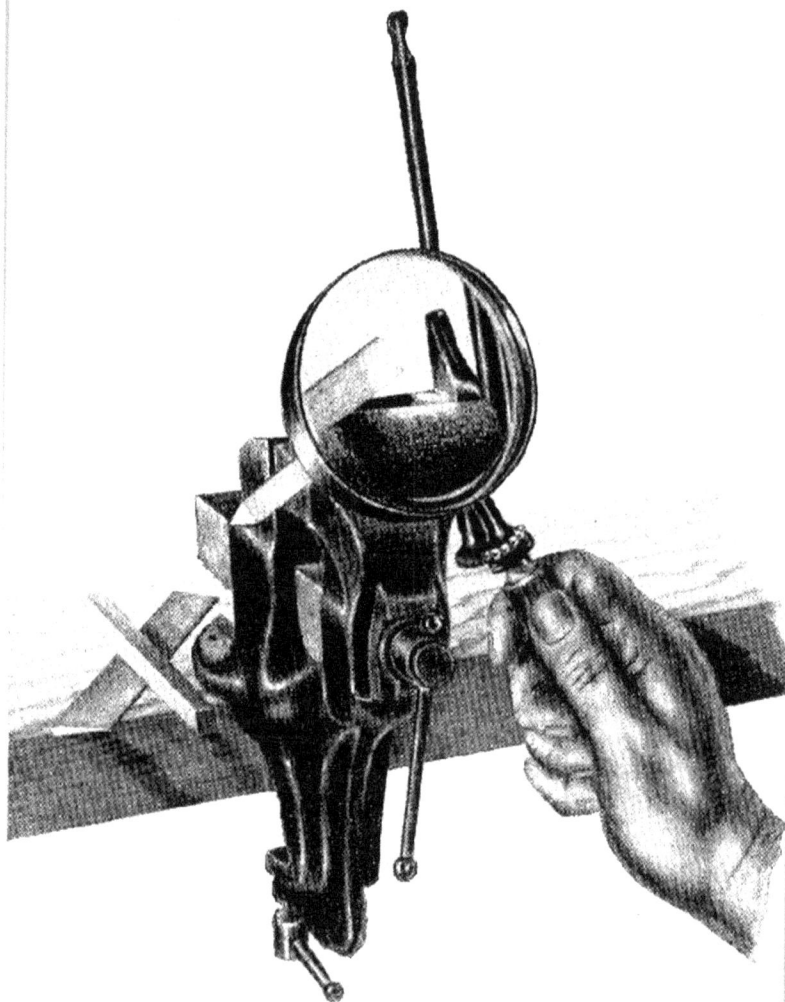

Trigger-Pull Adjustment

Stoning-off the sear-notch face of a Krag cocking-piece, to obtain a cleaner pull. The proper placing of the notch face between the vise jaws, in order to retain a square bearing, is of greatest importance, as is also the frequent use of the magnifying glass to examine progress of the work. Use only fine-grained slip-stones for this operation—the shapes illustrated will all come in useful at times.

The Memory of
That Master Firearms Inventor JOHN M. BROWNING

FOREWORD

The following pages contain a number of suggestions and ideas which I hope will prove useful and instructive to the reader. Some of the operations described may be beyond his equipment or facilities, especially in producing tools necessary to do the work. Should this prove to be the case, this part of the job may be done in a local or the nearest city machine-shop which has the tool equipment to handle it.

I have tried to avoid the highly technical descriptions often found in books of this character, and have given alternate methods where possible, in order to reduce tool requirements. This has resulted in a larger work than was first contemplated — and at that, I have not even touched upon much basic data and many operations essential to the beginner. However, there was no need to do so, as all this information can be found in Frazer's splendid "Elementary Gunsmithing," a companion hook to this one. Also, in order to avoid further duplication, I have restricted the scope of this work to the barreling, chambering, action and other metal-working operations involved and have not touched upon the equally essential operations of re-modeling, stocking, stock finishing and gun stock de sign; these subjects will be comprehensively treated in a companion volume, to come later.

A book of this character is necessarily the work of many men, each of whom contributes some methods of his own, some invention forced upon him by the circumstances, to make the whole. Many of us are located in large cities, where intricate parts of the work can be farmed out to specialists in those lines. Others of us are located in small towns or in the tall timber, where we must produce the work entire and alone. I have endeavored to make this book practicable and workable in either case.

Different parts of the country use different firearms, thus producing specialists in the building and repairing of each type ; rifle, shotgun or handgun — -but the rifle rules as king. A man will specialize also in the branch of the work that appeals to him most strongly, or he may possibly be temperamentally unfitted for doing certain parts of the work. No matter what branch of it he takes up, it will teach him one thing, that is — patience.

Guns have been my love from early days, preceded only by my attachment for tools. This combination soon resulted in alterations to guns in my personal collection and was later followed by desires for guns not in existence but which, after study and experiment, were produced. As my ambitions grew I acquired more tools and machinery, still making or remaking my own guns as a hobby. Friends with whom I hunted soon began to ask for small repairs or alterations to their own guns and I was gradually forced to the point where I gave up all other work to devote my entire time to professional gunsmithing.

I recall that almost twenty years ago I tried to persuade a leading gunsmith to produce for me a .22 caliber rifle, by necking down the .250-3000 cartridge to .22 caliber and re barrelling a Springfield action for it. This man refused to do so, telling me that the cost of the experimental work would be prohibitive and that very likely a balanced load could not be produced for it. What a name he could have made for himself and his business if he had produced that requested rifle at that time ! Remembering this experience, I have often since given my time, with small profit, to experimental work to fulfill someone's desires — and what a satisfaction it was when successful.

If, by the writing of this book, I can kindle in some reader the spark that will enable him to follow in the footsteps of such a man as John M. Browning, I shall feel amply repaid for the work it has involved.

W. F. Vickery
1021 Hays Street,
Boise, Idaho
November, 1939

Chapter 1 SHOP EQUIPMENT

The first requirement of the gunsmith is tools. He never has enough, in fact, no matter how many he acquires a job is sure to turn up on which he could use some tool he does not have. As a great many of these tools must be made by the gunsmith himself, he needs machine tool equipment.

As the lathe is the tool from which all other machine tools derive it is the major machine tool, in fact at a pinch it can be made to perform almost any operation performed by other machine tools, such as drilling, grinding, milling, shaping and profiling.

A lathe of large swing is not required for the gun-smith's work but it should have length enough between centers to handle the longest barrel ordinarily used. Another thing in a lathe that is of great advantage is a hole through the head spindle large enough to take the largest diameter barrel, which is about 1 1/4" usually. Many of the older lathes of ten to twelve-inch swing lack this large spindle hole, but the more modern lathes now have it. Lathes of this type are made by the Sebastian Lathe Company of Cincinnati, Ohio, in ten and twelve-inch sizes, in three price ranges, one of them very moderate. Pratt & Whitney Company of Hartford, Connecticut, make small lathes with large spindle holes in a higher price range, the construction of which are very good.

Chucks are a major requirement of lathes and a good set of collet chucks will pay for themselves in handling round bar work, as they run true with no adjustment necessary as long as they are kept clean.

Jaw chucks are necessary for work of such size or shape that it cannot be held in a collet chuck. These jaw chucks come in two, three or four-jaw models, either with concentric or with independent^ adjusted jaws. At least one four-jaw chuck of the independent jaw type should be on hand, to handle odd shaped work which must be centered. The two-jaw type of chuck is one that is seldom required by the gunsmith but he will find use for a good three-jaw chuck of the concentric type.

A chuck, or rather a pair of them, which the gunsmith should make for himself is the barrel chuck. These are merely a shell of steel or cast iron, threaded to screw onto each end of the head spindle of the lathe.

Through the body of these chucks, at right-angles to their bore, four set-screw holes are tapped, 90-degrees apart and headless set-screws of the socket type are used in each chuck. With these chucks in place on each end of the lathe spindle a barrel may be centered by the set-screws for many operations on either end.

A small and a large drill chuck mounted on taper shanks are necessary for using drills, taps, reamers, laps, etc., in the lathe.

A protractor collar, graduated in degrees, is a very handy item on the lathe spindle. This is made by boring a hole in a piece of steel so that it is a press fit over the lathe spindle at the head or chuck end. Press this piece in place, right up against the shoulder on the spindle, then machine it square with the spindle on its outer face for a distance of about half an inch from the outer diameter of the spindle. From this point to its outer edge, face it back on a bevel of IS or 20 degrees and machine its outer edge true. Polish the beveled face and the edge, then divide the beveled face into 360 degrees. This can be done with a sharp-pointed tool in the tool holder to mark the beveled face and a circular protractor of the cheap variety

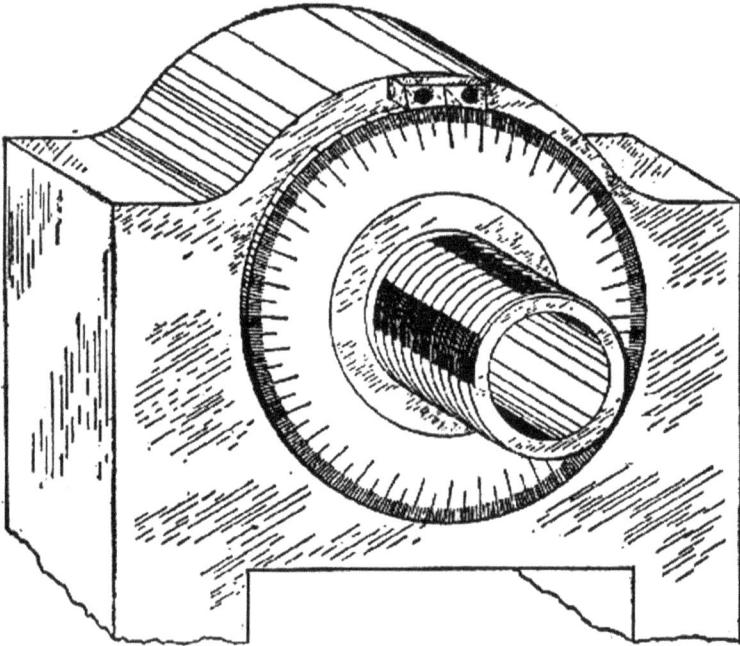

Protractor mounted on lathe spindle.

fastened on a piece of round stock by a machine screw and held in a drill chuck on a taper shank in the lathe spindle. A pointer is fastened to the tail stock spindle so that it almost touches the face of this circular protractor, then the lathe spindle carrying the circular protractor is revolved to bring each division in turn to the pointer and a division is then marked on the beveled face of the protractor machined on the lathe spindle.

This protractor will speed-up a job of facing back the shoulder of a barrel, as when the action is screwed up to the barrel shoulder you can see just what fraction of a complete turn, in degrees, it lacks to come to place and, knowing how many threads per inch the barrel has, this will tell you how many thousandths of an inch to face back the barrel shoulder to bring the barrel and receiver to their proper meeting place.

The protractor can also be used to lay out reamer flutes, flutes in special taps or any other divisions on circular work.

The companion tool to the protractor is the micrometer carriage stop. This is merely a piece of steel or

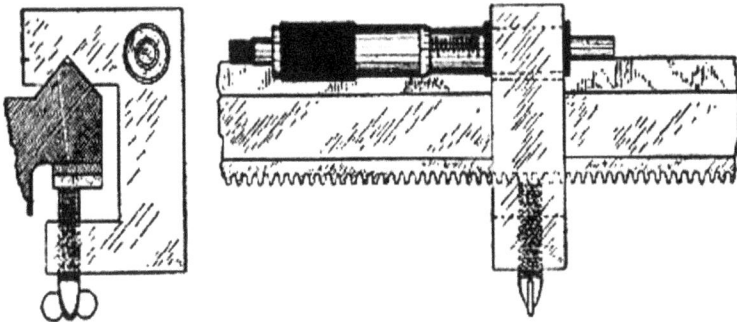

Micrometer carriage stop for lathe carriage. Uses a standard 1″ micrometer head mounted in a shop-made clamp.

cast-iron, with a clamp screw so that it may be fastened to the lathe bed, and with a hole through it parallel to the bed in which a micrometer head can be fastened so that the end of the micrometer spindle comes against the end of the lathe carriage, so that it can measure the travel of the lathe carriage on the lathe bed in thousandths of an inch. These micrometer stops can be purchased from the lathe companies or a micrometer head can be bought for four or five dollars and fitted to a piece of metal cut to fit on the bed of the lathe.

The lathe is equipped at the factory' with pointed or male centers but a useful item is a pair or at least one female center, to support small-diameter work which is too small to carry a hole for a male center. These female centers should be hardened and be polished to a high degree in the 60-degree center-hole. One of these female centers in the tail stock may be used as a ball-bearing center, to reduce friction, by inserting a single ball-bearing in it and bringing the center-hole of the work against the opposite side of the ball. This is especially useful in turning work with the tall stock set over to produce a taper.

Plate I

Making rim cut in chamber end of barrel with lathe — using micrometer carriage stop for depth. In cutting this rim space in the chamber end of a barrel for a rim-type cartridge, the barrel is centered in the lathe chuck so that the bore or chamber runs true. The cutting tool is then brought against the rear end of the barrel and the micrometer carriage slop is brought against the end of the lathe tool carriage and a reading taken from it. The micrometer carriage stop spindle is then backed off the required number of thousandths for the rim space and is locked. The rim space is then cut into the rear end of the barrel until the carriage comes against die micrometer stop.

If possible the lathe should be equipped with a taper turning attachment, for it isn't always easy to set over a tail stock just the right amount nor is it easy to return it to its true center position. The taper attachment is graduated in degrees on one end and in inches on the other end, so it is easily and quickly put in the proper adjustment for the taper desired.

A milling attachment is very desirable on a lathe, if a milling machine is not available. The type sold by the South Bend Lathe Co. is low in price and, with a few homemade attachments, can do a variety of work. A small set of index centers can be made, to be held in the vise of this milling attachment with the centers extending far enough out from the vise so that a reamer or tap can be held in them and fluted with a cutter on a taper arbor in the lathe spindle. As the vise of this milling attachment tilts and is graduated in degrees, taper reamers can easily be fluted with it. A small square-type machine vise, such as those put out under the Yankee trademark by North Bros, of Philadelphia, can be held in the clamp-type vise of this milling attachment and small parts can be held in this vise.

Another attachment for this milling attachment is a second milling attachment with a simple-type live spin- rile mounted on a piece of cast-iron or a piece of heavy steel plate, which also carries a small motor of 0.25 horse power, driving this live spindle with a vee-belt. As this live spindle is to turn slowly, it may be mounted in bronze bearings or Timken roller bearings may be used. The spindle should be about one inch in diameter, so that it will be stiff enough to carry milling cutters on one end. A small pulley is used on the motor shaft and a large one on the. live spindle, of the proper size to give the correct speed to the milling cutter used. This attachment is clamped in the vise of the regular milling attachment and as this vise has an elevating screw, a reamer blank held in the lathe chuck can be fluted with this attachment without removing the blank from the lathe chuck, then after being fluted an electric grinding attachment may be mounted on the lathe in place of the milling attachment and the reamer can be ground.

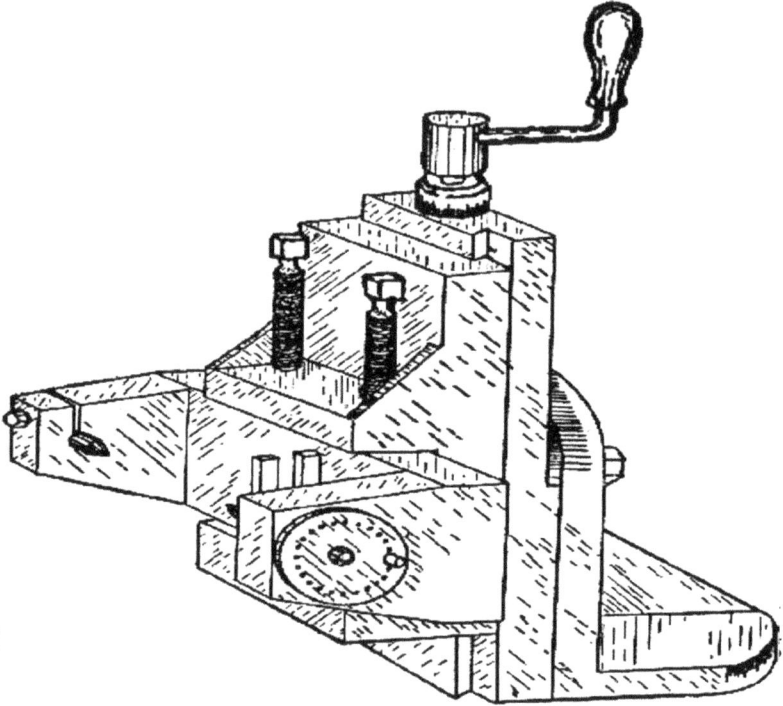

Another lathe attachment that is a necessity for tool making is an electric tool post grinder. As this is a precision tool and works to close limits it pays to have a first-class one. About the best commercial model will be found in the Dumore line of grinders, made by the Dumore Company, of Racine, Wisconsin. These grinders are made in a number of different sizes to fit various size lathes and are built in a wide price range.

A grinder is a necessity to keep the lathe centers in proper condition and these centers, to be accurate, must be ground while in the live spindle of the lathe. Reamers can be ground in the lathe with this tool post grinder and taps can be resharpened with it. A good tool post grinder is also an excellent tool to remove a small amount of metal from the outside of a rifle barrel, either to lighten the weight of the barrel, to change its contour slightly or to smooth up the military-type barrel for refinishing. The grinder leaves no scratches on the surface of the barrel, so that all that is required after grinding the barrel is the fine polishing of it. Grinding the barrel is not nearly so liable to cause it to warp as machining it with a lathe tool bit, because the grinding wheel exerts an almost negligible amount of pressure against the barrel while a cutting bit exerts quite a bit of pressure. Needless to say, the vees, or sliding ways on the top of the lathe bed, should be well protected from the grinding wheel particles when using a grinder upon the lathe. These vees should be well washed with kerosene after using the grinder and should then be recoiled.

An electric tool post grinder can be built in the shop, if you desire, by buying good high-grade annular ball- bearings for the spindle and a high-speed type motor for the power. One advantage of the high-speed type motor is that for the power developed the body diameter of the motor is small and the weight is light. The Dumore Company can supply these motors. The ball- bearings must be of the high-speed type, which are more expensive than the usual run of ball-bearings. The frame of the grinder need not be elaborate but must be stiff enough to be vibration proof. An iron casting of simple design will best accomplish this.

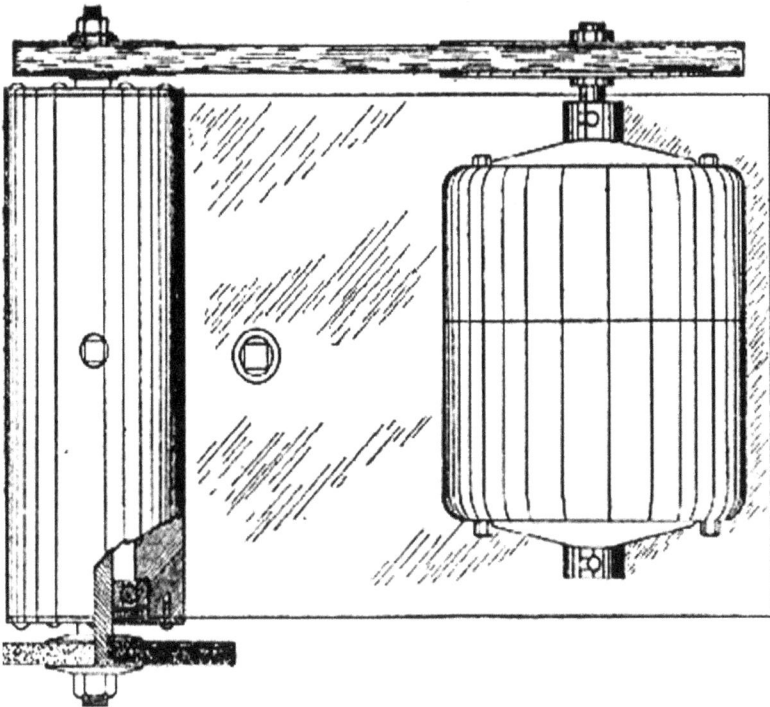

Home-made electric tool post grinder for lathe.

This casting should be as wide as the top of the compound rest of the lathe. A flat portion thick or a trifle less, about as long as the compound rest, with a heavier cylindrical portion large enough to bore out to carry the spindle bearings, extending across one end. This heavier section should be bored out for the spindle and its bearings, at the same height above the top of the compound rest as the height of the lathe centers above the rest.

These spindle bearings must be protected with dust- tight caps on the outer sides and a hole can be bored in the casting between the two bearings and threaded for a plug, so that lubricating oil can l»e introduced be- tween the bearings in the hollow' portion of the casting. The motor is mounted on the flat tail-portion of the casting and before boring out for the spindle bearings, the casting should be surfaced on the bottom. It can be clamped to the tool post slot of the compound rest by a bolt, or two bolts through the flat part of the casting engaging nuts in the tee slot of the rest.

The grinder, whether purchaser! or built in the shop, should be provided with a diamond dresser to shape the wheel, as desired for the work in hand, and to true up the wheel. A wheel must always be trued up when placed upon the spindle, or the wheel will leave chatter marks upon the work and also may burst with disastrous results to the operator.

For reamer and tap grinding, a thin finger-type rest must be provided to support the reamer teeth at the proper height for grinding. This must be adjustable in height so that the correct height may be made for different size reamers, as the tooth is ground in a different position when making a reamer than when sharpening it.

If the reamer is ground on two centers, as is done when it is being resharpened, a coil-spring of the pull- type is fastened to a face plate stud by one end and to the dog on the reamer shank at the other end, so that the reamer is held down against the finger supporting the tooth. In resharpening, reamers are ground on the face of the tooth with a cup wheel and not on top of the tooth, which would reduce their diameter. Taps are ground in the same manner for sharpening, as are formed-type milling cutters.

Another lathe attachment, which is sometimes almost a necessity, is a dial gauge indicator. This mounts in the tool post as a regular tool holder does and carries a pointer with two ball tips, one of which touches the work held in the chuck and the other bears against the plunger of a dial gauge whose face is divided into thousandths of an inch, which on the dial appear about 1/16" apart. With this tool, work can be centered in the chuck either by its outside or its internal diameter, so that it runs dead-true. This is very handy in chucking a barrel, to cut it off one or more threads, to set it back in the receiver and is equally valuable for chucking other finished work, to do additional machining upon it. This tool may also be used in the milling machine to equal advantage in cutting tapers or flat surfaces. The L. S. Starrett Co., of Athol, Mass, and The Brown & Sharpe Mfg. Co., of Providence, Rhode Island, both make this type tool.

The milling machine is a great asset to the gunsmith in making parts, complete actions, integral sight bases on barrels, barrel ribs, extractor cuts, tools and, according to some gunsmiths, in rifling barrels. This operation however, requires a universal milling machine of fairly large size and these run into real money.

If the gunsmith does not wish to buy a universal miller, hut still desires a milling machine of wider scope than the plain type miller, the VanNorman Machine Co., of Springfield, Mass, make a miller called the VanNorman Duplex which has a universal head that can be swung into any position, from vertical to horizontal, so that cuts can be taken at different angles without changing the position of the work in the vise or without a lot of expensive fixtures to hold the work in various positions. These milling machines are made in various sizes, so that the size of machine to fit the type of work can be chosen.

The milling machine is really at its best as a production tool in producing duplicate parts with formed milling cutters, yet it is almost a necessity to the custom gunsmith, saving as it does hours of hand work and at the same time producing a more accurate surface. With it, with the aid of standard cutters and index heads, reamers of all sizes and shapes can be grooved, as well as special cutters to use in the milling machine itself for cutting dovetail sight slots, etc. However, most of the cuts upon gun parts can be accomplished with standard cutters which are supplied in a wide range by cutter manufacturers.

Not many fixtures are required for the milling ma- chine, the two principal ones being a vise to hold the work in machining small parts and a set of index centers for holding reamer and tap blanks to be grooved. Barrels can be clamped directly onto the table of the milling machine, with simple clamps, for machining ribs and sight bases. In some operations a circular milling attachment is desirable, but these are expensive and often there is not enough work of this type to justify them. These are usually hand operated and consist of a stationary base bolted to the table of the miller, upon which is mounted a circular top equipped with slots upon which a vise or angle plate can be bolted. This lop is fitted with a worm gear and worm turned by a hand wheel, so that work can be turned in a circle while being milled.

Of late years a small milling machine is being offered by the Lewis Machine Tool Co., of 550 Fifth St., San Francisco, California. This is a bench type machine and is offered in three price ranges, as rough castings only, as semi-machined and as completely finished. The semi-machined miller can be finished with the aid of a small lathe and a drill press. These machines are for light operations only or for use on small parts, not having length enough to machine a rib the full length of a rifle barrel.

A drill press is, of course, a necessity in the gun shop and today a very wide range of types is available. A heavy drill press is not necessary in the gun shop and usually one with a capacity of half-inch holes is sufficiently large, as most of the drilling required is sight mounting or for action pins, screws and sling swivels. Tool making will sometimes require larger holes than half-inch, but not very often, and these can be drilled in the lathe or taken to a jobbing shop cheaper than the larger drill press of required accuracy can be purchased with its greater power requirements.

Accuracy is the essential requirement in a drill press for the gunsmith and the new, so-called home shop line of drill presses, such as Atlas, Driver, Duro, Delta, etc., with their annular hall-bearing spindles answer this requirement admirably. The highest grade Jacobs chuck should be obtained with the drill. This is the one called the Jacobs Super chuck, which takes drills from the smallest to half-inch. Unless only high-speed steel drills are to be used, buy your drill with a low- speed attachment or it will be too high speed for carbon steel drills. Either the bench-type or the floor-type drill may be chosen, personally I prefer the floor-type, because it is sometimes desirable to drill a hole in the «nd of a piece too long for the bench-type drill.

Twist drills may be obtained in two types; carbon- steel and high-speed steel, and in four size ranges ; the wire gauge, the alphabetical, the fractional inch and the millimeter sizes. The first two size ranges cover small sizes only but the last two go on up through the large sizes.

In smaller sizes, the four size ranges enable you to obtain drills only a very few thousandths of an inch apart, which is a great advantage in drilling holes that arc afterward to be reamed, as it speeds up the work, lessens wear on reamers and gives a better finish to the hole.

Another type of twist drill besides the common two- groove type, is the three and four-groove type, which are more properly reamers than drills, as they are used only for enlarging drilled or cored holes, not for drilling holes in solid stock. They are more properly machine reamers, except that they will remove far more stock than can be handled by a machine reamer, due to their deeper grooves. They leave a very good finish in the hole and can be supplied with pilots, but are only sup- plied in fractional inch sizes from 1/4" up in size.

In connection with drills there is still another type to be mentioned, which is the combination drill and countersink. This is used to cut centers in pieces to be machined on centers in the lathe and is also used to locate holes to be drilled from a center-punch mark. These drills consist of a large straight body tapering on a sixty degree included angle to a small point, which is made like an ordinary twist drill. This point has a short straight body of its own and is sharpened like an ordinary twist drill, the two grooves of which lose their helix when they meet the taper of the larger body which forms the countersink, and run up the taper of this in straight grooves, giving it a cutting edge. These combination drill and countersinks are supplied either double-ended with a straight body, to be used in a drill chuck or are supplied in a single-end type with a taper shank. The double-end type are least expensive and more economical, but the taper-shank type is usually a little more accurate.

High-speed steel drills usually do not pay in the gun shop, as they are much more expensive than the carbon- steel types; more drills are broken than are worn out and high-speed steel drills break about as easily as carbon-steel drills. There is, however, an exception to this statement that high-speed drills do not pay in the gun shop, and that is in the sizes used for drilling holes to mount receiver sights and telescope sight base blocks.

It is often necessary to mount these two items on hardened receivers, and while it is always necessary to soften these receivers at the point at which they are to be drilled, it is not always easy to soften them enough at this point to be easily drilled with a carbon- steel drill, without extending the softening process farther than you wish it to reach. In this case, a high- speed steel drill will easily drill through steel that is still too hard to be drilled readily with a carbon-steel drill, thus making it unnecessary to soften the receiver so completely at this point that the heat used extends farther than you wish. A tap will cut threads in steel that is too hard to be drilled readily with a carbon- steel drill.

An important tool in the gun shop is the tool grinder, and we can again thank the home workshop for the development of annular ball-bearing grinders at a reasonable price. A one-third or one-half horse power electric grinder is sufficient in size and these can be purchased at prices ranging from about eighteen dollars upward, equipped with tool rests and two grinding wheels.

A good investment in connection with the grinder is a disc grinding attachment. This can be purchased with some makes of grinders, but can always be made in the shop if necessary. It is simply a metal disc of seven or eight inches diameter, with a thickened hub, threaded to screw onto one end of the grinder spindle. It must run true as to both face and edge, and discs of either sandpaper or carborundum cloth are cemented onto its outer face with a quick-setting cement. These discs are used, in connection with an enlarged tool rest across the face of the disc, to surface flat metal parts, thinning them down to the point of final hard fitting by hand and at the same time giving them a good finish. For this reason, the work rest should be solid and at exact right-angles to the face of the disc, or should be capable of angular adjustment to the face of the disc. This disc is also useful for finishing the edges of recoil pads fitted to gun stocks. Sandpaper is used on the disc for this purpose.

Cloth or canvas buffers can be used on a grinder spindle for polishing metal parts such as gun barrels and receivers. For this purpose, emery cake is applied to the revolving buffer until the surface of the buff is impregnated with it. This cake can be purchased in various grades from coarse to fine.

One of the most important attachments for the grinder, which is often neglected in the small shop, is a drill sharpening attachment. Remember that the man never lived who can sharpen a twist drill accurately by the free-hand method, and the smaller the drill the harder it is to sharpen. A dull or poorly ground drill will not drill an accurate hole, and ac- curate holes are important in gun work. A properly sharpened drill is not so liable to break, and as broken or very dull drills will not drill holes the salvage in twist drills soon pays for a moderate-priced drill sharpening attachment, as drills are used up to the limit of their life instead of being thrown away and replaced by new ones. These drill sharpening attachments cost from about twelve to twenty-five dollars and the Atlas, a notably good one selling at $21.75, is thoroughly modern in design.

The air compressor, while not a necessity to the gun shop, is a very handy adjunct. A gun action can be blown clean of drill chips from a sight mounting operation in an instant with a good blast of air; the locking lug recesses of a bolt action can be quickly cleaned with it ; parts can be dried with it. A simple nozzle can be made by closing down a piece of copper tubing at one end, drilling a small hole in it and attaching a second piece of tubing to the first near the rear in a vee shape, so that this second piece can be put down into a can of gasoline and the air hose attached to the large end of the first piece to wash out the cuts inside of a receiver to clear them of oil, sand or other grit in no time. .

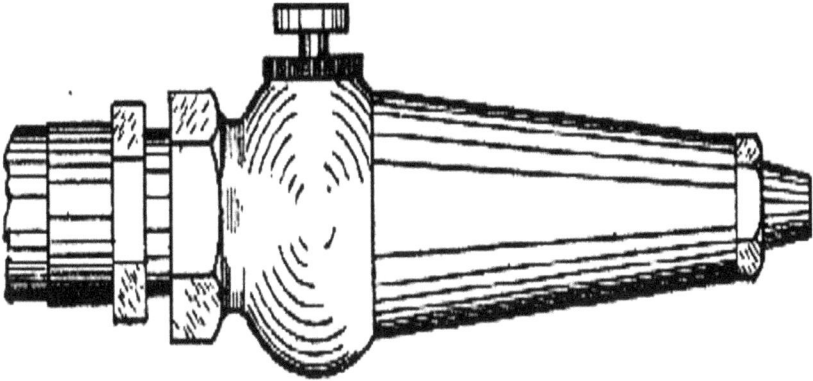

Another use of the air compressor is to supply air to air-driven tools and by that I do not mean riveting hammers but the line of small hand grinders, filers and chisellers made by the Madison Kipp Corp. of Madison, Wisconsin. While the gunsmith does not have much, if any, use of the filing or chisel tools, he can make good use of the grinders. These tools weigh but a few ounces, cost from $7.75 up, handle mounted grinding points of various shapes, also small grinding wheels, polishing points of any shape in small sizes, small metal-cutting burrs and have speeds up to 100,000 revolutions per minute. The exhaust air from these tools is expelled at the lower end, just back of the grinding or cutting point being used, and by this keeps the work blown clean at all times, and this blast also keeps small metal particles away from your face and eyes. They do, however, howl like a banshee and take about four to five cubic feet of free air at 40 to 50 pounds pressure per minute. This air requirement means that it will require the average garage-size compressor to supply them.

Small electric hand grinders with speeds of 25,000 to 27,000 revolutions per minute can be purchased for $16.00 to $18.50 and these tools use the same grinding points, polishing points and cutting burrs as the air grinders mentioned above. These speeds are too high for cutting burrs, except the smallest sizes, for use on steel but these electric grinders can be reduced in speed by foot-controlled rheostats, such as those used on an electric sewing machine. Incidental these burrs, running at low speeds, will drill harder steel than a twist drill will penetrate, but the feed is necessarily slower.

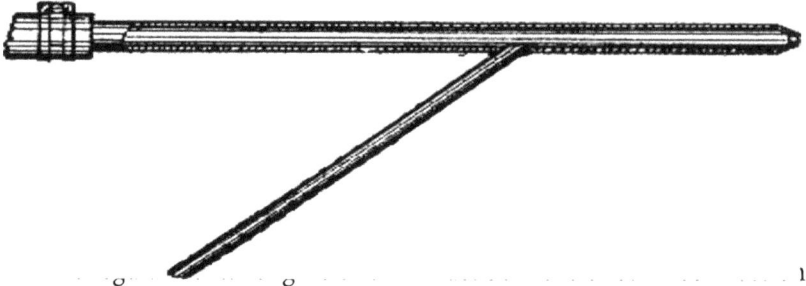

with these power-driven hand tools mainly because of it being exactly the proper speed for using the cutting burrs on steel. Another reason for mentioning it is that it can often be obtained from a dentist for next to nothing, after it has been replaced by a later type. Also old burrs may be obtained from the dentist that arc too dull to cut teeth well but will still cut steel easily. These dental burrs may be purchased new, from dental supply houses, if your dentist cannot supply certain shapes or sizes that you desire. These dental engines do not usually have a high enough speed to do good work on steel with grinding points or with polishing wheels, but can be used for this purpose at a pinch. The flexible-shaft style dental engine made by the Dumore company has a double speed range, one by attaching the shaft directly to the motor spindle and the second by attaching it to a reduction gear at the opposite end of the motor spindle. These give a high enough speed to handle grinding and polishing points in good shape while the low-speed side does well with the cutting burrs.

A hammer attachment may be obtained for these dental engines that changes the revolving motion into a reciprocating one. It looks a good deal like an ordinary dental hand piece and slips onto the lower end of the regular hand piece. It has removable points or tips, and you can shape the ends of these tips into various shaped points, such as sharp point, diamond point, etc., and do matting work on receiver rings, bridges, barrels or anywhere else you wish. The stroke of these hammer attachments can be regulated from light to heavy, after some practice very good work can be done much faster and more evenly than can be done with a hammer and punch.

An arbor press should be in every gun shop, as the gunsmith is sometimes called upon to do experimental work which requires special cartridge cases to be formed in a die, special bullets to be made in dies, all of which work can be done much faster and easier in a press than with a vise. Also, full-length case re sizing is best done in a press and it is very good, with a few shop-made attachments, for regular reloading. Besides this work, the press is needed for press-fits in tool making quite often and for fitting new hinge pins in double or single-barrel shotguns, as well as for straightening or bending work.

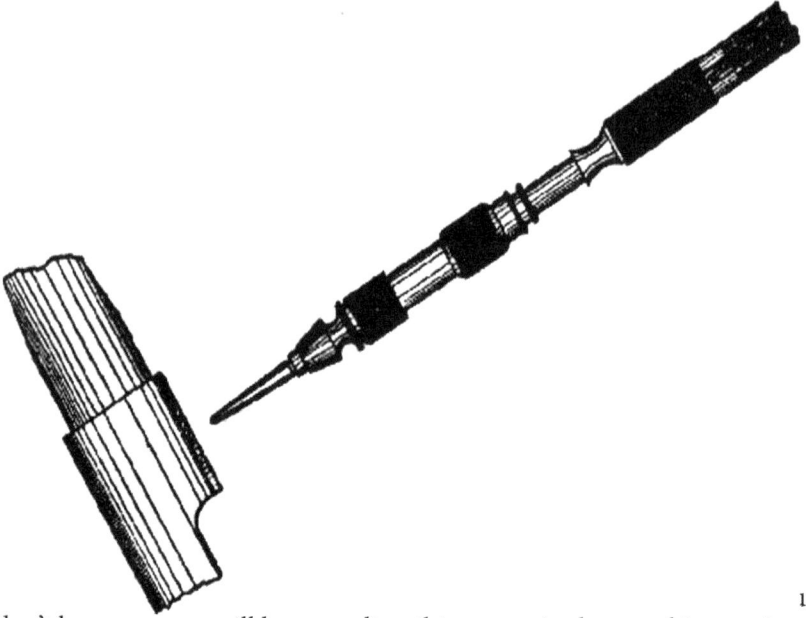

don't have one you will be pounding things on vise bars and jaws ; vises were never designed for this service and won't stand it very long either.

A good vise must be in the shop of course, in fact, two of them, one a regular bench type of good size with swivel base and also a swivel body if possible, so that the vise may be laid upon its side with the jaws vertical instead of horizontal. Until you use a vise of this type, you cannot realize how much superior to the horizontal jaw type it is. The usual thickness of a vise jaw from top to bottom is slightly more than an inch and in working on the ends of rods, barrels or gun stocks this gives you very little gripping power, but your vise jaws are five or six inches in length and when the vise is turned onto its side you have all this length available for grip, which makes a great improvement in the holding power of the vise. There are several makes of vise which can be turned upon its side in this manner.

There is one point to watch for in picking out or fastening a bench vise, and that is to see that the inner jaw-face extends beyond the edge of the bench, so that the bench edge will not interfere with long work held in the vise and extending down toward the floor.

The second type of vise necessary is the so-called machine vise with smooth and square bottom and sides, so that it may be used upon the drill press or milling machine to hold work being machined. These come in a number of sizes and types, a low-cost type of several sizes being made of cast-iron by North Bros. Mfg. Co. of Philadelphia, under the Yankee brand. These vises have swivel bench bases which enable you to use them upon the bench, but by loosening one screw you can remove them from the bench base to use on the drilling or milling machine. Other machine vises made of steel or semi-steel are supplied by various companies ,at various prices. One made by the Chicago Tool & Engineering Co. can be tilted upon its base to various angles. This vise, in cast-iron, sells reasonably.

Vise jaws of various types should he on hand, of copper, lead, brass, fiber and of heavy felt, such as rubbing felt. These felt jaws will last a great deal longer if they are cemented to a fiber back-piece about thick. Rak elite jaws are useful for holding small finished steel parts and they are tougher than the fiber. Old style radio panels will supply the bakelite at low cost, these can be picked up from any junk dealer.

A taper steel jaw should be supplied for the bench vise, to hold barrels and rough stocks or other tapered pieces. If the vise manufacturer does not supply this it can be easily made by taking a piece of steel half an inch or more thick, the same size as the face of the vise jaws, and grinding it on a taper on one side from the center point to a thin edge at each end. To hold it in position at the proper height, drill a 1/4" bole in the lower edge at the center and fit a piece of 1/4" rod into this hole to reach into a 1/4 hole in the top of the vise bar in front of the outer or movable jaw. This will keep the taper jaw at the proper height and it will move back and forth with the movable jaw.

chambering a barrel in the lathe by using a boring tool, the barrel is adjusted in the chucks so that the bore runs true. The compound rest is then set at the proper angle to the center line to bore the chamber at its correct taper, but undersize so that a finishing type chambering reamer can afterwards be used by hand to complete the chamber. All feeding of the boring tool in this operation is done by the compound rest screw.

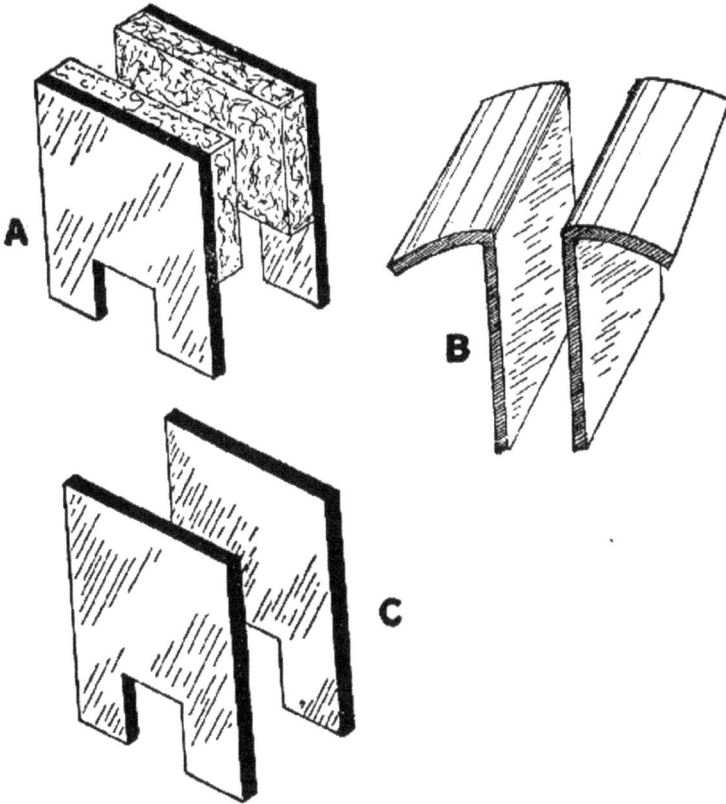

Vice jaws necessary for gunsmithing jobs. A are heavy felt jaws, backed with ¼" red or black hard fibre. B are soft-type jaws, made of lead, brass or copper. C are of ¼" sheet Bakelite.

A rifle barrel clamp, for removing barrels and re- placing them in receivers, can be made of cast-iron, cast at a foundry from a pattern like a pillow block of the split type, with the top or cap fully removable and held to the base half with two steel bolts of at least half-inch diameter. This casting should be bored out in the bearing portion to about 1 1/2" diameter. It should be about 3" wide and 8" to 10" long, so that it can be bolted or clamped to a heavy bench leg or a roof supporting post. Steel bushings 3" long and 1 1/2" outside diameter are bored to a taper to fit the contour of the outside of the rifle barrel to be removed and this bushing is then split lengthwise, so that it matches the split in the pillow block.

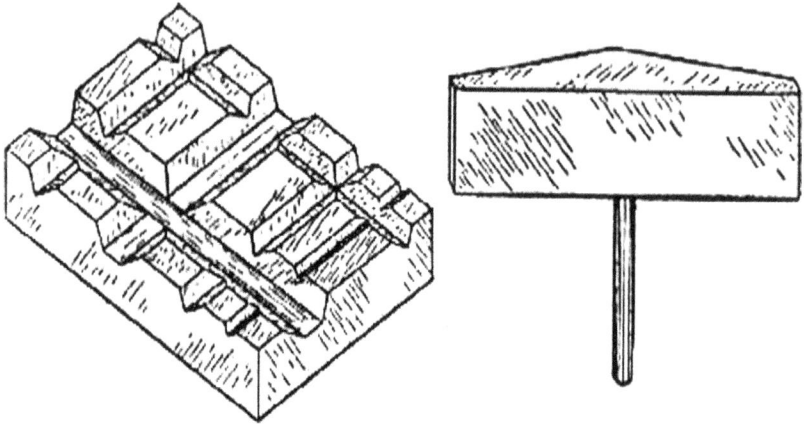

Vee-block jaw for machine-typo vise and swivel-jaw of steel to
hold tapered work.

The gunsmith has more use for the Swiss-type files than for the
ordinary type. The Swiss-type is more expensive but is a longer-lived
file, leaves a better finish and is supplied in more shapes, especially in
the small sizes, than is the common file. Swiss-type files are made in this
country by the American Swiss File & Tool Co. of Elizabeth, New Jersey,
by Nicholson File Co. of Providence, Rhode Island, Heller Bros. Co. of
Newark, New Jersey and Carson-Newton Co. of New- ark, New Jersey.
Imported Swiss files of Antoine Glardon (the famous fish brand) are
supplied by William Dixon, Inc. of Newark, New Jersey.

In looking over these file catalogs you will notice files with double
ends, sharpened at the ends only, called die sinkers rifflers in the small
sizes and silver- smiths rifflers in the large sizes. This type of file will be
found very handy, as they are extremely sharp clear to the point and in
a place where you can get a stroke of only a very short length, where an
ordinary shape or type file will not work, these rifflers cut nicely.

Another advantage of the Swiss-type file of the needle file and escapement file series, is that the edge- type files, three-square, slitting, etc., really
come to a knife edge, which the ordinary file does not do.

A few large flat files of the pillar type, in a fine cut, are necessary for
striking barrels and in squaring flat surfaces, which is very hard to do
with a small file. Remember, in buying files, that the larger the file is the
coarser the cut becomes for the same number. This means that a #2 cut
file in a 6" length is a very much finer cut than a #2 cut in a 12" file.

For laying-out checking on steel surfaces there is a file available called a checking file. It is a flat file and the teeth on it are set in rows, so that when used it cuts shallow grooves. These may be obtained cutting various numbers of lines per inch. They are used only for marking-out the checking, which is then finished and brought up to points with a three-square file of the escapement or needle type.

Files may be bent to various shapes by heating them red-hot and bending the points against a piece of brass, meanwhile keeping the file red-hot. The file may be rehardened by heating it to a cherry-red and plunging it into cold water. If a file is heated in a forge or blow-torch flame, the teeth must be protected to pre- vent them from scaling, which is caused by oxidation.

For protecting the teeth, a substance called file hardening compound is used. This is made of one part pulverized charred leather (put this through a #45 sieve) one and one-half parts fine family flour and two parts fine table salt. Mix these dry and add water slowly while stirring, to avoid lumps, until the mixture is about as thick as varnish, then apply it to the file teeth, before heating the file, in a thin, even coat with a brush and dry it thoroughly over a slow fire. After the file has been heated and bent, brush the compound from the teeth and recoat them, drying the compound as before, then heat the file to a cherry-red and plunge it into cold water to reharden it.

If the file is heated, to be either bent or hardened, in a flame of acetylene gas such as Prest-O-Lite gas, it is not necessary to protect the teeth in any way, as the oxygen is burned in the gas flame and oxidation of the surface of the steel does not occur. If the gas torch has an air line on it for compressed air, be sure that this air line is shut off while heating the file, as this excess air will cause oxidation of the file teeth.

Dental chisels are a useful item to the gunsmith as they are made of very good steel, can be obtained in a variety of shapes and widths and will cut soft steels easily. They are excellent as small scrapers. When front sight ramps are soldered to barrels, they will re- move excess solder squeezed out from under the ramp better than anything else.

Standard-type reamers ma} r be obtained in two types, hand and machine, both types in either solid or expansion. Then the machine reamers two types are also supplied ; the rose reamer, which has no radial clearance ground on the teeth and cuts on the end only ; and the chucking reamer, which has clearance ground on the teeth so that they cut on the sides or edges as well as upon the ends. In the expansion-type reamers there are also two kinds ; the solid blade type, which expands only a few thousandths of an inch; and the Critchlcy type, in which the blades are inserted separately in a solid body, with an expansion of 1/16 ".

Reamers of the above types are supplied in both fractional-inch sizes and in millimeter sizes. These millimeter sizes are made by The Morse Twist Drill & Machine Co. of New Bedford, Massachusetts. The Alvord-Polk Tool Co. of Millersburg, Pennsylvania, supplies Critchley type reamers in sizes as small as 1/4". The Greenfield Tap & Die Corp. of Greenfield, Massachusetts, makes an expansion reamer of the Critchley type from 3/8" up called the Reamrite Hand Adjustable Reamer, in which shims are inserted beside the blades. To sharpen these reamers, you place the shims in front of the blades, insert the reamer in the lathe on centers and proceed to grind the blades circular while the reamer is turning, by using an electric tool post grinder, just as you would grind a shaft to reduce its diameter. After the blades have been ground sharp, the shims are removed from in front of the blades and are placed behind them, thus moving the cutting edge ahead of center and giving a circular relief to the cutting edge of the blades. These reamers can be sharpened by a novice in one-third of the time necessary to sharpen the other type.

Fine taper reamers in wire gauge sizes, called English broaches, are listed by William Dixon, Inc. of Newark, New Jersey. These are fine reamers for enlarging peep sight holes and also for tapering firing-pin holes in single-shot rifle actions and in shotguns, after bushing the breech-block for a smaller firing-pin nose.

Taps and dies are supplied by Greenfield Tap & Die Corp. and in dies, their Little Giant type are the easiest to adjust oversize or undersize, for tight or loose fits.

Gun screws arc a finer thread than standard threads and must either be cut on a lathe or by a special die. Special dies are usually expensive, so it is cheaper to cut these screws on a lathe, unless there are certain sizes quite often in demand and if this is the case a simple button die of the solid type can be easily made.

The screws used to fasten receiver sights and telescope sight base blocks to rifles are at times stripped or broken, or sometimes you need a longer screw of this size for the job on hand, so it is a good idea to make dies for these screws. They are both the same size, #6 screw, and the same thread, 48 per inch, but the receiver sight screws are a U-thread and the scope base screws are a V- thread, so get a new tap for each from a sight company, then cut a disc of tool steel the size to fit a button die holder.

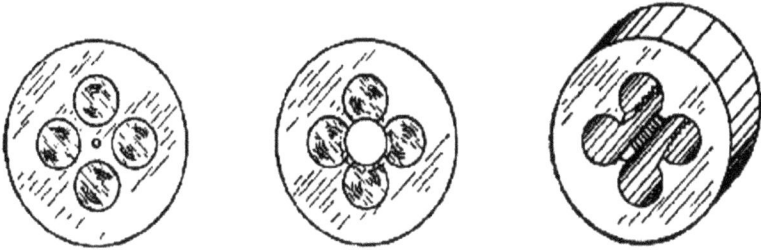

Stages in the making of a button die blank for cutting small receiver and sight base screws.

Mark the center of this disc with a fine prick-punch mark and, using dividers, make a circle around this punch mark of the proper diameter, so that 1/8" holes drilled on this circle will cut into a number 6 screw hole drilled on the prick- punch mark. Make three center-punch marks equidistant from each other on this scribed circle and drill three holes. Plug these holes with soft steel pins and then drill the center hole on the prick- punch mark with a. #32 wire gauge drill. Tap this hole out carefully with one of the new taps, then drive out the soft steel plugs and slightly taper out one side of the die for starting the thread, using a small file for this work. Now heat the die to cherry-red and plunge it into an oil bath, then polish it and heat until it just starts to turn a pale straw color and then quench it again in the oil bath. Make a second die just like this, using the other tap to cut the thread with and you can then turn out any length screw you need in a very few minutes. Dies for other size screws are made in the same way, but for large sizes use a larger drill than 1/8" to drill the relief holes.

Special taps may be made on the lathe and hardened by the same method as was used for the dies. These may be relieved by hand with a file, using a standard tap of the same diameter for a pattern. In making taps on the lathe, cut the grooves first before cutting the thread on the blank, or metal from the grooves will be turned out in a burr into the threads and it is very difficult to clean out. Use drill-rod to make the tap blank, as this hardens easily, and in tempering the taps heat from the shank end, letting the shank and the first thread or two below the shank come to a purple color before quenching.

Hack saws are supplied in several different thicknesses, for cutting and slotting purposes. For ordinary cutting work, the standard high-speed steel blade works the best, and for slotting the L. S. Starrett Co. of Athol,

Massachusetts makes several different thicknesses of blades, thicker than the standard blade, in both fine teeth and coarse teeth, in 8" length. A thinner blade, which is also narrower and about 6" long, can be obtained in most hardware and ten-cent stores, this is good for slotting screws for standard screw-driver blades.

The hack saw frame should be of a heavy type, adjustable for different length blades up to 12" and this is the length blade to buy for ordinary purposes.

For some reason the American screw-driver manufacturers do not see fit to make screw-driver blades of the proper form to fit screw slots, they make the blades wedge-shaped so that very often the screw- driver blade slips out of the slot of a tight screw because of the fact that the greatest pressure comes on the weakest point of the screw slot, the top, instead of at the bottom of the slot as it should. Sometimes the commercial blade may be reshaped by being ground or filed back of the edge, so that the blade is thicker right at the edge than it is just back of the edge, which is the proper shape for a screw-driver blade. After doing this, the blade must usually be retempered, as the degree of hardness and toughness that was proper for the wedge-shaped blade is not proper for it after it has been made thinner, and that is where the trouble be- gins, for often these blades are of a steel that requires some special heat treatment, and while ordinary methods used for carbon-steel will often harden these blades,

Proper shape and construction of screw driver blades.

it is impossible to maintain the correct degree of toughness unless you know the proper temperature at which this steel should be drawn. It is, therefore, usually necessary for the gunsmith to make his own screw-drivers out of octagonal chisel-steel. This is better than drill -rod, as it has a lower carbon content and is not quite so brittle.

The blades of these screw-drivers should be rather short, 2 1/2" to 3" long below r the handles, as this gives you a better control over the screw-driver. The blades should be made in five or six different widths and thicknesses, governed by the size of screw slots in various gun screws, from butt-plate and guard screws down to sight screw's. The handles should be made of hard-wood, treated with linseed oil, and they should be larger than like sizes of commercial screw-drivers. The handles should be fluted to give a good grip and a fairly heavy brass ferrule should be used. The blade is pinned to the handle by a cross-pin through the ferrule, handle and blade. These pins should be of steel and be a tight, driving fit through the blade shank.

The blades should be brought to a low cherry heat and quenched in oil, then polished and heated slowly until the color just changes to blue from purple, upon which they are again quenched in the oil.

A few center-punches and a prick-punch, which is a slender, pointed center-punch, will be required. Commercial punches arc alright if you choose a standard brand.

Straight pin-punches from 1/16 " up to about 3/8" will be necessary to handle action pins of revolvers, some rifles and of shotguns.

Scribers for marking and laying out cuts arc best made of steel phonograph needles, as these are very hard, have true-ground surfaces and are cheap. They may be set in a handle made of 3/16 " rod by drilling a small hole in one end of the rod, holding the needle in the vise jaws and tapping the rod onto the needle, or the needle may be held in a Starrett #162 pin vise. When dull, the needle is discarded and a new one inserted.

These #162 Starrett pin vises are very handy for holding small pins to taper them slightly, reduce them in size or to round the ends of them. They come in four sizes and are inexpensive.

Steel scales in various widths, lengths and thicknesses are a necessity and in this connection I wish to call your attention to the set #423 of Starrett short rules, with handle. These come in four lengths in. this set; 1/4 , 3/8, 1/2 and 1". The handle clamps onto them at any point, making it easy to reach into small spaces to make measurements. A scale graduated in tenths of an inch is very useful in setting scope bases the proper distance apart for target scopes.

A bevel protractor will be needed to measure angles or slope of cartridge cases in body and shoulder and tapers of other items such as ramps, sear angles, etc.

Two small hardened squares are used in setting scope blocks and receiver sights, these should be of high-grade such as Starrett or Brown & Sharpe make.

Starrett makes an adjustable small square, the #457 Improved Die Makers' square, which adjusts eight degrees each way from center, with which it is often possible to take an angular measurement in places into which nothing else will reach. It has two narrow blades, one of which is offset.

A center gauge is necessary for setting thread tools in the lathe and for checking lathe centers when re- grinding them.

Screw pitch gauges will be needed to measure the threads per inch of screws, as gun screws are not standard pitch.

Inside and outside calipers and dividers must be in the tool kit and in this connection I wish to mention that the round-leg dividers arc much easier to sharpen than the flat-leg type.

The smaller sizes of telescoping gauges, such as the #229 Starrett, can be used to measure the diameter of holes from up and the gauge may then be measured by an outside micrometer to get the dimensions in thousandths of an inch for close fits.

In buying micrometers, the one inch size should be graduated to read to ten-thousandths of an inch. The larger sizes will do well enough graduated to thousandths of an inch. Do not buy cheap micrometers, but .buy standard makes, the service they give will be worth the price paid.

For measuring the diameter of small holes the Starrett company make a tapered gauge of eight leaves, graduated to read in thousandths of an inch. This is the number 269, it sells for $5.50 and will measure holes from 1/10" to 1/2". Both Brown & Sharpe and Starrett make an inside micrometer graduated in thousandths of an inch to measure from 2/10 " to 1". This is operated by turning the spindle, just as an outside micrometer is, but it reads in the opposite direction. These each sell for $14.00 and are well worth their cost.

Parallel clamps are used to hold receiver sight bases and scope bases in place, while drilling holes for screws. They are also handy for other uses in the shop, such as holding small parts for filing, by putting the small part in the clamp and putting the clamp in a vise. The small jaws of die clamp make it easier to get at the part for filing than if the part is placed directly in the vise jaws.

A pair of parallels or true-blocks make the best thing to place beneath the action of bolt-action rifles to square it up on the surface plate for mounting receiver sights, scope blocks or lining up a front sight straight.

Vee-blocks are used beneath the barrel, in connection with the parallels under the action on the surface plate. Vee-blocks are also used beneath the barrel on the drill press, or for holding any round stock to be drilled. One of these vee-blocks should be equipped with a clamp, so that work placed in them will stay in position.

A good inexpensive surface plate can be made from a piece of heavy plate-glass. Get a piece eight or ten inches wide and forty inches long and mount this on a piece of flat board, placing padding beneath the glass next to the board. Felt can be used for this padding, or newspapers do very well if used in thicknesses of ten or twelve pages, simply to take up small inequalities in the board. The glass can be held in place with a few wire lath nails driven in carefully around the edge, so that one side of the nail heads extend just over the top of the glass.

A good powerful magnifying glass is a very good thing to have to examine or measure fine threads, sear and hammer surfaces, bullet bases, etc. Swift & Anderson of Boston make a two-lens glass of ten diopters power with a pen-type flashlight inserted in one side of the barrel to act as a handle and to supply light for the* subject being examined.

Small flat, square and triangular carborundum stones may be bought from the Carborundum Company and white Arkansas stones, either soft or hard, can be bought from the Norton Company. These are used for hard fitting of small parts and for dressing sears and hammers in adjusting trigger-pulls.

Abrasive cloth in rolls 1" to wide is about the most economical way to buy it, but you will need a few sheets of the abrasive cloth also in the standard 8 1/2" X 11" size. These come in almost any grit, down to crocus cloth. The wet or dry black sandpaper sold for automobile finish work is fast cutting and gives a smooth finish also and it is cheaper than carborundum cloth, but the backing, of course, is not so strong.

Emery cake can be bought in various grits for use in muslin or canvas buffing wheels. Carborundum powder in various grain sizes and flour of emery are used for lapping. Automobile valve-grinding compound makes a fast cutting lapping or polishing compound, but is too fast for use in barrels, although it docs well on bolt smoothing jobs.

The gas welding torch is a better tool on almost all gun work than the electric welding machine. The gas torch is better for joining two pieces of metal, as it heats the metal more thoroughly and makes a better bond thereby, for the electric welder heats only the point of contact in the small sizes applicable to gun work. On the other hand the electric welder of the spot-weld type is, perhaps, a little better for building up parts, especially hard parts, for the reason that it does not spread its heat so far as the gas torch does. Another drawback to the small type electric welder is that it often leaves a scale as hard as glass, that can be machined only by grinding. As much of the welding work on gun parts is done on very small parts, the airplane-type of gas torch is the easiest to handle on account of the fact that it can be cut down to a smaller flame than the larger type torch.

A small forge can be used for much work in the gun shop such as case-hardening, bending jobs, etc., but is not so good as a gas furnace for tempering work.

A gas furnace is usually an expensive item to buy, but a very service-able one can be built cheaply by experimenting somewhat on the type and size burner necessary. The furnace itself is built of firebrick, cemented with asbestos. A sheet-iron form is bent to the shape of a half-circle and the bricks are laid over this to form the upper part of the furnace. This is set on a fire brick and asbestos cement base and the steel form is withdrawn after the cement has set. One end is bricked and cemented up, leaving a small hole for an outlet flue pipe connected to a chimney. The other end is fitted with a steel door faced on the inside with asbestos cement in or on expanded metal lath. After the cement is all set hard, the whole interior should be lined with fire-clay.

The burner may be made of iron pipe, a line of pipe running along each side of the furnace, inside, about two inches away from the wall and from the floor. These pipes are connected to a supply-line. Along the sides of the J4" burner-pipes a line of small holes should be drilled, facing inward and upward to- ward the center of the furnace, and here is where the experimental work comes in, getting these holes the proper size for the furnace you build. Your gas company may be helpful in designing this burner. The inner ends of these burner-pipes arc capped, of course, and the connection to the supply-line should be on the outside of the furnace, with a good needle-valve between the supply line and each burner-pipe, so that proper adjustment of the gas supply can be made. Cast-iron pipe with screw caps on the ends can be used to place parts in while being tempered as they should not be exposed directly to the flame. For pack-hardening, parts are packed in charcoal, bone or whatever you use inside this cast-iron pipe. The caps of this cast- iron pipe should have a few small vent holes drilled in them on the upper side. Cast-iron pots can also be used inside this furnace, with sand, lead, nitre or other mediums in them, in which to place small parts. The cast-iron pipe and the pots can be set up on firebrick, or on cast-iron holders, to bring them about to the center of the furnace or a little above center. The size of the furnace you build will depend upon the largest size items you think you will ever wish to put into it for heat treatment. If you think you will wish to use high temperatures of two thousand degrees or more, an air-blast must be added to the gas flame. This can be run into each y 2 " burner-line after the line leaves the y supply-pipe and each air line should have a needle valve on it for fine adjustment to get the best results. Pyrometers to control temperatures inside the furnace, or rather to show temperatures inside the furnace so that they may be controlled, can be bought from Russel Electric Co. of 338 W. Huron St., Chicago, at very reasonable prices or from Illinois Testing Laboratories, Inc., 420 N. LaSalle St., Chicago.

For ordinary tempering work in a lead, sand or oil bath in a forge fire, or over a plumbers gasoline furnace, deep, fat-frying thermometers, registering up to 600 degrees, can be bought from $1.00 upward, or the tempering may be done in an electric oven of the common range type, which has temperature controls of the automatic type registering to 550 degrees. A gas- range oven will work as well, of course, just so temperature controls are accurate.

Chapter 2 BARREL CHANGING AND ITS ADJUSTMENTS

One of the commonest major operations on guns is barrel replacement. When the new barrel is a factory standard for the gun in the case this is usually a simple job on rifle or shotgun, as these factory barrels practically always screw right up to the proper place.

Removing the old barrel is not always so simple. If it is an octagon barrel, remove the tubular magazine, if the rifle is so equipped, and withdraw the breech-bolt far enough so that the extractor clears its slot in the end of the barrel by a safe margin. Next, place copper jaw-facings on the bench vise jaws and grip the barrel tightly in the vise, with the receiver close to the jaws. Pad the sides of the receiver with heavy card- board, sheet lead or copper and place a heavy monkey-
wrench on the receiver, being careful to place it as close to the front edge of the receiver as possible, so as to avoid crushing in the thin sides of the receiver back of the receiver ring. In the event that a monkey- wrench is not available, a smooth-jawed machine vise of iy 2 " to 3" width can be used, by turning it upside down and clamping it onto the receiver, and then clamping an old rifle barrel or a piece of steel shafting on the bottom of it with C-clamps of a heavy type, so that the old barrel forms a handle.

If the receiver resists all your attempts to unscrew it from the barrel, remove the wrench from the receiver and, using a torch, heat the receiver ring until it just starts to change color, then replace the wrench on the receiver and try again to unscrew it. If it still resists, remove the wrench and heat the receiver again, but keep cold running water on the barrel just ahead of the receiver, being careful not to pour it on the receiver. Keep this water running onto the barrel while keeping the receiver just hot enough so that the color does not change, until the barrel is cool to the touch, then quickly place the wrench on the receiver and give it a sudden, heavy pull — which will usually break it loose.

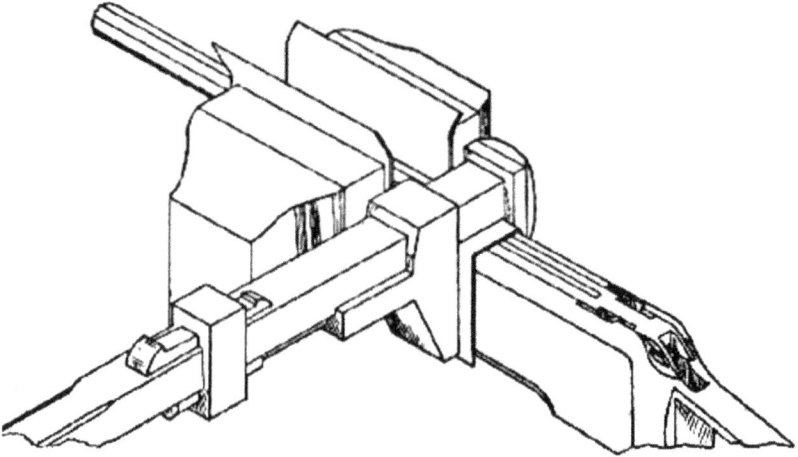

Removing octagon barrel from receiver by the use of a monkey wrench.

If this method fails to loosen the barrel, get the best penetrating oil that you can obtain and, standing the rifle with its breech up and the breech-block open, pour some penetrating oil around the edge of the barrel at the rear end. Let this stand for several hours, examining it now and then to see if any more oil can be poured around the edge of the barrel. Keep putting a little oil there if it seems to be working down any. I find that "Caseite" is a good oil for this purpose. It is made by J. R. Case Mfg. Co., Jonesboro, Arkansas— your garage man probably has it. Let this oil soak in until the following day, then put the rifle through the same procedure as you did before and if you cannot then move things it is a case of sawing off the barrel ahead of the receiver and cutting the remaining end out of the receiver. This is best done by drilling it out with a drill almost as large as the bottom of the threads on the barrel. An expansion reamer is then carefully used, until the top of the threads in the receiver just show through what is left of the barrel. The remainder of the barrel is then picked from the receiver threads with a small, fine-pointed punch.

Nearly all rifle barrels are fitted to the receiver with a right-hand thread, but there is always the exception, as I once found out when removing the barrel from a 6.5 m/m Norwegian Krag rifle. As it happened, I was able to move this barrel slightly in a left-hand direction and then it tightened up and would move no farther so, in spite of disbelief, I reversed operations and the barrel unscrewed to the right. The old, hammer-model, Marlin shotgun is also a left-hand thread.

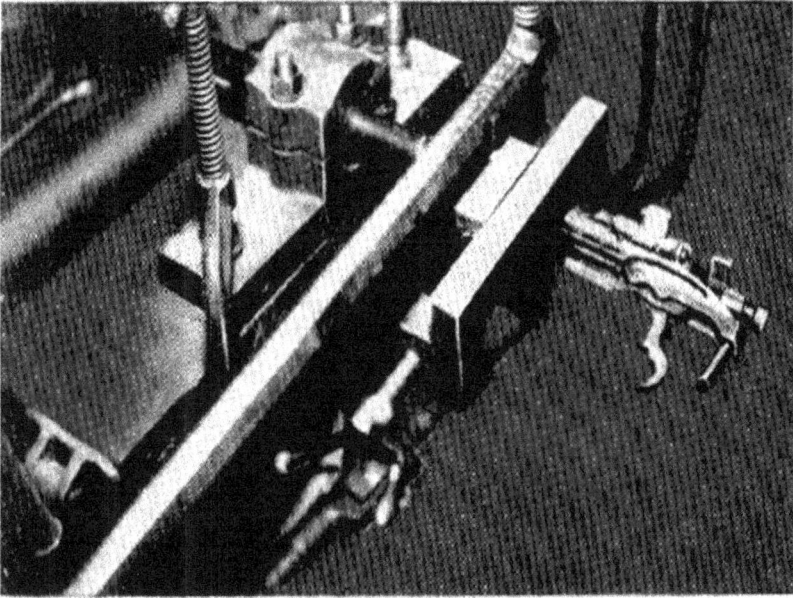

Plate III
Barrel removal, using a clamp upon the barrel and a vise (with old rifle barrel extension for handle) upon the receiver. The heavy, cast iron, split clamp is clamped firmly to the bench top, with its split, tapered steel bushing, which closely fits the barrel, in place. The barrel is inserted in this bushing and the clamping bolts drawn up light. A smooth jaw machine vise is tightened up on the receiver and an old 26" rifle barrel is clamped to the bottom of the vise, to use as a handle. The receiver is then unscrewed from the barrel.

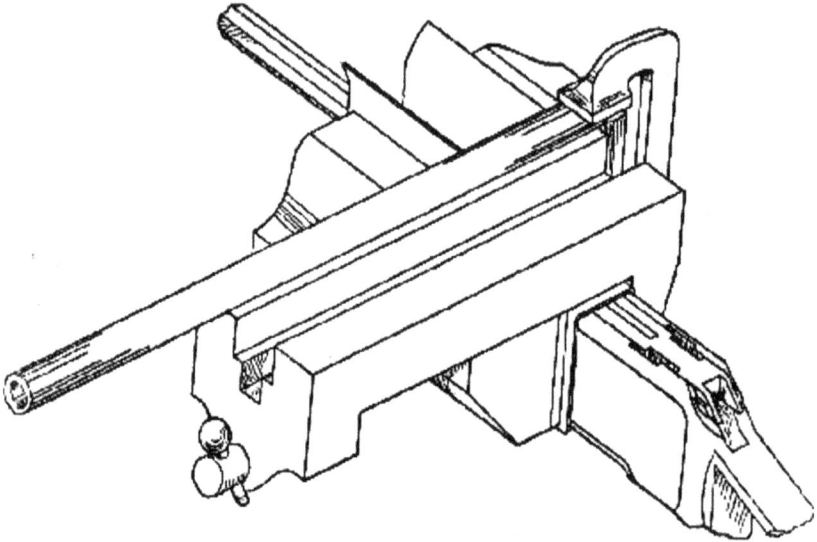

Removing octagon barrel from receiver, using smooth-jawed vise with un old barrel clamped to its base for leverage.

Shotgun barrels usually unscrew easier than rifle barrels do and, as they are round, the same method is used as for round rifle barrels. A split clamp, like a pillow-block, is fitted with a split sleeve of steel or cast-iron which, before being split, is bored to the same taper as the outside of the rifle or shotgun barrel, the boring being done in a lathe. The finish on the inside of this taper-bored sleeve should be as smooth as possible. Polish it with fine carborundum cloth, for other- wise it may mar a barrel.

Before clamping a barrel in one of these clamps, coat the surface of the sleeve that is to be against the barrel with powdered rosin. This gives it a much better grip and protects the surface of the barrel, not even mar- ring the blueing. This rosin may afterwards be cleaned from the surface of a barrel with high-test gasoline or turpentine.

The clamp is anchored to a ceiling support post, or to a bench-leg if the bench is solidly fastened. Be careful not to set the clamp up too tightly on a shotgun barrel if it is a new barrel, or a barrel you are going to use again, as you may crush it. But when setting it up on a high-power rifle barrel, oil the threads on the bolts holding the two parts of the clamp together, and pull the nuts up tightly with a long-handled socket- wrench.

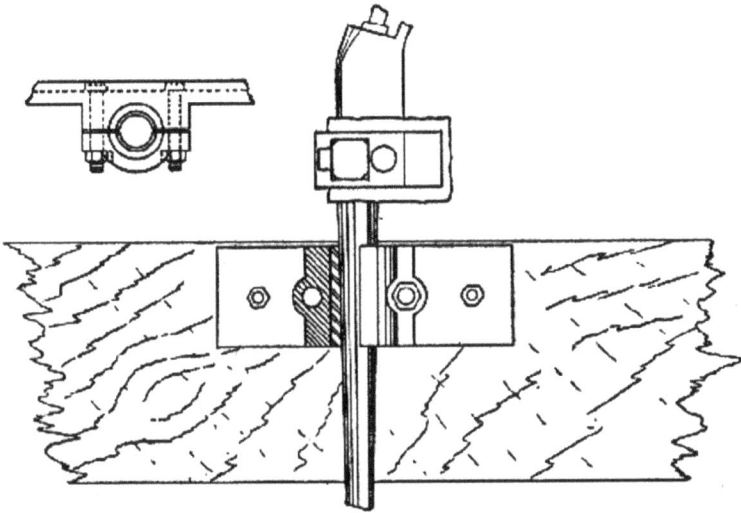

Removing a round barrel from receiver, using a split-clamp bolted to a post to hold barrel. Monkey wrench is placed as shown on receiver. Small drawing shows details of clamp and split bushing, taper bored to fit barrel.

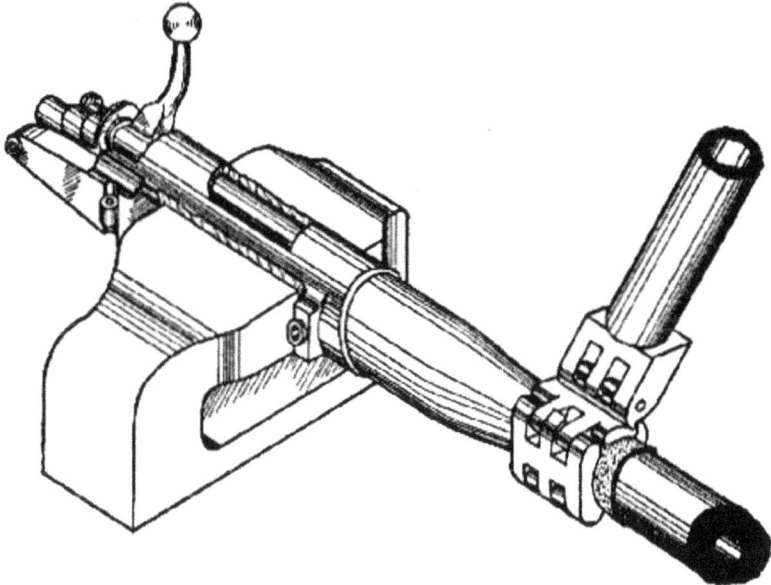

Removing a round barrel from bolt-action receiver, using Parmalee pipe wrench on barrel.

A shotgun barrel has a fairly straight taper from the breech, so the clamp can be fitted back close to the receiver, but on a high-power rifle it has to be fitted several inches ahead of the receiver, on the straight-tapered portion of the barrel.

Most shotgun barrels and many high-power rifle barrels, including the Springfield and Krag barrels, can usually be removed from their receivers with a Parmalee wrap-around type pipe-wrench. This wrench can be purchased from plumbing supply houses — the size that comes for girths for *4" and £4" pipe is the correct one. Two or three thicknesses of emery-cloth in the receiver in making one complete revolution in the threads. After the barrel is chucked in the lathe, bring the facing tool lightly against the end of the barrel, or against the barrel shoulder, and set the micrometer carriage stop against the forward end of the lathe carriage. Next, back off the micrometer stop the required number of thousandths of an inch for one revolution of the barrel, less the amount required to make the marks on receiver and barrel meet. It is easy to determine this amount, if the lathe has a pro- tractor collar on the spindle, graduated in degrees. In this case, place the barrel, with the receiver screwed up on it, in the lathe chuck and bring a sharp-pointed tool in the tool rest up to either the mark on the barrel or on the receiver and take the reading from the pro- tractor collar, then revolve the lathe spindle until the other mark is at the tool point and read the protractor again. The difference in degrees is then figured for what part of the full circle of 360 degrees it is, and this is then reduced to thousandths of an inch by dividing the number of thousandths of an inch that the barrel moves in a full revolution by this number. This number of thousandths of an inch is then deducted from the number of thousandths of an inch the barrel moves in a full revolu-tion, and the answer is the amount the micrometer stop is to be backed away from the lathe carriage.

A thread must be machined from the rear end of the barrel, on such barrels which have a blank section at the rear machined to a diameter of the root diameter of the thread. Sometimes, a section the width of a thread must be machined to thread-bottom depth ahead of the front end of the thread, but sometimes the threads are machined out of the front end of the receiver far enough hack so that this is not necessary.

If the rear end of the barrel is slotted for an ex- tractor, this slot must be deepened. This is easily done while the barrel is still in the lathe, using an electric tool post grinder, with a grinding wheel narrow enough to enter the extractor slot. It may also be done on the milling machine or, if necessary, it can be done by hand, with files.

The foregoing method of bringing a barrel to its proper place in the receiver when it screws past the register mark can only be used if a chambering reamer for this caliber is on hand because, of course, after shortening the barrel at the breech end the chamber must be deepened the same amount.

If no chambering reamer is available and there is no rush about the job, the gun may be returned to the factory for rechambering, after the barrel has been firmly screwed up to its proper place. If, however, the gun is needed at once, instead of shortening the barrel so that it can be seated one turn deeper in the receiver, a steel shim must be placed between the barrel shoulder and the part of the receiver against which this shoulder bears, so that the barrel screws up tightly at the register mark. If shim stock of steel the proper thickness for this job can be obtained, this is the best thing to use, but if this is not obtainable in proper thickness or width, some other thin stock must be used. When using this steel shim, lubricate it either with oil or collodial graphite to prevent it tearing under the twist- ing pressure.

There is another method which I saw used which worked perfectly, yet I would not recommend it. A man was up at a mountain ranch with a Luger pistol, the barrel of which loosened up, and when he screwed it up tightly', it went past the register mark. There was no thin steel available there, nor anything else to use as shim stock, but the rancher had some dry, powdered litharge and glycerine with which to mix it. The man with the Luger. mixed a rather stiff paste of this, applied it to the threads of the barrel and receiver, are covered with powdered rosin on the cloth side, wrapped tightly around the barrel with the emery side out , and the wrench is then placed over this in the right, direction to tighten when unscrewing the barrel. It is often necessary to add a foot or two of pipe to the wrench handle to give the power necessary to loosen the barrel. Enfield barrels cannot be unscrewed with this wrench. The clamp must be used on these latter, quite often the receiver must be heated and also must be tapped on the bottom with a hammer.

After the old barrel has been removed, clean out the threads in the receiver with an old tooth-brush, or a new one from the ten-cent store, dipped in gasolene. Also, clean the threads on the new barrel with brush and gasolene, to remove the heavy oil and any dirt that may have collected upon them. Oil the threads of the new barrel with a light oil that is acid free, and screw the barrel into the receiver as far as it will go by hand. Place the barrel in the vise or, in the case of a round barrel, in the barrel clamp, with the meeting mark of the barrel upright, and screw the receiver up to place with the monkey-wrench. If you cannot make the receiver screw quite up to the mark on the barrel, un- screw it from the barrel and, using a large, flat, dead- smooth file or a large carborundum stone, dress off the front of the receiver slightly and, after cleaning it, screw it onto the barrel again.

Repeat this process until you can screw the receiver up to its proper position. If, however, the receiver screws up too far on the new barrel, the proper procedure is to place the barrel in the lathe, face-off the end of the barrel and the barrel shoulder far enough so that the barrel can make another complete turn, less the amount required to make the marks on receiver and barrel meet. Knowing how many threads to the inch are on the barrel, it is easy to figure just how many thousands of an inch the barrel will move and screwed the barrel up to the mark. He heated the barrel and receiver ring slightly to hasten drying and laid the gun in the sun until the following day, when he again put it into use and had no more trouble with it. I had occasion to replace this barrel with a new one the following year, it was the tightest Luger barrel I have ever removed and I have changed a number of them.

Shotgun barrels of the take-down type have an adjustment by which they can be kept at the register marks, but sometimes a solid-frame type goes past the mark in fitting a new barrel and the steel shim may be used in this case or, as the threads are fine, the neces- sary amount may be filed from the end of the receiver to bring the register marks together.

Revolver barrels do not screw up to their proper places, as rifle and shotgun barrels usually do, but must be fitted. The threads on the barrel are usually oversize and must be lapped into the frame threads with fine grinding compound. The barrel may be held in hardwood blocks, grooved out to fit closely and lined with powdered rosin. These blocks are placed in the vise around the barrel and the vise is drawn up tightly, a small amount of valve-grinding compound is placed on the barrel threads and the frame is screwed onto the barrel by hand. Screw up the barrel as tightly as possible without jamming it, then reverse it a revolution or two and then screw it up again a little farther than before. Work it back and forth in this way a few times, then remove the frame from the barrel and add a little more grinding compound, repeating this procedure until the barrel shoulder is screwed up tightly against the face of the frame. Unscrew it again and wash out all grinding compound, then oil the threads with light, acid-free oil and screw the frame onto the barrel, this time using a hammer handle, or other piece of hardwood, through the cylinder opening in the frame to screw it up tightly but be careful not to spring the frame.

If you happen to be a fool for luck, the barrel may be in the right place, or so close to it that it can be forced there, but as most of us are honest men it will probably be as far from the proper place as possible. In this case, measure the distance from the rear face of the frame to the rear end of the barrel, then remove the barrel from the frame, after estimating as closely as possible what part of a full revolution the barrel must

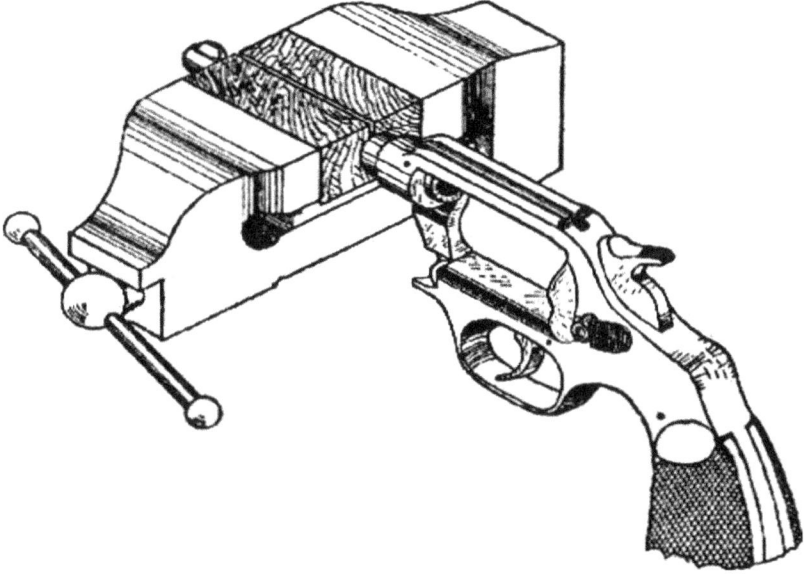

Revolver barrel clamped in grooved wood blocks in vise jaws, in order to unscrew frame from barrel.

take to bring it to its proper position in the frame. Count the barrel threads and figure how many thousandths of an inch the barrel will move back when screwed to its proper position, and deduct this amount from the measurement you made of the distance from the rear face of the frame to the rear end of the barrel. Place the cylinder in the frame and measure the distance the front end of the cylinder is from the rear face of the frame, and deduct from this the distance from the rear face of the frame to the end of the barrel when the barrel will be in its proper place in the frame. Add to this .0025" for clearance and cut this amount from the rear end of the barrel, in the lathe. Cut the barrel shoulder back the required number of thousandths of an inch to allow the barrel to screw up to place, and remove any burr from the rear end of the barrel with a round, tapered oil-stone or fine carborundum stone. Now, screw the frame onto the barrel again, and if your measurements are correct, the barrel will come to the proper place in the frame and have the correct clearance at the front end of the cylinder. The the barrel does not quite come to place, a small amount may be removed from the front face of the frame, where the barrel shoulder bears. Check the clearance of barrel from cylinder with a thickness gauge, checking each chamber, because now and then a high spot shows up on a cylinder and this must be dressed off.

Sometimes it is desired to fit a factory barrel to some action other than the one for which it was designed. When the threaded end of the barrel is larger than the threaded opening in the receiver to which it is to be fitted, it is necessary to place the barrel in a lathe and turn down the breech end to the proper diameter and length to fit the receiver, and then thread it with the same thread as the receiver.

Some actions use the regular U. S. form of vee- thread, while others, such as the Springfield, Krag and Enfield, use the square form of thread. In this square form of thread, the thread-cutting tool must be the same width at the front edge as the groove in the receiver thread, and the thread tool, when viewed from the front, must incline to the right for a right-hand thread and to the left for a left-hand thread, at the same angle as the lead of the thread, so that the thread tool will clear the sides of the thread below the cutting point of the tool. The nose of the thread tool must also have clearance ground on the sides from top to bottom, leaving the top edge the widest part. The cutting edge of the tool must be straight and parallel to the axis of the lathe, and the top of the cutting tool should slope back or down from the cutting edge.

Cuts should be very light at each pass of the tool and the cutting edge should be just slightly above the center line of the lathe. The cutting edge of the thread tool should be oil-stoned until it is very smooth and sharp, and should be examined after each pass to see that the corners are not dulled.

In fitting a square thread, .001" clearance should be left at both top and bottom of the thread. This is done by machining the blank to be threaded .002" smaller in diameter than the bottom of the threads in the receiver, and cutting the groove of the thread on the barrel .001" deeper than the depth of the receiver thread.

The lathe should be thrown out of gear before the thread tool reaches the end of the cut (but do not re- lease the half-nuts of the lathe carriage from the lead screw to do this) and the lathe is then turned by hand until the tool reaches the end of the cut. This is necessary because of the broad edge of the cutting tool, for it is not possible otherwise to stop the tool right at the end of the cut and the shock at the end of the tool, if it is not stopped at the end of the cut, may cause it to dig in and displace either the tool position or the work. This is not necessary in cutting a vee- type thread, as this is a shear type of cut and the low speed at which the lathe is driven while thread cutting will enable the vec-type cutter to continue to cut without being displaced or displacing the work if you miss the stopping point by a degree or two. In cutting left-hand threads, the cutter is started in the work at the shoulder end and, before beginning the threading operation, a groove the full depth of the thread to be cut should be cut at this point for either the square or the vee form of thread, so that the threading tool can be placed in this groove each time to start cut.

In fitting rifle barrels to actions other than those for which they are designed, it will be necessary to cut out the original extractor groove in the end of the barrel, if it has one, unless the position of the extractor groove for the action to which you are fitting the barrel comes at the right place. As cutting off enough of the barrel to remove the extractor groove usually means shortening the chamber, a chambering reamer must then be used to lengthen it enough to give proper seating depth to the cartridge.

If the barrel to be fitted is smaller than the receiver to which you wish it to fit, the receiver may be bushed or, more properly, the barrel at the breech end may be built up large enough to thread for the receiver. This may be done by turning down the threaded end of the barrel to remove the threads upon it and to bring it to some standard fractional-inch size for which you have a die. Carry this size down the barrel farther than the distance the barrel is to screw into the receiver to which you are fitting it, so that a new shoulder may be made on the piece of steel that you screw onto the barrel to enlarge it.

After threading the barrel with a die, drill and tap a piece of steel to screw onto it that will be large enough to thread for the receiver and to leave a substantial shoulder at the end of the thread. Clean the die-cut threads on the barrel with gasoline, to remove all oil from them and do the same with the tapped threads in the piece of steel, then tin both of these threads with solder and screw the steel piece onto the barrel as tightly as possible, keeping both parts hot so that the solder remains soft. After the barrel is cool and the solder well set, a new end is machined on it the proper size to thread for the receiver, and the front end of the steel piece fitted to the barrel is brought down in a taper to barrel contour at that point.

Barrel blanks are fitted to actions in the same manner as has been described for fitting factory barrels to actions other than those for which they were designed. In chucking either a blank or a barrel for threading to fit an action, the blank or barrel is centered by the bore or chamber and not by the outside of the blank, as the bore may be slightly off-center. This can usually be done closely enough by eye or, if you wish, the dial

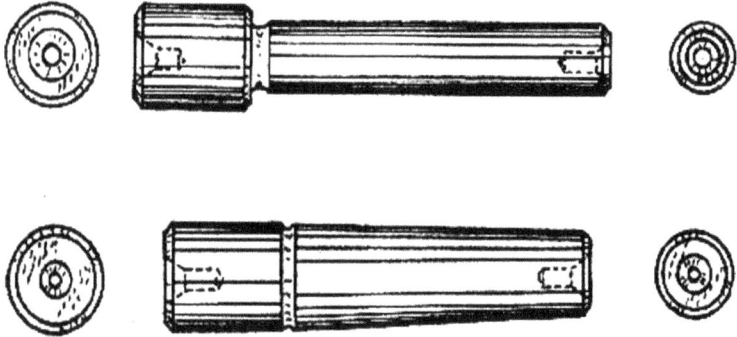

Hardened steel plugs or mandrels, ground on centers, to insert in muzzle and chamber of rifle barrel when it is to be machined on centers in a lathe.

gauge may be used to check the centering of the bore. When the blank is machined on centers and threaded, the bore is, of course, centered by the lathe centers, and the breech end may be faced off square with the thread if it is out of true, by using a narrow facing tool ground to an angle to go between the end of the barrel and the slope of the center point. A special tail stock center is sometimes used for this job that has had part of one side ground away for a distance back from the point, either flat or in a groove, so that the point of the facing tool will go to the bore or chamber opening. This is not necessary' however, as with a regular center in place the barrel end may be faced from the outside toward the center and when the point of the facing tool touches the lathe center, the center may be very slightly with- drawn, the barrel will raise slightly on the point of the tool and the small remaining fin will be cut off smoothly. Leave the facing tool in position after this occurs and stop the lathe before withdrawing the tool.

In fitting barrels to actions in which the end of the barrel comes against the face of the breech-block, as it usually does for rimmed cartridges, a Starrett micrometer head with lock-nut can be used as a micrometer depth-gauge by fitting the head into a steel block that will reach across the front end of the receiver ring, The hole through the block for the micrometer head must be at right-angles to the face of the block and the lock- nut must be recessed so that it is below the surface of the block, yet holds the head in place in the block without tightening on the spindle. Some actions for rimless cartridges have a rear shoulder in the receiver for the rear of the barrel to bear against, such as the Mauser has, and in this case the distance between the rear shoulder and the front edge of the receiver ring is measured in the same way as described for rimmed cases.

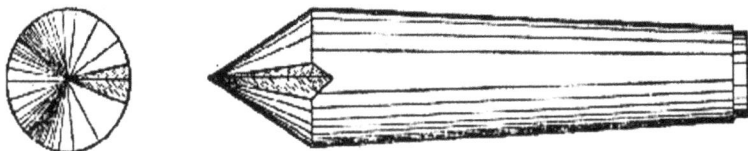

Vee-grooved tail center for lathe. Used when facing ends of work on centers, so that cutting tool cleans off the end completely.

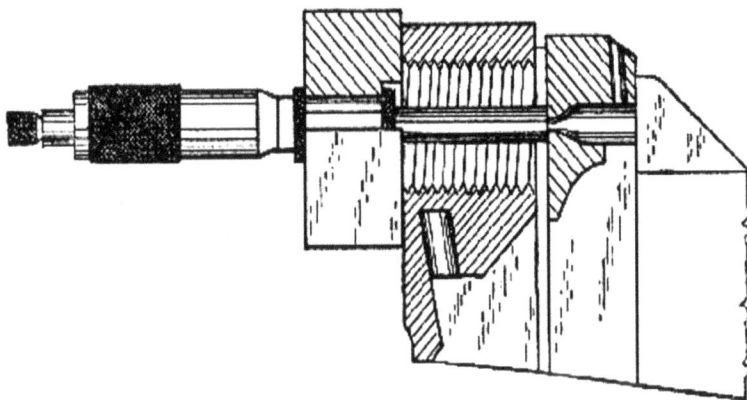

Method of using micrometer spindle, recessed nut clamping it into steel block, to measure length of threaded barrel extension to fit into a single-shot action.

Other actions for rimless cartridges, such as the Springfield, have no rear shoulder, and the length of the portion of the barrel extending back into the action is measured on an old barrel or may be taken from the front end of the receiver to the face of the bolt, while the bolt is locked in place.

Some barrels, notably the .22 long-rifle, are very touchy concerning the contact between the barrel shoulder and the receiver, and have to be spotted-in to get a perfect contact. The front of the receiver is

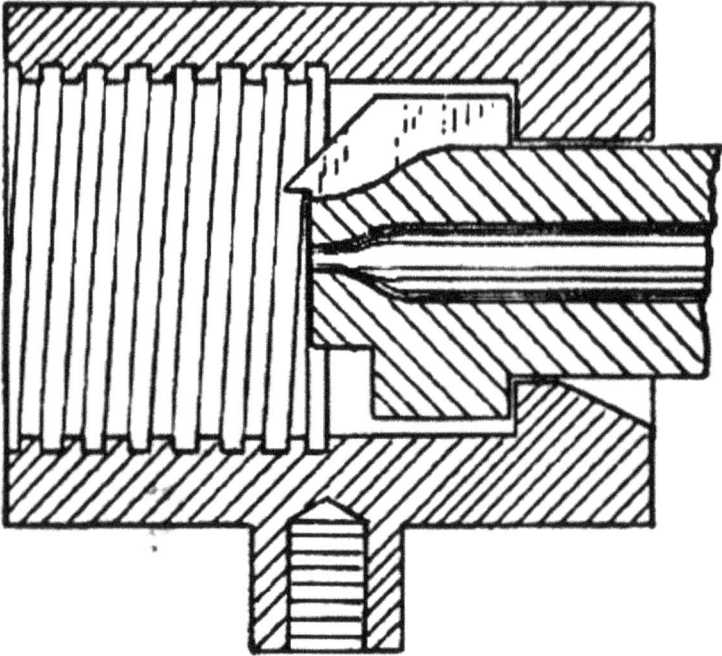

Details of external barrel shoulder at front of receiver of Spring-field action.

lightly coated with prussian-blue and the barrel is then screwed up tightly against it, then when the barrel is removed from the action the high spots on the barrel shoulder are coated with the blue. These high spots are then carefully worked down with a very fine file of the Swiss pattern and the barrel tried in the receiver again, the performance being repeated until the con- tact between barrel shoulder and receiver is perfect.

The recess in the breech end of the barrel for rimmed cartridges controls the head spacing of the cartridge. This may either be cut with a facing-type cutter, with a pilot in the barrel or, if the barrel is held in a chuck in the lathe spindle, it may be cut with a lathe tool at the time the rear end of the barrel is faced off.

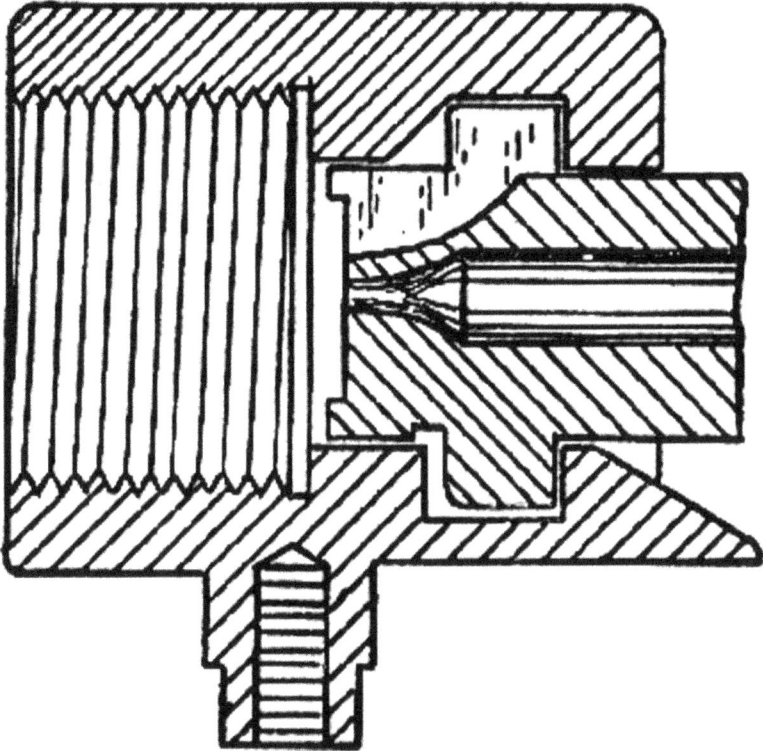

Details of internal barrel shoulder, just ahead of bold face, of '98 Mauser action.

In case the thickness of the standard rim for the cartridge in question is not known and there is no gauge available, measure the rim thickness of a number of cartridges with a micrometer and, taking an average of these, cut the recess to that depth for the rim of the cartridge. The micrometer carriage stop should be used on the lathe for this operation, so that it may be done to the correct number of thousandths of an inch.

Barrels or barrel blanks may be cut down to a smaller diameter in the lathe, if care is used. Ordinary sporting-weight barrels should not be turned down to a smaller diameter, as these are properly designed by the factory or the arsenal to be as light as possible. If it is desired to smooth up the outside of them, this can be done in the lathe, with the barrel on centers, either by filing or with an electric tool post grinder. Center plugs should be made for both the breech and the muzzle, of tool-steel, hardened and then ground on centers. The tailstock may be offset so that the tool post grinder may be used to make a cut the full length of the taper of the barrel, but it is better to leave the centers in their true center position and use a lathe with a taper attachment, resetting it each time the grinder travels the length allowed by the taper attachment.

In turning down barrel blanks or heavy barrels the back rest cannot be used to support the barrel, due to the taper of the work, therefore, as the barrel must be supported to keep it from vibrating under the cut, a

Principle of detecting crooked barrels. Left view shows shadow cast by a straight barrel—other two show shadows cast by crooked barrels.

short straight portion is turned upon the barrel and the steady rest is set up at this point to support it. It may be necessary to make two or three different positions to set this steady rest along the length of the barrel and after each short portion between the tail stock and the steady rest is finished, the rest is moved to another position along the barrel and another portion of the barrel is finished. The barrel is equipped with center plugs and the lathe centers are left in the true center position and a lathe equipped with a taper attachment is used to machine the barrel. Light cuts must be taken, so as not to spring the barrel, and the centers must be carefully watched to see that the barrel docs not heat from the turning operation and become tight enough between centers to spring it. After machining the barrel it should be checked for straightness, as the removal of very much metal from its outer surface may release strains in the barrel that will cause it to spring out of true. A wire is stretched across a window and the barrel is pointed toward it and held in a rest so that is may be revolved while watching the shadow cast by the wire in the bore. If the shadow is a true line, the barrel is straight but if there are breaks in it and part of the line of the shadow is to one side of the balance of it, the barrel is crooked.

Plate IV

Facing back a barrel shoulder in the lathe, using micrometer carriage stop. Tins micrometer carriage stop, which you see fastened to the lathe bed, measures the travel of the lathe tool carriage along the bed. in thousandths of an inch, so that the shoulder of the barrel is cut back the exact distance necessary to allow the barrel to screw up to its proper place in the receiver.

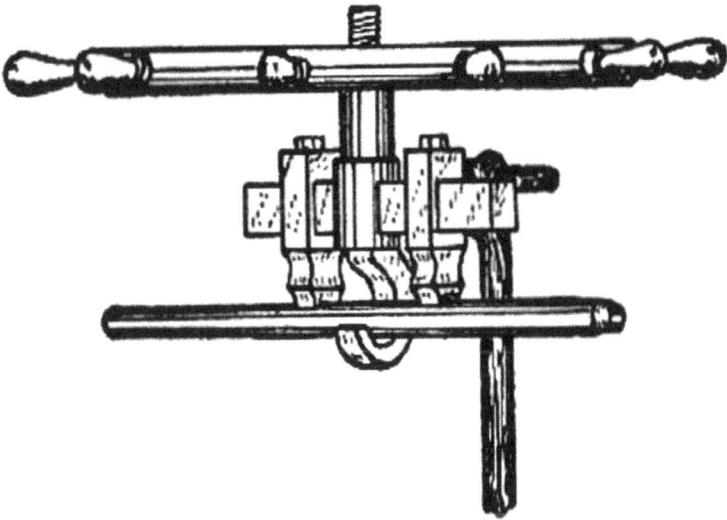

The modern, overhead press for straightening rifle barrels.

Some barrel makers claim the barrel should not be straightened, as when it becomes heated later, in firing, it may come back to its crooked position. Others claim it should be straightened. This straightening process is now almost entirely done in an overhead press, while the barrel is pointed toward the window with the wire stretched across it and the shadow in the bore that is cast by the wire is watched during the straightening. This overhead press has two stationary fingers several inches apart and between these a third finger with screw adjustment comes against the barrel from the opposite side. The crooked portion of the barrel is placed between the two stationary points, or fingers, and the barrel is turned until the outsprung portion of the crooked part of the barrel is against the movable finger. This movable finger is then used to spring the barrel back to a straight position. As the barrel has some spring in it, it must be sprung past center, so that when it springs back it will be straight.

Old method, using lead blocks and lead hammer to straighten rifle barrels.

The other method of straightening a barrel is to lay it upon two lead blocks, having the crooked portion be- tween the blocks with the crook upward, and it is then struck with a lead hammer to straighten it. This requires considerable more skill than the press method. Skill is also required to properly locate the crooked portion of the barrel to know where to straighten it.

In filing barrels upon the outside to get a smooth finish, a twelve or fourteen inch file of an inch or more in width should be used. This file should be either of the second cut or about a #2 cut in the Swiss pattern pillar-type tile. The lathe should turn in the next to the lowest speed on open belt. To prevent the file picking up cuttings of the barrel between its teeth (known as

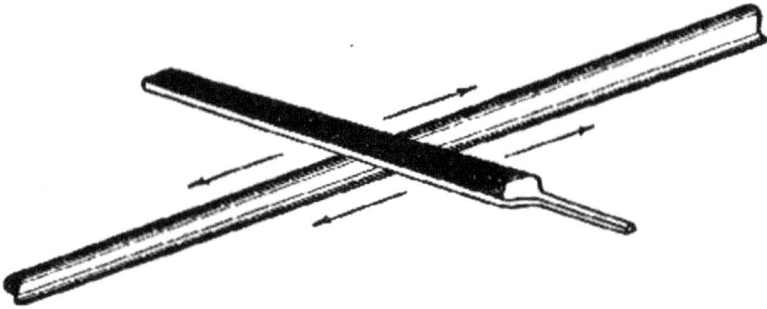

Striking or draw-filing a barrel to remove circular tool marks.

pinning) and scratching the surface of the barrel, the file should he chalked with common chalk. Clean the file often and rechalk it.

Striking a barrel, before polishing it, is done by holding a flat file in both hands, one at either end, across the barrel at a right-angle to the axis of the barrel, then moving it back and forth lengthwise of the barrel. This is often done to remove the circular tool marks on the barrel. The barrel is given its final polishing, before being buffed, with carborundum cloth while the barrel is turning at high-speed in the lathe. This removes all file marks.

Buffing a barrel for final finish may be done on a muslin buff, an inch or more thick, by applying emery paste in brick form to the buff, which will more or less impregnate the surface of the buff with the emery or carborundum in the brick. If you desire a wider range of grain size of carborundum than can ordinarily be obtained in these emery bricks, the buffing wheel may be coated with the stick-type belt dressing by holding the end of a stick of it against the buff while it is revolving and carborundum grains of any size you desire may then be rubbed into the surface of the buff, the belt dressing causing a large part of it to stick.

Another type of buffing wheel is made of thin pieces of chrome-tanned leather, enough pieces being used to make a wheel an inch or more thick. These pieces of

Muslin and leather buffing wheels and their use in buffing gun barrels.

about one-half inch of the outer diameter of the wheel. This leaves the wheel with a yielding face, which will follow the barrel contour better than a solid face would do. The face, or properly the

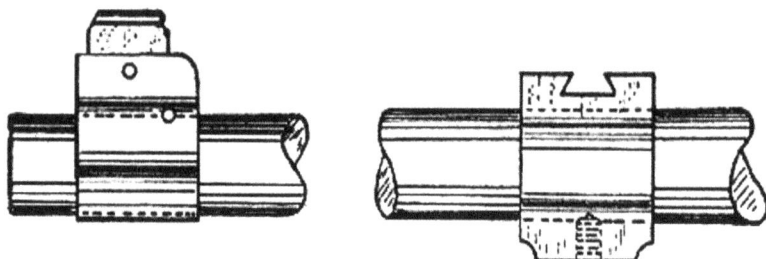

Front sight band attached by a cross pin with half its diameter in the top of the barrel. Rear sight, dovetailed barrel band, attached with set screw underneath.

the wheel is rolled on carborundum powder spread evenly on a paper laid on a flat surface so that the wheel takes an even coating of the carborundum grains. Usually carborundum grains of #120 to FFF size are used on either type of buff. Buffs should be eight inches in diameter and turn at a speed of at least 1750 R.P.M.

Cuts for sights in barrels, especially barrels of sporting weight, should be avoided as they cause uneven vibrations of the barrel, which causes inaccuracy.

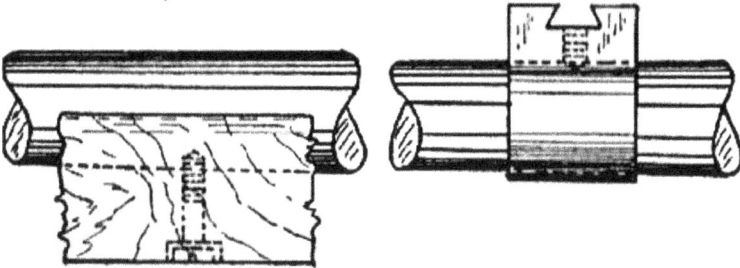

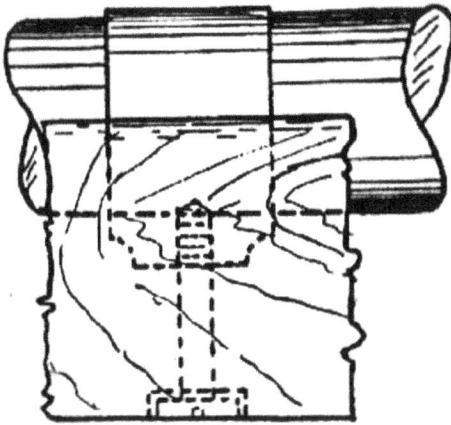

Various methods of attaching forearm and rear sight bands to rifle barrel with screws.

s.

These barrel bands can be held in place on the barrel with light cross pins, as are the sights of the Springfield service rifle ; or the rear sight band, if an open rear sight is desired, may be held in place by leaving a heavy portion on the bottom of the band in- side the forearm and running a headless set-screw, tapped into this heavy portion, through the band and into a slight depression in the bottom of the barrel, made by the point of a drill. If, due to the construction of the rifle there is not room to leave a heavy portion on the bottom of this rear barrel band, a set-screw may be run in flush on the top in the bottom of the dovetail slot for the open sight, although this is not as .good practice as putting it through the lower side of the band as it tends to lift the upper part of the band away from the barrel.

Forearms of single-shot rifles may be held to the barrel with a band

and screws running through the fore- arm, through the heavy portion of the bottom of the band and into a depression made in the bottom of the barrel with a drill point. These forearms may also be held to the barrel with a screw tapped directly into the barrel, in which case the screw should be carefully cut

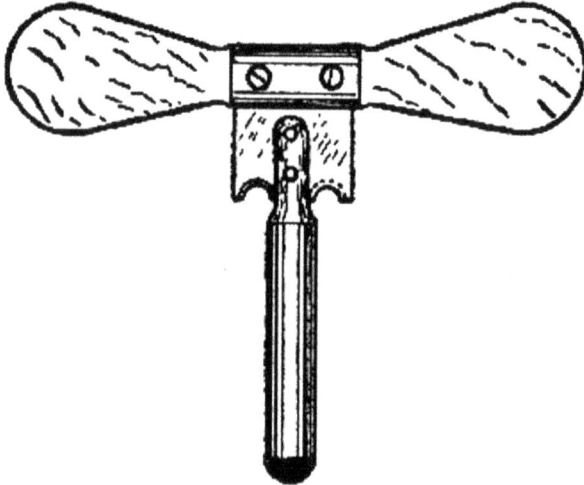

Muzzle crowning tool for rifle barrel.

for length so that it bottoms in the hole in the barrel, thus filling the hole completely, which will help pre- vent uneven vibrations of the barrel.

In cutting off the muzzle end of barrels, they may be sawed off with a hack-saw and then finished up true in the lathe, or they may be cut off in the lathe. After the cutting-off operation, the muzzle may be shaped up with a lathe tool, but if the inner or bore part of the muzzle is shaped up with a lathe tool be sure that the bore runs dead true or opposite sides will be of uneven length. The muzzle may also be finished, or crowned, by a crowning tool having a pilot that enters the bore and rides on top of the lands. The cutter is made of flat tool-steel, shaped to produce the crown on both the inside and outside of the muzzle at one operation. This cutter passes through a slot in the shank of the pilot and is held in place with two flush pins. The edge is relieved on opposite sides from the cutting edge. It may be operated by hand, in a drill chuck in the lathe, or in a drill press. It is turned slowly and should be kept lubricated with cutting oil.

Barrel Thread Sizes of Various Rifle Actions

Name of Action	Barrel Extension Diameter	Threads Per Inch	Type
Winchester #1 & #2 Single Shot Action	.821″	16	Vee
Winchester #3 Heavy Single Shot Action	.935″	16	Vee
Ballard Single Shot	.950″	18	Vee
Sharps Borchardt Single Shot Hammerless	.945″	16	Vee
Stevens Ideal #44 Single Shot Action	.8125″	20	Vee
Stevens Ideal #44½″ Single Shot Action	.875″	16	Vee
Remington Single Shot Navy Action, Pistol	.850	12	Square
American Krag Action	.980″	10	Square
Norwegian Krag Action	1.056″	12 L.H.	Square
Springfield Action	1.040″	10	Square
Enfield Action (Model 1917)	1.118″	10	Square
Mauser Model '98 Action	1.100″	12	Vee
Winchester Model 54 Action	1″	16	Vee

Chapter 3 CHAMBERING , BORING AND REAMING TOOLS

Chambering reamers may be purchased from firms specializing in this work, from barrel makers, in some cases from gun factories — or the gunsmith may make his own reamers.

Reamers for popular calibers for which the gunsmith often fits barrels should be made in sets of three, a roughing, a finishing and a burnishing reamer. These reamers should be made of high-speed steel to minimize wear. Reamers for a caliber which is seldom called for, or a reamer for a special job, may be made of carbon- steel and a single reamer of the finishing type may be made to do in place of a set of three reamers. The roughing out of the chamber in this case may be done in the lathe with a small boring tool, the proper taper being obtained by swiveling the compound rest to the desired angle.

Chambering reamers should have six or more cutting edges and these edges should be an uneven distance apart to prevent chatter of the reamer. The roughing reamer may be, and often is, made with four grooves instead of six and the lands of the tapered body part of the roughing reamer are usually nicked with a narrow lathe tool, about 3/32" wide and to a like depth. This is done to break up the chips and allow them to wash out easily with the flow of oil. If this is not done a taper reamer has a tendency to allow the chips to pack in the flutes. A catalog cut of Morse or Brown & Sharpe taper reamers for reaming sockets or spindles for these tapers will show the lands of the roughing reamer nicked as mentioned. This is especially desirable in a machine-drive reamer and the roughing reamer . is practically always machine driven. These nicks or grooves around the reamer may be 3/16" to 1/4" apart.

In cutting the flutes of a reamer the face or cutting edge of the flutes should not be on the center line of the blank, with the exception of those on the burnishing reamer. This cutting edge should be about .010" ahead of center, which gives a shearing cut and prevents the reamer digging in. This feature, combined with the eccentric relief stoned on the flutes in the hand-finish stoning, helps prevent chatter. This feature is illustrated and described very well in the Greenfield Tap & Die catalog in describing their "Reamrite" hand adjustable expansion reamers.

As in cutting our reamer flutes an uneven distance apart we cannot have them all with their cutting edges .010" ahead of center we cut #1 flute in this position. The next flute, #2, is cut .008" ahead of center, #3 is cut .006" ahead of center, but on #4 we return again to .010" of center because #1 and #4 are directly opposite to each other and by making them the same distance ahead of center we are able to get a truer micrometer measurement of the reamer for size, there- fore #5 flute is cut .008" ahead of center as was #2 and #6 flute is cut .006" ahead to match #3 flute. The four-flute roughing reamers may have their flutes cut .010", .008", 006" and .004" ahead of center, respectively as their diameter need not be measured accurately closer than .001" as it is made .010" to .015" smaller than the finish chambering reamer.

The roughing and finishing reamers are fluted with a standard reamer-fluting milling cutter of sixty to eighty degrees included angle as made by the tool companies that make milling cutters, but the burnishing reamer is fluted with a radius cutter of the convex type, with its center set exactly on the center of the blank. The lands left between the flutes are next milled at the top, on each side of the center, so that the center of each land is left as a sharp, or almost-sharp edge, with an included angle of about 120 degrees.

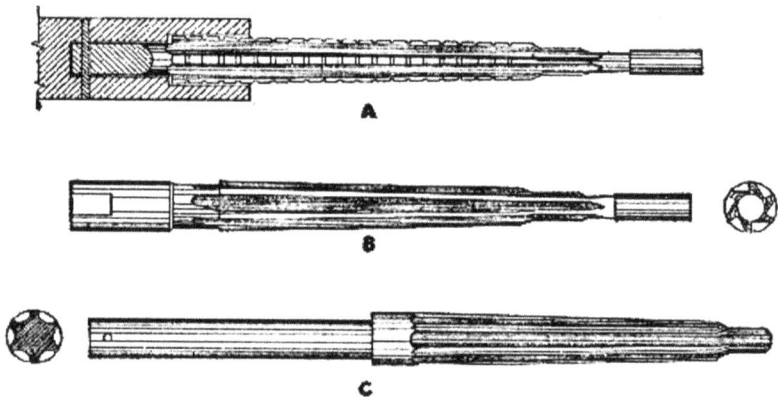

A is roughing type chambering reamer, four groove, with floating drive for machine use. Driving sleeve comes far enough down on the reamer to act as a stop for depth. **B** is finishing type chambering reamer, for hand use. **C** is burnishing reamer, without pilot, with long shank for use in chambering a barrel screwed up in the receiver.

After the burnishing reamer is hardened and then tempered at a light straw color, about 420 degrees Fahrenheit, it is ground cylindrically, on centers, until it is about .002" oversize. This leaves a radius on the top of the lands and the side angles milled on the tops of the lands are now stoned by hand until the center of the lands are sharp. The reamer is still oversize and a slight flat is stoned, by hand, on the sharp edges in the center of each land, reducing the reamer to exact size.

Roughing and finishing reamers are left .015" or more oversize when the blank is turned to shape and after being hardened and tempered they are ground, on centers, until they are within .002" to .003" of the proper size. Clearance is then ground on the lands back of the cutting edge but this edge itself is not touched with the grinding wheel. This unground cutting edge on each land is then stoned with a fine hand stone in an eccentric shape until the reamer is brought to size.

Some gunsmiths use a separate throating reamer, of six flutes, tapered with an included angle of about 2 1/2 degrees, to throat the rifling just ahead of the chamber to give clearance for the bullet when a loaded cartridge is in place in the chamber. These reamers have flutes

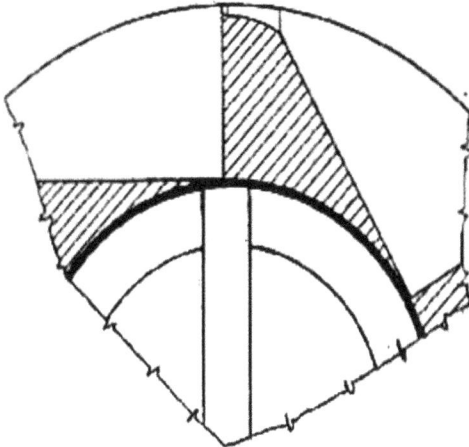

Detail of how the teeth of a finish-type reamer are stoned.

of the same shape as the finish-type chambering reamer with the cutting edges .010" ahead of the center of the blank and the flutes unevenly spaced as are those of the finish chambering reamer. These reamers have a pilot which fits the bore closely and rides on top of the lands.

Other gunsmiths, in making the finish chambering reamer, make this throating reamer as an extension of the finish reamer rather than make a scparate reamer. Some of the older type bullets made it necessary to throat the barrel ahead of the chamber and as some of these bullets are still in use. barrels for these must be so throated. As the chamber must be made at least y 32 " longer than the cartridge case, to allow for forward stretch of the case, and as the front end of the lands of the chambering reamer must be sloped forward at an angle of 45 to 60 degrees and these edges given clearance as the lips of a twist drill are in order to enable them to cut, the chambering reamer cuts away the lands of the barrel for some distance ahead of the mouth of a new cartridge case. This fact, taken in relation to our modern shape bullet which starts to taper toward the point from the mouth of the cartridge case, results in bullet jump if the throating of the barrel ahead of the chamber is carried very far. In fact, a barrel for a

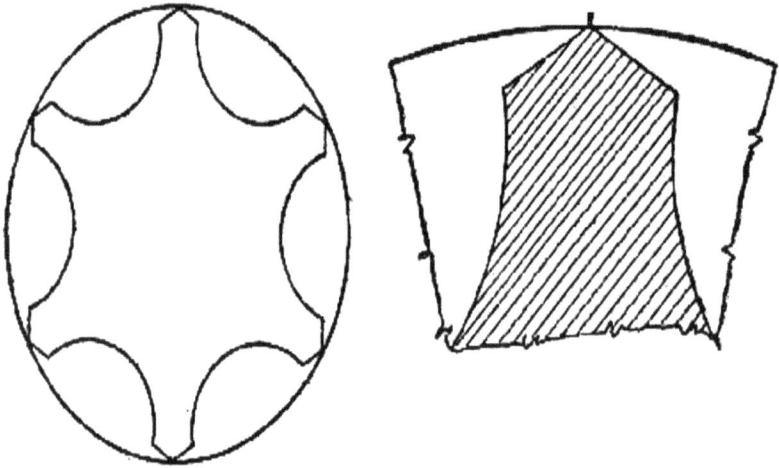

Detail of how the teeth of a burnishing reamer are stoned.

cartridge using a modern shape bullet needs only a touch with a throating reamer to give clearance for the bullet and if the chamber is more than 1 1/32 " longer than the cartridge case, the barrel will usually need no throating at all.

High-speed steel, hardened and fluted with four flutes, can be pur-chased from steel companies, one of which is the Central Steel and Wire Co. of 4545 South Western Blvd., Chicago, Illinois. This would require grinding to shape and size for a chambering reamer of the roughing type. This can be done in a lathe with an electric tool post grinder. This four-fluted shape is known as the standard cruciform section and is sup- plied in a number of sizes 1/2 " from outer diameter with 7/32 " solid-center section on up to 2 1/2" outer diameter.

Roughing reamers are usually driven by machine, using a floating drive so that the reamer lines up properly with the bore. A simple type of this drive is a machine attachment shank for the reamer with a hole drilled in it slightly larger than the reamer shank which slips into it. A pin hole, at right angles to the axis of the reamer, is drilled through the shank of the reamer for a drive pin. This pin hole in the reamer shank is slightly larger than the drive pin which is a tight drive fit in the hole drilled for it through the machine drive shank. This drive shank is sometimes used for a reamer stop on the roughing reamer, in which case the reamer shank is short and the hole in the front end of the drive shank is drilled out, for a short distance, large enough to go over the flutes of the reamer the proper distance to act as a stop against the end of the barrel, the hole in the shank being enough larger than the reamer flutes to allow the reamer to float.

In using this machine drive shank for a reamer stop on a barrel such as the Krag or the '98 model Mauser, which are flat across the breech end, the end of the reamer drive shank is left flat, but in rough reaming barrels such as the Springfield or Enfield which have a tapered lead into the rear end of the chamber the front end of the reamer drive shank is machined with a 45- degree slope forward. This same type of reamer stop may be used on the finish chamber reamer if it is ma- chine driven to within a few thousandths of an inch of the finish size, after which the reamer is removed from the machine and driven by hand for the last few thousandths and a reamer stop slipped over the shank and held on a flat ground on the shank of the reamer, using one or two set-screws in the side of the stop.

Both the roughing and finishing reamers have pilots on the front end which ride upon the tops of the lands in the barrel to keep the chamber in line with the bore. These pilots should be a very close fit in the bore, not more than .001" smaller than the bore diameter and are hardened as the balance of the reamer is and are ground and polished to a very high polish to prevent scratching the lands. Half an inch is a sufficient length for these pilots and the front and rear edges of this pilot section are slightly rounded off to prevent a sharp edge which would scratch the lands of the barrel. These pilots are solid, being part of the reamer itself.

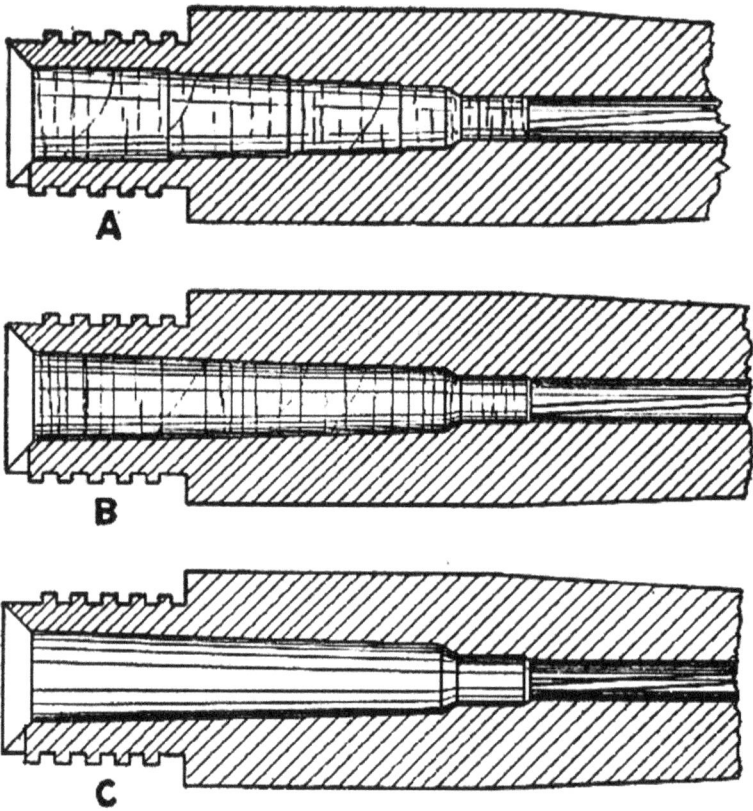

Sectional views of rifle chambers showing the metal removed by the various reamers—A, the rough chambering reamer—B, the finishing reamer—and C, the burnishing reamer.

Some gunsmiths prefer a floating pilot, which has an advantage when a number of barrels are to be chambered, as the bore diameter of barrels may vary enough so that a pilot that fits the lands of one may be too tight for another one. By having a few pilots in each size varying slightly in diameter, these varying bores may be fitted. This floating pilot is a sleeve, the out- side of which is bore diameter and the inner diameter of which rides on an extension of the chambering reamer slightly longer than the sleeve. This extension on the reamer is drilled and tapped in the front end for a screw with a thin fillister-type head, this head being

just slightly less in diameter than the outer diameter of the sleeve, thus holding the sleeve in place on the reamer extension.

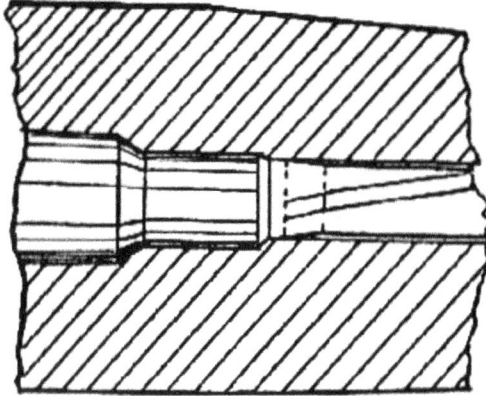

Sectional view of barrel at front end of chamber, showing metal re-moved by throating reamer just ahead of the chamber neck.

Throating reamers, if used, have the same type of pilots as the rough-ing and finishing reamers. Burnishing reamers are used either with or without pilots, being a matter of choice of the factory or individual gun-smith, some claiming that a better burnish is obtained if they are used without pilots. If pilots are used they are of the same type as those used on the other chambering reamers.

When reamers are machine- driven a supply of oil should be pumped into the barrel under pressure to wash out the chips, or the reamers will lodge in the chamber and break or cut an oversize chamber. If reamers are used by hand, the oil may be supplied by hand from a spouted can, then the reamers must often be removed from the chamber and both the reamer and the chamber thoroughly cleaned, after which a patch is pushed through the barrel to clean the lands and grooves. Lard-oil or black sulphur oil compound may be used, but never machine oil.

If the dimensions of the chamber desired are not at hand in making a chambering reamer, twelve or fifteen factory cartridges of various makes should be obtained and carefully measured for size and angle. A clear-ance, above the maximum cartridge found, of .002" in all dimensions will produce a good chamber. If head- space gauges are not available the largest cartridge you can obtain in that caliber should be used as a head-space gauge and the chamber carefully cut until the breech will just close without any perceptible effort upon this cartridge.

In using chambering reamers the cutting edges of the reamers should be carefully examined and any scratches or small nicks stoned out. Watch particularly for wire edges upon the cutting edge of a new reamer, using a magnifying glass of good power for this examination. The front of the cutting edge should be well stoned to remove all marks left by the milling cutter on this face. If a scratch appears in the chamber that is not later removed by the burnishing reamer its effect may be minimized by buffing the chamber with a crocus buff, of circular form, held on a small mandrel and driven by a high-speed polisher such as these electric hand grinders which reach speeds of about 25,000 R.P.M. This applies only to scratches that are not deep or wide and are not quite removed by the burnishing reamer.

In stoning the cutting edges of the reamers, to remove

Plate V

Lathe setup for milling the flutes in a chambering reamer—with the milling attachment driven by flexible shaft and an adjustable tail center to raise tapered reamer to a level. After the reamer blank is turned to shape, an adjustable tail center that can be raised or lowered by screw slides is placed in the tailstock and is raised above the live spindle center so that the tapered body of the reamer is raised until its top surface is level. The flutes are then milled in the reamer with the milling attachment. The live spindle is locked with the back gear of the lathe while each flute is being milled.

small nicks or scratches, be careful not to flatten the relief at the edge, as this is of eccentric form, not flat, but do not overdo this eccentric form or you may drop the cutting edge of a reamer tooth below the top of the land and the edge will then do no cutting. If the edge appears slightly dull it may be stoned on the front face to sharpen it, as this will not change the form nor will it reduce the diameter much.

In making chambering reamer blanks, cartridges can be measured for angle with a protractor. Take measurements at several different points around the body of several cartridges, as the cartridge case is not a perfect form, due to air or lubricant in the forming dies. Be careful that primers do not protrude on cases that you are measuring or this will throw your measurements off.

Barrel drills are short, about 2" long, and instead of having two cutting edges and two grooves as the ordinary twist drill has, it has a single cutting edge and a single vee-shaped groove running straight back from the point. The included angle of the drill point is the same as of the twist drill, 118 degrees. The vee-groove cut the length of the drill and almost to its center in depth, has an included angle of 90 to 100 degrees. The front end of the drill is ground for relief all around, back of the cutting edge, just as the lips of a twist drill are relieved. A small flat is left on the point of the drill, corresponding in size to the thickness of the web of a twist drill of like diameter. On the opposite side of the drill from the vee-groove a small hole is drilled lengthwise through the body of the drill for the passage of oil under pressure from the oil tube to which the drill is attached. On the rear end the diameter of the drill is reduced for a length of about so that the drill drive tube, which also carries the oil supply, may be brazed onto the drill. The drill itself is of high-speed steel and the drive tube is of high-carbon- steel. The drive tube has a vee-groove pressed into it, longer than the length of the barrel blank, matching the groove cut in the drill. This groove carries the returning oil and the chips out of the barrel. After the drill is brazed to the tube the joint is ground or filed smooth. The tube should be very slightly less in diameter than the drill, so that it will not lodge in the bore. The drill is ground with a slight taper to the rear from the front, matching the tube for diameter where they meet, and giving a slight body-clearance to the drill.

A split cast-iron block is mounted on the tool rest of the lathe. It is the full width of the top of the compound rest and has a tongue on the bottom that fits into the tool post slot in the rest. This tongue is just thick enough to extend a short distance down in the tool post slot and the block is held down by two cap-screws passing down through it and into a bar of steel in the wide groove at the bottom of the slot. This block is drilled and reamed, out beyond the tool post slot, on the exact center line of the lathe, clear through from side to side. This hole is a close fit around the drill drive tube which has no vee-groove in it at this point.

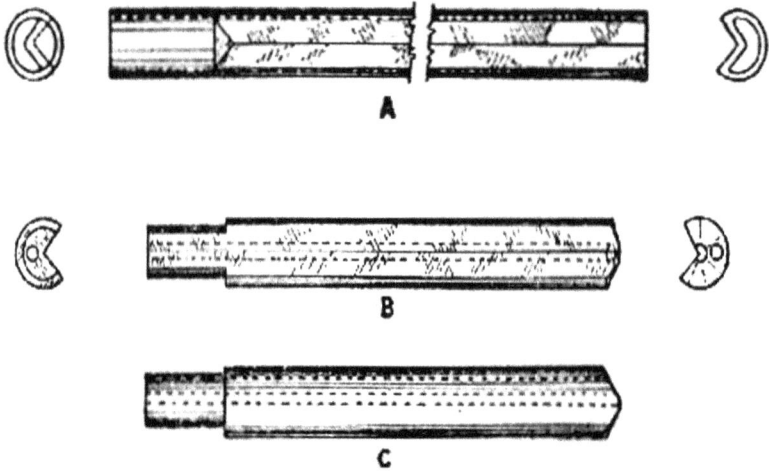

Barrel drilling tools. A is plan and detail views of oil tubing used on barrel drills. B is plan and end view of barrel drill while C is underside view of same.

This block is slotted with a saw-cut from the outer end back through this hole for the drive tube to a short distance back of the hole, the full width of the block. Out beyond the drive tube hole two cap- screws, from top to bottom through the block, clamp the sawed outer end of the block together, squeezing the tube tightly in its hole.

The speed the barrel turns during the drilling operation is high and the feed of the drill into the blank is slow, as you have but one cutting edge on the drill. Oil is pumped under pressure through the tube from the rear end where a connection for a flexible oil tube from the pump is sweated onto the tube. This oil passes through the oil hole in the drill, comes out below the point, and returns, carrying the chips with it in the vee-groove on top of the drill and drive tube. The drill is ground to drill a hole .010" to .012" smaller than the diameter the finished bore is to be made. The blank is carefully centered in the barrel chucks and the hole is started with a center drill and then drilled for a distance with a twist drill to give the barrel drill a true start.

After the barrel is drilled it must be reamed to size and for this operation three reamers are used, a roughing reamer and two finishing reamers, the last really being a burnishing reamer. Reamers arc made of high- speed steel and are made with six grooves, except the roughing reamer which may be made with four or six grooves. These barrel reamers have a rather long front pilot, the front end of which is turned down for a short distance so that the tube which draws the reamer through the barrel can be brazed to the reamer pilot. . The ends of the reamer flutes just behind the pilot are given a slight taper to bring the reamer diameter at this point to just under the diameter of the drilled hole in the barrel blank so that the reamer will start to cut easily. The cutting portion or flutes of the barrel reamers vary from 6" to 7" in length. A hole of small size is drilled lengthwise of the pilot from the front end to a necked portion just ahead of the flutes so that oil may be pumped to the reamer through the pull tube. From the end of this hole in the necked portion of the reamers, three small holes spaced equidistant around the neck are drilled at right- angles to the axis of the reamer so that the oil comes out at the front end of the flutes. These front pilots are made to just fit the drilled hole of the blank on the roughing reamer, to fit the rough-reamed hole on the finishing reamer and to fit the finish-reamed hole on the burnishing reamer. The roughing reamer re- moves .005" to .006" from the drilled hole in the blank, the finishing reamer removes .003" to .004" and the burnishing reamer finishes the bore to size.

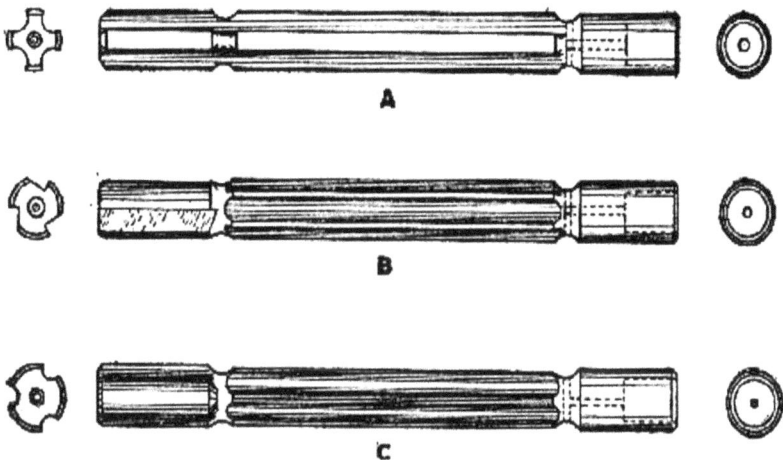

Barrel reamers. A is roughing type reamer, four groove, all carried through rear pilot. B is finishing type reamer, six groove, three grooves carried through rear pilot. C is burnishing reamer, six groove, three grooves carried through rear pilot.

The flutes of the roughing and finishing reamers are cut .010" ahead of center as are those of the roughing and finishing chambering reamers, while those on the burnishing reamer are cut on center and finished to shape as are those of the burnish-type chambering reamer. Barrel reamers do not have clearance ground upon them as do the chambering reamers, their clearance is stoned upon them by hand. Barrel reamers with spiral flutes are more efficient than those with straight flutes as they have a shearing cut but these spiral flutes are far more difficult to stone than are straight flutes. Barrel reamers are sometimes made with rear pilots as well as front pilots and in this case the flutes are milled out through the rear pilots so that the chips can pass off the reamer and on down the barrel.

In using the barrel reamers, the reamers are held stationary and the barrel blank revolves at a low speed as the reamer is drawn through the barrel by the oil tube which is attached to a movable carriage such as the lathe carriage in case a lathe is used. A floating connection at the end of the oil tube should be used, so that the reamers are entirely guided by the bore of the blank. The end of the oil tube may be plugged for 2" and a simple universal joint used, attached to this plugged portion, or a floating drive of the type described on chambering reamers may be used. The flexible oil line from the pump is led into the side of the hollow portion of the oil tube ahead of the plugged end through a screw connection like a nipple. This connection must be removed to pass the oil tube through the barrel blank, as the oil tube is brazed to the reamer, and then put in place and the oil line connected to it before starting the lathe.

Shotgun barrels are made from steel tubes and al- though they may therefore be reamed to size with a series of barrel reamers, such as those used on rifle barrels, they are usually bored with a long, four-sided, square bit of high-speed steel, ground to size on a surface grinder. These bits are 10" to 12" long and have a tapered lead at the front end, about long on the roughing reamer and an inch long on the finish- ing reamer or bit. The driving rod for these bits is brazed to the rear end of the bit, the opposite end from that which has the tapered lead, and the bits are pushed through the bore as the barrel tube revolves.

A wood packing strip, turned on one side to the con- tour of the barrel bore, is placed against one side of this bit, its full length, and on the roughing bit the two edges of the side diametrically opposite the side upon which the packing strip is placed do the cutting. Strips of paper are placed between the wood strip and the boring bit to cause it to cut larger after each trip through the barrel.

A wood strip of the same type is used on one side of the finish or fine boring bit but the leading edge of the opposite side has a small radius stoned upon it so that it does no cutting, which is all done with the trailing edge of this side opposite to that on which the wood strip is placed.

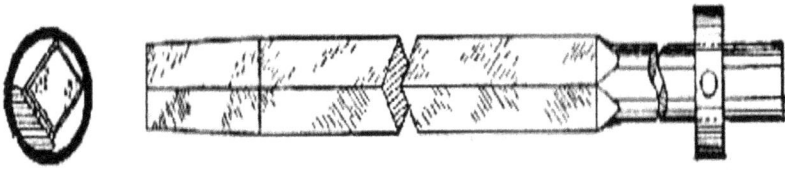

Shotgun boring bit, also sometimes used on rifle barrels. End view shows how wood packing strip and shims are used.

A third square bit, the choke boring bit, is used in shotgun barrels. After the finish or fine boring bit is used this choke boring bit which has a tapered lead an inch long which tapers about .050" in this distance is used to bore out the choke portion of the barrel which is not bored out by the finish boring bit, but only by the roughing bit. A wood packing strip is used, with paper shims on the tapered portion of this choke boring bit and this bit cuts upon two edges as does the roughing bit. These shotgun boring bits are run at a low speed and plenty of cutting oil is used. In making the bits they are hand honed after being ground to shape by a surface grinder. They must be carefully checked for straightness. In doing the grinding, if much stock is to be removed, do not grind a lot off of one side and then off the opposite side but take a small amount off of the first side, then a like amount from the opposite side, then take the same from an adjacent side and the same from the last side and repeat this until the bit is ground to size, as this method of grinding will prevent warping the bit.

Drills for boring out old barrels for relining (the insertion of rifled tubes) may be made from standard, high-speed steel, three or four-groove drills with the regular twist flutes as made by all drill making firms. These manufacturers will grind a pilot on these drills, to order, to fit the old bore of the barrels to be re-lined, or by using an electric tool post grinder you can grind your own pilot upon them. The cutting edges at the rear end of the pilot must be ground with relief, as were the cutting edges at the end of the drill originally. These drills will not drill holes in solid metal but are used to enlarge cored or previously-drilled holes. A carbon-steel shank of any length may be welded to the shank of these drills.

If you wish to make your own drills for drilling out barrels for relining they may be made of a short section, l 1/2" to 2" long, of high-speed steel by turning a pilot upon the front end to fit the old bore in the barrel and turning down a short section of the rear end to a smaller size so that an oil tube may be brazed onto it. The body usually has three straight grooves milled lengthwise of it with a fluting cutter. The front end of the lands between these grooves are relieved or ground as are the lips of a twist drill. A small hole is drilled lengthwise of the body from the shank end about halfway through the body and holes are drilled into this at the end toward the point of the drill from each of the grooves so that oil pumped through the oil tube can be forced out into the flutes, washing the chips out of the barrel ahead of the drill and keeping the cutting edges cool. The pilot is grooved with the milling cutter which cuts the flutes so that the chips have a free passage.

After the old barrel is drilled out with one of these drills it is usually reamed with a barrel reamer of the regular fluted type to straighten the hole perfectly and bring it to size to take the lining tube used.

Six-groove barrel reamer, of the type commonly used in sets of three, in graduated sizes.

Chapter 4 RIFLING TOOLS AND THE RIFLING OF BARRELS

In rifling barrels, a rifling head to hold the cutter is used, to which is attached the rod or tube which draws the cutter through the barrel. In its simplest form this rifling head is a steel cylinder, three inches or more in length, which will just pass through the drilled and reamed barrel blank. In one side of this a slot is cut lengthwise of the cylinder, just wide enough to accept the cutter which fills the slot from side to side and end to end closely enough so that it has no shake. This slot is cut nearly through the cylinder, seating the cutter as deeply as possible.

The rifling cutter is of high-speed steel, square-sided, flat-bottomed and its cutting edge is of the hook type, like a file tooth. The cutting edge has a rake of five to six degrees, both on the face and on the top. The top of the cutting edge is not flat but is rounded to conform to a circle, the diameter of which is the groove diameter of the barrel. The cutter is about V/ 2 " long and the cutting edge is slightly back of center, leaving a space in front of it sufficiently large to hold the chips.

When the cutter is seated on the bottom of the slot the cutting edge is just below the surface of the rifling head. The cutter is raised to rifling position by placing very thin shims beneath it in the slot. These shims should be only .0002" to .0005" in thickness, preferably the thinner one. After the cutter makes a cut in each groove, another shim is placed beneath the cutter, another cut made in each groove and this process continued until all grooves are cut to the proper depth. A small hole is drilled through the rifling head in the bottom of the cutter slot so that a small pin- punch can be inserted through the hole to push the cutter up out of the slot in the rifling head.

The commercial, or factory-type rifling head, is a hollow or tubular piece of high-carbon tool steel, hardened. The hook-type cutter is set in a port within this tube and the hook or cutting edge is about one fourth of the length of the cutter from the rear end. The tail of the cutter is beveled off at a thirty-degree angle on the top side and the rear end of the port in the rifling head is beveled at this same angle. The cutter is beveled both ways on the bottom from a point directly beneath the cutting edge. This bottom bevel is ten degrees. At the rear of the rifling head a beveled wedge goes in, which rests beneath the beveled rear of the cutter. The bevel of the wedge is the same as the bevel on the bottom of the cutter, ten degrees. This beveled wedge is pushed forward by a screw, threads for which are tapped into the rear of the rifling head. Screwing this screw forward in the ri- fling head results in pushing the beveled wedge farther forward under the tail of the cutter thus raising the cutting edge. A cut is taken in each groove of the barrel before moving the wedge farther forward to raise the cutter for a deeper cut. The front end of this hook-type cutter, which comprises three-quarters of the length of the cutter, butts against a steel plunger within the tube which has a coil-spring in front of it. The front end of the cutter is not finished off at right-angles to the top surface of the cutter in front of the hook but is beveled back from the top at about ten degrees. The end of the spring-backed plunger is beveled at ten degrees in the opposite direction, so that its included angle with its top surface is 100 degrees. This is done so that the front end of the cutter is held upward against the top surface of the rifling head. The cutter is about two inches long over all and the rifling head six inches long. The top or cutting edge of the hook is cut on the arc of a circle the same as was described for the simple-type cutter.

Hook type of commercial rifling cutter and rifling head.

The cutting edge of a rifling cutter is ground and honed to a gauge or template, so that when it is re- sharpened or rehoned during the rifling operation its form is not changed at any point. This cutting edge must be kept very sharp and very smooth to do good work, as barrel steel is tough and tends to tear, rather than cut clean, unless the tool is perfect.

The scrape-type of rifling head leaves a better finish in the grooves than does the hook-type but it is more difficult to keep sharp and requires very careful honing. Its cutting action is a scrape rather than a shearing cut and the shavings are extremely fine, rather like very fine shavings cut from wood with a fine file.

The rifling head is a hollow cylinder of high-carbon steel with a port for the cutter cut lengthwise, about two inches long, in one side. This port is very accu- rate in shape and size as the scrape cutter must fit it closely with no shake whatever, as this cutter cuts in both directions while traveling through the barrel. This rifling head is about six inches long and is internally 7 threaded at both ends, a thread at one end for attaching the pull-tube, which also carries a supply of oil to the cutter, and a fine thread at the opposite end for the adjusting screw to raise the cutter. In the bottom of the rifling head between the port for the cutter, but upon the opposite side, and the fine threads for the adjustment screw, a narrow slot is cut length- wise of the head. This is for the head of a screw to ride in which is screwed into the bottom of the adjusting wedge.

The cutter body is a very exact fit in the port in the rifling head and the bottom of the cutter body is ground on a taper of about ten degrees from one end to the other. The face of this taper is at an exact right-angle to the sides of the cutter body. The cutting edge of scraper on top of the cutter body is not at right- angles to the sides of the cutter body and rifling head but extends across the top of the cutter body at a forty-five degree angle to give as much shearing effect to the scrape as possible. This scraper is at the central point of the cutter body and the body of the cutter is cut away at each side of the scraper to give chip space. The actual edge that docs the scraping is an included angle of eighty degrees, the sides sloping down and away from the edge equally in both directions to the top of the cutter body. This scraping edge also has the contour of the arc of the circle the diameter of which is that of the groove diameter of the barrel. This edge must be ground and honed to a template so that its shape will be true and will remain so. The template is cut from thin sheet-steel.

The wedge which raises the cutter in its slot in the rifling head has a circular contour on the bottom to fit the contour of the inside of the rifling head upon the bottom. The top of this wedge is ground off on a ten-degree taper to match that upon the bottom of the cutter body. The thickness of this wedge is such that its thin end extends slightly beyond the thick end of the cutter body, which is toward the end of the rifling head to which the pull-rod is attached. This thin end of the tapered wedge is ground square on the end and this square end butts against a square-ended plug, backed by a spring, which spring is in turn backed by the end of the pull-rod inside the rifling head. In the bottom of the wedge a hole is drilled and tapped for a small screw, the head of which closely fits the slot cut in the bottom of the rifling head. This screw prevents the wedge from turning and should be hardened to prevent undue wear. The adjusting screw for the wedge has an unthreaded portion beyond the threaded part, smaller than the threads. The end of this un- threaded portion is ground square and butts against the large end of the adjusting wedge. As this adjusting screw is screwed forward in the rifling head it moves the tapered wedge forward under the cutter, raising it as necessary.

Now that wc have the rifling heads and cutters made, the next thing is a rifling machine to use them. These are of several types, from the regular factory rifling machine to the lathe and the various types of hand- rifling machines, usually called a rifling bench.

We shall consider the simplest type, the hand-rifling machine first. In this type, the most intricate fixture is the rifling guide, and probably one of the simplest guides is another rifle barrel of the same twist as you wish to use. It need not have the same number of grooves however. A good solid clamp or preferably a pair of clamps are bolted to a good solid bench to hold the barrel. In line with these, and at the same center height, a third clamp is bolted to hold one end of the barrel that is to be used as a guide. The fourth clamp, which is also used on the barrel being used for a guide, must be a different type from the other, for this clamp must hold a flanged sleeve which is clamped tightly to the guide barrel and in this sleeve are as many holes drilled in a line around its circumference as you desire grooves in the barrel to be rifled. A pin passes through this last clamp at a point in line with the holes drilled in the sleeve, so that when the guide barrel is loosened in its clamps, the guide barrel and sleeve can be turned, so as to bring one of the pin holes in the sleeve in line with the pin hole through the clamp in which the sleeve operates. This pin must fit the holes in clamp and sleeve very closely, the sleeve must fit closely in the clamp, and it can also be locked by having the clamp split at one side and a clamp bolt passed through the two sections. The flange on the sleeve is to prevent end motion of the guide barrel.

A rod or tube long enough to pass through both the barrel to be rifled and also the guide barrel, with some several inches to spare, is attached to the rifling head. This rod or tube must have a guide block upon it to ride in the grooves of the guide barrel to cause the rifling cutter to turn. The simplest way to make this is to place the rod inside the guide barrel, packed with waste at a point four or five inches below the muzzle. Fastening the barrel muzzle-up, heat the barrel and the rod from the muzzle down to the packing point, with a torch until it is pretty hot and, making sure that the rod is central in the bore, pour in melted nickel-babbit around the rod until the barrel is full to the muzzle. After it has cooled, withdraw it partly from the barrel and shave off the outer end, where it overflowed the muzzle. Now, make a punch mark on the muzzle of the barrel at one of the grooves and mark the babbit slug on the end opposite this mark on the barrel, so that if this guide block is removed from the guide barrel you will get it back in the same position in which it was cast. Remove the waste from the barrel and clean the barrel out well. Reinsert the rod and guide block in the guide barrel, then attach to the rear end of the rod a sturdy cross-handle, mounted on the rod on ball-bearings.

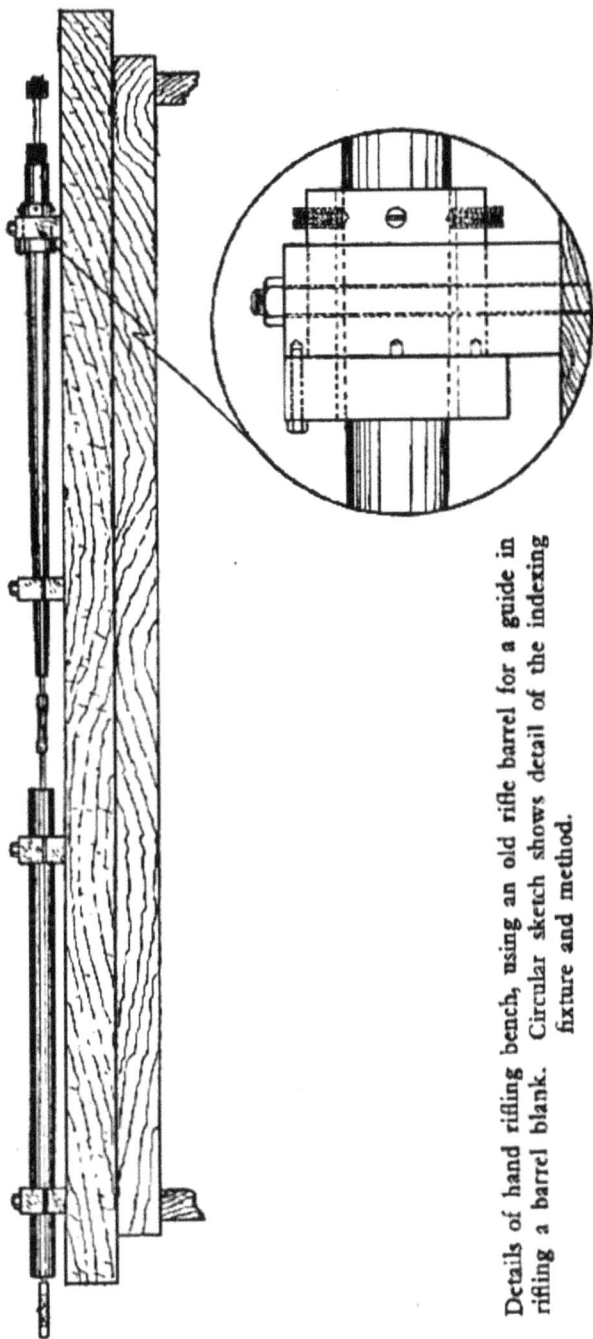

Details of hand rifling bench, using an old rifle barrel for a guide in rifling a barrel blank. Circular sketch shows detail of the indexing fixture and method.

The rod, with the guide in place in the guide barrel near the end closest to the barrel to be rifled, should be long enough so that the rifling cutter clears by an inch or more the opposite end of the barrel to be rifled. With the clamps all locked and the rifling cutter in position in the head, the rifling cutter is now drawn through the barrel to be rifled, making the first cut. The cutter is then dropped down, or, if it is the shimmed-up type of hook cutter, it is removed from the rifling head and the head is pushed back through the barrel. The cutter is replaced and the clamps on the guide barrel are loosened then the index pin is withdrawn and the guide barrel revolved in the clamps to the next pin hole, the pin is replaced, the clamps are tightened and the cutter is again drawn through the barrel to make a cut for the second groove. This process is repeated with the same cutter setting until one cut has been made in each groove. The cutter is then raised and a second cut is made in the first groove, and all this is repeated until the grooves are all cut to the proper depth. The guide barrel must be kept well oiled on the inside and the barrel being rifled must be flooded with cutting oil, either lard-oil or black surphur oil compound. This cutting oil should be fed into the barrel under pressure so that it will wash out the chips and for this reason it is better to use a tube for a pull-rod, as the oil line from the pump can be attached to the end of the tube opposite the rifling head and the oil can be pumped into the barrel by this method by having oil outlet holes drilled in the rilling head. An automobile oil pump driven by a small electric motor can be used, or the oil can be forced through the barrel by air pressure, if you have a compressor. As the oil leaves the barrel it is screened to remove chips and is returned to the sump from which it is pumped.

The next step in improvement over using another barrel for a guide is a steel shaft, grooved on the out- side with spiral grooves and run through an indexing fixture held in a clamp. The barrel to be rifled is held in a clamp fixture on a bench, just as the barrel was held by the first method described, and the spiral cut shaft is held in two clamps, in line with the barrel to be rifled. One of these clamps, or more properly guides for the spiral shaft, is plain and while the shaft must be a close fit in it, it must not bind, for it passes through it with a twisting slide. The second fixture for this spiral guide is the indexing fixture, which has as many pin holes, equally spaced around its circumference, as you desire grooves in the barrel. A rather heavy pin fits tightly in these holes, one pin being used and all holes being the same size, as this pin passes through the fixture rim and engages the spiral groove in the shaft. A ball-bearing cross-handle is fitted to the end of the spiral shaft, so that it may be moved back and forth and, of course, on the opposite end of the spiral shaft from that to which this handle is attached, the tube connected to the rifling head is attached. A single groove is all that is necessary to be cut in the guide shaft. If this spiral guide shaft is made too small in diameter, it will not move as freely or last as long as a shaft of larger diameter. To cut down the weight incident to a larger diameter shaft, a fairly heavy- walled steel tubing may be used for this purpose. In large cities, jobbing machine shops may be found that have lathes with a spiral attachment on them and if they have the proper gears with this spiral attachment to cut long spirals, the guide shaft may be machined in one of these lathes. If it is not possible to find a lathe with this equipment, this spiral groove may be cut in the guide shaft with a milling machine which is equipped with a spiral-cutting setup. It will require a milling machine of pretty good size, in order to have a table long enough and with enough travel to cut this

Plate VI

Circular grinding of a chambering reamer in the lathe, using a Dumore electric tool post grinder and an adjustable tail center. After a chambering reamer is fluted and the clearance is ground on it, the reamer is hardened while still .012" to .015" oversize. It is then replaced in the lathe and with the lathe centers in line the pilot of the reamer is ground to size, using the electric tool post grinder. The tailstock is then set over to bring the slight taper of the neck portion of the reamer parallel to the center line of the lathe. This portion of the reamer is then ground to size. The tailstock is then set over the additional amount to bring the body portion of the reamer parallel to the lathe center line and this portion is then ground to size. Instead of offsetting the tailstock center an adjustable tail center, as shown above, can be used.

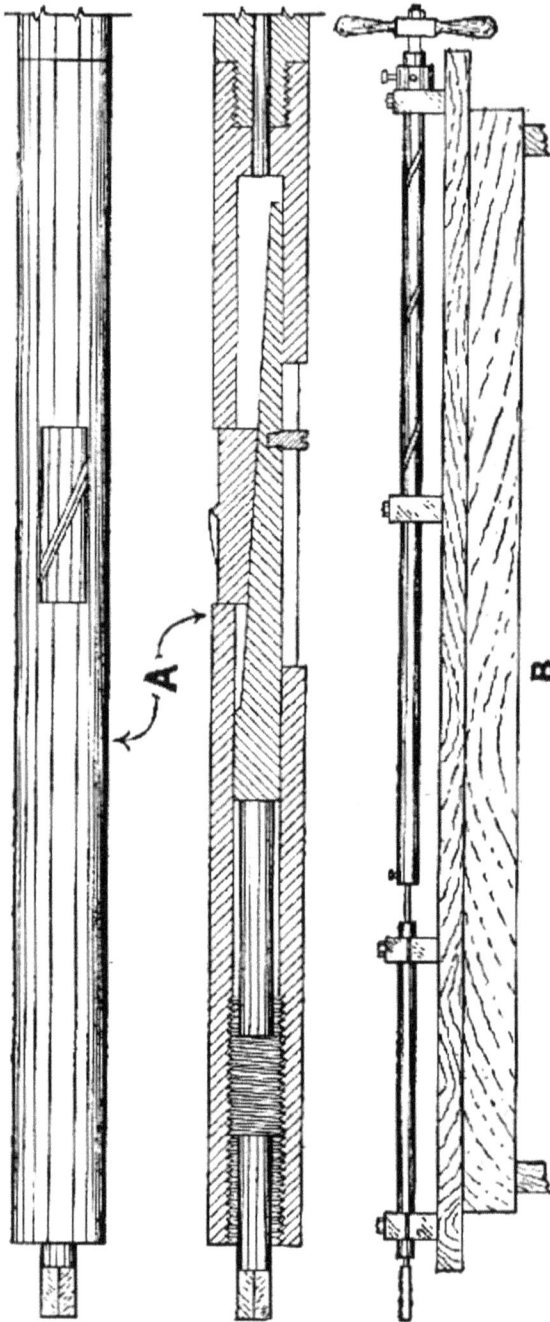

A shows simple type of scrape rifling cutter, showing how adjustment is made with a tapered raising wedge, held from turning by a set screw screwed into the bottom of the tapered wedge and riding in a close fitting groove in the bottom of the rifling head.   Bottom sketch B shows method of rifling a barrel blank in a hand rifling bench by using a grooved steel shaft for a rifling guide.

long spiral. Each spiral will only cut grooves of one twist, so that in rifling barrels of different twists, different guide shafts must be used, each with its own twist of spiral groove.

The engine lathe of the screw-cutting type can be used to rifle barrels and the setup is not expensive. Some makers of engine lathes supply spiral attachments for their lathes. These have a set of gears with them and these gears, in connection with the gears regularly supplied with the lathe, will cut almost any required spiral. If the lathe has a large hollow spindle, the barrel can be passed through the spindle and held with the regular barrel chucks mounted on each end of the spindle. The oil tube which is attached to the rifling head can be held in a clamp fixture mounted upon the tool rest of the lathe. This is the most satisfactory method and requires the least fixtures. If however, the spindle is too small to allow the barrel to pass through it, the rifling head may be driven by the lathe spindle and the barrel can be held in a clamp fixture mounted upon the tool rest. In this case the clamp fixture holding the barrel should be fairly long and heavy, so that it may grip the barrel at two rather widely separated points. This method requires a longer lathe bed than the first method, as the bed must be long enough to accommodate the barrel length plus sufficient length for the rifling head with yet enough length of tube or pull rod on the rifling head so that it can pass clear through the barrel.

The lower priced lathes are not supplied with spiral attachments by their manufacturers but the higher grade lathes can be so supplied. These spiral attachments usually include an indexing attachment but if it does not, a simple one may be devised so that the rifling cutter is started in the barrel with the spindle in the correct position each time. An accurate pro- tractor mounted on the spindle nose will do the trick.

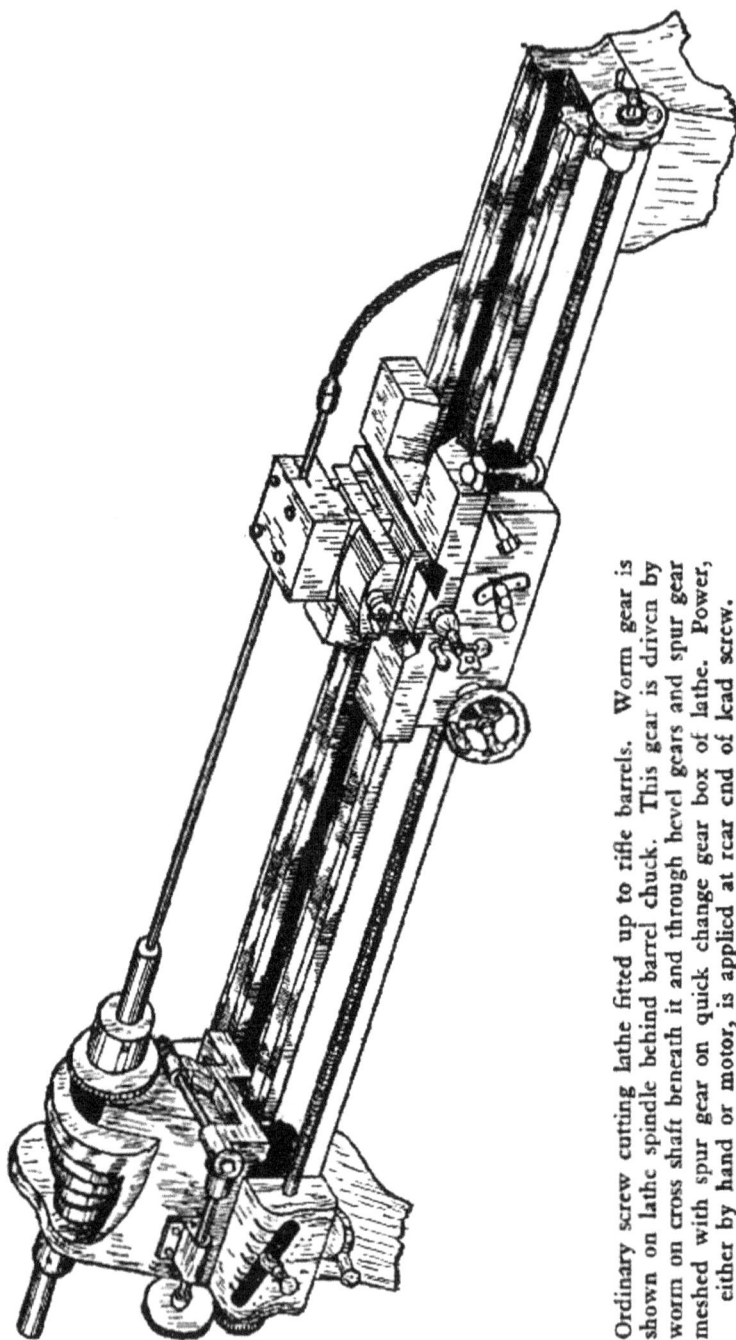

Ordinary screw cutting lathe fitted up to rifle barrels. Worm gear is shown on lathe spindle behind barrel chuck. This gear is driven by worm on cross shaft beneath it and through bevel gears and spur gear meshed with spur gear on quick change gear box of lathe. Power, either by hand or motor, is applied at rear end of lead screw.

A spiral attachment may be built for a screw cutting engine lathe of the quick-change gear-type with- out much expense, outside of the labor involved, so that barrels may be rifled upon the lathe, driving it either by power or by hand.

To make this spiral attachment, obtain a stock worm gear and worm, the gear being large enough so that it may be bored out to slip over the lathe spindle nose with a close fit. This gear is held in place with a barrel chuck screwed tightly up against it. A bracket is now made to fit the lathe bed, just as the tail stock or center rest does, and on the upper part of this bracket, which can be clamped to the lathe bed with the clamp plate used with the center rest, a shaft is mounted, at right-angles to the center line of the lathe, and on this shaft the worm that mates the worm gear on the spindle nose is mounted so that it meshes with the worm gear. This worm shaft is long enough so that it extends to the front of the lathe, a little past the headstock. On this outer end of the shaft, a standard miter or bevel gear is mounted and a second miter or bevel gear meshes with this and is on a shaft extending to the head end of the lathe. A bracket for this shaft may be bolted to the side of the head- stock. At the head or gear end of the lathe, a gear is mounted on this shaft so that it meshes with the gear train leading from the lathe spindle to the quick- change gear box. This gear may have to be a special gear, if the gears on your lathe do not happen to be standard gears which can be purchased from some standard gear works. It may even be necessary to use two gears at this point to reach the lathe gear train. The ratio of these gears, and of the worm and worm gear, must be figured out for your particular lathe to bring the spiral produced within reach of the gear box gears of the lathe, so that all the common twists in rifling may be reached by simply shifting the gears.

In use, the belt pulleys of the lathe are disconnected from the spindle so that the spindle turns freely and the drive is applied at the tail end of the lead screw of the lathe. A hand crank may be applied to the end of the lead screw and after the half-nuts of the lathe carriage are closed upon the lead screw, the carriage is moved as the lead screw is turned ; the lead screw in turning operates the gears at the head of the lathe and through the special shafts added, turns the spindle with the worm and worm gear. If desired, a pulley may be placed upon the end of the lead screw and a motor can be used to drive the lead screw. Vee- pulleys and vee-belt will make the best drive at Ibis point. The gears necessary for this setup should not cost more than twelve or fifteen dollars, unless special gears have to be made for use at the head of the lathe. If the lathe is a small type, the cost for gears will not run more than half the above amount. Standard gears can be obtained from Boston Gear Works or from Chicago Gear Works or any other company producing what is known as standardized gears.

A goud grade of cutting oil must always be supplied under pressure to the barrel being rifled, to lengthen the life of the rifling cutter, to make a smoother cut and to keep the barrel clean of chips.

Forms of rifling of widely divergent types have been experimented with in years past, but rifling has finally settled down to two main forms, one in which lands and grooves are of equal width and the second in which the grooves are wide and the lands are narrow. These two types seem to give equally good results, although the groove and land of equal width are usually preferred for the jacketed bullet. Grooves in barrels to use lead bullets are often deeper than those in barrels for jacketed bullets, with the exception of the .22 caliber, although all manufacturers do not follow this practice.

Grooves should not be deeper than is necessary to grip the bullet well, as extremely deep grooves lead to rapid throat erosion and sometimes to fins upon the base of bullets which act as rudders and give the bullet an erratic flight. It is a good plan to follow the practices of some of our best rifle manufacturers, but this does not mean that it is useless

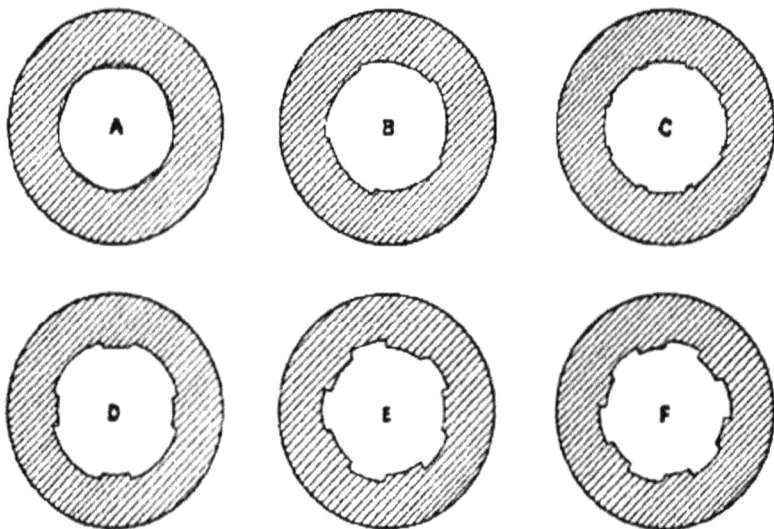

Various types of rifling. A Charles Newton's segmental type, 5 grooves. B Newton's parabolic type, 5 grooves. C Harry Pope's 8 groove rifling. D standard type 4 groove. E standard type 5 groove. F standard type 6 groove rifling.

to experiment, for who knows what you may develop.

In the work of relining barrels, the original barrel is bored out by a drill with a pilot to fit the original bore as previously described, the drill being started at the chamber end of the old barrel so that it will be well centered. The barrel is then reamed with a barrel reamer to bring it to the size of the tube to be inserted in it. These tubes come in two sizes, 1/2 and 3/8" and are already rifled, although some barrel reliners prefer to insert an unrifled tube in the old barrel and rifle it after it is in place.

Split brass bushings, tapered on the outside, are supplied with the relining tubes. These slip over the outside of the tube at each end and the ends of the old barrel must be reamed out with a reamer of the same taper as these bushings. These reamers have a pilot which fits the reamed barrel and thus the bushings center the liner in the barrel.

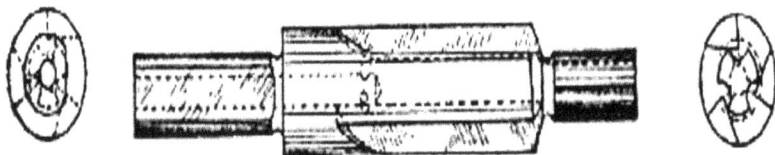

Three groove drill of high speed steel, with straight grooves, to bore out old barrels for relining.

The barrel to be relined is placed on a soldering stand, while gas jets play upon it, along its full length, from each side. When it reaches the proper heat it is tinned all over, inside, with a stiff wire brush or with a special copper tool supplied with grooves to hold the solder. If the brush is used, it is dipped into and saturated with regular tinners solder and the barrel is tinned by running the tool or brush through the barrel.

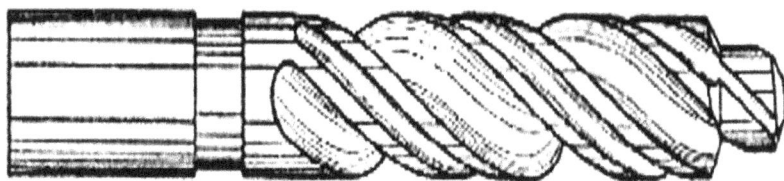

Standard commercial three groove twist drill, with pilot ground on it, to drill out old barrels for relining.

The liner has its ends plugged with wood plugs and is tinned on the outside. It is inserted in the barrel and worked back and forth so that excess solder is worked out and surfaces of both barrel and liner are evenly tinned. The liner is left about three inches longer than the barrel, an even amount being allowed to extend from each end of the barrel.

The split brass bushings arc tinned all over, then placed around the tube and tapped into the taper reamed for them at each end of the barrel.

Set the barrel upright while cooling. After it is cold, hang it up with a wire and strike it with a small hammer. If the job is well soldered, it will ring. If it does not ring, the liner will have to be removed and the soldering operation repeated until it does ring, showing a good tight job.

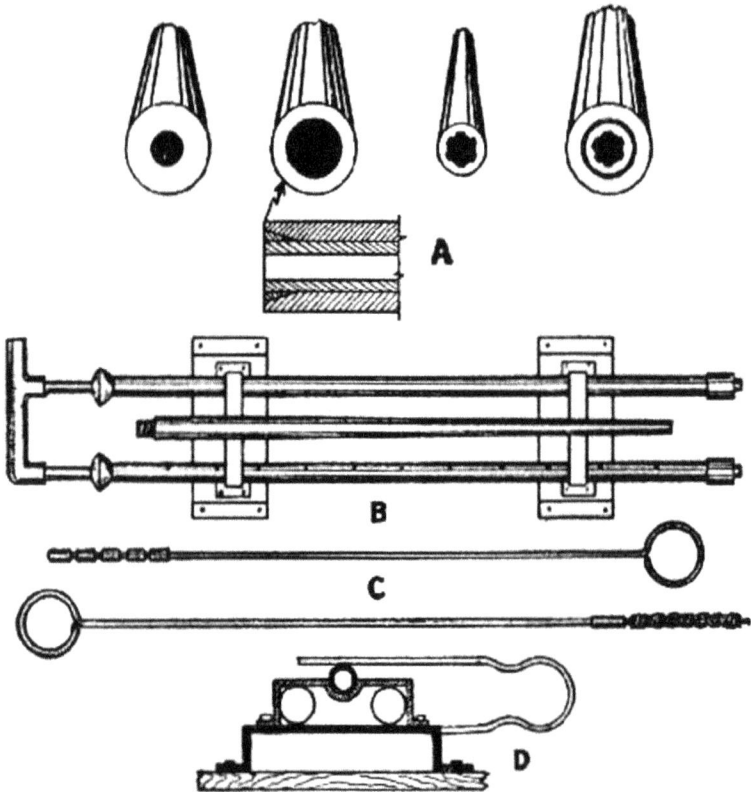

Details of relining old barrels. A shows steps in boring out old barrel, the relining tube and the assembly of same. B is gas burners and barrel rest necessary for soldering liner in barrel. C is the two types of tinning tools for coating inside of old barrel and D is spring clamp for holding barrel on stand.

After the liner is cut off flush with each end of the barrel and fitted to the action, the extractor cut is made, the liner is then chambered for the cartridge and the muzzle end is finished with a countersink equipped with a pilot fitting the bore.

In rifling a barrel or a reliner tube, the rifling cutter sets up a small burr along the edges of the grooves and these must be removed by lapping. Insert a grooved lapping rod in the barrel after wrapping about two of the lower grooves with string, the rod being inserted from the breech end of the barrel and stopped just a little short of the muzzle. The barrel is stood or rather held upright in a vise, muzzle-up, and in the case of a new barrel, is heated so that the lead casts a full lap. If it is heated to just a light straw color, it will be sufficient and the heating is done only for the length of the lap at the muzzle, about two inches. The melted lead is poured into the muzzle and is just allowed to come flush with it. As soon as the lead cools, which it does very quickly, the lap is pushed out of the muzzle just a short distance and examined to see that it is perfect. If it shows an overflow at the muzzle this is trimmed off with a sharp knife. Do not allow the lap to come entirely out of the barrel at any time until the lapping work is finished.

Give the lap a coating of light oil and withdraw it to the breech end of the barrel, allowing it to extend slightly from this end, so that the string may be re- moved and the lap coated with a fine grade of optical emery. While the lap is at the rear end of the barrel, coat the barrel from the muzzle end with oil.

The lapping rod is equipped with a ball-hearing cross-handle at the opposite end from the lap so that it may easily be grasped and worked back and forth through the barrel. Stops are placed at both the muzzle and breech end of the barrel so that the lap will never be pushed or pulled entirely from the barrel. Lap the barrel for eight or ten minutes, adding fresh emery and oil frequently.

At the end of this time withdraw the lap from the barrel and wash the barrel out with gasoline or solvent and examine it to see that all burrs have been re- moved. If further lapping is necessary, an entirely new lap must be cast on the rod in the barrel, as be- fore, for the old lap cannot be reinserted.

If you desire an extra high polish, as is often given to .22 caliber target barrels, the barrel can be polished with rouge and olive-oil after the lapping operation. Leather washers about two or three-thousandths of an inch larger than the groove diameter of the barrel are placed upon a polishing-rod with ball-bearing cross- handle, these leather washers being separated from each other with small brass washers and retained in place by a brass nut on the end, which is made bore diameter. During the polishing operation, this nut can be tightened a little from time to time, to swell the leather washers slightly. The polishing operation may be kept up for an hour or more.

In casting a lap in a relined barrel in which an un- rifled tube has been inserted and later rifled, the barrel cannot be heated as hot as the one-piece barrel, or the solder holding the tube in place will be melted, there- fore keep temperatures to not much over 250 degrees.

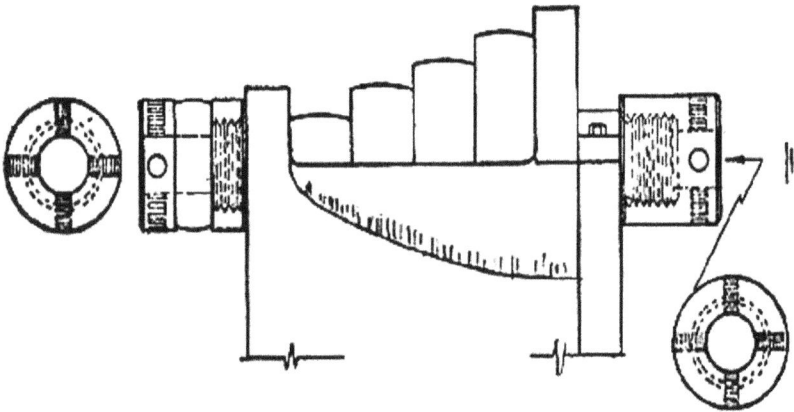

Lathe spindle, showing barrel chucks at each end.

Chapter 5 REBORING AND RECHAM-
BERING OLD RIFLES

Rifles with worn-out barrels may have the barrel recut to a larger caliber and rechambered for a cartridge that the action will handle. For instance, the .25-20 Winchester repeater, model 1892 may be recut to .32-20. The .25-35 model 1894 Winchester can be recut to .30-30 or .32 special. The Savage model 1899 in the .22 Hi-power may be recut .25-35, etc. Single-shot rifle barrels may, of course be recut to any larger caliber, as it makes no difference to the action in this case whether a cartridge is long or short.

There is often a difference in the pitch of rifling between cartridges of different calibers, so in recutting these old barrels to larger calibers be careful not to use a twist that is too slow. A little faster twist won't make much difference, in fact may make bullets that are slightly out of balance travel a little truer, but slowing down the twist will result in poor accuracy and keyholing of bullets unless a light, short bullet is used. For instance, the .22 Hi-power barrels are rifled with one turn in 14" for the Savage .22 Hi-power cartridge, while the .25-35 barrels are rifled with one turn in 8", so if a .22 Hi-power barrel is recut to .25-35 caliber and the twist left the one turn in 14" the barrel would not handle the 117 grain or the 100 grain bullet with much accuracy. It might do fairly well with the 87 grain bullet loaded to its highest permissible velocity and it would prob- ably handle the 60 grain very well. Therefore, in recutting old barrels it is not possible to use the old barrel itself for a rifling guide unless the twist of the old barrel and the required twist for the new cartridge are the same or very nearly so. Two instances of this are the .38-40 being recut to .44-40 — the twist in this case is the same, one turn in 36 inches, — and in recutting the .30-30 to .32 Win- chester Special. The twist of the .30-30 is one turn in 12 inches while that used for the .32 Special is one turn in 16 inches. Cutting the barrel for the .32 Special with a twist of one turn in 12 inches will not matter much, as the increase in twist in this case will not raise breech pressures to any great extent.

The recutting of the barrels for the above cartridges, using the twist of the original barrel, is mentioned be- cause this requires a minimum of equipment, the original barrel being used as the rifling guide while it is being recut. To do this, the old barrel must have a fair amount of rifling left in it. A lead slug is cast in the barrel, about 4" long, on a rod of steel, as is described in the chapter on cleaning and lapping barrels, and the oil and emery are used to lap the barrel first, so that it runs even for size, with no very tight or very loose places within it. The barrel is then thorough^ washed out with gasoline and cleaned, after which a new slug of nickel-babbitt, 6" in length, is cast upon a heavy steel rod of a diameter that will just enter the bore easily. Two inches of one end of this rod is turned down to a smaller diameter. In the case of recutting a .30-30 to .32 Special caliber the rod would be turned down to y 4 " diameter for 2". This section is then filed square and the edges notched at four or five places with a three-square file. This rod is inserted from the breech of the barrel, with a piece of cotton waste or string wound on the rod at the point where the squared portion joins the round portion of the rod. This squared portion is stopped with its end 4" below the muzzle and, with the barrel set muzzle-up, the last 6" of the barrel is warmed with a torch until it is about ready to change color, whereupon the melted babbitt is poured steadily into the muzzle until the bore is filled for the last 6". As soon as the babbitt cools, the cast is pushed a short distance out of the muzzle so that any overflow may be cut off. It is then with- drawn slowly through the barrel, to see that it slides through all right and is not too loose.

The old rifling grooves appear as ridges on the cast and in one of these ridges a slot is cut, the full width of the ridge and 1 1/2' to 2 " long, following the angle of the ridge exactly and not quite going clear through the cast, leaving about 1/1 0 " thickness at the bottom of the slot. A rifling cutter of the hook type is then made to fit this slot very closely and of a depth so that when it is on the bottom of the slot the edge of the cutter just comes flush with the top of the ridge in which it sets. This cutter may be ground to shape from a piece of high-speed steel, such as a lathe cutting bit or it may even be made from a large flat file by heating the file red-hot and burying it in slaked lime to cool, after which it is soft and may be sawed and filed to shape. Leave plenty of chip room in front of the culling edge by filing or grinding out a space half an inch long and a little over half the depth of the cutter at this point. If the cutter is made from a file, it is heated red-hot after being shaped and is quenched in water to harden, after which the edge is honed with very fine oil stones. If the cutter is of high-speed steel, ground to shape, no hardening will he required, merely the honing to give it a smooth, very sharp edge.

A hole is drilled through the bottom of the cutter slot, so that a small punch or nail may be used to push the cutter up out of its slot. The cutter is set in the slot with the hook pointing backwards and the rod is inserted into the barrel from the breech, with the cast carrying the rifling head and cutter going in last. A cross-handle, equipped with a ball-bearing center, has the center drilled and tapped so that the end of the rod opposite the rifling head can be threaded to screw into this ball-bearing center of the cross-handle. Probably the easiest way to make this ball-bearing center cross-handle is to get a ball-bearing bicycle hub or pedal and anneal one end of the shaft by heating to a red-heat and burying in slaked lime, after which it may be drilled and tapped. If it is not hardened this will not be necessary. Two pieces of hardwood are clamped together and a hole is drilled through them where they meet, just the size of the outer case of the ball-bearing hub or pedal. These two pieces are bolted together at right-angles to the hole drilled through them. A little is planed off the edges of these pieces where they meet each other so that when they are placed around the hub or pedal and the bolts drawn up they will clamp tightly upon it. The ends of these wood pieces can be shaped-up into handles with a draw knife.

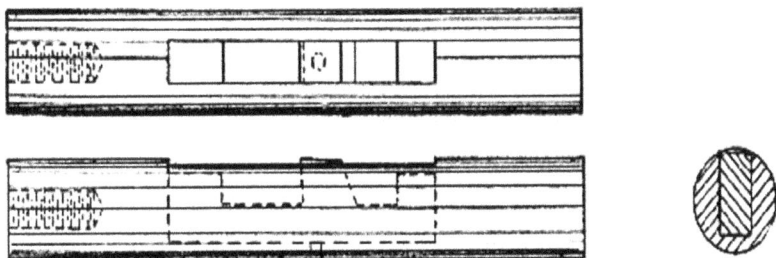

A simple design of hook type rifling cutter, using shims to raise the cutter. This is the type which can be made by the individual for use in rerifling old barrels.

rod projecting from the muzzle, the rifling head is carefully started into the breech end of the barrel so that the ridges upon it enter the grooves in the barrel. The barrel is clamped tightly in a vise and the rod, carrying the cutter, is drawn steadily and slowly through the barrel and out the muzzle. The barrel is cleaned out and a punch is used to push the cutter out of its slot, and both cutter and slot are thoroughly cleaned. Remove the rod from the handle and put the rod through the barrel from the breech again and attach it to the handle at the muzzle. Start the rifling head into the grooves again, but with the cutter in another groove, and draw the cutter through the barrel a second time. Each time the cutter is passed through the barrel, examine the edge of it and hone it if necessary. After the cutter has passed once through each groove, place a shim of very thin paper beneath it in its slot and, after oiling the barrel with lard-oil, draw the cutter through each groove in turn again, oiling the barrel each time after it has been cleaned out following the passage of the cutter. The cutter may be run through each groove more than once if it will continue to cut without the addition of another shim but be sure and run it through each groove the same number of times. After all the grooves have been recut with one shim under the cutter, the babbitt rifling head will be loose in the barrel and must be melted off the rod, then a new slug of babbitt cast on the rod as before and a slot cut in it for the rifling cutter.

After the grooves have all been cut to within .001" of the proper depth for the new cartridge, the groove- diameter of the barrel will be .002" less than is used for the cartridge in question. The barrel can be measured with a soft lead slug and an outside micrometer or it may be measured directly with an inside micrometer of a size from .2" to 1" as sold by both L. S. Starrett Co. and Brown & Sharpe, price $14.00.

The bore of the barrel must now be increased for the new cartridge and for this purpose reamers of left-hand spiral with right-hand cut are used. These reamers are used in sets of three, are equipped with pilots and are drawn through the barrel by a rod attached to the pilot end of the reamer. The first two reamers each remove .005" and the third reamer re- moves .002". In the case of recutting a .30-30 to .32 Special caliber these three reamers will remove just the right amount, leaving the bore .001" small. Lard-oil is supplied in quantity during this reaming opera- tion, being poured in from the muzzle end of the barrel as the reamers are drawn through from the breech. As you arc facing the front end of the barrel reamer turn it to the left, which gives the reamer a right hand rotation as you draw it through the barrel.

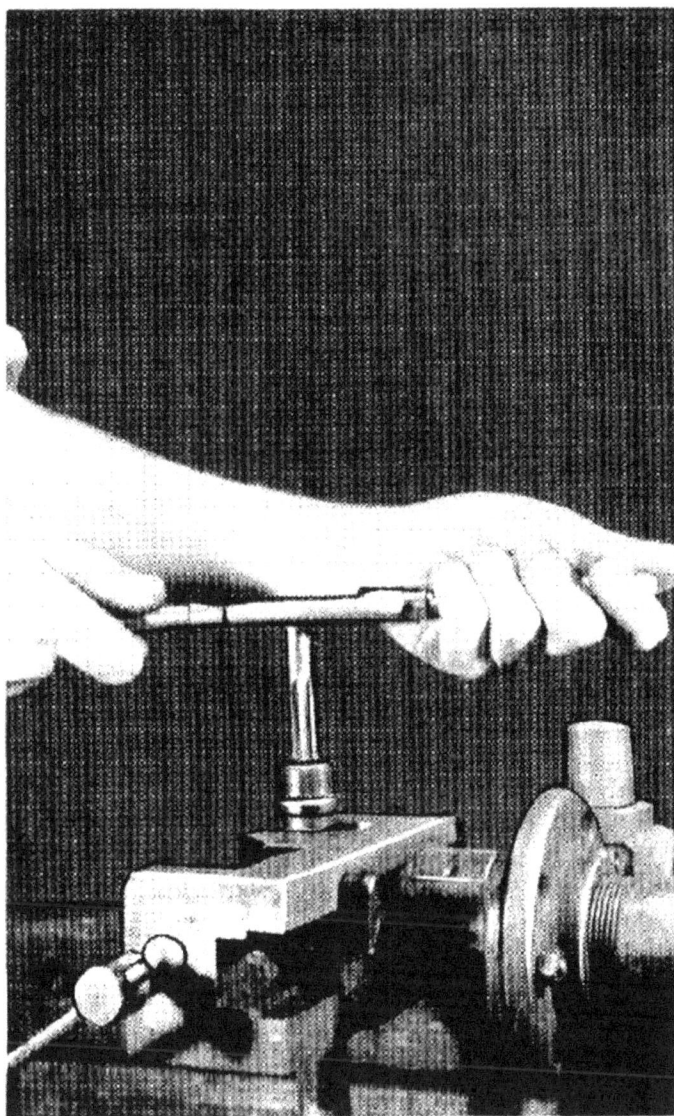

Plate VII

Chambering a rifle barrel by hand.

In using the finishing chambering reamer by hand, the barrel is mounted vertically in the vise, as shown, and both hands exert an equal pressure in turning the reamer wrench. This helps to keep the reamer running true, cutting equally on all sides.

with emery and oil until the bore is brought to size.

The regular chambering reamers are used to chamber the barrel for the new cartridge.

In recutting a barrel for a cartridge requiring a different twist, such as recutting a .25-20 Repeater barrel to .32-20, there are the two ways of obtaining the desired twist with a hand rifling bench. One way is to obtain a barrel with the desired twist, in this case one turn in 20", and mounting this on a heavy bench in line with the barrel in which the rifling is to be cut. It does not matter what diameter the bore of this guide barrel is, nor does it matter how many grooves it has. The rifling head is made of steel in this case and has the pull rod on one end as before, and from the rear end of the rifling head a rod extends through the guide- barrel, and upon this rod a length of nickel-babbitt is cast within the guide barrel. This guide barrel is kept well oiled with machine oil and the ball-bearing cross-handle is attached on the end of the pull-rod beyond the muzzle of the barrel being rifled, as before.

The babbitt guide block in the second barrel runs always in the same grooves, and either the guide barrel or the barrel being recut is turned to give the position for each groove being cut.

The second way of rifling the barrel is to have a shaft with a single groove milled upon its surface by a milling machine with a spiral attachment, the groove having the proper twist, in this case one complete turn in 20", to produce the correct twist of rifling. This shaft passes through two blocks, with close fitting smooth bearings, fastened to a heavy bench in line with the clamp blocks holding the barrel being rifled. In one of these blocks holding the shaft with the spiral groove upon it is a pin passing through the block and bearing and entering the groove in the shaft, which it fits closely. Only one pin is used but there as as many holes for it, equally distant from each other around the circumference of the bearing, as you desire grooves in the barrel being rifled.

In connection with this groove business is an argument as to just how many grooves, and whether of an even or odd number, a rifle barrel should have. Win- chester and Remington contend that six grooves give the best results, Springfield armory claims they do just as well with four grooves and Savage joins them in this to some extent. The British government says five grooves are the thing, which is the reason our 1917 model adapted from the British Enfield has five grooves. Charles Newton was also an exponent of five grooves, while Eric Johnson turns out eight-groove barrels and other barrel makers make five and seven-groove barrels. This argument has never been settled, as barrels with all these different numbers of grooves have shot well, but the contenders for the odd number of grooves really have what looks like the basis for a good argument, as they say that with an odd number of grooves the part of the rifling head directly under the rifling cutter is supported with the solid steel of the bore, as in odd-number grooved barrels the grooves are not opposite to each other, while in barrels with an even number of grooves the rifling head has a groove beneath the part directly under the cutter and, of course, this groove can give the rifling

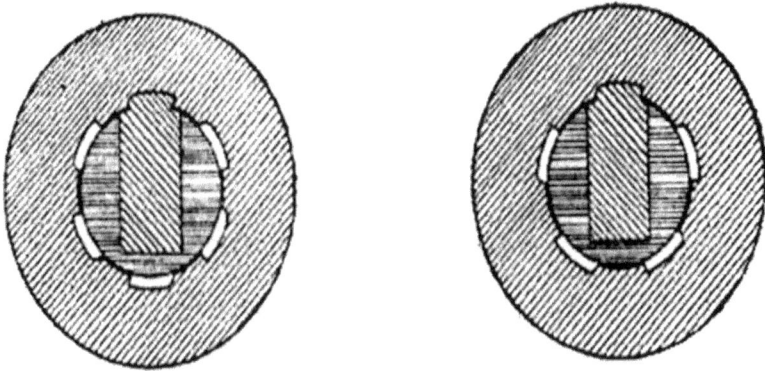

Odd versus even number of grooves. Showing how rifling head, directly beneath cutter, is unsupported in rifling an even number of grooves while, in rifling an odd number, the solid portion of the barrel, the lands, support the rifling head by being directly beneath the cutter.

In recutting barrels in which the twist of rifling is to be changed, the barrels are first rebored to their new bore diameter before being rifled. The bore diameter of the .25-20 is .250" while the bore diameter required for the .32-20 is .305". A three or four-groove twist drill with a pilot on it may be used to rough-bore the barrel to a diameter of .292", or a spear-type drill, as was described for drilling out barrels to be relined, may be made of high-speed steel and used to rough-bore the barrel. Following the rough-boring, which is done in the lathe, the three spiral-type bore reamers with pilots are used, being drawn through the barrel with the pull rod attached to the pilot end. The first two each remove .005" and the third removes .002". The barrel revolves in the lathe spindle while the pull rod of the reamers is held in a clamp bolted upon the tool-rest slide of the lathe. Plenty of lard-oil is used in these drilling and reaming operations, supplied under pressure by a small pump. The draw rod is really a tube with outlet holes drilled at three points around its circumference just ahead of the reamer pilot. The line from the oil-pump connects to the rear end of the tube back of the clamp on the tool rest of the lathe.

After the bore is reamed it is lapped with a lead slug cast on a rod, to remove tool marks and raise the bore the last .001" to size. Emery of a fine grade in a light oil is used upon the lap.

Now that the barrel is ready to be rifled, it is placed in the two clamps upon the rifling bench so that it lines up with the guide barrel or guide bar, whichever is used, in its two clamps or bearings upon the rifling bench. The rifling head is of steel and is a close fit within the bore. It may be made with a simple slot, straight with, not angular to the axis of the rifling head, in which slot the cutter sets and is raised with paper shims as was described for the babbitt rifling head, or it may be the more complicated type with a wedge beneath it to raise it as is described in the description of rifling head types. Whichever type is used the rifling process is the same, the rifling cutter is drawn through the bore, then without changing the setting the index is changed to bring the position of the next groove beneath the cutter and a cut is made in this groove and then in the third groove, etc., until all grooves have been started with the cutter at the same height setting. The cutter is then raised and the second cut is begun and carried through each groove again, before the setting is changed. This is repeated until all grooves are cut to proper and equal depth. The barrel may be left without lapping the grooves if they are sufficiently smooth, or the grooves may be left .001" to .002" undersize and the lead lap cast upon a rod in the bore used with emery and oil to lap the barrel after the rifling process. The lapping process is usually necessary to remove the wire-edge from the edge of the lands that is left by the rifling cutter, but this may be done without deepening the grooves if the finest grade of emery is used. Before doing the lap- ping, scrub the barrel thoroughly with a Parker bronze bristle brush which will remove most of this wire-edge from the lands. Grooves for the .32-20 are cut .003" deep.

As the rifling cutter comes out of the muzzle each time iri rifling a barrel it leaves the muzzle slightly bell-mouthed, so the barrel must be faced off in the lathe to remove this bell-mouth. This may be avoided if the muzzle is faced off smooth and square at first and a piece of steel sweated to it, which is later drilled and reamed to bore size before the barrel is rifled so that it becomes a continuation of the rifle bore. After the barrel is rifled this sweated-on piece is re- moved which does away with the bell-mouth on the bore.

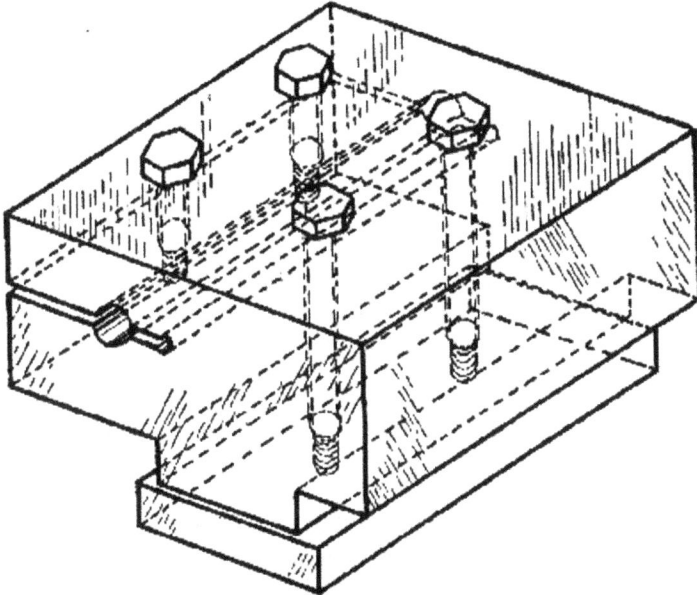

Clamp block, mounted in tool rest on compound slide of lathe, to hold oil tubing shanks of barrel drills or rifling heads.

The .22 rim-fire barrel may be rebored to .25 rim- fire by the reboring process in single-shot rifles such as the Stevens #44 1/2 Ideal or the single-shot Winchester. The barrel is rough bored, then reamed and lapped to a bore diameter of .250". The Stevens company cuts the grooves for these .25 rim-fire barrels only .002" to .0025" deep, using six grooves. Winchester barrels were grooved .0025" to .003" deep for the .25 rim-fire. Grooves may be made two and one-half to three times the width of the lands, which is the usual practice for jacketed bullets, or the grooves may be cut very wide and the lands left quite narrow as shown in the illustration of Pope rifling, used for lead bullets.

In changing the .22 rim-fire to the .25 rim-fire, the position of the firing-pin nose must he changed in the breech-block, so that it strikes in the proper place for the larger-headed .25 rim-fire cartridge. The old firing- pin hole in the breech-block is filled up by drilling it out with a 7/32 " drill and tapping it 1/4" x 32-threads per inch and screwing in a piece of 1/4" drill-rod threaded 32 threads per inch. Either a new firing-pin is made with the nose in the proper place to strike just within the rim of the .25 rim-fire cartridge, or if the body of the old firing-pin is large enough, the nose is cut off and the body is drilled, a piece of drill-rod is screwed in so that it bottoms in the hole and is then shaped up for the firing-pin nose in the new location.

In marking the location for the hole in the breech- block for the .25 rim-fire pin, the plug is put into the breech-block and the face finished off. It is then assembled in the rifle and a piece of rod closely fitting the bore and pointed, centrally on the end, is passed down the barrel from the muzzle and a small mark is made on the breech face by tapping the outer end of the rod. This will locate the center of the bore on the breech face, and the distance from this to the proper place to strike the rim of the .25 cartridge may then be measured on the breech face and the hole for the firing-pin nose drilled in the face of the breech-block.

The extractor must be cut out to handle the larger cartridge, and this can be done with the chambering reamer. The extractor is put in place in the barrel either by sweating it into its slot and the barrel re- chambered for the .25 cartridge while it is out of the action or the barrel may be screwed into the action, the extractor put in place on its pin and swung into its slot in the barrel and wedged there with a piece of steel or hard-wood extending back to the rear end of the receiver. The barrel is then rechambered while in place in the action.

The recess in the end of the barrel and in the ex- tractor for the cartridge rim can be cut on the lathe, with the extractor sweated in place in its slot in the barrel, while the barrel is out of the action or it may be cut with a face reamer, like an end-mill, with a pilot riding on the lands of the bore, while the barrel is in place in the action with the extractor held in its slot with a wedge.

Head-space in a rifle for rimmed cartridges is the distance from the face of the breech-block, in the closed positions, to the bottom of the recess cut in the end of the. barrel for the cartridge rim. Head-space is important, for if it is excessive so that the cartridge is not heLd forward to its proper place in the chamber upon the moment of firing, the cartridge case backs up until its head contacts the face of the breech-block, which stops it and, as the chamber in the barrel tapers in form, as the cartridge backs up, its walls are not supported by the chamber walls. When this happens, especially if a cartridge case is not exactly the proper anneal, the head blows off from the body of the case, allowing the gas to come back into the action, wrecking it and often injuring the shooter badly.

The required amount of head-space for a rimmed cartridge is easily measured, as the thickness of the rim of the cartridges to be used can be measured with a micrometer in thousandths or ten-thousandths of an inch. As there is some difference in thickness of cartridge rims between different manufacturers, several different brands should be measured for rim-thickness and as there will also be some variation in rim thick- ness among cartridges of the same caliber made by the same manufacturer, due to being turned out in different dies, several cartridges of each brand should be measured. The amount of head-space required will be the measurement of the thickest rim found on any of the cartridges, although the variation between the thickest rim and the thinnest one should not be over .005" for best results and not over .008" in the interests of safety.

Head-space in a chamber for rimless cartridges (with the excep- tion of the magnum cases, which have a belt raised around the case just ahead of the extractor groove which acts as the rim does in a rimmed case to determine head-space) is the distance from the shoulder slope in the chamber to the face of the breech-block or bolt. As you can readily see, this is an extremely difficult measurement to take. Rifle factories use steel gauges, hardened and ground to the measurement of maximum and minimum cartridges, to test rifle chambers with. These gauges are not available for sale except in caliber .30'06 in which caliber they can be purchased from L. E. Wilson of Wilson Bros., Cash- mere, Washington, for $4.50 each. The average gun- smith must rely on new, maximum and minimum cartridges for his gauges in chambering barrels and, in using the chambering reamer, cuts the chamber until the action will close easily on the minimum case but requires a little force to close it on the maximum case. To pick out these cartridges, a rifle in good condition, preferably new, that turns out fired cases with next to no expansion showing upon them, is the best medium to use. A number of unbred cartridges are run through this rifle to pick the cases desired, being placed in the chamber one at a time, with a piece of steel shim stock laid on the head of the case and the bolt closed upon it. The maximum case, of course, is the one which will only accept the thinnest shim, or none at all, and allow the action to be closed. The minimum case being the one that will accept the most shim stock upon its head and allow the bolt to close. This steel shim stock can be supplied in ribbon shape at 34^ per foot by the L. S. Starrett Co., or from automobile parts companies.

In cutting the chamber it is cut with the roughing reamer and then with the finishing reamer, to a length which you know is less than the required length, while the barrel is out of the action. The barrel is then assembled in the receiver and the finishing reamer run in a little distance, withdrawn, and the chamber thoroughly cleaned. The bolt is then placed in the action, the minimum case placed in the chamber and the bolt is closed upon it. If the bolt encounters any resistance in closing, the cham- ber is not deep enough so the cartridge and bolt are removed, the chamber is cut a little deeper and tried again. This is continued until the action closes upon the minimum cartridge. Thereafter the maximum cartridge is used as a gauge and the chambering continued until the bolt will close upon it, but requires an effort to close it. The burnishing reamer is then used until the bolt just closes on the maximum case without effort. In case the gauges arc used, the maximum gauge is a "no go" gauge and the bolt must not close upon it but must close with no effort upon the minimum gauge. Head space is important, respect it.

Old rifles with worn-out heavy barrels can be renovated by relining the barrels with other rifle barrels, the original barrel, or a still heavier, old, worthless barrel picked up for the purpose, being used for a jacket. In one case of this kind the model 67 Winchester single-shot barrel was used. The action used was a #44 1/2 Stevens Ideal. An old heavy barrel was picked up and was drilled out with a 9/16" drill having a pilot ground upon it to follow the original bore of the old barrel. A 1/2" steel rod was carefully welded to the shank of the drill, using a jig set-up to make sure the rod and the drill were in alignment. The breech end of the old barrel was then drilled out to 3/4" to a depth of about 6". The 9/16 " hole in the old barrel was then reamed out to 5/8" and the old threaded end of the heavy barrel was cut off an inch, leaving the 3/4" hole five inches long.

The .22 barrel was then turned down slightly in the lathe so that it would just clear inside the heavy barrel except at the breech and muzzle where the contacts were tight. As the receiver in the model 67 Winchester is a continuation of the barrel, this was cut off and the rear end of the barrel was turned down and threaded to fit the Stevens action, so that it screwed up tightly against the closed breech-block, but not strained against it. The barrel was then loosened one-eighth of a turn and locked in this position by tightening the barrel screw on the under side of the receiver. The outer barrel was slipped over the liner and turned back one- eighth turn (it being an octagonal barrel) from its proper position. . A mark was then put upon the outer barrel with chalk and a chalk mark was put upon the receiver, lining up with the mark on the outer barrel.

The outer barrel was removed and placed in a stand holding it horizontally over gas-jets about 4" apart. This outer barrel was swabbed inside with soldering acid and was placed with its muzzle tight against an asbestos pad and clamped in the stand in that position. The gas-jets were started and when the barrel was hot enough it was tinned inside with solder. A special tool was used for this purpose like those used for tinning the inside of old barrels bored out for the regulation relining tubes. A brass brush will do this tinning job just as well. After the outer barrel was tinned, some more solder was placed within it and the inner .22 barrel, still attached to the action, was started into the outer barrel slowly and allowed to heat up as it was worked in with a twisting motion. This .22 barrel was plugged in each end with asbestos before being started into the outer barrel to prevent solder or flux from entering its bore. When the .22 barrel was all the way in the outer barrel, the chalk marks on the outer barrel and the receiver were lined up and the gas-jets turned out, allowing the barrel to cool.

The recess was cut for the head of the cartridge with a recessing cutter, so that when the barrel was screwed up tightly in the action the breech-block closed on the cartridge closely but without marring it. The groove for the extractor was cut in the rear end of the barrel and the job turned out to be a heavy-barrel target rifle showing good accuracy, while the expense was low. This model 67 Winchester retails for less than $6.00 complete.

This same system may be used where it is desired to retain the old original octagon barrel, by buying a barrel blank, bored and rifled but not chambered, from a barrel-maker. This blank can be fitted to the action as this .22 barrel was fitted and the old octagon barrel used as a jacket.. The blank may be chambered for any cartridge desired that the blank will handle.

After high -power .25 and .30 caliber barrels are too badly worn or pitted to perform well, they may be recut by the amateur to use a larger jacketed bullet, just as the lead-bullet barrels used to be recut when worn. The .25 calibers may be recut to use a .256 or 6.5 m/m bullet and the .30 calibers can be recut to use a .303 British or an 8 m/m bullet. A .270 Winchester can be recut to use 7 m/m bullet, etc.

As an example we shall recut a .30 caliber, the model '06, to use .303 British bullets of .3125" diameter. The first thing to be done, after removing the barrel from the receiver, is to clean it thoroughly and scour it well with a brass brush. Next we take a piece of 1/4" round drill-rod and file two inches of its length, at one end, square. We then gash the corners of this square in four places on each corner with a three-square needle file. These gashes need not be very deep, about 1/32 " is sufficient. Just below the square portion we wrap the rod with tow or string so that it is a tight fit in the bore, wrapping it evenly so that it is centered as well as possible in the bore. This rod is inserted into the barrel from the breech and pushed to within 4" of the muzzle. The barrel is set muzzle-up in a vise and heated for 6" back from the muzzle with a torch, but not hot enough to make it change color. Melted nickel- babbitt is poured into the muzzle in a steady stream until the last 6" of the barrel is full, level with the muzzle. When this babbitt cast has cooled, it is pushed forward out of the barrel and the overflow (at the extreme muzzle into the countersunk portion of the barrel muzzle) is trimmed off with a sharp knife. We now have a cast 6" long, 2" of which is upon the rod. We now cut a slot in one of the raised ribs of this cast, which represents a groove in the barrel, 1 1/2" long and the full width of the rib plus .005", .0025" of which extends beyond each side of the rib.- This groove is cut at the same angle on the cast that the rib lies, or in other words, it follows the angle of the rib. This cut starts about 1" from the outer end of the cast and extends toward the rod on which the cast was made. The slot is cut to within 1/8" or a trifle less of the opposite side of the cast. A small hole is drilled through the remaining lead in the bottom of the slot, at the center, so that a punch or small nail can be inserted through this hole to push the cutter up and out of the slot.

The cutter to fit in this slot is ground to shape and size from a high-speed steel lathe bit, being ground in length and width so that it can be inserted into the slot without any shake and yet does not bind at any point. A portion in the center is 1/4" long and is ground with a slope toward one end. The top of this portion is ground with a slope of 5 1/2 degrees down from the direction in which this portion inclines, forming a hook cutter. This top is ground and honed to a height that brings its cutting edge just level with the top of the rib in which it is sunk in the babbitt casting. In front of this cutting edge a recess 3/8" long is ground 1/8" deep and behind the inclined cutter portion another recess 1/4" long and 7/8" deep is ground. These recesses take care of the chips or cuttings. The remaining portions of the cutter body at each end are ground down on the top to .010" below the cutting edge. The cutter portion in the center is carefully ground and honed to the exact width of the barrel grooves, .1767". The cutting edge of the hook is not straight across but is ground to fit the bottom of the barrel grooves which is a slight radius.

A handle of hardwood, 2" thick in the center and a foot long, is drilled through from side to side, at the center, so that the rod on which the cast was made is a close slide-fit in the hole. One side of this hole in the handle is drilled out so that a ball thrust bearing, such as are sold to slip over the shaft of small electric motors with shafts to convert them for vertical use, is a close push fit in the hole. The hole in the thrust bearing is bushed to to fit the rod and a washer is placed in the bottom of the hole in the handle before the thrust bearing is placed in the hole.

A 3/32 " hole is drilled through the rod from the end opposite the babbitt cast and a cotter-pin is used in this hole with a washer beneath the pin against the thrust bearing.

The barrel is now fixed in a horizontal position in the bench vise and the end of the rod opposite the babbitt casting is inserted into the barrel from the breech and pushed forward until the end comes out of the muzzle. The handle is now slipped onto the rod, the side with the thrust bearing in it going on last. A washer is slipped over the end of the rod and the cotter-pin is inserted outside the washer.

The barrel is oiled with lard-oil from a pump oil-can, pumped into the bore. The cutter is seated in its slot in the babbitt casting with the cutting edge forward and is oiled with lard-oil and the casting is inserted into the bore with its raised ribs in the grooves. A mark is made at the breech, where the cutter enters, so that we can be sure which groove it enters. The handle of the rod is now grasped in both hands and the cutter is drawn through the bore. As it comes out at the muzzle we must be careful not to bend the casting. The barrel is now cleaned by running a patch through it and the cutter and casting are cleaned, the handle removed from the rod and the rod again inserted through the barrel from the breech, the barrel again oiled in the bore and the cutter oiled. Wc now insert casting into the rifling with the cutter in the next groove and again mark the end of the barrel at this point, place the handle on the rod and draw the cutter through the second groove. This performance is repeated until the cutter has been drawn through each groove in turn. f We are now ready to start over again at the first groove, but with a shim beneath the cutter to raise it so that it will take a full cut. A very thin paper shim the full width and length of the cutter may be used in the bottom of the slot or a piece of cellophane such as is used for wrapping cigarettes, cough drops, etc. may be used for shim stock. This cellophane is just .001" thick so we will use that. A piece is cut and fitted into the slot and the cutter placed in the slot, the rod inserted through the barrel, the bore and cutter oiled and all marks removed from the breech of the barrel. The cutter cast is now inserted in a groove, the position marked on the breech again, the handle placed upon the rod and the cutter drawn through the barrel. The bore, the cutter and the casting are thoroughly cleaned and the bore and cutter again oiled and started into the barrel again in the same groove and pulled through the barrel. This is repeated in this first groove until the cutter no longer cuts any more, the second groove is then cut in the same manner, and so on, until all grooves have been cut with the shim under the cutter. The same number of cuts are made in each groove. After all the grooves have been cut with one shim under the cutter, the cast will be loose in the bore so we melt the cast off of the rod and, proceeding exactly as we did in making the first cast on thc rod inside the barrel, we make a new cast and sink a groove or slot into one of the raised ribs to receive the cutter as we did before. By measuring the cast over the ribs with a micrometer we find out how much we have removed from the grooves. It should be .001", plus or minus an imperceptible amount, from each groove, deepening the groove diameter .002".

Starting with the new cast, we first run the cutter through each groove with no shim beneath it. In cutting the slot for the cutter in this new cast, we were careful to cut the slot to the proper depth, so that the edge of the cutter was the same height as the rib in which the slot was cut. This measurement was made with a micrometer with the cutter in the slot and compared with the micrometer reading of the casting measured over the ribs.

The shim is now placed beneath the cutter in the slot and each groove is again given the same number of cuts, the number being that required to free the cutter in the tightest groove. The barrel should now have a groove-diameter of .312" and to prove this we start an oversize soft-lead bullet through the barrel by gently tapping it into the breech end of the bore with a wood stick and a hammer, after oiling the bore with a thin gun-oil. We push this bullet through the bore with a stiff square-end rod and catch it on loose- piled rags as it falls from the muzzle. We now measure over the raised ribs on this bullet with the micrometer and find that the bore measures .312" in the grooves, as it should.

We must now enlarge the bore diameter between the grooves to a diameter of .303" so we melt the old cast off the rod and make a new cast upon it as before. We now cut a groove or slot in one of the grooves in this casting as these grooves in the casting correspond to the lands in the barrel. We make a new cutter of high-speed steel, ground from a lathe bit, because this cutter has a different contour on the cutting edge from that upon the rifling cutter as the contour of the edge of this cutter will be the arc of a circle with a diameter of .303". Also the width will be less than that of the rifling cutter, the official width of the lands being .0589" in Springfield barrels. The width of the cutter for the lands should be a trifle wider than the lands so that it will be sure to clean up the full width of the land each time, so we will make it .070" wide.

The cutter is ground and honed down until, when it is placed in the slot with no shim beneath it, its cutting edge is level with the groove in the babbitt casting. This is ascertained by placing a thin steel scale edgewise into the groove over the cutter.

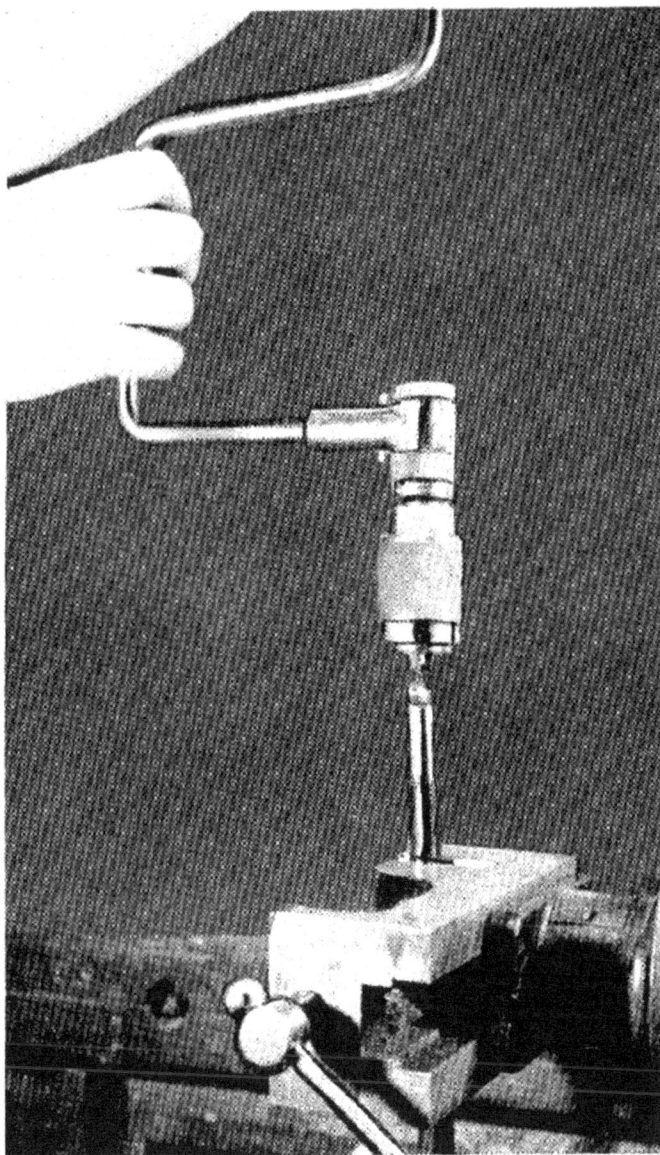

Plate VIII

Using a ball cutter with a bit brace to round out, or crown, the muzzle
of a rifle barrel. The special ball shaped cutter is of tungsten steel and
is turned at low speed.

A cut is now made over each land in the barrel, with no shim beneath the cutter and after each cut is made a very stiff bronze brush of the Parker type is used to scour any burr out of the barrel. After each land has been passed over by the cutter, a .001" shim of cellophane is placed beneath the cutter and the first land is given a cut, after which the bronze brush is used and the same land is again run over by the cutter and the bronze brush again used, this being repeated until the cutter no longer cuts on this first land. The second land is then cut in the same way, with the same number of cuts, then the balance of the lands arc cut, which should increase the bore diameter of the barrel to a diameter of .302". This may be measured by pushing a soft-lead slug through the bore, as was done to measure the groove diameter. As the ribs raised by the grooves in the barrel upon the lead slug prevent taking a measurement of the grooves made in the lead slug by the lands of the barrel unless these ribs on the slug are cut away with a knife a simple way to take this measurement is to lay two pieces of drill rod of small size in the grooves of the slug, one in one groove and the other in the opposite groove, and measure over these with a micrometer, after which the diameter of the drill rod is taken with the micrometer and the diameter of both pieces deducted from the first measurement.

As the smoothness of the cuts we have made in the grooves and upon the lands of the barrel depend upon how well the cutter is dressed and honed, this cutting edge must be watched closely and will need to be honed with a hard Arkansas stone quite often. A good magnifying glass is used to examine the edge, which should have a mirror-like finish. As our shims have been .001" thick, which is too thick lor the smoothest work, the interior of the recut barrel will not be as smooth as we should like to have it so, as the barrel is still tight we can lap it with a lead lap and very fine emery powder mixed with oil.

A regular lapping rod with ball-bearing handle is used for this work. The simplest way to make it is to get a bicycle pedal of the ball-bearing type and make a short nipple, drilled and tapped in one end to screw onto the threaded end of the pedal spindle. The bicycle shop can do the threading for you if you have no tap this size and in attaching this nipple to the pedal shaft you can sweat it on so that it will not unscrew. Clean the threads well and use a good soldering flux on both sets of threads. At the nipple upright in a vise or hold it in a pair of pliers and heat it so that the solder flow's readily. Put the solder in the nipple and continue the heat for a minute then dump the excess solder and screw the pedal shaft in while again applying the heat. After it has cooled drill a hole in the opposite end of the nipple to insert the lapping rod.

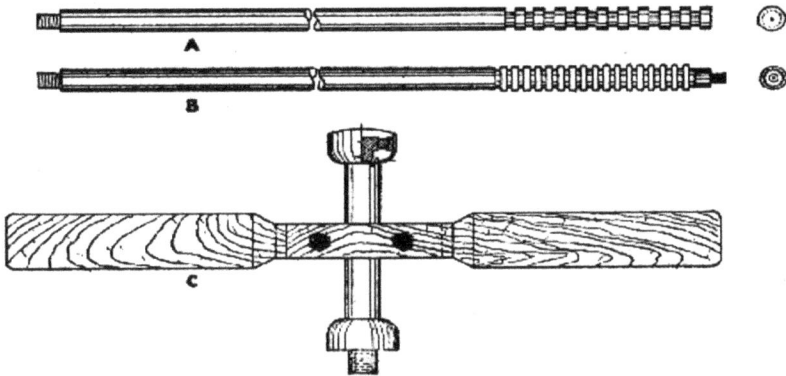

Details of construction of steel lapping rod, to hold lead laps cast upon it. A is special head for lead laps. B is special head equipped with leather washers, used in burnishing rifle bores to a high polish. C shows ball bearing lapping rod handle made from a bicycle pedal.

This may be threaded into the hole and pinned with a straight pin to prevent it unscrewing. The last three inches at the outer end of the rod are squared and nicked on the corners as was done with the rod on which the babbitt rifling head was cast. Two pieces of wood bolted together on opposite sides of the pedal in a right-angle position to the rod will supply a handle. The rod is wrapped with tow or string below the squared portion and inserted in the barrel from the breech and the tip brought just level with the muzzle. Melted lead is used for this lap casting and the barrel should be heated for the last 3", as it was in pouring the babbitt rifling head, so that the shrink of the lead cast will be held at a minimum. After the cast has cooled, gently push it from the muzzle and carefully examine muzzle end of the cast and measure it at the end to see whether the rifling cutter or the land cutter has bell-mouthed the muzzle of the barrel. This is the usual case and as the length of barrel in this condition will be short the barrel will have to be cut off slightly and the muzzle refinished, but do not do this until after the lapping is completed.

In making this examination and measurement of the lap do not push more than 1" of it out of the muzzle, as the lap should never be entirely removed from the barrel or it will be necessary to cast a new lap upon the rod. Use a sharp pocket knife to cut down the expanded portion of the lap at the end so that it will slide freely down the barrel or in casting the lap you can stop the rod about 1" short of the muzzle and the expanded (portion of the lap at the muzzle end can then be cut off with a fine-tooth hack- saw and the burr left on the end by the saw cut off with a knife.

Flour of emery is mixed with sperm-oil or olive-oil to a sirupy mixture and, with the lap withdrawn to the breech end of the barrel, apply the lapping compound to the bore with an undersize bristle brush on a clean- ing rod. A .25 caliber brush is right for the .30 caliber barrel. Push the lap well up the barrel and pour a little of the mixture into the breech end and then turn the barrel muzzle-up and allow the mixture to drain out. Push the lap about 1 J4" out of the muzzle and apply some of the mixture to the lap with a small brush like a glue brush. Mark the rod so that when the lap is just even with the muzzle, the mark can easily be seen on the upper surface of the rod at the breech, just even with the rear end of the barrel. Withdraw the lap to the rear and make another mark upon the rod when the rear end of the lap is just entering the neck of the chamber. Watch these marks closely while lapping the barrel so that the lap does not pass out of the bore at either end of the barrel.

Push and pull the lap back and forth through the barrel and if any tight spots are noticed, make three or four short strokes back and forth at these points. After lapping for about ten minutes, push the lap an inch or more out of the muzzle and apply fresh lapping mixture with the brush. The lap may be withdrawn part way into the chamber and some lapping compound applied to it at this end with a smaller brush, such as a small camel-hair brush or a, pipe cleaner. Reapply the lapping compound each ten or fifteen minutes for about an hour then apply only sperm-oil or olivc-oil to the lap and lap for about fifteen minutes to a half hour more. This should leave the bore pretty smooth but if it still lacks a polish to suit you the barrel should be carefully cleaned and washed out with gasoline, a new lap cast upon the rod and the barrel lapped for another hour with crocus powder and olive-oil.

We now have the bore finished and can cut off the enlarged muzzle portion, usually half an inch or less, and refinish the muzzle. This may necessitate moving the front sight farther back on the barrel. Remove locking pins in the sight band if any are present, ex- tend the key slot back with a small milling cutter or drill and file it out and make a new key and drive the sight band back to its new position. If the band is too tight to drive back readily, peen it all around with a Stanley composition-face hammer, which will not mar it but will loosen it sufficiently so that it can be driven to its new position. If the key for the front sight band is integral with the barrel a slot may be cut behind it and a key inserted.

We now must enlarge the neck of the chamber, as the larger bullet has cut down the neck clearance so that probably the loaded case will not enter the chamber fully. We make a neck reamer from an 11/32 " straight hand reamer by grinding a pilot 1" long on the front end to ride on the lands of the barrel. The teeth behind the pilot are ground to a 45-degree angle with the center line of the reamer, on their ends leading down to the pilot ; clearance is ground or stoned on these beveled ends of the teeth and the teeth are honed on their cutting edges to a slight taper, .002" in the length of the chamber neck. Plenty of cutting oil is used on the reamer, which is operated by hand, and it is not forced, the weight of the reamer and reamer wrench supplying the feed. This will cut a fairly tight chamber neck and if it is tight enough to show signs of high pressure on the fired cases, it may be lapped by drilling out the primer pocket of a fired case and threading the case for a 1/4" steel rod screwed into the hole. Flour of emery or fine carborundum powder is mixed with sperm or olive-oil to make the lapping compound and this is applied sparingly to the neck of the case and a tap wrench is placed upon the end of the steel rod so that the case may be revolved back and forth. Only a few turns can be made at a time and then new lapping compound must be applied. Clean the chamber and the case thoroughly each time to prevent the lapping compound getting to work on the shoulder of the chamber.

Others calibers may be recut as has been described for the .30 '06 and in choosing reamers, or making them to enlarge the neck portion of the chamber, allow a minimum clearance over the diameter of the neck of the loaded case of .003" and a maximum clearance of .005". A 19/64" will hone down nicely to handle the .25 calibers enlarged by using the .256" diameter bullets. In connection with this job do not get reckless and try to use 130 grain and heavier bullets, as these are too long to be handled by the ordinary .25 caliber rifling twist. Limit your bullets in this caliber to the 100 grain, or if these are too expensive make a swage and increase the diameter of the cheaper .25 caliber bullets to .256".

The neck clearance of the .270 Winchester enlarged by using the 7 m/m bullet is taken care of by an 8 m/m reamer. The 139 grain 7 m/'m bullet will work nicely here.

Chapter 6 ACTION WORK AND ALTERATIONS

Bolt-handle bending, or cutting-off and replacing the bolt-handle at a different angle, is a job often desired on military and other rifles but this is a job that must be carefully done if the working parts of the bolt are to be properly protected from the heat.

In bending a bolt-handle to a different angle, all removable parts are stripped from the bolt and its interior is filled with a long, narrow strip of cloth, packed into place with a rod or narrow-bladed screw- driver. This cloth is now thoroughly saturated with water. The bolt is placed in a heavy vise, after the jaws are covered with copper to prevent marring, then more cloth is placed over the rear of the bolt and pressed into the open end upon the strip that was previously packed in there. Water is kept running over this cloth while the handle is being heated.

Heat the bolt-handle, at the point at which it is to be bent, with a narrow flame from the acetylene torch and heat it as quickly as possible , for the longer the time it is heated the farther that heat will run. Have a narrow-jawed wrench ready to be tightened on the bolt-handle at a point beyond the heated portion, or use a piece of heavy steel with a notch cut out of it to fit the bolt-handle closely and, as soon as the handle is hot enough, bend it to the position you wish. Keep the water running over the cloths after the bending is done and as soon as the heated portion of the bolt- handle turns blue in color, pour water upon that until it is cool. The bolt-handle is then repolished with fine carborundum cloth and crocus cloth.

In cutting off a high-rising bolt-handle to weld it back on the bolt in a lower position, so that it may clear low-mounted scopes, the position and shape may be copied from the Remington, Enfield or model 70 Winchester. The bolt-handle may be sawed off with a high-speed steel hack-saw blade unless it happens to be case-hardened, in which case a groove must be ground around the bolt-handle at the place it is to be cut, just through the case-hardening, using a narrow grinding wheel dressed to a vee-shape, or you may use a 3/32" thick cutting-off wheel if you have one.

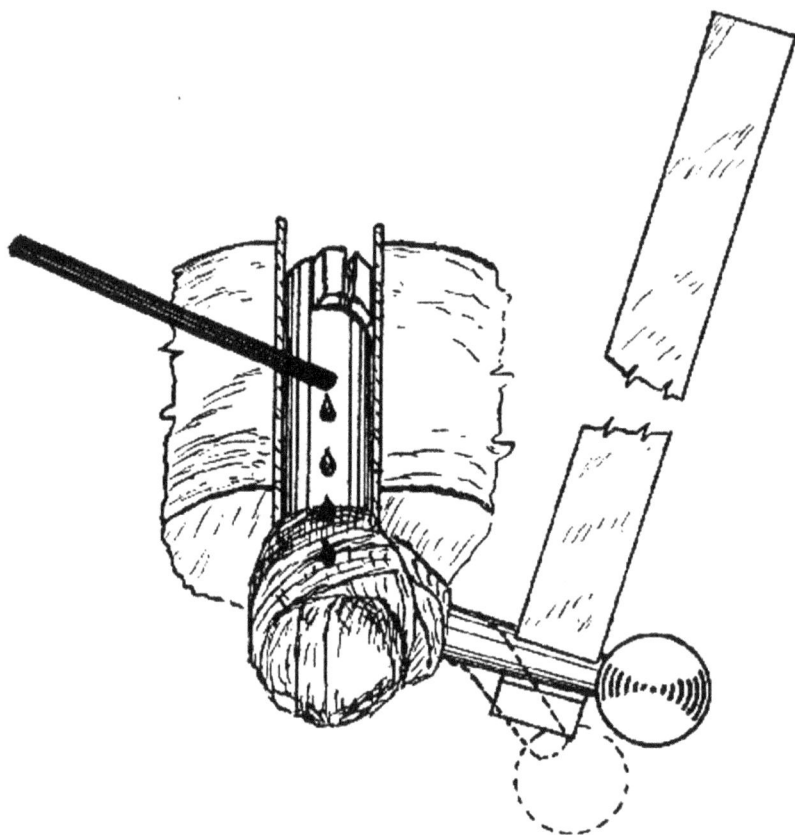

Rifle bolt handle bending setup. Bolt packed and wrapped with wet cloth, with water kept dripping on cloth.

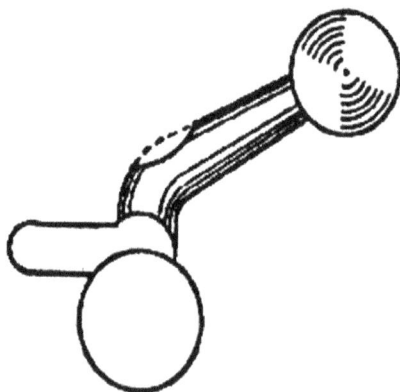

Notch ground out of bolt handle, so it will pass telescopic sight tube.

The hollow of the bolt is filled with a cloth strip saturated with water, as in the case of bending the bolt- handle, and the bolt must be covered with cloths with water running upon them as before. In some cases the bolt can be placed in a shallow pan of water, as it is not necessary to grip the bolt in a vise as in the bending operation. It may be necessary to arrange some kind of a jig or holding device for the bolt and handle to keep them in the position in which you wish to weld them.

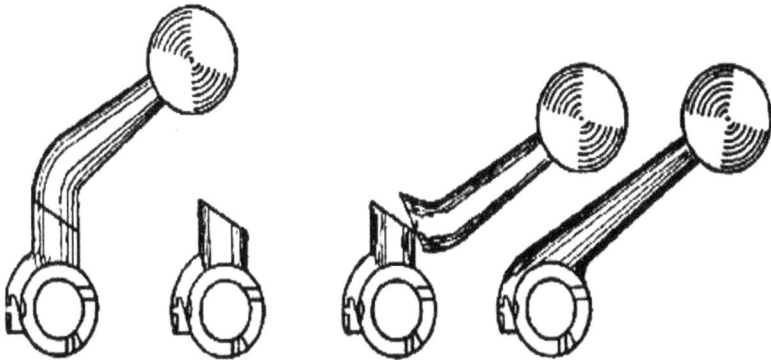

Method of cutting off a bolt handle and welding it back onto the bolt in a lower position.

The ideal welding method for this operation is the electric arc welder, as it does not spread its heat as far as the acetylene torch does. After the weld is made and filled in above the old surface of the bolt-handle, the bolt-handle is dressed down at the weld and smoothed up by grinding, filing and polishing with carborundum and crocus cloth.

In changing over bolt actions which cock upon the closing of the bolt to make them cock upon the opening of the bolt, the cam of the bolt which engages the cam on the left receiver wall to extract the cartridge must be protected from the welding heat. For which reason the electric weld is almost imperative in this operation. However as this cam is on the opposite side of the bolt barrel from the bottom opening that must be filled up, this weld or build-up can be made with a gas torch if care is used. In using either type of weld the bolt barrel is plugged with a closely fitting carbon rod and the bolt is laid upside down in a pan of water so that the extraction cam is under water, then cloths are laid over the bolt so that both ends are in the water and these are kept wet over the bolt to prevent the heat from running back to the lugs.

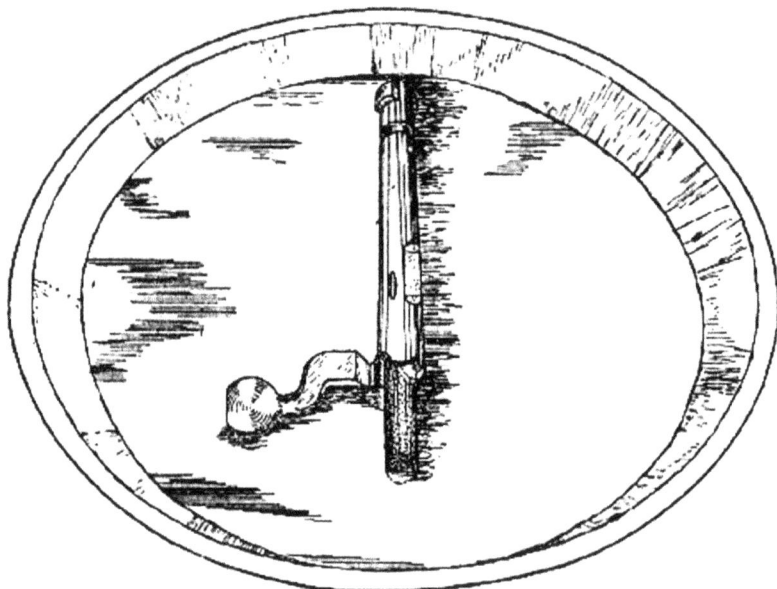

Portion at rear of bolt barrel (in white) to the right of cocking piece notch to be filled in by welding, on Enfield bolt, to make this rifle cock upon opening the bolt. Bolt barrel lies in water to half its depth, and carbon rod is inserted inside the bolt barrel.

The bolt must be filled in at the rear end on the bottom, so that a new cam groove can be cut resembling that in the Springfield or other bolt-actions cocking upon the opening of the bolt. It is necessary to cam the cocking piece clear to the rear end of the bolt barrel, so this bolt barrel notch (on the type that cocks on the closing of the bolt) must be filled up so that the new notch can be cut with an easy sweep from the deepest point to the rear of the bolt barrel. As this takes considerable wear at this point, a build-up steel of very tough quality must be used. Each manufacturer of welding rod has his own pet formulae for this type of steel but they can all supply it.

In making the weld, handle it carefully as it must be hot enough so that the steel flows readily and makes a perfect, close-grained surface to get the greatest wear but be careful not to carry this heat high enough to burn the steel in the slightest or to get pin-holes in it or it will soon roughen up the cocking-piece surface.

Modern bolts of the nickel-steel type may be readily machined without annealing but the older type of case- hardened bolt must be annealed and after the machining is completed must be rehardened. Springfield arsenal will supply upon request the proper heat-treatment information to reharden these bolts in the modern manner.

Sometimes an extractor is broken off just where the hook end joins the body and a new one is not available. A repair can be made by brazing a new piece of steel to the end of the body of the extractor to make a new hook. This should be a piece of spring-steel heavier than the original hook and after the end of the body of die extractor is ground square, a piece of brass is laid here between the ground end and the new piece of steel for the hook and, using the regular brazing rod, the two are brazed together. The new hook end is then filed to shape and proper thickness. This is only a temporary repair and the extractor should be replaced with a new one as soon as possible.

New hook brazed upon end of Mauser type extractor.

It is often desired to use a smaller cartridge than the original extractor was designed for and in this case, in any type of action, the original extractor can be lengthened by welding on a new piece of steel, to be cut to fit the smaller cartridge. On the Winchester single shot action extractor, and extractors of a similar type, the side extension of the extractor can be entirely cut off, the shank notched at the top, leaving part of the shank in place at the rear and a new piece of steel is brazed in to make a new side extension to the chamber.

Winchester factory extractors for this action are made in this manner.

Chisel-steel is the best material out of which to make new firing-pins. It is bought in the annealed state and after the pin is machined to size it is hardened by heating to a cherry-red and quenching in oil. Either a light machine oil or a special quenching oil may be used. The pin is then polished and reheated slowly and evenly to a deep blue and again quenched in the oil. All quenching of parts much longer than their width, such as firing-pins, should be done by being dipped end- wise into the quenching bath, heavy end first, and be agitated in widening circles while cooling. The end- wise quenching is to prevent warping. In drawing parts to proper temper after hardening, where no furnace or lead bath is used, they can be heated more evenly by laying them upon a heated iron plate and turning them over and over as they slowly heat to the proper color.

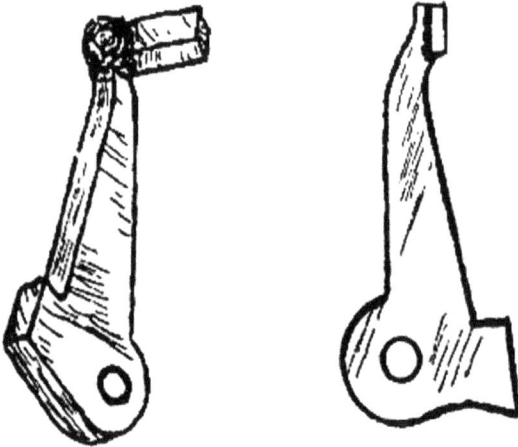

New extension brazed upon single-shot extractor of Winchester type.

Correct profile of center-fire firing-pin nose.

Coil-springs of desired size are easily wound from spring-steel wire on the lathe. This wire comes in many different sizes and is already tempered. A rod is mounted in the lathe chuck upon which to wind the spring. This rod must be smaller in diameter than the desired inside diameter of the spring coil, as the spring will expand somewhat in size after it is wound. If the rod or spring mandrel you mount in the lathe chuck is very long, it will have to be supported at the outer end with the tail stock center, as the wire must be pulled tight at right-angles to the mandrel while it is being wound. One end of the wire must be fastened to the lathe chuck or passed through a hole at the inner end of the mandrel, so that it can be held tightly, or it will not wind around the mandrel.

The lathe should turn in a left-hand direction, so if it is placed so that you cannot stand at the back of the lathe, the direction of the spindle travel must be re- versed. The coils of the spring are spaced by slipping a washer or a loop of wire of the desired thickness over the mandrel. If a washer is used, a hole is drilled through it and wire attached in the hole, so that it may be held in one hand to keep the washer tight against the mandrel as it travels along with the spring being wound. The hole in the washer must be larger than the outer diameter of the spring being wound. A very tight pull is kept on the wire with one hand while the spacer is held tightly with the other hand. This tension on the wire out of which the spring is being wound is necessary in order to produce a spring of even diameter. - This method will do very well for making springs out of fairly light spring-wire, but sometimes a spring of much heavier wire is needed. In this case tension on the wire is controlled by a simple tension device in the tool post of the lathe and the carriage of the lathe

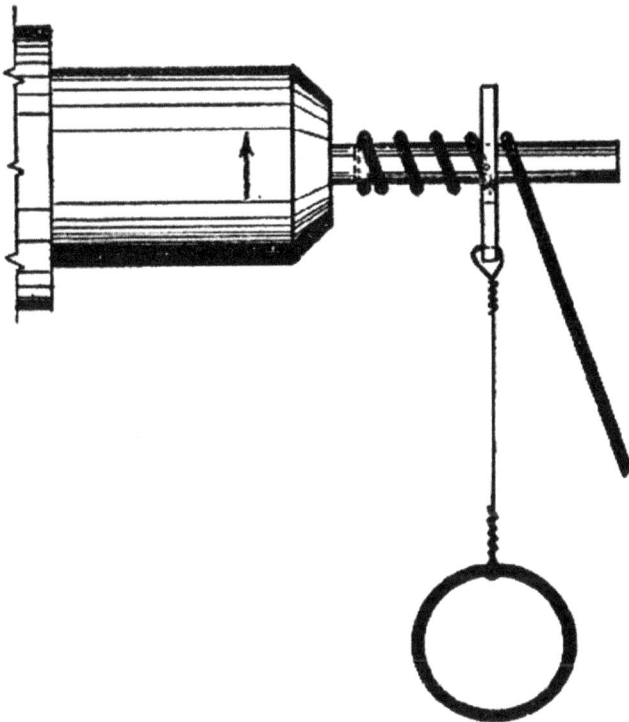

Winding a spring of light wire on a mandrel in the lathe chuck, using a large washer for spacing the coils.

is moved along the bed by the lead screw with the lathe geared to the same number of threads per inch as the spring being made has coils.

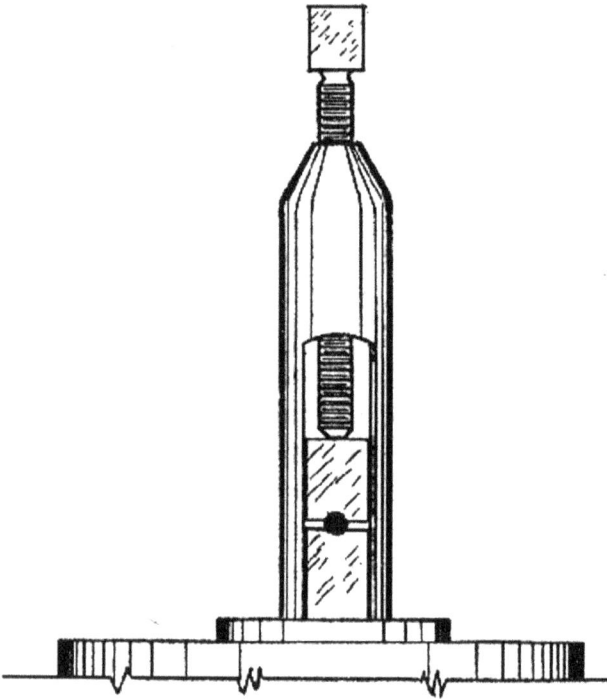

Steel tension blocks in tool post of lathe to keep heavy wire tight while winding coil springs on a mandrel in the lathe chuck.

This tension device is simple and is made of two steel blocks held in the tool post, with a groove slightly smaller than the wire cut between them. By tightening the tool post screw the proper amount the desired tension is put upon the wire. The wire must be oiled for this operation.

Flat steel-spring making, with its attendant forging and tempering, is quite an art and the proper steel is not always easy to get. The English steel is considered to be the best but our spring-steel is improving in quality.

Flat steel-springs are heavier at the fixed end than at the operating end and this is accomplished, not by grinding or filing down the steel at the operating end, but by forging it. While bringing the bar to the proper thickness and width, the steel must be kept at a cherry- red, for if it is hammered while at lower temperatures it will develop cracks. Between 1400 and 1500 degrees is the proper heat and in heating do not heat it too rapidly but keep it out of the hottest part of whatever fire you are using, so that it heats up gradually. In doing the forging, make your hammer blows as even as possible as you draw the steel out to its proper width and thickness. As soon as it shows any signs of cooling much, return it to the fire for reheating.

If the spring is of the sharp bent or vee-type, after it has been forged to size, cool it in lime, file it to the desired dimensions, then mark the place where the bend is to be made. Place it back in the furnace and reheat to the same temperature used in forging, then bend it, using a piece of steel of the proper thickness to space it at the bend. It is hardly possible to make this bend without having the steel cool too much, so bend it only part way and then reheat it to complete the bend.

After this sharp bend is made, the spring is again heated to the same temperature as before and curved the proper amount at each end, being sure that the steel does not cool too much during this operation, which will also include squaring the two sides so that the spring is in line all over.

The spring is now ready for hardening. As it is difficult to control the temperature evenly all over the spring in an open flame or forge, due to its varying thickness at different points, the best way to heat it is in a lead bath that has the proper temperature. Use an old ladle for the lead bath, one that has been heated many times before, if possible, so that all im- purities, especially sulphur, have been burnt out of it. Use a good chemically-pure lead, not scrap lead, to guard against impurities and cover the surface of the melted lead with powdered charcoal, which prevents oxidation of the lead. Suspend the spring on a wire in the melted lead and, as lead is heavier than steel, the wire must be stiff to keep the spring below the surface of the lead. Coating the spring with alcohol and chalk, or dipping it in a solution of potassium cyanide, one pound to one gallon of water, will prevent the lead from sticking to the steel.

The lead should be brought to a bright red heat or if a pyrometer is available, to 1450 degrees, and the spring left in it until it is the same temperature or a bright cherry-red. Have a quenching bath of sperm-oil at hand and quench the spring in this when it reaches the proper temperature.

For tempering flat-springs, a bath of melted salt- peter is considered the best. It should be heated to a temperature of 700 to 725 degrees and the spring placed in it long enough, about twelve minutes, to take the temperature of the bath. The spring need not be quenched after temper-ing, as its temperature cannot rise higher than that of the bath.

Action-pins often need replacing in old guns, especially those in single-shot actions. Sometimes it is necessary to ream out the holes, in which the pins fit, to a larger diameter as these holes may be worn out of round. If the parts containing these holes are of nickel- steel or of carbon-steel heat-treated, not case-hardened, all that is necessary is to ream the hole so it is round and fit a new hardened pin. If however, the parts are case-hardened and are worn out of round in the action- pin holes, it means that the pins have worn through the case-hardening and, after the holes have been reamed to a larger size, the part must be rehardened by the case-hardening method.

A simple type of case-hardening can be used for this work, consisting of the cyanide process. The part to be rehardened around the action-pin holes is heated red- hot and dipped into powdered cyanide of potassium at the point to be rehardened, reheated to red heat and held there a short time, redipped into the cyanide and again reheated. This is done three or four times and the part is then quenched in cold water while at a red heat. Do not inhale the jumes of cyanide of potassium as it is a deadly poison . A small electric fan can be used to blow the fumes away from you, so that you do not inhale them or, if a forge is used for the heating, it should have a hood on it connected to a chimney so that the fumes are drawn to the outer air and dissipated.

The new action-pins to be fitted in the enlarged holes are turned to size or made from drill-rod of the proper size. The pins are heated to a cherry-red, quenched in oil, polished, reheated slowly until the color shows straw-yellow upon them and quenched again in oil.

Never weld a cracked action, except at a minor point such as tangs, trigger-guard or parts of the cartridge feeding mechanism of a repeating gun; in other words, points on which little or no strain is placed by the firing of the cartridge. If gas welding is used, be sure to protect other parts of the action from heat running to them by immersing all of the action except the part being welded in water or covering them with water-soaked cloths.

Operating levers and lower tangs may be easily bent to conform to modern, close, pistol-grips. This is often required on single-shot actions, if they are made of steel and not malleable-iron the bending is a simple process and can usually be done cold, although if tangs are case- hardened and have a screw-hole close to the end, the hardening has sometimes gone completely through the steel around the screw-hole and bending cold will result in a break at the screw-hole. If in doubt about this and you do not desire to shorten the tang any, heat the end around the screw-hole to a bright red heat and hold it at that for about live minutes, then allow it to cool before starting the bending operation.

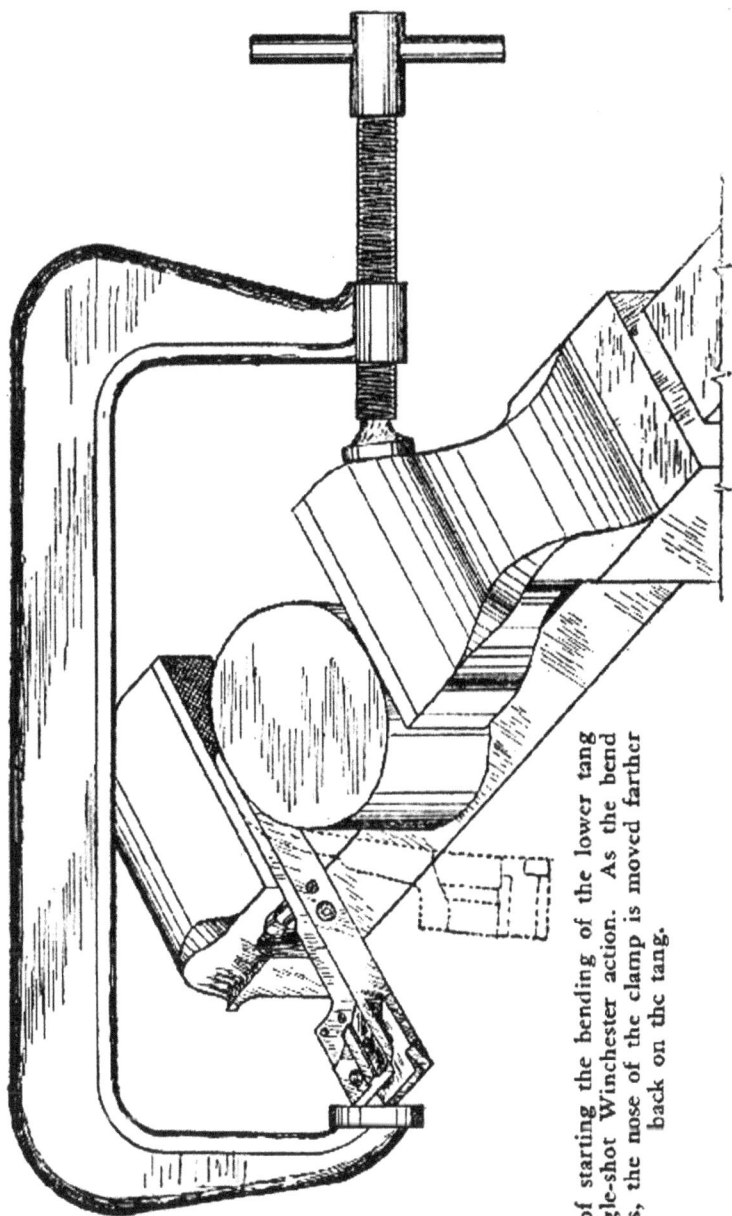

Method of starting the bending of the lower tang of a single-shot Winchester action. As the bend progresses, the nose of the clamp is moved farther back on the tang.

To make the necessary bend, remove all parts from the lower tang and plug all screw-holes with steel plugs to prevent them closing up. The threaded hole for the tang screw that passes from the upper tang through the stock and into the lower tang, should have a threaded, hardened steel plug in it. This plug should have a square head, which can be larger than the threaded body, and it should be screwed in from the top surface of the lower tang, just coming flush with the lower surface.

A short steel cylinder, cut from a piece of shafting, is stood upright upon the bar of the sliding jaw of the bench vise, and the end of the lower tang is held be- tween the back of this cylinder and the rear jaw of the vise, with a piece of copper between the steel cylinder and the lower surface of the tang. The vise is set up rather tightly and a large C-clamp is used to draw the tang in a bend around the steel cylinder. The size of the steel shaft from which the cylinder is made is varied to suit the bend desired in the tang. The position of the cylinder and the tang in the vise is varied, as is necessary to get clearance, as the bending proceeds.

Operating levers, if of the single type, will usually have to have a piece welded on them to lengthen them, in order to bring them to the bottom of the pistol-grip. A ball may be welded on them to finish off the end, or the steel may be bent around in a close curl. The lever is bent around the cylinder of steel in the same way the tang was bent.

If the lever is of the loop type, such as is often found upon a rifle, the bending is a more complicated process. It is best done in an arbor press, using three steel rods or brass rods, but it can be done with a vise. In doing it on a press, two rods are laid on the pressure plate of the press, spaced a short distance apart, and the lever is laid upon these, bottom up, then the third rod is laid upon -the inner surface of the back strap of the lever, midway between the other two rods. A piece of heavy strap-steel is bent to the shape of a square-U, so that its open ends may be placed upon the third rod, and the ram of the press brought down upon the bottom of the U, which is turned upwards above the front strap of the lever. Pressure is now applied and the rods moved along as is necessary to make the proper bend. The front strap of the lever can usually be bent by direct pressure of the ram of the press, bending it a little at a time as you move it, so that no sharp kinks develop in it, until it parallels the back strap.

This same job can be done in a vise if the ends of the rods used in the bending process are bent over at a right-angle, so that the rods will hang in place on the vise jaws but, due to the width of the vise jaws you do not have the clearance that you have in an arbor press for the lever to make its curve. This can be corrected in bending the back strap by using a steel cylinder against the movable jaw of the vise, between it and the lever.

In remodeling a heavy-type, single-shot action for a modern high-velocity cartridge, the firing-pin hole in the breech-block usually has to be bored out from the front, a bushing fitted in the breech-block with a smaller firing-pin hole in it than the original hole in the block, and a smaller nose made on the firing-pin. This is

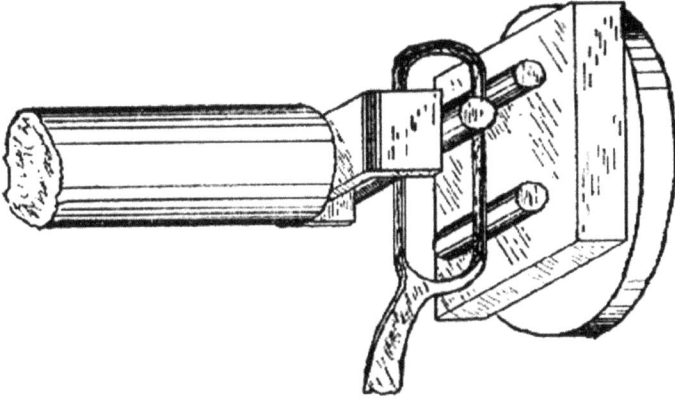

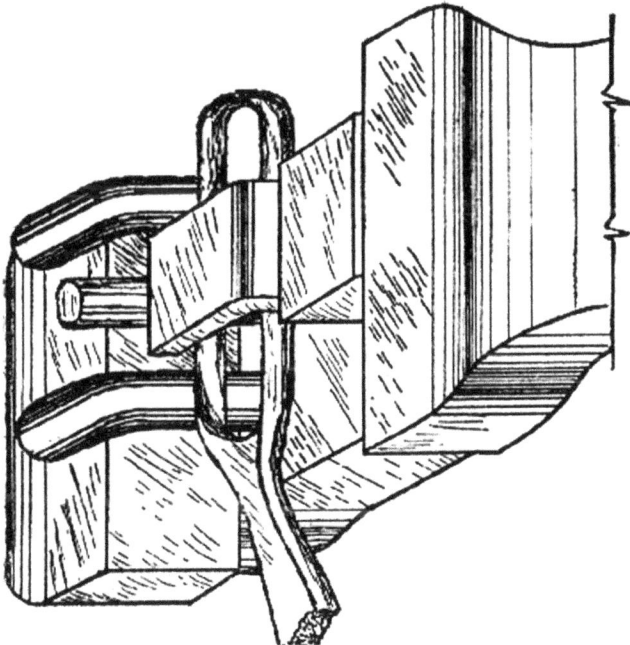

Method of bending a loop lever in a vise and in an arbor press.

vise and necessary to prevent the primers puncturing from high pressures of 35,000 pounds or more per square inch.

The best way to make and fit this bushing is to chuck the breech-block in the lathe chuck and bore out the old firing-pin hole to a diameter to be threaded with a fine thread, of 32 or more to the inch, of diameter to a depth of about 1/8". The front of the hole is then counterbored to 1/2" diameter, to a depth of 1/8" and a flanged bushing of tool-steel is made and threaded to fit this counterbored hole. Two small holes are drilled

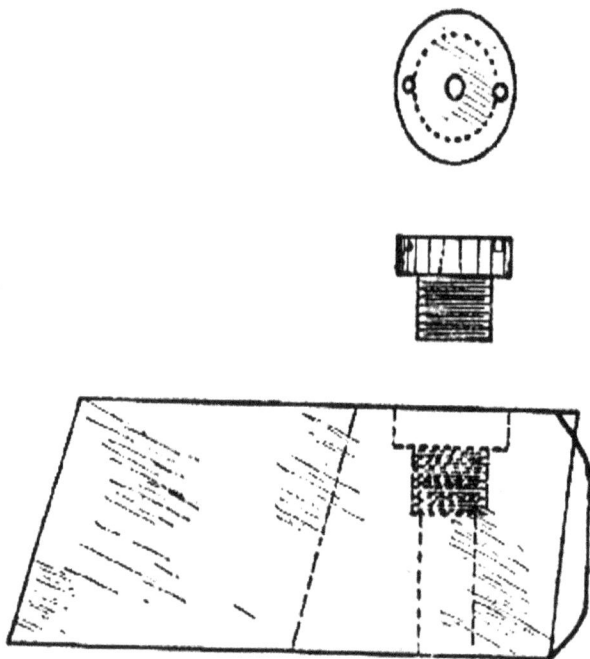

Flange-type bushing for firing-pin nose as fitted in breech block of single-shot action.

near the outer edge of the flange of the bushing, at each side, opposite each other, and a pin spanner wrench is made with pins to fit the holes, so that the bushing may be screwed into place. The threads should fit very tightly so that there is no chance for the bushing to loosen.

A piece of drill-rod that will just slip down the bore and which is slightly longer than the rifle barrel is pointed, centrally, on the end and the point hardened. The breech-block with the bushing in it is placed in its fully closed position in the action and the rod is tapped on the outer end, to mark the location of the bore center on the breech-block bushing. The breech-block is then removed and, with the block in a vise on the drilling machine, the firing-pin hole is drilled in from the face of the breech-block. Make sure that the breech-block is tilted at the proper angle in the vise, so that the original hole in the breech-block for the body of the firing-pin is vertical to the table of the drilling machine.

The firing-pin hole in the bushing is first drilled with a Vis" center-drill and then redrilled with a #44 wire- gauge drill, after which it is reamed from the rear, either with a firing-pin reamer or a tapered broach reamer. I prefer the tapered English broach reamer for this work, so that the firing-pin hole is slightly relieved just back of the face of the bushing. This can also be reamed with a small, round, tapered Swiss-type file turned in a left-hand direction.

As the firing-pin hole through the bushing may not be central with the original firing-pin body hole in the breech-block, it will be necessary to make a firing-pin with an off-center nose if this is the case. The original firing-pin, if it is an odd shape, may be cut off square, after being annealed, replaced in the breech-block and the location of the off-center nose located with a drill run through the firing-pin hole in the hushing. The old pin is then drilled and tapped for a piece of chisel-steel to be screwed in and turned up for a new nose, after which it is hardened and the temper then draw to a deep blue, in oil.

The bushing is removed from the breech-block, hardened, the temper drawn in oil at a dark purple and the bushing replaced in the block. Check the surface carefully to see that it is flush with the face of the breech-block, if not grind it down flush and polish it.

An alternate method of bushing the breech-block is to bore the block out to a square-bottomed hole, to a diameter to thread for 1/2" with a fine thread of 32 or more per inch, to a depth of 3/8".A piece of 1/2" drill- rod is then threaded to fit this hole tightly and screwed in against the bottom of the hole. A drill fitting the body-hole of the firing-pin in the breech-block is inserted from the rear and the bushing is drilled deeply enough with this to take the body length of the old firing-pin. A 1/16 " drill is then used to drill on through the bushing for the firing-pin nose, which hole is then enlarged with a #44 wire-gauge drill and reamed out as in the previous method.

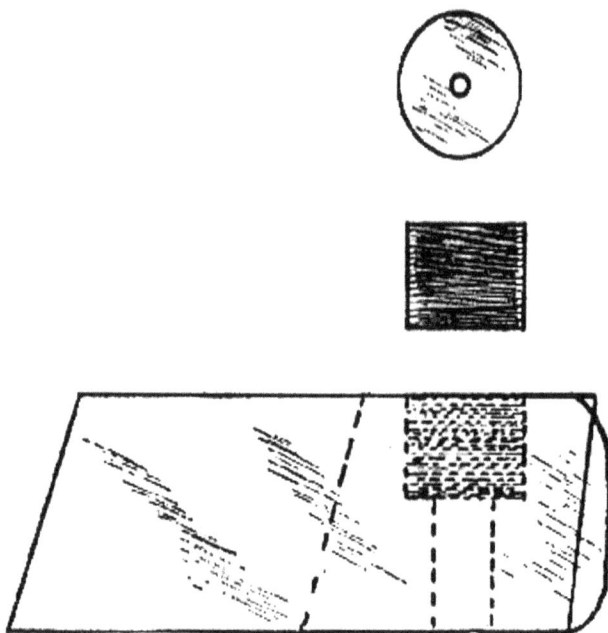

Straight-type bushing for firing-pin nose as fitted to breech block.

The bushing is still part of the original drill-rod, several inches long, and is now unscrewed from the breech-block, hardened and then the temper is drawn in oil to a dark purple, verging into blue. The bushing, still on the several inches of rod, is then screwed tightly back into the breech-block and, using a high-speed steel hack-saw blade, is cut off just beyond the face of the breech-block, after which it is ground down Hush with the breech-block face. This method is applicable to the Winchester single-shot ac- tions because of the fact that the thickness of the head of cartridges used determines just how high the breech- block rises in clos- ing this action, so even if the firing- pin hole location is marked centrally with the bore, there is no assurance that the firing-pin will always strike a primer centrally.

Firing-pins should have a protrusion of .050" beyond the face of the breech-block when in the fired position, with the exception of those in the Sharps Borchardt action. These latter firing-pins must be made with as little protrusion as possible and still fire the cartridge with certainty, for this breech-block moves straight down when the action is opened but it starts to move down before the firing-pin begins to retract so that the nose of the firing-pin is dragged partly through the primer before being retracted mechanically, which results in a broken firing-pin if the protrusion of the pin is greater than .040" beyond the face of the breech- block, and .035" is better yet, if it will fire with certainty every time. There will be a variation in the thickness of heads of rimmed cases, so this firing-pin protrusion on this Sharps action must be carefully checked with several different makes of cases, to be sure that primers will fire every time.

Lock-time on these single-shot actions may be speeded-up by lightening the hammer, stiffening the main-spring and, in actions of the Sharps Borchardt type, by lightening the firing-pin and shortening the hammer fall or the firing-pin travel.

While shortening lock-time usually results in better accuracy, this is not always true and this especially applies to rim-fire actions, as these seem more sensitive to variation in firing-pin blow than do the center-fires. Some target barrel makers refuse to guarantee as good accuracy with shortened lock-time in the .22 long-rifle as they will with a standard lock-time.

In the open-hammer type actions, the hammer may be lightened by drilling holes in the web below the hammer spur, or by cutting a triangular-shaped piece out of this web. A second method is to cut a new cocking notch farther forward than the original, so that the hammer travel is shortened. As hammers are hardened, it will be necessary to anneal them before making any cuts or holes in them and then reharden them after- wards.

If the hammers are lightened, or their travel shortened, a stiffer main-spring is nearly always necessary to produce a heavy enough blow to fire the primer properly. In the flat main-spring type, this is easily accomplished by making a heavier spring, which in- creases the tension on the hammer, or by fitting a block or tension-screw so that the bend of the spring is shortened in use.

The the coil-type spring, a new spring is made of heavier wire. In this case it is sometimes necessary to use wire of a keystone shape, instead of round wire, to get the necessary stiffness. This usually occurs in actions of the Sharps Borchardt type, or of the regular bolt-action type where space around the firing-pin is too limited to use a heavy enough spring of round wire.

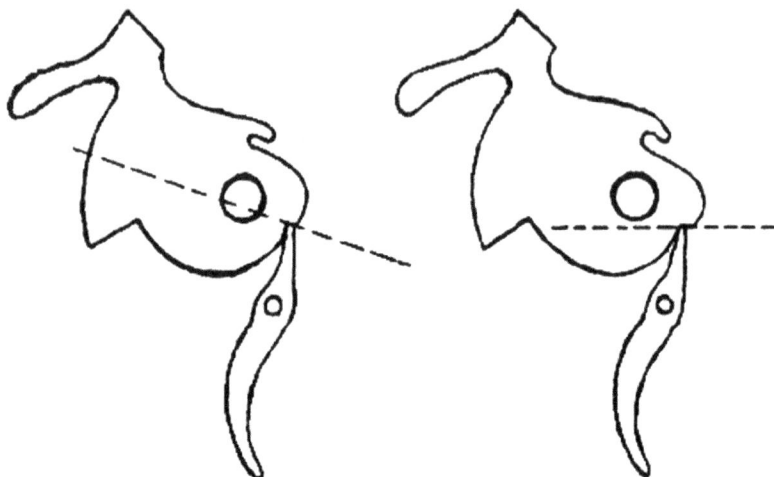

At left is shown incorrect shape of sear notch in hammer. The hammer will be cammed back against main-spring pressure when trigger is pulled. At right is shown correct shape, so hammer will remain stationary as sear point is withdrawn from notch by pulling the trigger.

The lock-time of the Sharps Borchardt action is fairly fast as it was made originally, due to the short firing-pin travel but it may be speeded-up still more, as is done with bolt-actions, by lightening the firing- pin, from the rear, to remove weight but, due to the sear notch in the pin, this hole cannot be made very large, although drilling the hole off-center enables you to make a larger hole than if the pin is centrally drilled. Some weight may also be removed from the heavy head of this firing-pin, on the top and bottom sides. If these methods do not increase lock speed enough, a new firing- pin may be made of light-weight metal to replace the steel pin.

Speeding-up lock-time on bolt-action arms is done by using stiffer springs of keystone-shaped spring-wire, by substituting alloy-steel firing-pins without cocking- knobs — as has been done at Springfield Arsenal on the "free" rifles — or by shortening firing-pin travel by grinding back the sear-notch and the face of the sear. The best results come from lightening the pin and using the stiffer spring of keystone-section wire.

Trigger-pulls can be greatly refined and lightened, thus improving accuracy, by carefully polishing the contact surfaces of triggers, hammers and sears and this is the first thing to be tried in changing a trigger- pull , before making any other alterations . Polish these contact surfaces with the hard white Arkansas stones, then examine them carefully with a high-power magnifying glass to see that the surfaces are flat and even.

When reassembling them for trial, coat the surface of one or the other lightly with prussian-blue, then all points of contact can be readily seen, so that high spots can be removed or the shape altered if necessary. On bolt-actions of the Mauser type, polish the under sur- face of the receiver, where the rear upper portion of the trigger bears.

If the polishing process does not result in sufficient lightening of the trigger-pull, check the depth of sear engagement in the sear notch and also see if the sear nose and notch are of such shape that the hammer or firing-pin is cammed back against the main-spring pres- sure by the first part of the trigger-pull.

If the sear engagement seems unnecessarily deep in its notch, except in bolt-actions, drill a small hole in the back part of the notch and drive in a Vie" diameter

At left is shown incorrect shape of sear notch in hammer. The hammer will be cammed back against main-spring pressure when trigger is pulled. At right is shown correct shape, so hammer wiU remain stationary as sear point is withdrawn from notch by pulling the trigger.

pin tightly, filing this off to the proper length so that it just allows the sear to engage a small amount of the notch, which will shorten its pull.

If the hammer or firing-pin is cammed back upon pulling the trigger, change the angle of the contact be- tween the sear and notch so that upon pulling the trigger the sear moves straight forward or down out of its notch without exerting this camming action. Be careful in this operation not to bevel these surfaces in the opposite direction but keep them level, so that during the movement of the sear out of its notch there is no move- ment in either direction of the hammer or firing-pin, as the case may be.

These three points ; polishing contact surfaces, giving the scar a shal- lower engagement in its notch, and straightening the contact surfaces so that no camming action occurs upon pulling the trigger, will practically always lighten the trigger-pull sufficiently. The one exception to this is when the sear-spring is too stiff, which sometimes, but very seldom occurs. If this is the case, a lighter sear spring may be fitted or the pres- ent one may be shortened by cutting it off a little at a time, but be very careful in this operation and check and recheck time and again to see that the spring remains stiff enough to return the sear to its proper seat in its notch each time the trigger is partly pulled and then released.

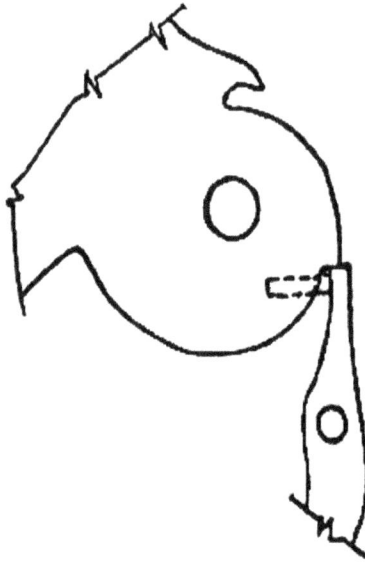

Method of pin insertion in face of sear notch in hammer to decrease depth of a notch that is too deep.

If the sear is not returned fully to its seat each time, a dangerous condition has been set up and the only remedy is a new sear spring.

Bolt-action trigger-pulls require a different treatment in some respects than other types. Most of the bolt actions have the double or military-type pull, to which many shooters object. In types of these actions which have an independent bolt-stop separate from the sear, this take-up or preliminary pull may be removed. One method of doing this is to place a small steel plate in the guard, on the upper side so that, its rear end prevents the trigger moving far enough forward to allow the sear to rise to its full height. This plate may be fastened in place with two small screws or two rivets. If screws are used make sure the threads fit tightly, so that they do not work loose.

A second method of eliminating the take-up pull is to drill and tap a small hole through the trigger, so that a screw passed through the trigger from rear to front will bear against the front edge of the trigger slot in the guard to prevent the trigger moving all the way forward. Here again the threads must fit very tightly, to prevent any movement of the screw' after it is adjusted.

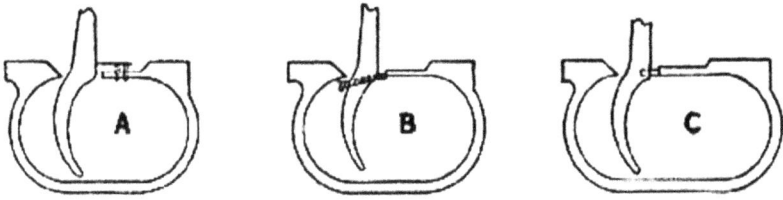

Trigger-pull adjustments for bolt actions. A shows plate riveted to guard, to take up part or all of preliminary pull. B shows same object attained by use of a small screw through trigger, while C shows this preliminary pull taken out by means of a pin driven tightly into a hole drilled into front of trigger so that its end bears against front edge of trigger slot in guard.

A third method is merely a modification of the second, in that a small hole is drilled only partly through the trigger from front to rear, then a pin is driven tightly into the hole and filed off to the proper length to limit trigger movement. This method is safer than the screw in that if this pin loosens it can only drop out, allowing the trigger to move completely for- ward, whereas if the screw loosens it is possible for it to screw' farther forward through the trigger, so as to shorten the trigger-pull below the safety point. This however, is a remote possibility.

In lightening the trigger-pull of bolt actions, all con- tact surfaces are polished and trued up so that no high spots remain and the rear top edge of the sear is given a very slight radius with a fine stone, merely enough to remove the sharp edge. The face of the sear notch in the cocking piece is stoned back on a slight angle from the vertical, so that the rear face of the sear bears only for short distance at the bottom edge of this notch. If these two contact surfaces here and the contact surfaces of the two cams on top of the trigger and the under surface of the receiver where these two trigger cams bear are given a good polish, the average bolt action trigger-pull can be brought to three pounds with no trouble. In some bolt actions however, the sear spring is unduly stiff and it will be necessary to shorten it by cutting it off, half a coil at a time and trying it. This spring should always be left stiff enough to return the sear to full engagement with the cocking piece when the trigger is given the preliminary pull and then re- leased without completing the release of the firing-pin.

Check the rear face of the sear to make sure that it is of the proper shape so that it does not cam the firing- pin back against main-spring pressure when the trigger is pulled, but be sure that this rear face of the sear does not have so much angle that it has to force the firing-pin back to rise to its full engagement when the preliminary pull only is given and the trigger is then released, as this condition makes a very stiff sear spring necessary and increases the weight of the pull.

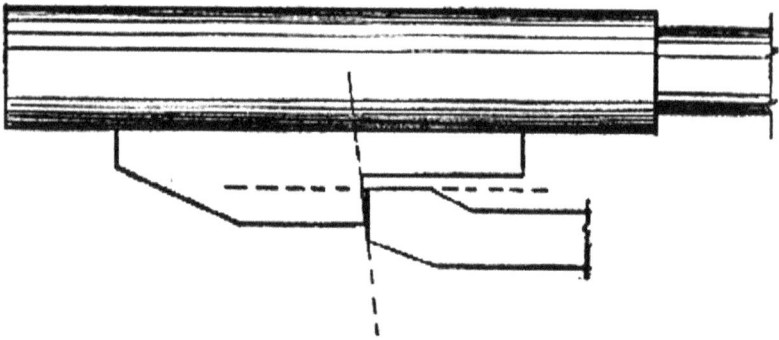

Correct shape of sear and face of sear notch of bolt actions.

If length of the preliminary pull is not objected to, a good short, snappy, final pull can be given by grinding down the top of the rearmost of the two cams on the upper part of the trigger which bear against the bottom of the receiver. By decreasing the height of the rear cam, more w r ork is thrown onto the front cam, which has the most leverage, and the sear is drawn farther down out of the notch by the preliminary pull before the second cam comes in contact with the bottom of the receiver to give the final pull. The increase in the length of the preliminary pull will hardly be noticeable, but a lighter trigger-pull will result.

The only work recommended on trigger-pulls of autoloading arms is a thorough polishing of all contact surfaces, as parts of these arms are usually fitted with more tolerance than other types and the action is sub-ject to far more jar and vibration, so that if trigger- pulls are lightened too much they may soon fail to hold when a little wear appears and the arm is then unsafe.

The smooth functioning of a gun depends upon the proper fit of parts and the closer this fit is made and the better the surface of the parts, the longer the life of the action will be. To get this condition, the parts are machined or filed as closely to size while in their soft state as is safe, which is usually within .002", and are then hardened and the surfaces brought to a perfect fit with small hand stones and lapping plates. This is called hard fitting of parts.

Plate IX

Using a small jeweler's lathe to make a composition front sight bead.
New white or red sight beads are easily turned to size, at high speed, in
a jeweler's lathe, using either a tool rest of the type shown or a hand
rest and a small chisel.

with the part being worked upon being held in these jaws with an almost imperceptible amount above their top, so that as it is brought down to size the stone slides across the tops of the jaws, which reduces the rocking tendency to a minimum. (See Frontispiece.)

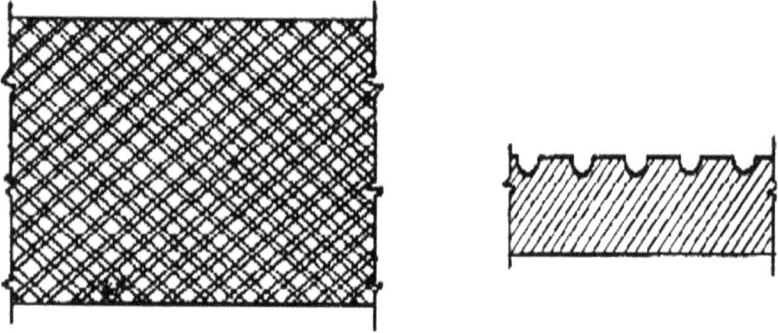

Construction of lapping plate of cast iron, for use in lapping flat parts.

A lapping plate of cast-iron is used to flat-finish parts by rubbing them over the plate, which is charged with diamond dust or other lapping compounds, by hand. The surface of this plate is crossed or checkered with small, shallow grooves and the lapping compound

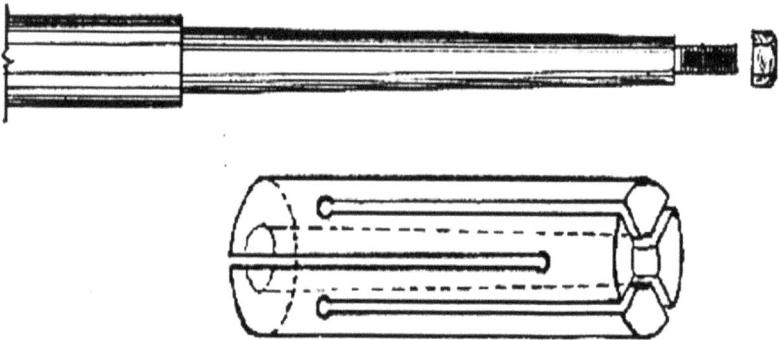

Construction of cast iron lap, for lapping round holes.

being used is mixed with oil of a light body and spread upon the plate. In using these lapping-plates, do not lap a piece continually in one place but move it about all over the plate, to reduce any tendency to wear the plate unevenly.

Holes are usually lapped to size with a round lead lap, which is charged with emery and oil, although expanding cast-iron laps are sometimes used with diamond dust to lap holes. The lead lap is merely upset to increase its size by bumping the end of it lightly from time to time, but the cast-iron lap is a sleeve with four or more slots sawed in it, half from one end to within a short distance of the opposite end and the other half sawed from the opposite end to within a short distance of the first end These slots alternate with each other, one from one end and the next from the other end. The interior hole or bore of this sleeve is a taper. A taper-pin reamer may be used to produce this taper and a corresponding taper is turned upon a shaft to fit the hole. Part of this shaft at the small end of the taper is turned straight and threaded for a nut smaller in diameter than the outer diameter of the sleeve and this nut forces the sleeve farther up the taper of the shaft, thus enlarging the lap as is necessary.

The sides of parts such as hammers, which must have a good finish but need not have as high a degree of fit on the sides as other parts, are polished or lapped upon a plate of steel or iron on which fine carborundum cloth is cemented. This may be cemented to the plate, either with the quick-setting wax put out for attaching grinding-paper discs to disc-grinders or water-glass may be used, although this is much harder to remove than the wax.

In choosing steel for making gun parts, the function of the part is studied to see if it is subject to impact or only wear from a sliding action. If the part is subject to impact, such as firing-pins, locking bolts or hammers, it should be made of alloy-steel or tool-steel. Locking-bolts arc best made of nickel or tungsten alloy-steel, while hammers and firing-pins should be made of carbon tool-steel, although hammers can be made of manganese alloy-steel as this is very tough. Firing- pins should not be made of tool-steel of too high a carbon content, chisel or rock-drill steel being better than drill-rod for this purpose. All these steels require proper heat treatment to bring out the required hardness and toughness.

Sliding parts require a high surface hardness but usually do not need interior hardness, so these parts are usually case-hardened to resist wear and the center left soft so that in the hardening process there is no danger of cracks developing, unless the part is too thin and is given too great a chill. As case-hardening is an impregnation of the surface with carbon, a tool-steel is not of the best type to choose for a case-hardened part as the structural grain is too fine to allow good penetration of the carbon. A steel of a coarser, more open grain will answer the purpose better as it allows a deeper more even penetration of the carbon, so machinery steel, commonly called cold-rolled, is a better case-hardening steel than tool-steel. Also, due to the fact that tool-steel already contains carbon, it will develop a hardness of its own throughout during the case-hardening operation, which will defeat the soft- center idea which is one of the objects of case- hardening.

Misfires are sometimes due to incorrect steel being used for a firing-pin or may be due to incorrect hardening methods being used. It might be thought that a firing-pin of machinery' steel, case-hardened, would be the best type, but the continual pounding of an action- hammer on the end of a case-hardened pin will gradually bulge the soft center of the pin, until it binds in its hole and softens the force of the firing-pin blow on the primer; or a tool-steel pin may be used and be case-hardened, which will cause cracks to appear, especially in the smaller point section of the pin which will finally break off and yet may remain in place and appear all right to a casual inspection. When the pin is in two parts, dirt will collect between the ends of the two parts or small particles of brass from primers or cartridge case will get in there and cushion the blow of the firing-pin. Using a steel of too high a carbon con- tent may result in the same thing, too brittle a pin which will cause breakage and misfires. Firing-pins made of chisel or rock-drill steel, then hardened and tempered in oil, will give the best service and the least trouble from misfires, as the oil hardening imparts less brittleness to the steel than does cold water and seems to develop the greatest toughness in this chisel-steel.

I have seen tiring-pins made of carboloy that were ground to shape, as they were too hard to machine with a cutting tool, but they were placed in a soft steel breech-block and as the firing-pin had a long slender nose and the hole in the soft steel breech-block soon wore to the point where it was far from a close fit on the firing-pin, the pin had so much side play that, being very brittle as it was, it soon snapped off ; so in this case a poor choice of steels to work together resulted in the defeat of the desired object, namely a long-life firing-pin.

Chapter 7 SIGHTS , SCOPES AND SMALL PARTS

Probably the poorest way to attach sights to the gun barrel is in the time-honored dovetail slot — but this has been done from the earliest days, is still being done and is often demanded by the customer, so a word or two about it will be in good order.

Is is sometimes necessary to cut a few inches from the muzzle of a rifle which has a front sight in a dove- tail slot, so if any great amount is taken off the barrel must be slotted further back. Small milling cutters to mill these slots must usually be made by the gun- smith or made to order by some cutter manufacturer, which is often expensive, so many times these slots are cut with a three-square file by hand, instead of in a milling machine.

Whichever method is used, the slot must be straight and level. With an octagon barrel it is easy enough to get it level by leveling the top flat of the barrel, if it is being held in a vise and the slot cut with a file. A small level is used in the slot, as the work progresses, to in- sure the bottom of the slot being kept level. If the slot is cut in a vertical head milling machine, the top flat is leveled but if a miller with a horizontal head is used, the top flat is set at right-angles to the surface of the table and the milling machine vise squared with the table.

If the rifle has a round barrel, the top of the barrel is leveled-up by leveling the top of the action or squaring it with the table top of a horizontal miller.

In cutting these dovetail slots by hand, the slot is marked out and then rough-cut with a fine-toothed hack-saw. Between the two ends of the slot, make several vertical cuts with the hack-saw, close together but not reaching the bottom of the slot. Then by turning the saw to a side-angle, this center portion can be pretty well sawed out, so that the work of the file is cut down a great deal and much time is saved.

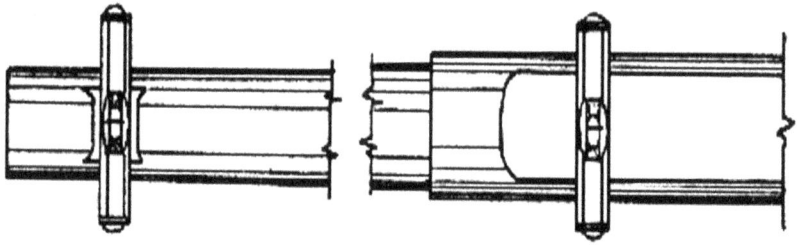

In cutting slots for sights, the rifle receiver is leveled by a small level, while barrel is held in padded jaws of vise. Dovetail slot is then cut with file, slot being kept level while cutting by a small level laid in the cut from time to time.

A regular three-square file is used, but it is better if one with parallel sides instead of tapering ones be used. Two sides of the file should be ground smooth, leaving only one side to do the cutting, as it is then easier to keep the slot true. Using a file with parallel sides makes it easier to keep the slot at right-angles to the axis of the barrel, as any deviation is more easily seen than with a tapered file.

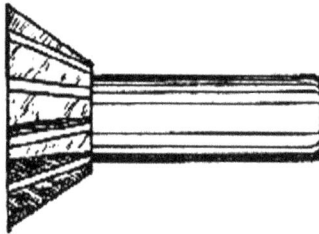

Special milling cutter for cutting sight dovetails in barrel.

Sometimes it is necessary to replace a front sight bead, either to replace a broken bead or to experiment with a bead of a different color to increase visibility, or to change a Patridge-type sight to a Call-type but using white, green or red instead of the conventional gold for this type of sight. These beads of various colors can be easily made from colored celluloid, bought in a ten-cent store. White knitting needles can be used to make the white beads, other articles such as combs or dress ornaments will furnish the other colors. The very light shades of red and green should be used, in fact a deep pink is superior for visibility to a genuine red.

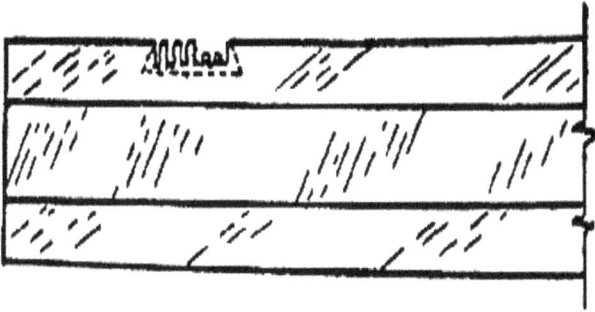

In cutting dovetail in barrel by hand, the slot is roughed out with hack saw cuts. A small chisel is then used to chip away the metal between saw cuts as shown, after which the slot is finished to size with a three-square file.

The material is turned at high speed and a very sharp tool is used to shape it. In the case of the regular beads, the shank should be about 1/8" long. The shank is made a fairly close fit in the blade and Dupont cement is first put into the hole, the shank of the bead is then pressed in and the bead lightly clamped in place. A spring-type, wooden clothes-pin makes a good clamp for this job. A small parallel clamp is clamped to the opposite edge of the blade from the bead face, to give the clothes-pin a square surface to clamp against at that end.

The regular Patridge-type front sight may be equipped with a colored bead of the Call-type, as mentioned above, or a square-type bead with a round shank can be made, the square being the size of the width of the blade. A shallow notch is filed on the rear face of the blade so that this square bead sets in flush.

A Patridge-type front sight, such as those supplied on the Colt auto-loading pistols, can be slotted with a 1 1/32 " slitting saw in a milling machine and then filed down on top to a height that will bring a bead sight to the proper height when its blade is filed down to the correct thickness and set into the sawed slot. A flush, tight-fitting pin is put through the sides of the original sight, pinning the bead sight in place.

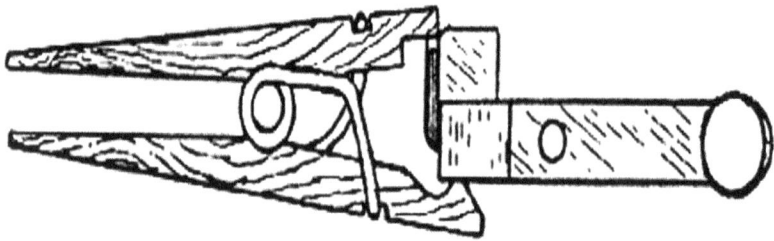

In cementing a new composition bead in a blade front sight, a parallel clamp is fastened on the blade below and opposite the bead. A spring clothes pin is then cut away as shown and used as a clamp while the cement sets.

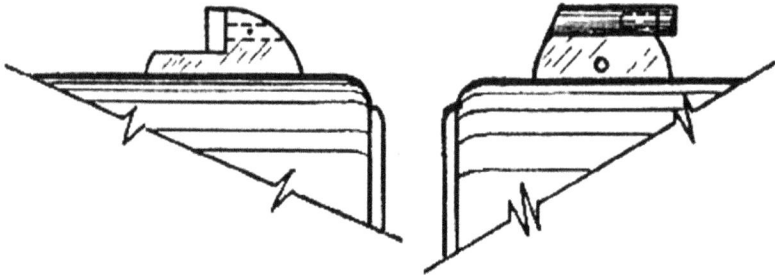

Left shows square face of red or white composition set into the rounded top Patridge-type supplied on the Colt Ace pistol. The rounded sight has a square notch cut out as shown and the square face composition with a round stem on it is set into a hole drilled through the blade from the front and anchored with cement and a small pin. Right sketch shows same front sight slotted lengthwise with a $\frac{1}{32}''$ slot, then cut down in height so that a standard bead sight with the blade cut to $\frac{1}{32}''$ thickness is pinned in place in the slot.

Gold-bead sights are made of phosphor-bronze wire, which may be obtained in various diameters. This should be brazed to a steel blade in making a regular bead-type sight, as solder does not hold it well enough. Solder, however, may be used to hold it in a hole in a steel blade, as the bead is protected better from hard knocks in this case.

The Patridge-type rear sight can be changed over to a U-notch, to work with a bead-type front sight, by taking a thin piece of steel and drilling a small hole in it the proper size for a U-notch, then countersinking this hole from the front side to give clear cut edges and filing the steel down to a straight horizontal line through the center of the hole, leaving a U-notch. The piece is then put in nitric-acid until it has a dull gray- black pitted surface, when it is washed in boiling water, dried and sweated with solder to the rear face of the Patridge sight.

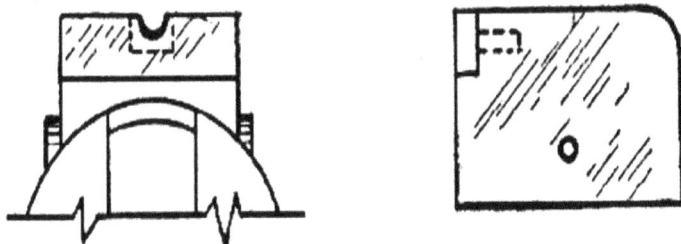

Left shows Patridge type rear sight changed over to U notch by solder-ing a thin piece of steel with U notch in it on the rear face of the sight. Right shows a square face of red or white composition set into a Patridge type blade front sight of flat rear-face pattern.

Receiver sights must be squared with the receiver, and the easiest way to do this is to set the action and barrel up on a surface plate. If you do not have a regular cast-iron surface plate long enough you can get a piece of heavy plate-glass from a glass company, as the surface of this is pretty true. Get a piece ten or twelve inches wide and about forty inches or more long. Lay this upon a true, flat surface, for glass is elastic and will bend if not well -supported.

In setting up a rifle on the surface plate for attaching a receiver sight, place a steel parallel or a well-squared piece of steel under the receiver, if it is a bolt-action rifle with a flat-bottomed receiver, and place a vee-block beneath the barrel. If the rifle does not have a flat- bottomed receiver, a 5 some lever-actions do not, place two vee-blocks beneath the barrel and square the sides of the receiver with the surface plate, using a clamp around the barrel and one vee-block to hold the rifle square. The receiver sight is then clamped in place on the receiver with parallel clamps, using a machinist's square set on the surface plate to square-up the sight base on the receiver.

High-speed steel drills are the best to use for spotting and for drilling the screw holes in receivers to attach sights, as they cut the alloy steels better and stand up longer without resharpening. A drill that just fits the screw holes through the sight base is used to spot these holes, just drilling the full depth of the drill point, so that the tap-drill used will center the hole perfectly. The base is left in place while tapping, so that it will act as a guide to start the tap straight.

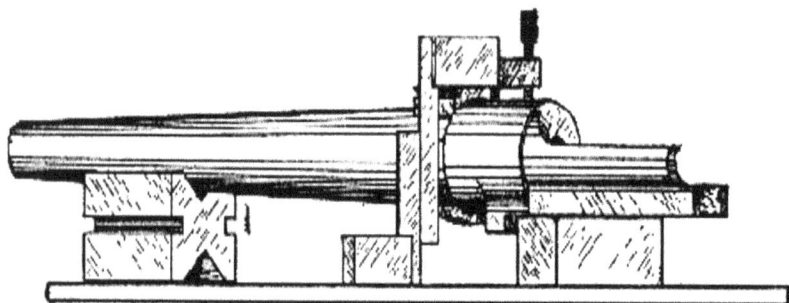

Set up necessary to square-up rifle barrel and action when fitting scope sight blocks.

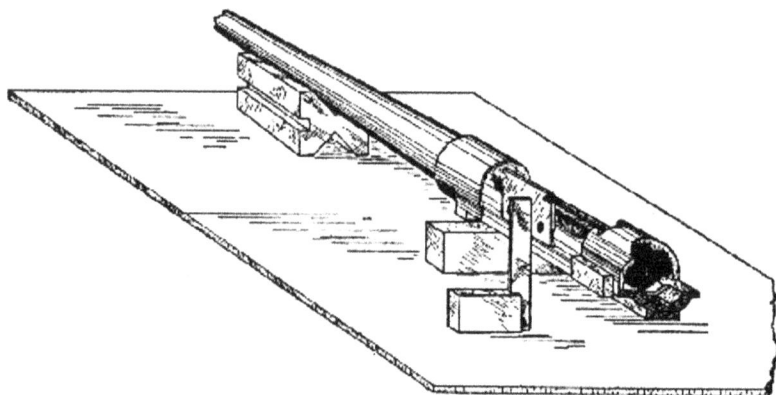

Set up of receiver and barrel supported on steel parallel and vee-block on glass plate, while side-plate for hunting-type telescope is squared on the side of the receiver with a machinist's square resting upon the glass plate.

Even a high-speed steel drill will not drill a hardened receiver but as most all hardened receivers are case-hardened, it is only necessary to get through this case-hardening in order to drill the hole, as the center of the steel is soft. Various methods may be used to penetrate this hardened skin, one of which is to mark the locations of your holes, then remove the sight base and, using a small mounted grinding-wheel or carborundum point in a high-speed electric grinder, grind through the case-hardening at the two points you wish to drill the holes. The base is then replaced, squared-up and the hole drilling is done as on unhardened steel.

Shows base of receiver sight clamped in place on receiver for mounting. Receiver bottom rests on steel parallel upon heavy glass plate and the sight base is squared up with machinist's square setting on the glass plate.

If the case-hardening is very thin it can often be penetrated with a heavy center-punch. In this case, the hole center is carefully marked and the center-punch placed thereon and struck a heavy blow. The drill is then started at low speed, using turpentine for a lubricant, and as long as the point of the drill does not contact the steel, the lips of the drill will cut. The center-punch is driven into the hole several times, as the drilling proceeds, so that the center of the hole is kept depressed below the reach of the drill point. An- other method to drill this case-hardening is to soften it with heat, at the points to be drilled. The best method to do this is by using an automobile storage battery. Use two heavy cables, such as old starter cables; attach one cable to some part of the receiver with a heavy cable clip or a clamp and attach a sun- lamp carbon to the loose end of the other cable (the positive lead is best for this) and touch this carbon point to one of the spots to be drilled. The carbon immediately becomes white-hot at the point and softens the case-hardening. The place for the second hole is then touched with the carbon and softened, and the drilling may proceed. Do not try this with A.C. house current unless you have a very heavily fused line and a variable control coil, in which case (after some experimenting and blown fuses) you may accomplish it.

Dental drills may be used to drill steel that is so tough or hard that even high-speed twist drills will not drill it. The ball shape is the best one to use. These are used in a drill press at low speed with a very slow feed, as they will not cut fast. After a small hole is opened up in tough steel with one of these dental drills, the hole can usually be enlarged to the required size with a high-speed steel twist drill running at low speed. These dental drills will not, how- ever, start to cut on case-hardened steel any better than a twist drill.

Telescope sight base blocks or mounts may be squared up on a rifle by using a small level. First, level the action while the rifle is held by the barrel in the padded jaws of a vise, then place your first block, level it and clamp it in place, drill and tap the holes, using the block clamped on the barrel with a parallel clamp as a drill guide for the spotting drill, after which the tap-drill is used, and, with the block still in place to act as a guide, the holes are tapped. The barrel is set in vee-blocks on the drill press to drill these holes and the barrel squared-up with a small level on top of the block, as the block has been clamped in the correct position on the barrel while the rifle was leveled in the vise. In the case of side mounts that separate from the clamping rings of the scope, a square with a level in it can be used to square-up the mount that attaches to the side of the gun. The surface plate may also be used to square-up scope base blocks or side mounts by setting up the barrel and action on parallels and vee-blocks, or vee-blocks alone, and using a square on the plate to square-up the side mounts, and a square on the plate and a small square on top of

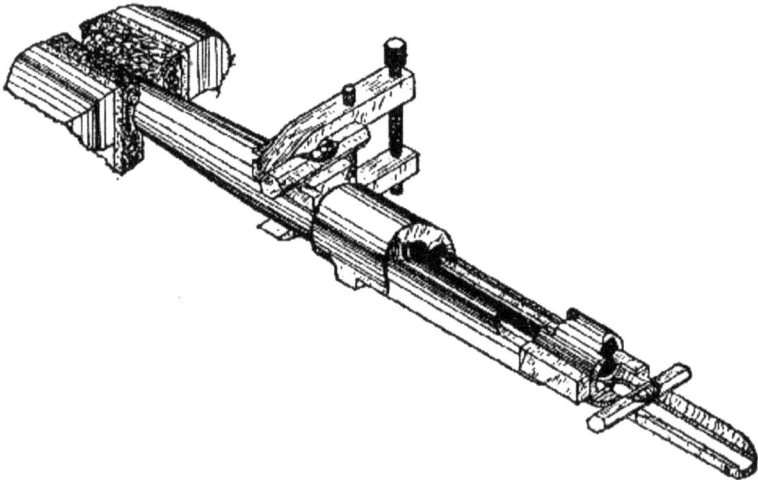

Illustrating how barrel is held in padded vise jaws while receiver is leveled with a small level, which later is used to level the telescopic base block on top of the round barrel.

For setting scope base blocks the proper distance apart, steel scales may be obtained graduated in tenths of an inch for part of their length. These are only obtainable in six-inch lengths now and as base blocks may need to be 7.20" apart, center to center, it will be necessary to clamp a short rule, a 2" one, to the end of the 6" rule. These can be clamped together with a small parallel clamp if you use rules of the same thickness, the width being immaterial as each rule is run in half the width of the clamp jaws and butted against the end of the other rule with their front edges in the same line.

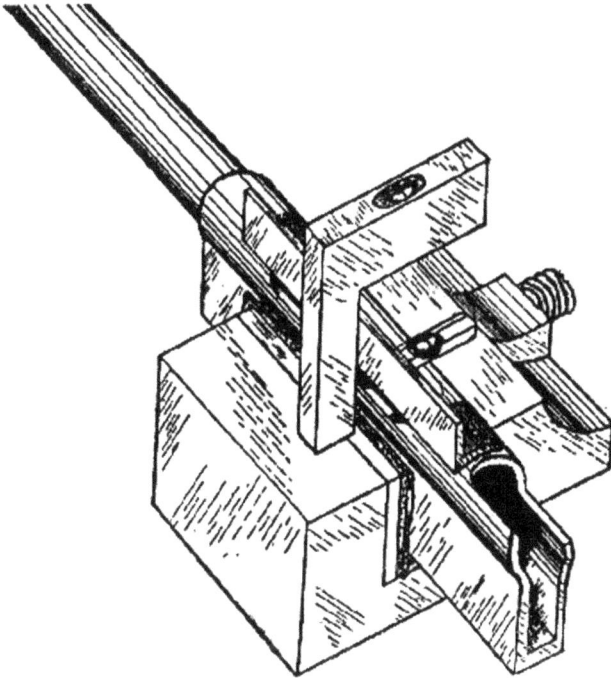

Receiver of light rifle held, leveled, in machine vise jaws while top fastening side mount of the Lyman type for light telescopes is squared on top of the barrel with a cross test level.

Telescopes sometimes need repairs, and unless you are sure of what you are doing, they had better be sent to their makers or to some expert who specializes in scope repairs but sometimes it is necessary to make certain repairs on the spot, due to the time element involved and if you are careful this can be done.

A simple trouble of the double lens cemented type, when they become old, is the separating of the two lens that are cemented together, either the objective or the ocular and sometimes both sets. The first evidence of this is small stars appearing in the lens which is sometimes caused by the scope being subjected to high heat, such as leaving it where the hot summer sun strikes directly on the lens for some time.

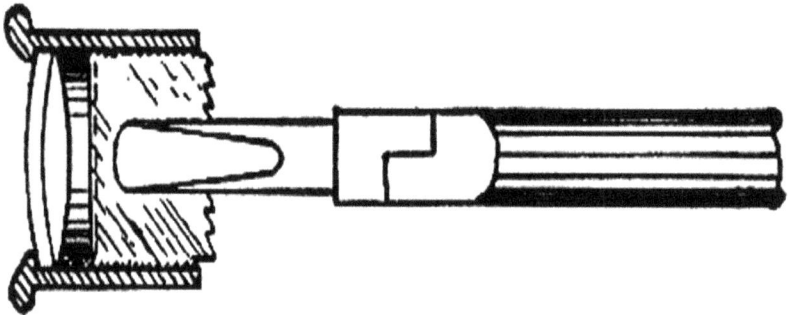

Removing a threaded telescope lens-retaining ring with a short piece of hack saw blade held in a pair of flat-jawed pliers.

When this occurs, the lens and holder are unscrewed from the scope barrel and upon examining the inside you will see a thin brass ring, with two notches in its outer edge, that is screwed down against the lens to hold it in place. Cut a piece of hack-saw blade just the exact length to reach clear across the lens holder from side to side, not quite touching the threads. Carefully place this, smooth edge down, into the two notches in the brass ring and, using a pair of thin but strong-jawed pliers, carefully unscrew this ring, being careful not to let the piece of hack-saw blade slip out of the notches. After this is removed, if the lens does not easily push out with your finger, place it upon a soft cloth upon a bench or table with the outer surface of Balsam gum is used to cement the two lens together* and if there is an optical company near by, take this lens to them to have them separate the two parts and re-cement it. If there is no optical firm available, heat an iron plate to a low heat and carefully lay the lens upon it. As soon as the heat has softened up the balsam used for cement, carefully separate the two parts of the lens, using only your fingers, but protect them from being burned by putting a cloth over them. After the lens has cooled, soak the old balsam off of them with benzine, using a soft, clean cloth like an old handkerchief to wipe them clean and dry.

Obtain some fresh balsam gum from the druggist and, carefully heating the two parts of the lens again on the iron plate, put a small amount of the gum in the cupped lens and let it melt. Now lay the other part of the lens in place upon the cupped part and, using a small stick of soft pine, preferably white pine, work the sec- ond part of the lens back and forth and around on the first lens, evenly distributing the balsam gum between the two parts and working the excess out of the edges. It may be necessary to set the lens back on the heated plate during this operation, to keep the balsam thin enough. After you have it as thin as you can get it between the two parts of the lens, and you are sure there are no air bubbles in it, see that the edges of the two parts of the lens line up perfectly and then set it aside to cool. After it is cool, place some melted beeswax on the threads, inside the lens cell at the point where the lens rested, replace the lens in the cell and screw the notched brass ring up against it carefully with a firm pressure but be careful not to overdo it and crack a lens. The excess beeswax is removed with a sharpened, soft, pine stick and the surfaces of the lens are cleaned by blowing and brushing with a camels-hair brush. This is also the proper method to remove dust from a lens, do not use a cloth to do this or you will scratch the lens.

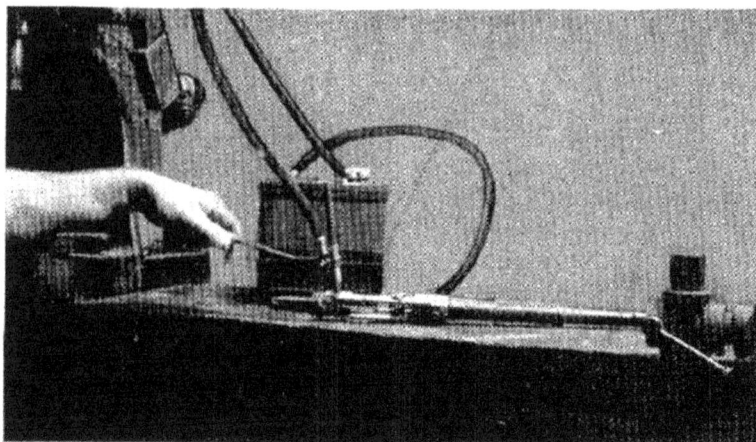

Plate X

Spot annealing a hardened steel receiver to soften it for drilling, using a
storage battery and a carbon point. In annealing case-hardened or heat treated
actions in small spots for drilling and tapping holes by which to mount receiver sights or scope mounts, the negative pole of a six-volt storage battery is
connected by a heavy cable to some part of the action, using a heavy spring
clamp to make this connection. The positive pole of the battery also has a
heavy cable attached to it, upon the other end of which is a clamp with an
insulated handle to hold a sun lamp carbon. This carbon point is held on
each spot to be annealed for one to two minutes, during which time the point
of the carbon becomes almost white hot.

In case no fresh balsam gum is available and the old gum is not
badly starred or the lens parts have not separated enough to let dirt get
between them, the lens can be gently heated as you did to separate the
two parts, then instead of separating them they can be worked around
upon each other as you did after putting in the new balsam gum, and if
there is sufficient gum remaining between the two parts of the lens to
spread around between them, the two parts can be re-cemented with the
original gum without separating.

Reticules in scopes are sometimes broken and must be replaced. If a
post reticule is broken, which seldom happens, obtain the very finest steel
embroidery needle that you can get and if it is to replace a flat-topped post,
stone the point off of the needle squarely, examining it under a powerful
magnifying glass to see that it is square. After removing the rear lens from

the scope loosen the reticule cell and remove that. You can then remove the broken post from the reticule cell and, cutting off the needle to the correct length, solder it in place where the original post was soldered, being careful to keep it in the center of the cell.

If the reticule to be replaced is a cross-wire type and you have wire of the desired size in platinum or steel, solder it in place or if the material you have is non- metallic, use Dupont cement to fasten it in place. The cross-wire is stretched across the ring to which it is fastened and a small spring paper clip with a rubber band around the jaws is hung on each end of the wire to keep it taut while being soldered or cemented. In case cement is used, leave the clips hanging upon it for twelve hours.

Platinum and steel wire may be obtained in fine enough size to use for reticule cross-wires. The size of this wire for cross-hairs may vary from .0005" (very fine) to .002" (very coarse). A medium fine cross-wire will be .0007" to .001" in diameter.

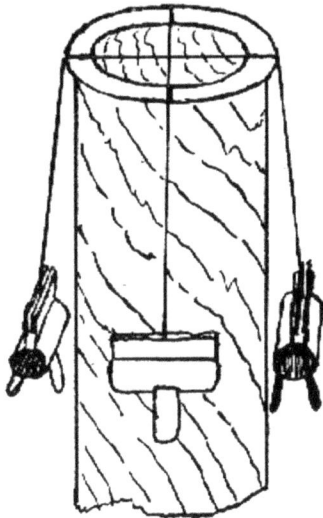

Steel cross-wires stretched over the reticule of a telescope, to be soldered in place. Spring paper clips on each end of the wires stretch them by the weight of the clips.

If steel or platinum wire is not available and you have no supply of other type of cross-wire material, a fresh spider-web may be used. The best way to get this is to find a spider-web that is in use and destroy most of it. In a few hours Mr. Spider will have it re- built and you can take some of the fresh-built web to make into cross-wires. Spiders come in various sizes and degrees of efficiency, and it may pay you to look about and find various kinds of web to use for your cross- wires. Field spiders arc supposed to spin a finer and stronger web than house spiders. I under- stand that the cross-hairs for fine surveying instruments are made from the web of field spiders. Women's hair, if of sufficient fineness, can be used. I say women's hair, as this is nearly always finer than a man's hair and by careful selection can often be obtained as fine as .001". Human hair is quite elastic and will stand a good deal. I have been told that certain types of real silk thread may be separated finely enough to get material for very fair cross-wires, but I have never tried it out.

If none of the above materials appeal to you or if they are unobtainable in the size desired, spider threads, taken from the cocoon of the spider, may be used. Late in August and early in September the large yellow' field spider with a cross on its back spins its cocoon in the fields. This cocoon is a round, brownish ball, found on golden rod and blackberry bushes. It should be cut open and thoroughly steamed to kill the eggs inside. Between the egg sack and the outer shell is a fine cushion of reddish down. This is the part to use for cross-wires.

Take a wire hairpin and spread the ends so that the distance between them is about inch greater than the diameter of the reticule cell, then place a small ball of beeswax on each of the ends of the hairpin. With a small needle, pick out one loose end of thread from the cocoon and, letting the cocoon hang down, wrap this end five or six times around one of the beeswax balls on one end of the hairpin. Now turn over the hairpin so that the thread comes around the other end of it, wrap it around this end about six turns and then pull off the cocoon. Hang this hairpin, with the spider thread stretched across it, some distance above a small vessel of boiling water and let it steam for fifteen minutes, so that it will absorb all the moisture it will take up. This is to prevent the thread becoming slack on a wet day, after it is in place in the scope.

Now take hold of the back end of the hairpin and, with the reticule cell lying flat on the table and with fine marks scored across it at right-angles to each other, lay the thread in place across one pair of these scores. The back end of the hairpin should lie upon the table but the front ends, to which the thread is attached, should be clear of the table top. It may be necessary to place a coin or two under the reticule cell so that the ends holding the thread do clear the table top, thus stretching the thread tightly across the cell. Use the magnifying glass to make certain the thread lies in the scores cut across the cell. If not, take a needle and gently place it there. Put a minute quantity of collodion or DuPont cement in these scores of the cell, on top of the thread. After ten minutes, cut the ends of the thread, place a new piece between the ends of the hairpin and put the second cross-wire or thread in position on the cell, in the other pair of scores.

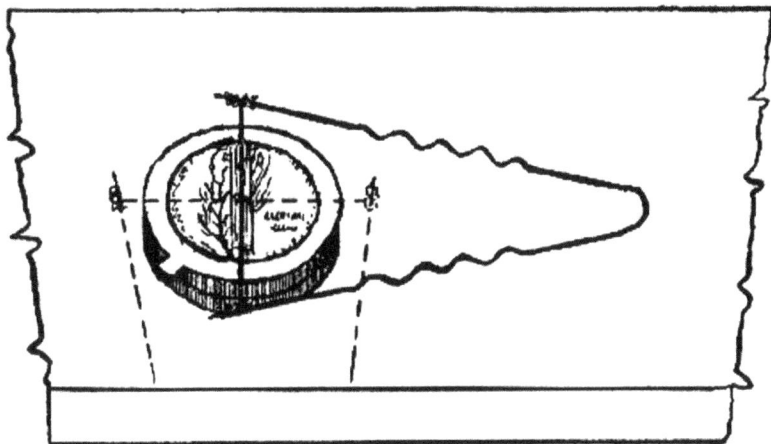

Cross-wires being made of spider cocoon stretched over the reticule of a telescope between the waxed ends of a heavy hairpin, ready to be cemented in place.

This spider thread is very fine and you may break a dozen before you get your cross-wires in place, but when you do get them there you will have a fine pair of cross-hairs of great uniformity.

Spider-web cross-hairs are entirely practical, but only in low-power scopes. They are used by many individuals and by the leading makers of transits. Some years ago Fecker wrote an article about cross-hairs in which he recommended the silk from the spider's cocoon, so I got some spider-web and some of the cocoon and saw at once why he recommended the latter. The web is much too heavy for target scope use, I could find none below .00175" which, in a high power scope, covers about 4" at one hundred yards. The silk of the cocoon, according to Fecker, runs an even .0005".

Woman's hair is easier to obtain than either spider web or cocoon silk, can be found down to about .0015" and is very elastic. I have often used it myself and it is excellent, but too heavy for anything over a three- power scope. I have replaced cross-hairs in transits and found that the ones put in them by the factories arc too heavy for target scopes. I now use a material which I buy from R. A. Litschert, Winchester, Indiana; this runs from .00075" to .001" in diameter, and 50<* worth will last quite a long while. I don't know what material it is made of but it looks to be some kind of vegetable fibre and it can be cemented in with either DuPont cement or finger-nail enamel. I have a Persian cat that has an under-fur which runs

.0005" in diameter and this would be ideal except that it is brittle and has little tensile strength. There may be other fine-furred animals whose fur has a higher tensile strength so that it can be used — but a target shooter would crown you for putting spider-web cross-hairs in his 15X scope.

Dents may be removed from a scope tube or a bent tube straightened, after removing all lenses and the reticule cell, by inserting a steel rod inside the tube. This rod should be a very close fit in the tube and the end inserted in the tube should be rounded at the edge and well smoothed-up. so that it cannot dig into the wall of the tube. A fiber-faced or composi-tion- faced hammer can he used on the outside to tap the dents out of the tube against the rod inside the tube. As these tubes are thin and soft, dents are easily re- moved and the hammering should be light taps, not heavy blows, as this would stretch the tube.

Front sight ramps are of two different general pat- terns, one a straight-blade type, cut to the contour of the barrel on the bottom and soldered and screwed to the barrel, the other a band- type, with the band, which is part of the ramp, encircling the barrel and either pinned or keyed in place on the barrel.

The first type is the simplest to make, merely being a flat piece of steel cut on the bottom with a radius cutter of the right size in a milling machine, the tail milled off at the correct angle and matted or cross-grooved, and a slot cut for the type of sight being used, either a blade or dovetail type. This type is soldered to the barrel but it had also better be held in place with a screw beneath the sight, tapped into the barrel. A ip 6 screw, 48 threads to the inch, with fillister head like a scope base block screw, is the best type to use. The position of the ramp is marked on the barrel, the blueing scraped off within the lines and the barrel tinned at this point. The bottom of the ramp is tinned and the ramp is then put into position on the barrel, the it 6 x 48 screw, for which a hole has been drilled and tapped into the barrel, is then put through the ramp and the ramp is drawn up tightly on the barrel with it. A piece of copper is placed on the tail of the ramp, near the rear end. and a parallel clamp is used to draw this part of the ramp down tightly on the barrel. The ramp is heated with a torch until the solder starts to run, and then both the screw through the ramp and the clamp on the tail are again tightened up and the ramp and barrel allowed to cool. Any solder that escapes from beneath the ramp onto the blued portion of the barrel is easily removed, when cold, without any injury to the blueing on the barrel.

If a milling machine is not available, this type of ramp can be made accurately with a lathe, although both the base contour and the sight slot must be cut by hand. A piece of steel, of the right width and thickness, is filed on the bottom to the barrel contour and a line scribed on one side from the rear end of the straight portion at the front to the rear end near the bottom, showing the slope of the tail. This sloped portion is then roughed off with a hack-saw or grinder. Now place the front portion of the ramp between two adjacent jaws of a rather heavy three or four- jaw chuck in the lathe, with the jaws in the position to hold work internally, and have these jaws faced with copper so that they will not cut the sides of the ramp. Ar- range the ramp so that the line scribed upon one side showing the tail slope is at right-angles to the center- line of the lathe. Now face-off the tail of the ramp to the line just as you would face any piece of steel, then, using a sharp-pointed tool bit, set to cut about .007" deep on the tail slope of the ramp, gear the lathe so that this bit moves about .015" per revolution of the spindle and, starting the lathe in gear, the bit will cross-rib the ramp tail.

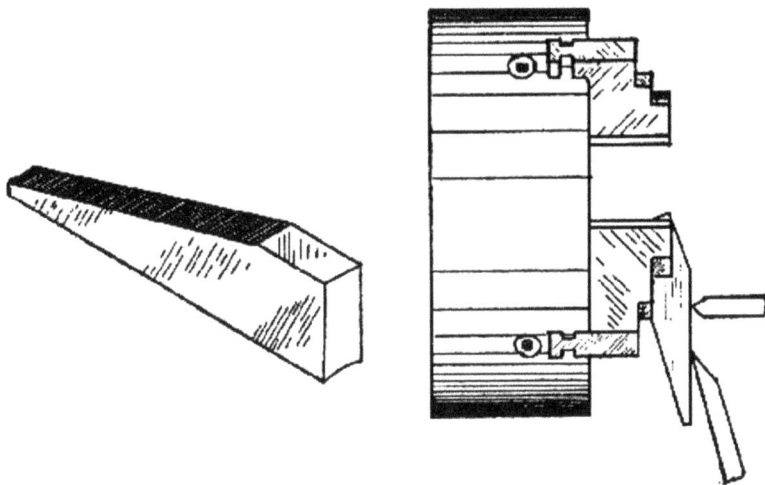

Left sketch shows blade-type ramp, ready to be soldered or soldered and screwed to the barrel. Right shows how such a ramp sight is held between adjacent jaws of the lathe chuck in order to face off the tail and cross-groove it.

In making the band- type ramp, a piece of steel thick enough to make the band and ramp in one piece is drilled from end to end, slightly under the diameter of the barrel, and then is reamed to the diameter of the barrel at the muzzle. This is then put in the milling machine vice and the sides of ramp are milled off to leave the ramp the correct thickness, but the cut is not made quite through to the hole drilled through the block. The piece is then set vertically in the vise of the miller, with the part that is to be the band held in the vice jaws, and a light cut made at each side cuts the bottom away from the ramp tail back of the band or the ramp may be held upside down in the vise of the miller and the bottom milled off be- hind the band. The tail slope is milled off and the ramp grooved with a sharp vee-cutter, then a corner- rounding cutter of the right size removes the corners around the band. This type of ramp will require some hand filing and polishing to turn the band out perfectly.

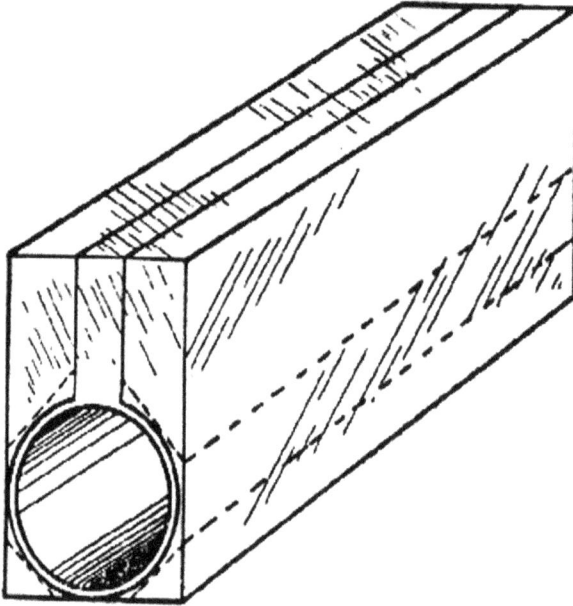

Band-type ramp cut from solid block of steel.

A second method of making the band-type ramp is to weld a piece of flat steel lengthwise of a piece of shelby steel tubing, then mill off the slope of the ramp tail and mill away the tubing, leaving only a short band at the front. This will require quite a bit of hand finishing where the weld is made.

Barrel bands are best made from thick- walled shelby tubing or from any piece of solid steel by boring or drilling and reaming the hole for the barrel. The excess metal is roughed off with a hack-saw, leaving a heavy part on bottom or top or both, depending upon what the purpose is of the band. After these have been roughed to shape, they can be finished more closely by grinding and then completed with files and carborundum cloth. All polishing of these bands should be done lengthwise of the barrel, so that after being blued they match barrel finish as near as possible.

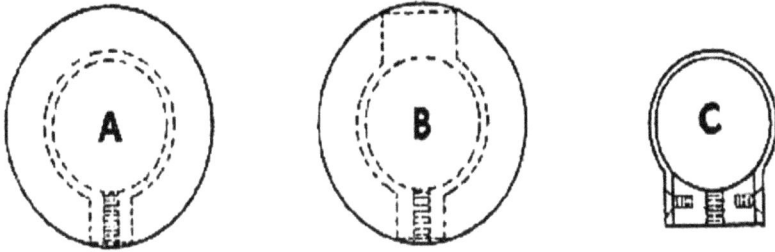

Barrel bands. A is front swivel band, cut from heavy-walled shelby steel tubing. B is band for open-type rear sight made from same material. C is makeup of a swivel barrel band with base, to go inside of forearm. Band is of spring steel, fastened to base block with four small screws.

If a tool post grinder is available for the lathe, the finishing time on these bands made from tubing or solid stock may be cut down by mounting the band on an arbor between centers on the lathe, putting a rather coarse wheel on the tool post grinder and grinding the band down to the finishing point. The arbor is allowed to turn free on the stationary lathe centers but a dog is attached to one end of the arbor so that it may be turned back and forth by hand, so that the band is ground down all around except at the heavy part left for insertion of sling-swivel screw, or rear sight, or what have you. The grinding is only done while the band is being turned slowly in a direction opposite to that in which the grinding wheel is running. On the return motion of the arbor and band the wheel is slightly backed off.

Hands with a heavy part or projection on top of the barrel are often used to hold open rear sights, the dovetail slot for the sight being cut in the heavy part of the band rather than in the barrel itself. In this case, a heavy part is usually left on the bottom of the band also, so that a screw may be tapped in here to seat in a shallow cup on the under side of the barrel, to keep the band in position and prevent any rotation while moving the sight from side to side in the slot for adjustment.

Barrel bands with a heavy part on the bottom are used to hold forearms to barrels, either with a screw only or with a sling-swivel screw, or they may be used to hold the sling-swivel only, either being set on the barrel ahead of the forearm or being set within the forearm with clearance in the forearm all around the sling-swivel screw.

A rapid way to make barrel bands with the heavy part on the bottom only is to use a piece of thin steel like an old phonograph or large clock spring, annealed, and passed around the barrel and fastened with four small screws, #4 or #5 machine screws, to a steel block, shaped with a half-round file to fit the contour of the barrel. This type of band may be put on or re- moved from a barrel without having to remove ramps or high front sights.

Another type of band with the heavy part beneath the barrel can be made by using a piece of tubing just slightly larger in outer diameter than the outer diameter of the band wanted and with an internal diameter slightly smaller than the barrel. This piece of tubing is brazed or welded to a steel block and is then reamed out to fit the barrel and finished on the outside.

Barrel bands should be fitted closely to the barrel about two inches ahead of the point where they arc to be finally seated and then peened lightly all around to stretch them, so that they can be tapped back to the point of final fitting. In case the band is quite thin, such as the clock spring type mentioned, this peening had better be done with a compo- sition-faced hammer such as the Stanley Company puts out, so that the sur- face of the band is not marred or it will have to be polished down thinner for finishing.

Sling-swivels can be made by turning a screw from cold-rolled, round, bar steel of y$ f diameter or more, leaving a head of about the same length as the diameter of the stock used. The shank is threaded to screw into whatever base the swivel is to be fastened to, a barrel band, or a nut set flush inside the forearm, and the head is then drilled for the sling loop.

The sling loop is made from J4" or a little heavier round, bessemer steel rod. as this steel is quite soft and will not crack when closely bent. The copper plating on this rod can be easily removed with a little carbo- rundum cloth before shaping the loop. To shape the loop, set a piece of flat steel upright in the vise and either catch one end of the rod between the vise jaw and one side of the piece of steel, or clamp one end of the rod to the steel with a clamp, or put it into a tight-fitting hole drilled in the steel and then wind the rod around the steel, tapping it on the edges lightly to square the bend slightly. Be sure to wind the rod closely around the steel, keeping the coils close together like a spring wound with closed coils. The coils can be sawed down one of the flat sides of the steel piece and they will then drop off as individual loops.

A small hole is drilled through the head of the swivel screw at right-angles to and in the same plane as the hole drilled for the loop. This hole need not be larger than 1/16" and after the loop is put in place in the head of the swivel screw, with its ends clearing each other by a small pin is driven tightly into this 1/16" hole and the ends finished off flush with the sides of the swivel screw head. This pin will prevent the loop moving from side to side in the head of the swivel screw".

Butt sling-swivels may be made of the plate type, such as the government uses, or a wood screw shank may be made in the lathe, with a head matching the front swivel, from round bar stock. A round-nose tool, rather narrow, is used to cut the thread in the lathe and the twist is rapid but the thread is shallow. The small pin is used to hold the loop in its base, as was done with the front swivel.

Quick-detachable swivels, several designs of which are upon the market, are usually simple in construction and the simpler they are the better they will usually be. The main thing in a quick-detachable swivel for use on a game rifle is quietness, meaning lack of rattle, which is where most of them fail. There is one design upon the market which, while not as rapidly detached as some others, is likely to be the quietest. This design employs a regular type swivel screw except that the shank is larger

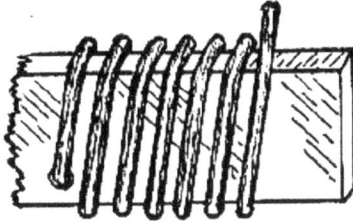

How bessemer-steel rod is wound around a piece of flat steel, to form sling loops.

than that usually used and is quite short, having only a few threads, and screws into a plate set in the stock. A few turns will remove it, and it should be as quiet as the solid-type swivel. All these designs can be examined and perhaps, using one of them as a basis, you can make an improved design of quick-detachable swivel.

You may sometimes wish to change a right-hand safety of the push-through type, located in the trigger- guard, to a left-hand one and as these are of simple construction and of two general types, a study of the thumb piece will show it is easily accomplished.

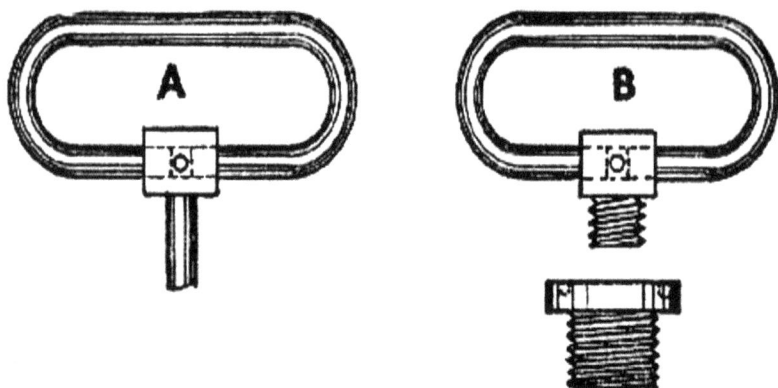

A indicates how cross pin through head of swivel screw keeps sling loop in place. B shows construction of a simple type of semi-quick detachable sling swivel.

One type of the push-through safety is a simple straight bar with a flat cut in it at one point so that when this is opposite a projection on the trigger, or beneath the sear point as is often seen when the safety is in the front of the guard, the trigger may be pulled.

When the thumb piece is pushed through so as to move this flat to one side the full diameter of the bar is beneath the trigger projection or sear point and the trigger cannot be pulled. In this type, it is only necessary to fill in this flat portion, either by welding or by sweating and pinning in a piece of steel and finishing it to the diameter of the round bar, after which a flat is cut at the opposite side, so that when the safety is pushed in from the left this flat comes beneath the trigger projection or sear point and allows the trigger to be pulled.

The second type of push-through safety, which is found only in the rear of the guard, has a groove cut around it into which the trigger projection enters when the trigger is pulled with the safety in the "off" position. To change this type to left-hand it is usually easier to make a new safety. This should be made from drill-rod, hardened and drawn or tempered at dark straw color. The groove location can he determined by putting a little prussian-blue upon the rear edge of the trigger projection and with the bar stock, after being cut to length, shoved in flush with the left side, the trigger is pulled so that an imprint is made upon the piece with the blue or this distance may be measured if the gun is disassembled.

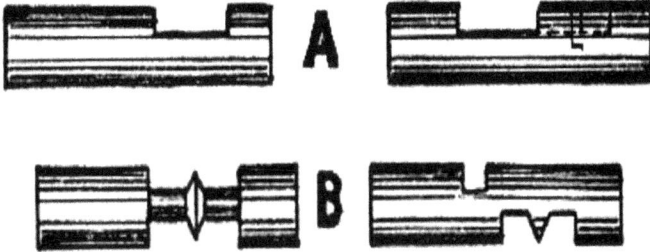

A indicates how a right-hand, push-through, trigger guard, shotgun safety is changed over to left-hand operation by filling the notch and cutting another to the left of the original. B shows how a right-hand, push-through safety in the rear of the trigger guard is replaced with a new type for left-hand operation. The double notch is for the poppet and the single slot for the extension on the back of the trigger.

The manufacturer of metal pistol-grip caps is either a machine job with heavy blanking presses or is entirely a hand job of cutting, filing and grinding, for the lathe will not produce the elliptical shape needed for the cap nor will the milling machine, except the profile miller which is not found in the ordinary shop.

The cap of steel may be rough sawed, ground, filed to shape and polished from steel of 1/16" or more in thickness. If a raised center section is desired, the steel should be 3/16 " to 1/4" thick. The edge may be rough-ground on a shop grinder for a distance of 1/8" to 1/4" in from the edge to a thinner section and then finished off smoothly around the edge of this raised portion with high-speed hand electric grinder with mounted grinding points or with round files.

The raised center portion may be left with a plain smooth border K" or m ore in width, and a plain smooth section around the grip-cap screw in the center, and the balance of the raised portion of the cap may be decorated by engraving or etching with acid some de- sign upon it, or it may be decorated by matting it with a punch with simply a point upon it or a matting punch with a design upon it may be used. These punches can be obtained from William Dixon Inc., of Newark, New Jersey, for about 30? each. Instead of a plain border around this raised center portion, a matting tool of a bead design may be used to decorate the border. Good effects in matting may be had by using dental burrs of different shapes, just as you would use a punch, by placing them upon the work and striking them with a hammer.

Pistol-grip caps of malleable-iron or bronze can be cast for you at any iron foundry and these can be cast to shape from a wood pattern that you make up. They may even be cast with a design upon them. They are buffed to a polish with stiff-wire buffing wheels. If a decorative design is used, do not have details too small or they will not come out well in the casting.

Plate XI

Cross grooving the tail of a ramp sight with a pointed tool in the lathe. Showing how a ramp is mounted between the sides of the lathe chuck jaws and a sharp-pointed tool in the tool post is used to cross rib the ramp tail. The power cross feed is used and the lathe is so geared that the serrations are .015″ apart. A depth of .006″ to .007″ will be found about right for these serrations.

Pistol-grip caps of ivory or of bakelite or other plastics are easily sawed with a hack-saw and cut to shape and decorated with small cutters in a high-speed hand electric grinder. They may also be decorated or carved with engraving or dental chisels and die-sinkers or silversmiths' riffle files. They may be polished with a buffer and any of the polishing compounds, even valve grinding paste, followed by opticians' polishing rouge. Small felt polishing points may be used in the high-speed hand electric grinders for polishing small designs.

Chapter 8 SHOTGUN REPAIRS

Looseness sometimes develops between barrels and action of a double or single-barrel gun of the break- open type. To repair this correctly requires quite a bit of work, as it usually means a new hinge-pin or new bolt, sometimes both. On cheap guns, peening parts to lighten the action is permissible if a low-priced re- pair job is necessary but it is, of course, a short-lived repair.

First, make sure that the barrels bed evenly upon the frame and see that the barrel lug does not bind in its cut in the action, if the barrels will not bed down evenly. If the barrels bear evenly on the frame (which can be determined by coating the bottom of the barrels with prussian-blue and closing the action) well and good but if high spots appear on the frame or barrel bottoms, dress these off with a very fine-cut pillar file until the fit between barrels and frame is even.

If the hinge joint is loose and a cheap job is necessary, peen the sides of the semicircular notch in the barrel lump which bears against the hinge-pin.

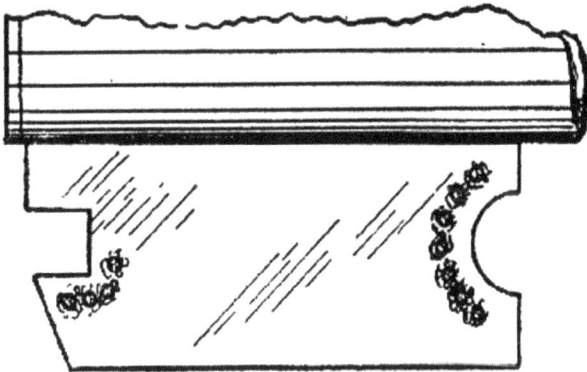

Punch markings show where an underlug is peened around the hinge pin and bolt notch, in order to tighten up a cheap shotgun.

Do not peen around the edge of this notch, but peen the metal around the notch a short distance back from the edge until the joint is tight. Dress off the sides with a fine pillar file so that it fits the cut in the frame.

For an example of peening shotgun lugs to take out play and retighten the action of a cheap double or single gun, we can take any gun of this type in which the barrels have play both up-and-down and forwards-and-backwards when the gun is closed- The first part of the play to take out is the forward- and-backward movement, as this occurs on the hinge- pin and taking this out will often take out much of the up-and-down play of the barrels.

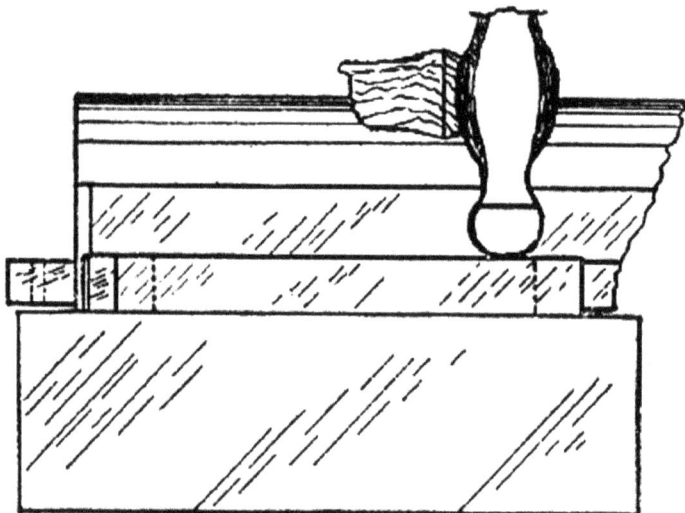

Showing how the underlug should be supported by being laid upon a smooth steel block while being peened.

Lay the barrels upon their side with the lug containing the semicircular cut for the hinge-pin upon a perfectly flat block of steel, and see that the lu^ lays flat upon this block , or you may bend it or loosen it from the barrels in the peening operation. Tt may be necessary to block up the barrels with pieces of wood to get the lug to lie flat upon the block. Use the ball end of the hammer head for the peening and do not strike too close to the edges of the cut for the hinge-pin, as you do not want to batter these edges but want to draw the lug out slightly longer toward the front end. Peen the lug some on one side, then turn the barrels over and peen the lug the same amount on the opposite side. If you have trouble in striking with the hammer around the hinge-pin cut near the top back of the cut, on account of the barrel being in the way, use a punch with a rounded end to place on the lug, striking the punch with the hammer. Try the fitting of the barrels on the action after a little peening, as there is no use in over- doing it. When you have all the forward-and-back-ward play taken out of the action by this method and there still remains up-and-down play with the action locked and the lock bolt is in good condition, peen around the locking notch in the rear end of the barrel lug, doing the peening on the lug below the notch and just around the lower, inner corner of the notch. Keep back from the edges of the notch as before, so that the lug is drawn out but the edges of the notch are not battered. Smooth up the sides of the lug each time, after the peening, with a fine flat file so that the lug does not bind in the frame slot.

If this peening operation does not take the up-and- down play out of the locking bolt notch, squeezing the notch together in the vise jaws with steel plugs in the chambers, as elsewhere described, should do the trick unless the lock bolt is badly worn, in which case it will have to be replaced.

If a new hinge-pin is to be fitted, examine the old pin to see whether it is screwed into the frame or pressed in. A screwed-in pin of course has a screw- driver slot in it, usually but not always. Small screws are often used to lock the hinge-pin in place, especially if it is a screwed-in pin. These may either be put in from the front of the action or from the flats on top. After these small screws are removed, if the hinge-pin is a screwed-in type with screw-driver slot, put the action in a vise and, using a brace screwdriver, remove the old hinge-pin. If it cannot be loosened with the brace screw-driver, try heating the frame, but not to the color changing point, and if it still cannot be re- moved it will have to be drilled out. To do this, center- punch each end of the pin carefully in the exact center

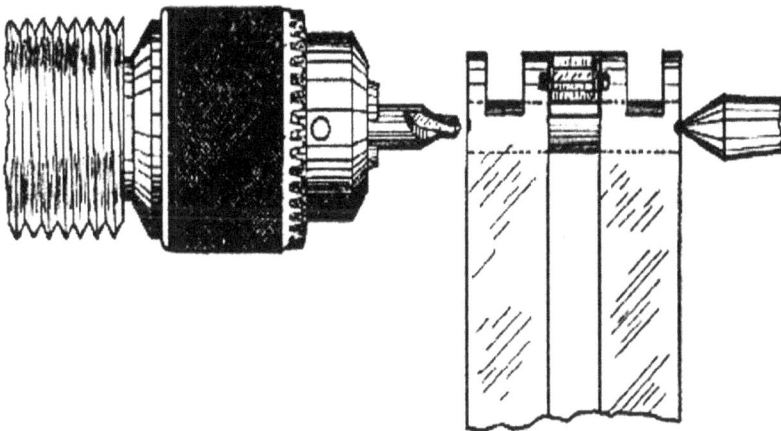

How the hinge pin is drilled out of a shotgun action in the lathe.

the tail center in the center-punch mark in the opposite end of the pin and drill into the pin with the center-drill. Take a high-speed steel drill about 1/16" smaller than the pin, replace the center- drill in the lathe chuck with this and drill through the pin from end to end and then, using reamers, ream out the remains of the old pin from the head end, but do not ream out the threads at the opposite end. At this threaded end, when the pin is reamed to the top of the threads in the action, the remains of this end of the pin must be removed with the point of a heavy, steel scriber or with small, pointed chisels, being careful not to damage the threads in the action.

If the pin is of the pressed-in type, examine the action for small screws holding the pin in place and remove them if there are any used. A steel support block must be placed between the two sides of the frame to prevent springing it together and a steel block must often be fitted to the frame, so that the hinge-pin is vertical in the press. Heat the frame to just below the color changing temperature and apply pressure to the pin. If the pin will not start, have some- one set a heavy brass block upon the lop of the press- ram, then strike it a heavy blow with a heavy hammer, as this will often start a tight pin. Keep pressure on the press-ram while the brass block is struck. If this fails to move the pin, it must be drilled out.

With the barrels tightly against the standing breech and clamped down tightly on the top flats of the action, the hinge-pin hole is lapped to a larger size if the wear is slight. Use an expanding cast-iron lap for this job. The arbor for this lap is a length of steel rod turned to the same taper as a taper-pin, to the foot, with a straight portion about M" Jong turned on the small end. This straight portion is threaded with a fine thread and fitted with a nut. The cast-iron lap is a piece of cast-iron, turned to a size that will just enter the old hinge-pin hole nicely, and reamed with a taper-pin reamer to fit the arbor. This lap is then sawed lengthwise, with a thin slitting saw, in three equidistant places, starting at one end but stopping about short of the opposite end. The lap is then sawed with three slots from the opposite end, between the first three, the slots again ending J4" short of the opposite end from which they are started.

An oil or water-mix grinding compound can be used on the lap to enlarge the hole, the nut being screwed up on the end of the arbor to enlarge the lap as the work

Hinge-pins should be made of chrome-vanadium steel for best strength. In case the pin is of the press-fit type and not the threaded type, after the hole has been lapped measure it carefully for size and turn up a pin .001" oversize. The surface finish of the pin should be as smooth as you can make it, with a mirror polish.

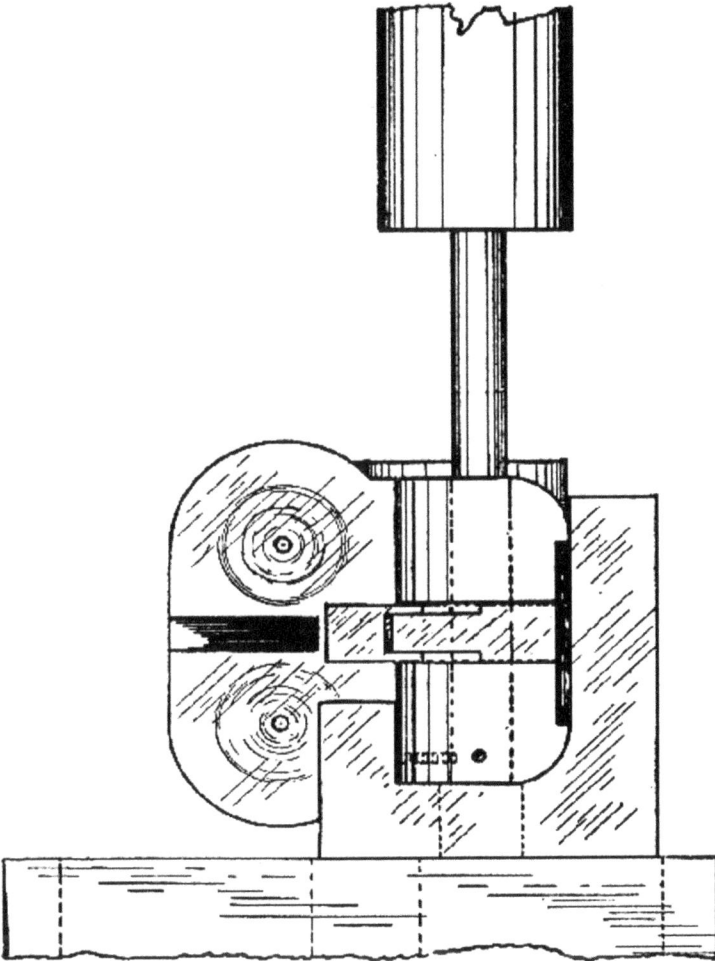

How the hinge pin is pressed out of a shotgun action. Note supporting blocks in slot around hinge pin and around the front end of the action. Two possible screw positions are shown for the locking screw in hinge pin, as this screw may be in either location.

Pack the pin in dry-ice and warm the frame thoroughly, but not hot enough to make it change color. Thirty minutes in the dry-ice will shrink the pin sufficiently and, placing the steel block between the two sides of the frame, press the pin into place.

In case the wear at the hinge-pin joint is more than .005" or .006" the lapping process had better be re- placed with a reaming process, therefore it will be necessary to soften the case-hardening of the action. To do this, pack the action, stripped of all parts, in slacked lime or powdered charcoal in an iron box, heat it in the furnace to a cherry-red and then allow it to cool in the box. Clamp the barrels in place on the action and ream the hinge-pin hole to the necessary size to clean it up of all wear, then case-harden the action again and fit a new pin as previously directed.

If the hinge-pin is of the threaded type, lap or ream the hole only as far as the threads, measure the hole carefully, and turn up a threaded pin to a very tight fit in the hole. Using a lathe dog on the unthreaded end of the pin, which should be left long, screw it into the hole, setting it up very tightly against the shoulder. When screwing the pin into the hole, oil it with a very thin oil. While it is screwed up tightly, measure the pin lengthwise of the action and mark it for length so that it may be cut off and a screw-slot sawed in the end, so that the slot sets lengthwise of the action when the pin is screwed home. Unscrew the pin, cut it off, slot it, finish up the ends properly and screw it into place, using a screw-driver in a bit-brace.

If the bolt is loose in the underlug, check the bolt carefully to see if it is loose in the frame. If it is loose at this point, a new bolt must be fitted tightly in the frame. If however, the bolt is tight in the frame and is loose in the underlug, a low-cost job can be done by peening around the back and under the bottom near the back of the bolt-notch in the lug. Do the peening well back from the notch, so as not to merely upset the edge of the notch. If this will not tighten the bolt in the underlug, fit steel plugs closely in the chambers of the barrels, then catch the ends of the barrels and the outer end of the underlug between the jaws of a vise, with the jaws faced with brass or copper, and screw up on the vise to close up the notch in the underlug enough to make the bolt fit tightly in its notch. In case the barrels have an extension rib, set a heavy piece of brass across them at the rear end, with a notch cut out of its under side to clear the rib, so that when the vise is screwed up the rib will not be distorted.

The proper way to take up wear in the bolt notch of the underlug is to fill up the old notch by gas welding and recut the notch, or to cut away the notch deeper at the bottom and fit in a piece of hardened steel with a tongue on it extending down into the lower part of the lug and held in place with a small transverse pin through lug and tongue. This is the system used on Parker shotguns.

A common trouble of lower priced double and single- barrel guns is the loosening of the forearm. These usually snap into place on the barrels, being held there with a curved, flat-type spring.

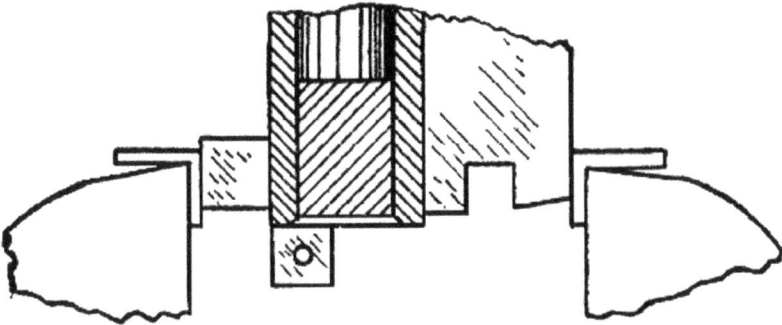

Method of closing up the bolt notch in the underlug of a cheap shotgun by squeezing it in the vise jaws. The brass block shown placed against top of barrels has a notch cut out over the rib. Be sure to place close-fitting steel plugs in the barrels.

The shortening of the curve of this spring, or wear upon the end of it where it goes against a lug on the underside of the barrel, is the cause of the loosening of it. It is usually soft enough so that it can be drawn out by peening, starting back half an inch from the point and working down to the end. If it is too hard to do this, heat it to a cherry- red, allow it to cool and then draw it out longer by peening it cold, reharden and temper it and then refit it by filing the end, trying it for length until it is correct length to fit tightly.

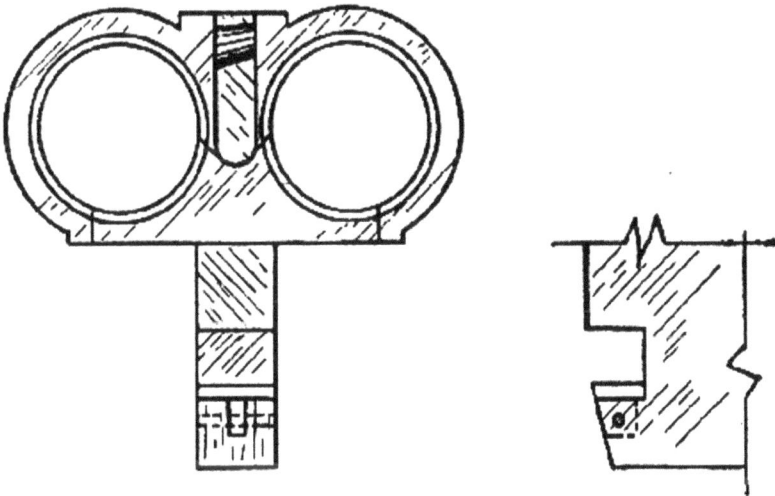

Method of fitting a piece of steel into the bolt notch of the underlug in order to tighten it up. This is a very good method.

If a loose fore-end of the above type shows very little wear on the end of the spring, the spring is probably too soft and has developed too great a curve. Straighten it out a little bit, going slowly and carefully, by placing it in the jaws of a vise and tightening the vise a little at a time, and checking the spring to see that it is straightening out. If it does straighten out, continue the short pressure treatments until it is the proper length to fit.

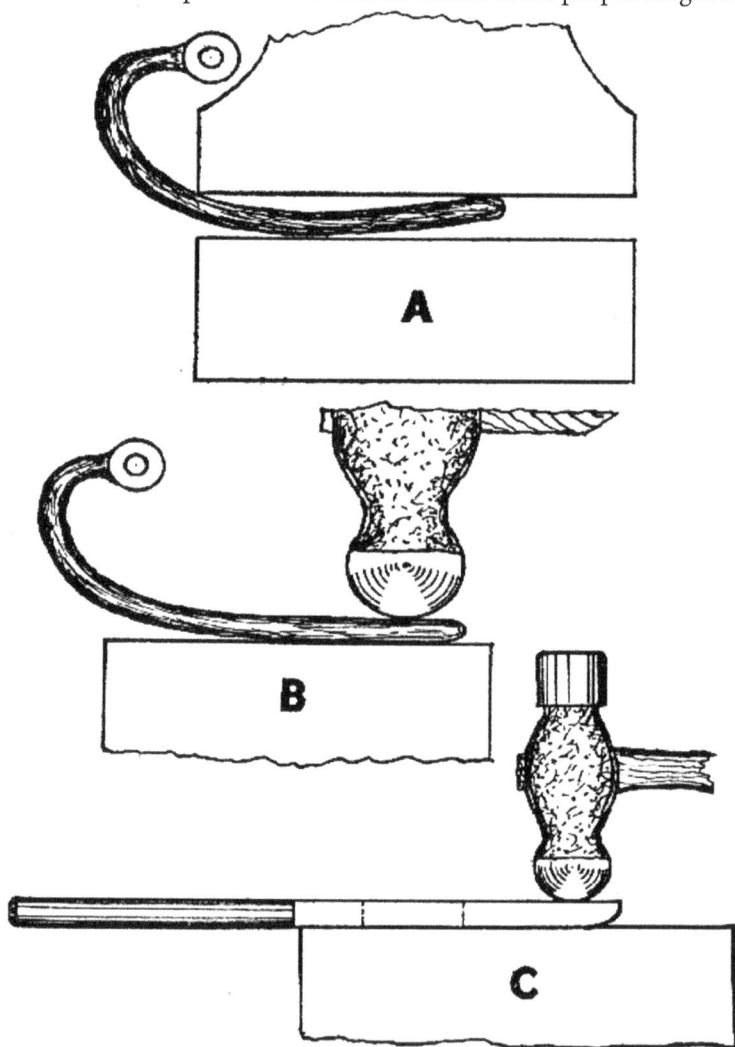

Various methods which may be necessary in fitting a loose forearm. A shows tightening the forearm by straightening out the curve of the spring in the vise jaws. B shows curved spring type forearm being peened out to lengthen it. C shows a sliding-type forearm catch being lengthened by peening the end with a ball pien hammer.

The sliding-type fore-end catch may become worn, until the forearm is loose. When this happens, the catch can be heated and drawn out a little by forging, filed to proper length and rehardened and tempered at straw color. If the old catch cannot be lengthened by forging, a new one can be made of tool-steel, hardened and tempered as directed above.

Broken parts such as the action frame should never be brazed or electrically welded. Any welding should be done with a gas torch, as the work is more thoroughly heated that way and makes a better weld. Brazing is usually too soft, as the brass used in making the joint will sometimes be pounded out a little, making parts bind upon each other and may throw strains, set up in firing the piece, upon the wrong parts of the action.

When new firing-pins are necessary they should be made of chisel-steel, hardened by heating to a cherry- red and quenching in oil, after which they are tempered by heating to deep blue and again quenching in oil.

Broken hammers should not be welded, new ones should be made up of tool-steel, hardened in oil and the temper drawn at deep blue or a light purple.

It is sometimes necessary to cut off the muzzle of a shotgun barrel, due to its having been burst or injured at this point. This means that the choke is removed from the barrel, as it lies in the last two or three inches at the muzzle. While the full amount of choke can- not be replaced, some choke can be put in the barrel unless it is extremely thin.

If the gun happens to be a single-barrel gun it can be chucked in the lathe and a new choke bored from the muzzle end. This choke should start 1 1/2 " to 2" back from the muzzle, leaving this length of barrel at the muzzle straight. The barrel should be bored out for a distance of about 2" in length to a diameter .007" or .008" larger than it was, with both ends of this recess bored on a taper so that no abrupt shoulder is left at the ends. As the boring tool will not leave a smooth enough finish in the recess, it will have to be polished after being bored.

A rubber expanding mandrel is the best thing to use to polish this recess choke. Make this rubber mandrel of a diameter so that after carborundum cloth has been cemented on it in short sections around its circumference, it will just pass into the muzzle of the barrel. For the polishing process use 000 carborundum cloth followed by crocus cloth.

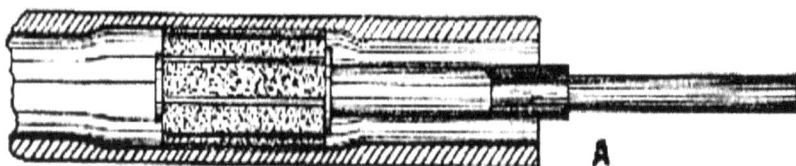

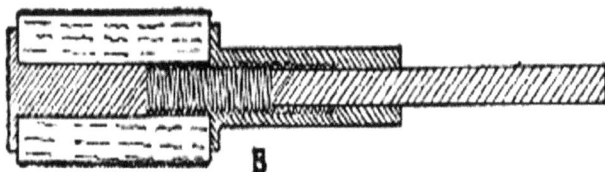

Expanding rubber mandrel (A) with strips of carborundum cloth glued onto the rubber being used to cut a recess choke in a shotgun barrel. This method may also be used to remove the choke from a barrel. B shows details of this expanding rubber mandrel.

A steel mandrel about 6" long with a solid head upon it is used to mount the rubber upon. The rubber can be about 1 1 / 2 " long and is slipped onto the steel arbor and pushed up against the head. The shank of the arbor, starting about 1" below the head, is threaded for the nut that screws onto it to expand the rubber. This nut is made quite long, although only part of it need be threaded, so that when the rubber mandrel is clear at the rear end of the choke, the nut is even with or only slightly inside of the muzzle. The purpose of this long nut is to allow the rubber mandrel to be inserted into the choke portion not expanded, and then expanded while in the recessed portion of the barrel by tightening up the nut.

The outer end of the steel arbor is held in a drill chuck in the tail stock of the lathe while the barrel is revolved in the lathe spindle. The rubber mandrel, with the carborundum cloth cemented on it, is moved back and forth from one end of the choke to the other, while the barrel is revolving, by the tail stock screw. The recess should be polished out to .010" or a trifle more. It may be necessary to replace the carborundum cloth with new pieces while polishing out the choke, as it wears down.

In case the gun is a double-barrel gun, or in case for some other reason the barrel cannot be chucked in the lathe to have the recess choke bored in it, the entire job may be done with the rubber mandrel and carborundum cloth. In this case, the recess is started and carried practically to finish dimensions with carborundum cloth, after which the polishing is done with the 000, followed by crocus cloth. The arbor upon which the rubber mandrel is mounted can be placed in a chuck in the live spindle of the lathe and revolved while the barrel is held in the hands, or a motor with a drill chuck mounted on its spindle can be used to drive the rubber mandrel, or the mandrel can be chucked in the drill press. Always unscrew the expanding nut of the rubber mandrel before drawing it out of the muzzle and do not tighten it up until the mandrel is replaced in the recess choke, so that the bore at the muzzle will not be enlarged.

It is sometimes desirable to relieve the factory choke of a shotgun barrel, as it may shoot too close with the loads used. This is done by enlarging the bore at the muzzle. This may be done with the expanding rubber mandrel with carborundum cloth cemented to it, by- placing the mandrel in position back in the enlarged portion of the barrel and expanding it with the nut, after which it is started revolving and brought slowly out to the muzzle then run back again and the performance repeated until the straight muzzle portion of the barrel is enlarged the required amount. Removing .012" to .015" inside the muzzle will reduce a choke from full to three-quarter. An automobile piston pin hone may be used for this job, if you can obtain one of the correct size.

Choke alterations can be accomplished by means of a proper sized piston pin hone, which will remove part of the choke. These hones are adjustable for size and burnishing blades may be obtained as well as hone stones.

Shotgun barrels will often require polishing out, due to neglect that has caused small pits or rust spots, or a new barrel may be rough enough to lead sufficiently to spoil the pattern after a few shots. The simplest method of doing this polishing is to mount a steel rod in the lathe chuck with a slot about 4" long sawed down from the outer end. Place carborundum cloth cut 4" wide around the outer end of the rod by placing the end in the saw-slot and wrapping it around the rod in the opposite direction from that in which the rod is turned. The fineness of grain of the carborundum to be used will depend upon what condition the barrel is in as to pits or rust. If little rust and only small pits appear, followed by gradually finer through the polishing stage will answer the purpose.

A steel rod slotted lengthwise for 4 inches at one end, so that carborundum cloth may be wound around the rod in 4 inch strips, to polish out the bore of a shotgun. The rod is held in a lathe chuck and revolved by power while the shotgun barrel is held in the hands and run slowly back and forth over the revolving cloth.

The final polishing should be done with oiled carborundum cloth of 000 grain, followed by crocus cloth used dry. These final polishing operations are done with the barrel held stationary in a vise or lathe chuck and the polisher operated by hand, lengthwise of the barrel. The polisher is turned a little from time to time during the polishing operation, so that all parts of the barrel are polished evenly. The barrel should show no scratches and should have a mirror polish if no pits are present.

A solid dent raiser, made of steel, used to start up deep dents in a shotgun barrel. It is driven through the barrel, beneath the dent, with a heavy steel rod and hammer, and should be a close fit in the barrel.

Dents are removed from shotgun barrels either with solid steel mandrels, graduated in size about .002" apart, or with expanding mandrels. The solid steel plugs or mandrels are expensive, as each barrel size requires several of them and they must be made of tool-steel, hardened, ground and polished. The ends of these solid steel dent-raisers are tapered off at 1 5 to 20 degrees, so they will start a dent up easily without tearing the inner barrel surface. Three inches is a good length to make them, and a heavy hard-wood dowel rod or a steel rod is used to force them beneath the dent, with taps from a hammer. The barrel and the dent- raisers are both oiled with a light oil like sperm oil.

Plate XII

Using a ⅝" steel rod with a carborundum cloth wound upon it, to polish out a 12 bore shotgun barrel held in the lathe. The steel rod shown in the lathe chuck has a hack saw cut lengthwise of the rod, 4" long, at the outer end. One end of a 4" wide strip of carborundum cloth is inserted in this cut and is wound around the rod in the opposite direction from that in which the lathe turns. The lathe is run in its lowest open belt speed while the shotgun barrel is held in the hands and pushed and pulled slowly over the revolving carborundum cloth, which should be a tight fit in the barrel.

The adjustable or expansion dent-raiser is made of two flat pieces of tool-steel sweated together. This type is also best made about three inches long, but in making them leave an additional inch of length, so that a lathe dog may be clamped on them. After sweating the two pieces together, cut the ends off at an angle of about 80-degrees to the sweated splice, the ends being parallel to each other. Now center the ends and, placing the lathe dog on the pieces, place them between centers on the lathe and turn them to bore diameter, plus .012" or .015" and taper off the ends at fifteen or twenty degrees for a short distance, will be enough.

Enlarge the center-holes to about 7/16 " diameter, if they are not that large, and drill the pieces with a 17/64 " hole from end to end. Drill out this hole from one end to the sweated seam with a drill and tap the remaining portion of the hole with a 24-thread tap.

Turn a groove three inches from one end, almost cutting the piece off, so that after it is hardened it may be easily broken off at this point.

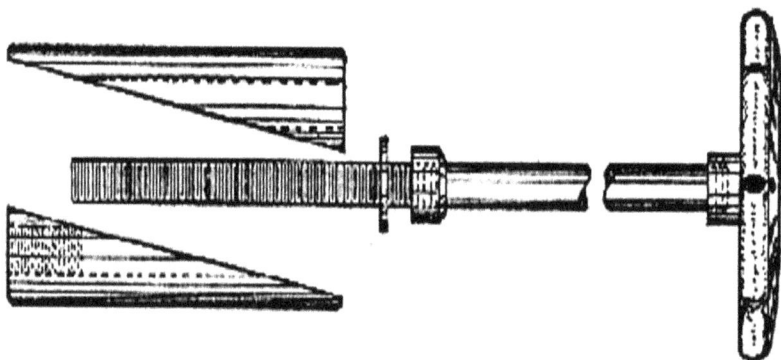

Details of expanding dent raiser for removing dents from shotgun barrels.

Heat the two pieces until the solder melts and they can be separated, clean the soldered faces of all solder and harden both pieces, drawing them slightly at pale- straw to relieve strains afterwards. Resolder the two pieces together and grind them to just under standard bore size, then polish the surfaces until no grinding marks remain. The one inch of extra length may now be broken off at the grooved place. Remove the solder from the pieces.

A piece of drill-rod is now threaded for 3" with a 24-thread die and a nut is screwed up very tightly to the end of the thread. This nut is turned off on the outside diameter so that it clears the thin end of the expansion mandrel and a washer of the same diameter is placed against the nut. An iron valve wheel is placed upon the opposite end of the rod and pinned in place. When the threaded end of the rod is placed through the drilled out portion of the mandrel and screwed into the threaded portion and tightened up, the mandrel expands in one direction. The barrel and mandrel should both be oiled with a light oil while re- moving dents.

A solid mandrel will be necessary to start bad dents up so that the expanding mandrel can be inserted, as its shrink and expansion is limited. In removing the dent a hammer with a composition face, such as made by the Stanley Company, is used to hammer the outside of the barrel lightly around the dent, while the expanding mandrel is tightened against the dent on the inside, as this hastens the removal of the dent and lessens the strain on the barrel set up by the expanding mandrel.

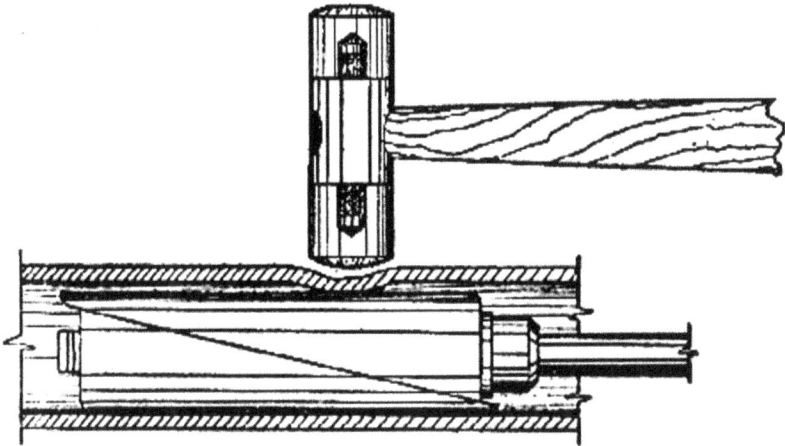

Showing method of using expanding dent raiser in shotgun barrel while the dent is being hammered lightly from outside with a Stanley composition-faced hammer.

Shotgun barrels sometimes become bulged for a short distance. This happens fairly often to a 12-gauge lull-choke gun, if it has a very soft barrel. It is generally a pump or autoloading shotgun that suffers in this respect and the bulge usually occurs just at the rear end of the choke, sometimes going as far forward as the front sight. The cause, in this case, is generally a heavy high-velocity load of #2 shot, which does not seem to chamber well in a 12-gauge choke. Bulges sometimes occur at other points in a shotgun barrel, but in that case the barrel usually bursts instead of merely bulging, for these bulges at points other than the rear end of the choked portion of a shotgun barrel are invariably caused by obstructions in the barrel when the cartridge is fired.

If the barrel survives without bursting or cracking, the bulge may be removed by turning up a steel mandrel in the lathe, to dimensions a few inches longer than the bulged portion of the barrel and a close fit to the bore, in fact the barrel should be oiled with a thin oil and the mandrel should fit closely enough so that it requires a heavy rod to push it to place in the barrel.

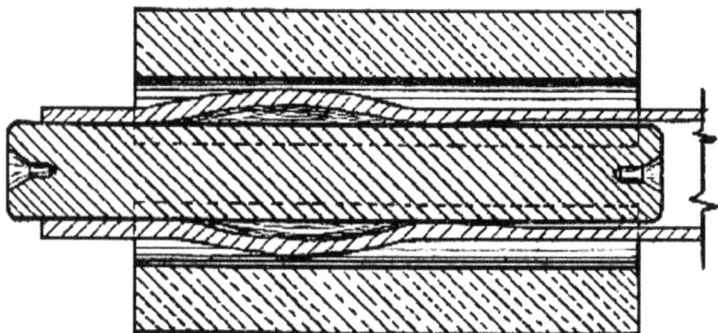

Cross section showing two brass blocks, cut out to fit around the outside of a shotgun barrel, to clamp together over a bulge, while a steel mandrel is placed inside the barrel.

Two pieces of brass an inch or more square and about two inches long, each of which has a circular cut in one side to fit across the outside of the barrel at right- angles to the barrel s axis, are clamped over the bulge from opposite sides. These brass blocks can be bored in the lathe by clamping them upon the face plate, separated about 1/4" , using a drill to bore the hole an under- sized part in each block, and then using a boring-bar mounted upon the compond rest to bore the circular notches in the side of the blocks to the angle of the barrel taper. Bore the notches just deep enough so that when the blocks are placed upon opposite sides of the barrel they fail to meet by 1/4".

The barrel may be held in a well-padded vise and the brass blocks damped around the barrel with a small machine-type vise like one of the " Yankee" vises. The vise is tightened up, causing the brass blocks to squeeze the bulged portion of the barrel in upon the steel mandrel, the vise is then loosened and the blocks moved around the barrel a short distance upon the bulge and again tightened. After the bulge is pretty well pressed out, oil the barrel well at that point and tighten the blocks upon it again with the vise, but not too tight. Take hold of the outer end of the vise screw and turn the vise and brass blocks around the barrel upon the bulge, tightening the vise a little from time to time, continuing this until the bulge is ironed out.

Roller pipe-cutter, fitted with three rollers, used to iron out a bulge in a shotgun barrel. A steel mandrel is placed within the bore, as in using the brass blocks.

Removing a bulge of this type can be done more rapidly if, instead of the notched brass blocks, a roller- type pipe-cutter is used. A #1 Trimo three-wheel pipe- cutter is then equipped with three rollers, instead of two rollers and one cutting wheel, and after the steel mandrel is placed inside the barrel, under the bulge, the barrel is oiled on the outside and the pipe-cutter with three rollers is used to iron out the bulge.

The notched brass blocks may be used to pound the bulge out of the barrel by placing the steel mandrel inside the barrel as before, placing one block upon the bench with the barrel lying in it, at the bulged point, laying the second notched brass block on top of the bulge and striking the top block with a medium- weight hammer. Turn the barrel as necessary to pound out all the bulge.

When the barrels of double-barrel guns are cut off for any reason at the muzzle, the opening between the ribs is exposed and must be refilled with solder. Scrape and clean the opening very thoroughly for a distance of about 3/16" back from the muzzle, cut a piece of tin to fit closely in the opening and press this in and back an eighth of an inch or more from the muzzle. Use rosin core solder to fill the opening above the piece of tin. After the solder has cooled, file it off flush and polish across the muzzles with fine carborundum cloth on a flat wood block. In cutting off the barrels at the muzzle, always use a machinist's square to mark the barrels for sawing and also afterwards, while filing the ends, to make sure that the muzzles are square. Use a piece of fine carborundum cloth glued onto a steeply- tapered, round piece of wood, small enough at the small end to go inside the barrels, so that the inner edges are slightly rounded off, to remove any burr that may be left at that point.

Ribs on double-guns sometimes loosen for a short distance at some point and must be resoldered. Lift the loosened portion as far up from the barrels as you can, without loosening any more of the rib, place a small wooden wedge beneath it to hold it up and, using slender scrapers or small needle files, clean the barrels beneath the rib and under side of the rib as well as you can, moving the wedge when necessary to reach all parts. After this is done, use a small soldering copper, with the tip hammered out flat like a screw-driver for a short distance, to tin the under side of the rib and the surface of the barrels where the rib is to be resoldered. Use powdered rosin for flux for this work, to prevent rust. Remove the wedge under the rib and wrap three or four turns of soft iron wire around the barrels in two places on each side of the loosened portion of the rib, then wrap the same number of turns around the barrels over the loosened portion of the rib. If the loosened portion is very short, one wrapping over it will be enough, but if it is more than 1 1/2" long place wire wrappings over it an inch apart throughout its length. Cut some small wooden wedges and place these under each wire-wrapping around the barrels, upon both upper and lower ribs. Along each side of the loosened portion of the

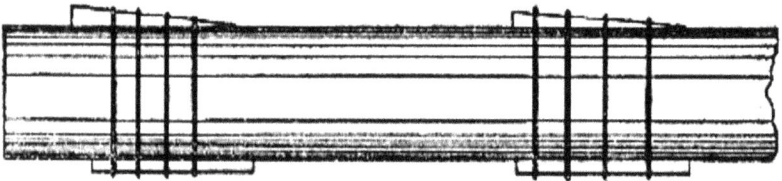

Showing how small wedges are wired around a double-barrel shotgun, used to hold the rib in place while it is being soldered.

rib place a small amount of powdered rosin and some fine solder shavings, then carefully heat the loosened portion of the rib and the barrels at that point with a small torch flame until the solder melts and runs. Remove excess solder along the edge of the rib, after it has cooled, with small three- cornered scrapers.

Shot patterns of guns, either single or double-barrel, that are equipped with ribs, may be raised or lowered by lowering or raising the rib for a few inches at the muzzle. It is easiest to raise the pattern as it is only necessary to lower the rib, which carries the front sight, to accomplish this. On double-guns, the rib is loosened for a few inches back from the muzzle and a little is filed off of each side of the rib, to narrow it. It is then pressed down into place on the barrels again where, on account of its narrower width, it takes a lower position and is then resoldered. The same result is accomplished with single-barrels equipped with a rib by loosening the rib and filing some from the bottom of the rib to lower it and then resoldering it in place.

Lowering the shot pattern by raising the rib is more difficult to accomplish but can be done by loosening the rib as before and soldering in place beneath it a piece of steel, to raise it the required amount, and then soldering the rib back in place on top of the steel shim. The sides will have to be filled in with solder on a double-gun where the rib is raised and also on a single- barrel gun with hollow rib. With a ventilated-rib bar- rel, the shims are cut the exact width of the rib sup- ports, so no filling-in with solder is required at the edges.

Some of the shot pattern can be made to go higher or lower by cutting a little from the muzzle, at top or bottom, inside the bore. This can be done with a carborundum file of round or half-round shape of the required size, or a reamer smaller than the diameter of the bore at the muzzle can be used to do the job by placing a steel shim beneath the reamer at the opposite side of the bore from where the cut is to be made. The shim protects the bore where it is not to be cut and raises the reamer so that it will cut at the side desired. After using either the carborundum file or the reamer, the bore is repolished at the point cut.

Cross-firing sometimes occurs with double-barrel guns. When this occurs at less than thirty yards the gun should be returned to the factory, for after correcting cross-firing at this short distance the barrels will usu-ally have to be refitted to the breech face. If the cross-firing occurs at a greater distance, separating the barrels more at the muzzle and for a few inches back will correct it.

The upper and lower ribs are both loosened with a small torch flame or a large soldering iron applied to the ribs for eight or ten inches back from the muzzle. The solder is also removed from the ends of the ribs at the muzzle. The distance between the barrels is measured and a piece of bright steel, thick enough to force the barrels farther apart, is pushed down between the barrels.

Showing how small steel piece is placed between barrels of a double gun, to force them apart to correct cross-firing.

This should be so adjusted in width that it will keep the top rib at the same height it was before, so that the gun will shoot to the same elevation. This piece of flat steel does not need to be more than two inches long. Apply flux and solder it in place, so that it will hold the ribs at the certain height, desired for the top rib when they are replaced. The ribs are then brought down into place and wires run around the bar- rel with wedges beneath them on top of the ribs, as was previously described for resoldering ribs. The bottom rib can be brought right back against both barrels for resoldering but the top rib, if maintaining the same elevation as before, will not quite touch the barrels and this gap must be filled in with new solder and the ends of the hollow beneath the ribs at the muzzle must be refilled with solder, as was previously described.

To determine the amount the barrels should be separated to cure the cross-firing is a difficult matter, but targeting the barrels beforehand to see where they cross-fire will also show the amount of cross-firing at distances within range of the gun. Laying the barrels, removed from the gun, on a support and training them upon a target, within shooting range, upon which a heavy cross line is drawn marked off with heavy vertical lines 4" to 6" apart, and looking through the barrels at this line will show where the barrels point. After the ribs are loosened, lay the barrel back on the support, in the same position, and use a wedge pushed between the barrels at the muzzle to separate them until the cross pointing is corrected within range of the gun. The distance between the barrels can then be measured and the flat steel piece of correct thickness to maintain this distance between the barrels is put in place.

Pump and autoloading shotguns sometimes throw loaded cartridges directly from the magazine out of the bottom of the action instead of passing them up to the barrel. This is due to failure of the magazine shell-stop, which may fail for a variety of causes. In an autoloading shotgun, if neither the shell-stop or its spring is broken or missing, the failure of the shell- stop is due to the breech bolt and the cartridge carrier (which lifts the cartridge from the magazine up to the barrel level) being out of time with each other so that the carrier is in the raised position instead of the lowered position when the breech bolt opens. This is caused by a broken or badly worn carrier tip, or dog as it is sometimes called. It may also be caused by break- age of the carrier tip spring. The remedy is, of course, a new part.

When a pump-type shotgun throws the loaded cart- ridges out at the bottom the cause may be the same as that mentioned for the autoloading gun, but is usually the failure of the shell-stop itself. In some of the cheaper shotguns of the pump-type this shell-stop is merely a piece of spring-steel, fastened to the side of the receiver, inside, with a bend in it so that its front end touches the head of the rear cartridge in the maga- zine, holding it in place until this piece of spring-steel is pushed aside, into a recess in the receiver, by the closing of the breech-block. This bending back and forth of this spring-steel shell-stop often results in it losing its spring, due to the fact that it is tempered a little too soft, and staying in its recess in the receiver wall instead of leaping forth at the time the breech- block opens to hold the next cartridge from sliding back out of the magazine. Remedy is to rebend and retemper the shell-stop after first hardening it when it is rebent to its proper curve.

This same spring-steel shell-stop has another trouble and that is that its front edge is sometimes too sharp and it catches on the indented ring on the head of a cartridge. This ring is rather close to the edge on some cartridges and in this case if the sharp edge of the shell-stop catches in it, it prevents the stop from moving far enough across the head of the car- tridge to hold it well. As cartridges have a rather loose fit in the magazine tube, there may be play enough of the cartridge in the magazine tube to allow the shell-stop to slip off the head of the cartridge when the action is operated. The remedy, in this case, is to oil-stone the edge of the cartridge stop at its front end, so that it slides easily over this indented ring in the head of the cartridge.

Shell-stops of other types than the spring device described above may sometimes give trouble from the same cause of having too sharp an edge, but this seldom occurs, and a failure on their part in a pump shot- gun is usually due to breakage or extreme wear. The remedy is to replace the stop with a new one, although spring-operated shell-stops such as on the model '97

Winchester sometimes become so dirty through neglect that the springs fail to operate, when the remedy is a thorough cleaning of stop, spring and recess in the receiver wall.

A firing-pin nose will sometimes break off and wedge in the face of the breech-block, and when this happens the gun fires as the breech-block closes and if it is an autoloading model it will continue to fire until it is empty, so if a gun fires upon closing the breech-block, look for a broken firing-pin at once. Hammer-notches may break or wear so that the sear does not hold the hammer back upon closure of the breech and this will also cause the gun to fire, so check this point too in case this trouble develops.

I once had a 20-gauge Remington pump shotgun stump me for two hours, because part of the time the trigger could not be pulled while the rest of the time that trigger had a normal pull. I took the trigger mechanism apart at least ten times and finally discovered a small piece of copper, from a pierced primer, rolling around in the trigger mechanism. Part of the time it would get under the forward extension of the trigger, so that the trigger could not be pulled, and then it would roll out of there and back into the hollow in the grip of the butt-stock, out of the way of every- thing. The first nine times I took the trigger mechanism apart, it was back in that hollow in the grip, but the tenth time it didn't get back that far and I saw it. After removing it the gun worked perfectly, so in case of action jams where all parts look normal, hunt for loose pieces of foreign material in the mechanism.

Extraction trouble in a pump or autoloading shot- gun is usually due to wear of the extractor hook. If the wear is slight, slightly sharpening the hook with a file and increasing the angle of the hook a small amount will correct it, but a new extractor is the best remedy. Faulty extraction is sometimes due to the ammunition used, the case rim being too narrow, or having too much slope on the front side of the rim. This trouble hap- pens more often with cheap ammunition than with the standard article, for one reason for the cheapness of the ammunition is very apt to be far less strict inspection standards at the factory.

Dirt under the extractor seldom bothers a shotgun, as there is room for considerable of it in the notch of the extractor, but it is well to clean the notch occasionally. -A broken spring can be the cause of poor extrac- tion, but as these are coil-springs they seldom break.

A fired case sometimes remains in the extractor hook instead of being ejected, so that it prevents a new cartridge rising to the barrel, whereupon the fired case is returned to the chamber. A broken ejector spring or an ejector jammed with dirt will cause this, or if the ejector is a long spring fastened in the top of the receiver, the weakening of this spring may cause the trouble. In guns with an ejector of this type, cartridges with an oversize rim will not eject from the breech-bolt. A different brand of ammunition generally corrects the trouble in such cases.

Autoloading shotguns have a fibre or composition pad fastened in the rear end of the receiver or in the rear end of the breech-bolt, so that the metal breech- bolt does not strike on the metal receiver wall. Do not neglect this pad, replace it when necessary, for if it is missing and the breech-bolt pounds against the receiver wall it causes crystallization of the operating rod or other parts of the breech-bolt mechanism and may crack the receiver.

Chapter 9 PROBLEMS OF THE 22 AND OTHER RIM -FIRE RIFLES

The .22 Rim-Fire rifle is in a class by itself, both as to price and for performance, and therefore deserves some special discussion. It has some troubles all of its own, so we shall devote some space to them.

One of its commonest troubles, even in new guns, is failure to extract the fired cartridge. In the case of a new rifle this is very often caused by heavy grease or dirt under the hook of the extractor and when ex- traction fails on a gun, either new or old, this is about the first place to look for the trouble. If this point is perfectly clean, then try the "spring" of the extractor. If the extractor is a piece of spring-steel, with no spring behind it, make sure that it has the proper

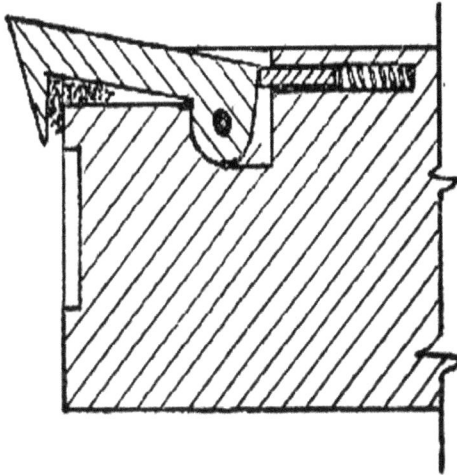

Dirt lodged behind the extractor may hold it back out of place, and make it fail to function.

"Spring" to it and is not too soft. If it also has a coil-spring behind it, make sure the action of this is positive and snappy, by pressing or drawing the ex- tractor hook outward and then letting it snap back into its slot. If it appears to be sluggish, remove the pin holding the extractor in place, then remove the ex- tractor and the coil-spring and clean out the hole in which the spring seats, also clean the spring thoroughly. It is seldom that the coil-spring is not of the proper temper, but this may happen, so press it together between your fingers and see that it springs back readily to its full length. If any of the coils of the spring are out of line, discard the spring and put in a new one, for it is almost impossible to straighten it up.

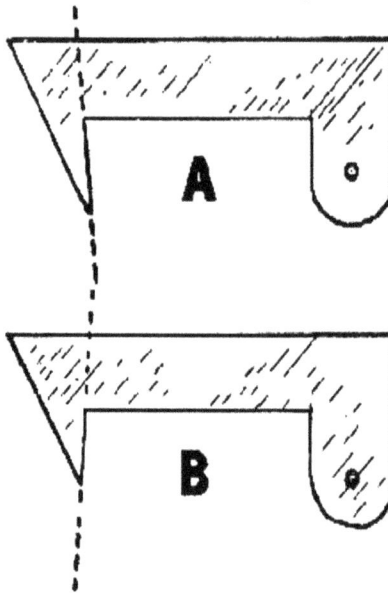

Showing correct (A) and incorrect (B) shape to hook of rim-fire extractor.

Next, examine the edge of the hook of the extractor to see that it has not been broken off and, if the gun is one that has had some use, make sure that the edge of the hook of the extractor has not been worn or rounded by use. This edge should be flat on the rear side right out to the limit, and when in place this rear face of the hook should have a rake to it, meaning that the edge of the hook should be closer to the face of the breech than the rest of the hook, so that the angle between the hook and the body of the extractor is less than a right-angle. An angle of 80 to 85 degrees is about right.

If the edge of the hook is very slightly broken away or rounded, file the rear face of the hook with a fine three-square file until the rear face is perfect clear out to the edge, then just remove the wire-edge left by the file on the edge of the hook with a fine carborundum stone or with a white Arkansas stone. The carborundum stone can be bought from the Carborundum Co. of Niagara Falls, New York, and the white Arkansas stone from the Norton Co. of Worcester, Mass. These square and triangular stones cost about 50^ each.

If the edge of the extractor is badly worn or has quite a piece broken from it, the only thing to do is to replace it with a new one. If the factory product is not readily available, a new one can be filed out of a piece of spring-steel. This steel is readily obtainable anywhere, for if your locality does not contain a shop which makes automobile springs or replacement leaves for them so that you can buy annealed spring-steel, get a piece of broken automobile spring leaf from a garage, heat this to a moderate red-heat and then bury it in slaked lime to cool. This will anneal it so that it can be easily cut and filed and after it is filed to shape, heat it to a low cherry-red and quench it in a light oil to harden, after which polish it and heat it slowly to a deep blue and quench it again in the oil to give it the proper temper.

Another cause of extraction failure is a rough or dirty chamber or a badly worn chamber. If the chamber is merely dirty it can usually be cleaned with a brass-bristle brush and a good powder solvent. If this fails to clean the chamber then use a chambering reamer with plenty of cutting oil, such as lard oil or black sulphur oil, but be careful not to force the reamer, use it gently or you may gouge the chamber or stick the reamer and break it.

Correct ignition is a main factor in the development of the potential accuracy of any .22 rim-fire rifle and is a matter which should receive constant attention from the rifle owner. These drawings on Plate XIII are intended to illustrate certain correct principles of rim-fire ignition and also to show certain common faults of action fitting and adjustment which will seriously affect this vital matter of accuracy.

It shall be called to mind that the "anvil" of any center-fire primer is a part of that primer itself — being contained in the primer cup, in the case of our American -type primers— or being formed in the primer pocket of the case, with the Berdan-type primer. However, in any rim-fire rifle this "anvil" is an integral part of that rifle — being formed by the breech-end of the barrel — that portion of the counterbored recess around the mouth of the chamber which accommodates the rim of the cartridge ease, and which lies directly under the point of the firing-pin. In llic Plate opposite, this "anvil" is indicated by the letter "X."

Figure "A" shows .22 rim-fire operation under proper conditions. Notice that the cartridge is fully seated into the chamber, with its rim solidly up against the rifle's "anvil" so that there is no movement or lost-motion when the firing-pin drives forward. Such condition gives instantaneous and consistent ignition for every cartridge fired. The gunsmith should see to it that all tolerances and adjustments — both in firing-pin and extractor — establish this correct relation of parts. The rifle's owner should see that this situation is maintained — by keeping grease and dirt out of the rim-counterbore and from around the extractor, and by avoiding any battering-down or cushioning of the "anvil."

Figure "B" illustrates a common fault of many .22 falling-block rifles one which seriously affects their accuracy. Here we have a condition whereby the cartridge rim cannot bear firmly against the "anvil" — causing erratic ignition and hang-fires. This is often due to dirt or heavy grease lodging behind the extractor, or it can be caused by a bent extractor — either of which fault prevents the cartridge from being fully seated in the chamber. Both faults can occur in a properly adjusted rifle after it has left the maker's hands — and their correction calls for either a thorough cleaning or a new extractor.

Figure "C" illustrates a similar condition, where the cartridge is prevented from being properly seated on account of an extractor which is a trifle too thick. A bit of filing or stoning-down will correct this fault.

Figure "D" shows the same condition in a bolt-action rifle. Here the cartridge is prevented from proper seating by an extractor which is too long. The remedy is to stone or file off a bit from the end of the extractor — or to file out the hook slightly. Dirt or hard fouling ac- cumulating in the recess for the extractor hook can cause this same fault — so keep this recess cleaned out at all times.

Figures "E" to "J" illustrate proper and improper firing-pin profiles.

"E" is a poor one — too pointed and edge too sharp. Will cause pierced eases, with accompanying gas-bursts.

"F" is also a pour one — striking face too narrow and too sharp. Will cause split and burst case-rims.

"G" is a good shape — but care should be taken to stone-off the sharp edges, just strike a slight bevel all around.

"H" is proper for the round-end firing-pin, but this is a poor shape to use for rim-fire cartridges.

"I" is proper profile for the round, flat-end firing-pin — but be sure to strike-off the sharp edge around its point.

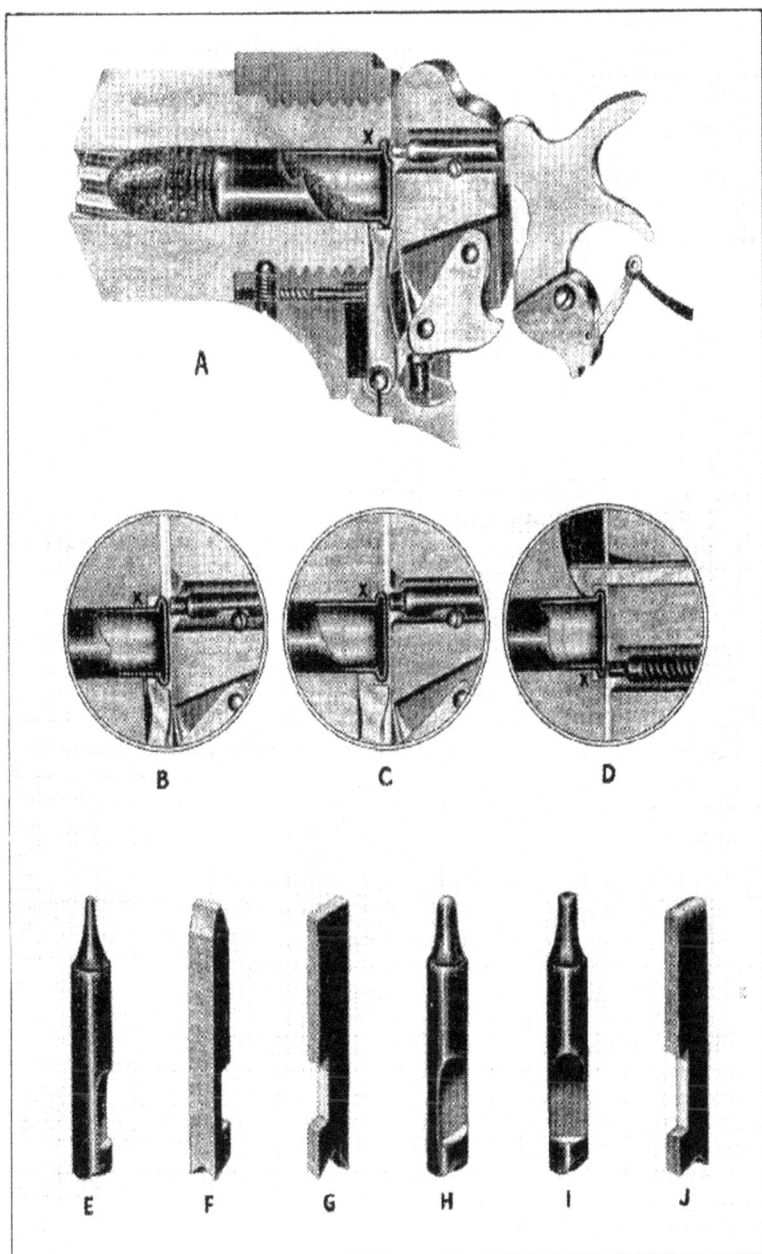

Plate XIII

(Descriptions given on opposite page.)

If a chamber is rough, try the chambering reamer to see if it will smooth it up, although a rough chamber is usually enlarged so that a chambering reamer will not touch it and if this is the case there are two things that can be done ; either replace the barrel with a new one or make a new chamber. This last can be done in two ways. One of these is to cut off the old chamber, rethread the barrel and set it back the amount it has been cut off, then cut the new chamber. The second method is to chuck the barrel in the lathe so that the bore is truly centered and bore out just the length of the chamber to a larger size, large enough to be tapped with a fine-thread tap to about 3/8". A piece of 3/8" drill-rod is then threaded with a die set slightly over-size, so that the rod will screw very tightly into the threads tapped in the barrel. Make sure that the piece of drill-rod bottoms perfectly in the bottom of the counterbore in the barrel, then set it up as tightly as you can and cut it off, facing it down to the rear end of the barrel. With the barrel still centered in the lathe, drill a center-hole in the piece of drill-rod, using a combination center-drill, then drill out the length of the chamber with a 3/16 " or 13/64" twist drill, after which bore it with a small boring tool, which you can grind to shape from a piece of high-speed steel lathe cutting bit, until it is just a few thousandths of an inch below chamber size, then use the chambering

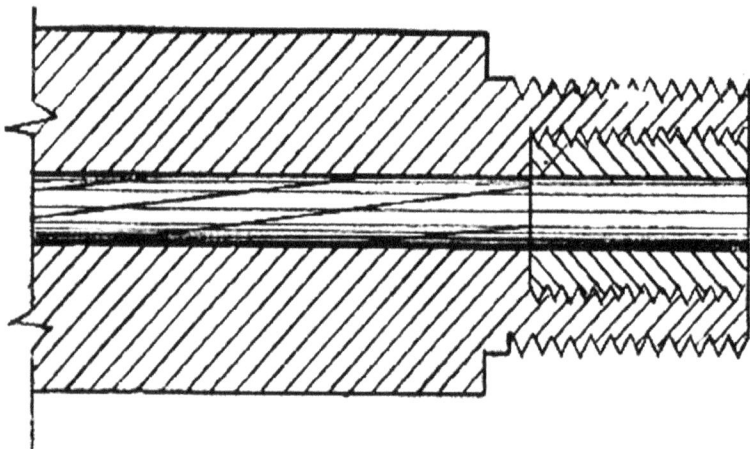

Illustrating how a piece of steel rod may be set into the rear of a barrel and a new chamber cut in it, replacing a worn chamber.

Once in a while you will encounter a new gun with the chamber so large that the fired case expands beyond its "spring-back" point, so that it grips the chamber walls very tightly. This usually does not give much trouble in a rifle where you have ample extraction power, but it is a tough break when it occurs in a revolver where six or more fired cases are extracted at once. The gun, of course, should be re- turned to the manufacturer at once, but if this is not feasible, then try brass-case ammunition, as the brass case is often stiff enough to have more spring than other types.

Extraction difficulties are one big reason why guns should be thoroughly cleaned each time they are used, regardless of what the ammunition manufacturer tells you about his noncorrosive ammunition making clean- ing unnecessary, for dirt that collects in a chamber may be of any nature, and it may readily absorb moisture so that the chamber is rusted and pitted, and a barrel with a ruined chamber is almost as badly ruined as one with pock-marked rifling. I prefer a brass or bristle brush of the Parker type, as these brushes will remove dirt better than a patch does. If the brush is dipped into a good cleaning solvent or oil, it will leave a coating of it in the chamber and rifling, then a dry patch run through the barrel before the gun is used again will remove anything loosened by the action of the oil or solvent.

The rim-fires, especially the .22s, arc very susceptible to ignition troubles, not necessarily misfires, but hang- fires and uneven ignition. A great deal of this is due to the ammunition. The primer space in a .22 rim- fire case is very small, the primer mixture is not always evenly distributed around the rim, and spots where it is thin may easily cause a slight hang-fire. Also the modern high-velocity brass case is pretty stiff and the firing-pin blow on many of the older rifles, and on some of the new ones, is a little too light for best ignition. This is sometimes caused, in a new rifle especially, by heavy grease inside the bolt barrel, so that the firing-pin is cushioned against the inside of the bolt head by this grease. A new rifle should always be examined at this point to make sure there is no grease inside the bolt. A very light oil is the only lubricant that should be used upon the firing-pin or coil-spring inside the bolt.

Poor ignition from a light or misplaced firing-pin blow can be detected by examining the impression made by the firing-pin on the head of a cartridge. To give the best ignition, this impression should be .015" or more in depth. If the firing-pin impression looks to be considerably less than this in depth, out on the cartridge rim itself, start to hunt the cause right away. First, make sure your bolt is clean of grease and dirt inside the head as mentioned above; next, make sure that the firing-pin protrusion from the breech face is sufficient. Sometimes a firing-pin is shortened by wear on the point and when this occurs it can often be lengthened by cutting back the shoulder of the pin slightly, thus giving it a longer point. If the pin is hard, it must either be ground back or be softened by heating to a red-heat and burying in slaked lime to cool, after which it may be filed or machined in the lathe. It is then rehardened by heating to cherry-red and quenching in a light oil, after which it is polished and then heated slowly until it becomes blue in color and then quenched again in the oil to temper it. Hardened pins can be chucked in the lathe and ground back slightly in the body with an electric tool post grinder, or this grinding can often be done on an automobile valve-grinder of the better type often found in garages.

If the firing-pin protrusion is sufficient, examine the rim of the chamber where the case rim is supported against the firing-pin blow (its "anvil") to make sure that the rim is not dented at this point, as in some rifles, especially older types, the firing-pin is long enough to strike the chamber rim if the rifle is snapped without a cartridge case in the chamber. If the rim is in bad shape at this point from this cause, the rem-edy' is to set the barrel back one thread, cutting it off and deepening the chamber the required amount. After this has been done, the firing-pin should be shortened so that it does not quite strike the rim when the empty gun is snapped.

Dirt in the counterbore in the end of the barrel for the case rim may cushion the blow of the firing-pin enough to cause hang-fires or misfires, so make sure there is no dirt or heavy grease at this point. Grease may easily collect there when greased cartridges are used, and the autoload-ing .22s are sometimes bad of- fenders from this cause because powder fouling blows back into the action with this type of gun and grease at the rear end of the chamber will pick up this fouling, so the rear end of the chamber should be cleaned after you are through shooting the gun for the day.

In examining the firing-pin impression on the head of the fired case, check carefully to see where the firing-pin strikes. If the firing-pin impression extends clear out over the edge of the rim, and your rifle gives ignition troubles, try' narrowing the pin enough at the outer side so that it strikes just inside the edge of the rim, for the rim is very much stiffer at the edge, due to the double thickness at this point, so a rifle on which the firing-pin blow is a little too light to give good ignition when the pin extends over the edge of the rim may give good ignition if it is narrowed enough to strike just inside the edge of the rim.

The round, flat-ended firing-pin has to strike a heavier blow to give as good ignition as the rectangular, so called "chisel -shaped" flat-ended firing-pin, unless the diameter of the pin is very small, for the greater part of the impression is made upon the case-head inside the rim and this tends to cushion the blow.

This may be corrected in two ways; either by grinding off the side of the firing-pin toward the center of the case, to reduce the amount of pin impression on the case head inside the rim, where it does no good ; or by grinding the sides of the pin parallel, to narrow it to the chisel-shape, thus concentrating the force of the blow. In making any change in the shape of the firing-pin point, the edges of the flat point should not. he left sharp, but should be slightly rounded with a fine hand-stone like the white Arkansas stones. Never make a rounded-nose firing-pin that is a hemispherical- shaped end like a center-fire pin for use on rim-fire cartridges, for this is almost sure to give poor ignition. The end of the firing-pin should be flat.

In some of the older make rifles of the falling-block types, the firing-pin strikes the case rim at the point where it is supported by the extractor. This nearly always leads to ignition troubles, due to the fact that dirt often gets behind the extractor and cushions the firing-pin blow, also very often the extractor is slightly below the level of the end of the barrel so that the rim is actually not supported by the extractor against the firing-pin blow. The best correction for this is to make a new firing-pin, with the nose in a different position so that it strikes the cartridge rim where it is solidly supported by the end of the barrel. The old firing-pin hole in the breech-block can be filled up by tapping it out with a fine-thread tap and screwing a piece of drill- rod into the hole tightly, after which the rod is cut off and filed down flush with the face of the breech-block.

At any time a cartridge case head blows out, examine the inside of the breech-block or bolt for small pieces of copper or brass that have come back through the firing-pin hole, as these will often cause enough friction to cushion the firing-pin blow or may even roughen up the firing-pin enough so that it binds in the hole in the bolt or breech-block.

Of course, weakened main-springs will always be a source of ignition trouble and the remedy is to replace the weakened spring with a new one.

If ignition troubles persist, another point to examine about the firing-pin is the angle the face or end of the pin makes with the body of the pin. This angle will sometimes be found to be greater than a right-angle at the outer edge where it strikes the case rim, which makes the inner edge of the firing-pin, that strikes on the case head inside the rim, the longest side of the pin, so that it strikes the case head first and cushions the blow before the outer edge strikes on the rim.

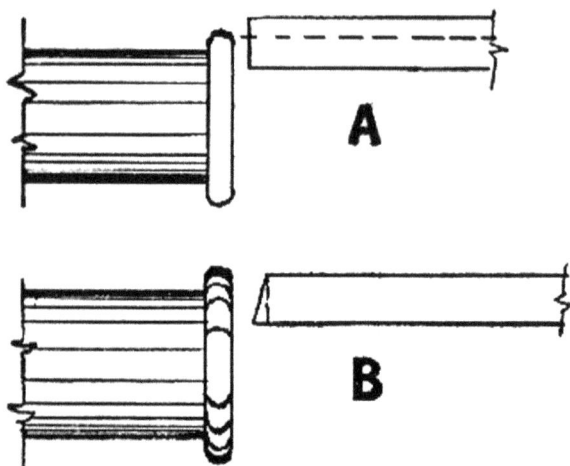

Showing importance of proper firing-pin impact. A shows pin nose striking too high across the side wall of rim. B shows firing-pin face of wrong shape, causing the blow to be cushioned by the pin first striking below the priming space in case rim.

Chisel-shaped firing-pins will sometimes wear into such shape, and they have also been put out by factories in this shape. The remedy is to carefully stone the end of the firing-pin at right-angles to the sides of it, using a fine carborundum stone and rounding the edges slightly with a white Arkansas stone.

The movement of the cartridge case into and out of the chamber, in a rifle with repeating action, has a certain degree of lapping action on the chamber as the number of cartridges fired mounts up into the thou- sands. The practice of some manufacturers of repeating rifles is to harden the chamber end of the barrel on their better grade guns to keep this wear at a minimum, but in any except the autoloading rifles this wear is not much of a factor in ignition troubles. It is more so in the autoloading rifles for two reasons ; one being that usually more ammunition is fired through an autoloading rifle than through any other type of repeating rifle in the same length of time ; and the other reason is that usually the chamber of the autoloading rifle is somewhat larger to start with, as more clearance is usually given the cartridge case in these actions so that they will function properly.

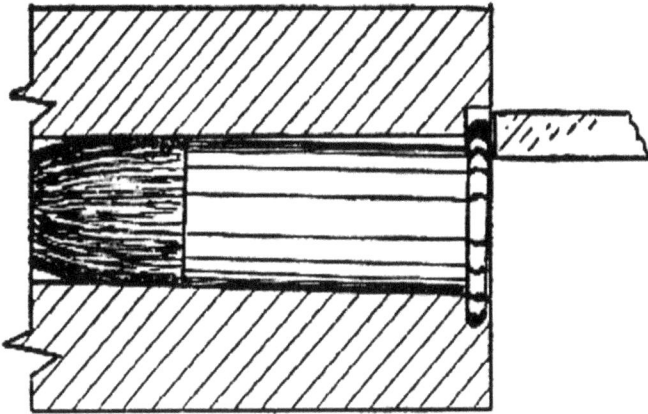

Illustrating how a badly worn chamber allows cartridge to drop to the bottom, causing a misplacement of the firing-pin blow and cushioning of the impact.

The part these worn chambers may play in ignition troubles is simply to allow the cartridge case to move far enough out of line until the firing-pin strikes on the edge of the rim where it is doubled over, so that the blow of the firing-pin has to compress this edge before it can crush the primer mixture. The remedy here, provided that the chamber is not so badly worn as to cause inaccuracy, is the same as before noted when the firing-pin strikes out over the edge of the rim, to narrow the firing-pin by grinding off its outer edge so that it strikes entirely inside the edge of the rim. If the chamber is worn enough to cause notice- able inaccuracy, a new barrel should be fitted or the old barrel set back and rechambered.

A badly worn or over-large firing-pin hole in a breech-block may allow the pin to move about so that it strikes over the edge of the case rim instead of just inside the edge, thus causing ignition trouble. The remedy for this is to bore out the firing-pin hole in the block or bolt so that it can he threaded for a threaded plug of drill-rod, which is screwed tightly into the hole and cut off flush with the breech-face, after which a new firing-pin hole of the proper size is drilled.

Speed-actions sometimes give ignition troubles on modern high-speed cartridges with their stiff cases and as manufacturers of ammunition are adding even more stiffness to the case material from time to time, to prevent case heads blowing out in older actions, a speed-action that may have given pretty good ignition a few years ago may fail to do so on a later-type am- munition. The only cure for this is a stiffer main- spring, if it is possible to get one stiff enough that will go into the action. If this is not possible, the speed- action will have to be replaced with a slower type having a longer firing-pin travel.

Main-springs of speed-actions often have to be re- placed, because usually a very small let-down in main- spring strength on these actions will result in hang- fires and sometimes in misfires. For the same reason, firing-pin length should often be checked on these actions, as wear on the firing-pin will shorten it so that the impression it makes on the case head is too shallow. This should not happen if the pin is made of the proper steel and is properly hardened.

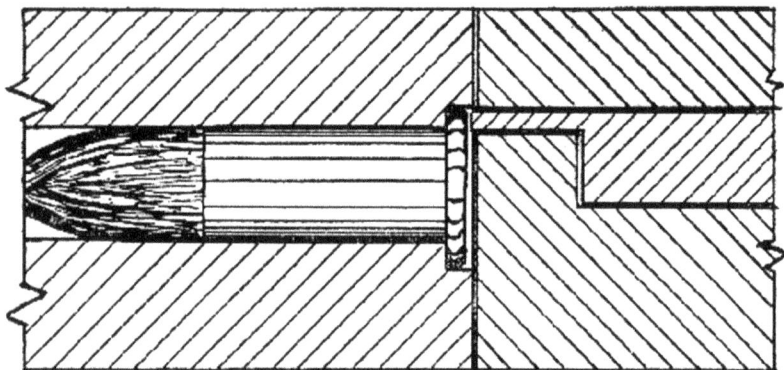

Excessive head-space causes a light firing-pin blow and poor ignition. In many rifle actions the forward travel of firing-pin is limited by a shoulder, as shown above.

Excess head-space seldom results in poor ignition, because before it becomes enough to cause this trouble, case heads will be blowing out due to not being properly supported. Excess head-space, however, does result in poor accuracy in the .22, because if the case head is not properly and very evenly supported the rifle does not group well. Most manufacturers of rifles try to keep excess head-space to not more than .003". The size of .22 rim-fire cases has been pretty well standardized by ammunition manufacturers, but dies for forming cases are subject to wear, so a certain small tolerance has to be allowed in the manufacture of cases. The rifle owner, however, should check head-space if the rifle does not group well. Steel shim stock that is used in garages can be bought cheaply from a garage and cut into small pieces, that can be placed upon the head of the cartridge and the action then closed upon it. As soon as the action closes with a slight effort, the shims can then be removed and measured with a micrometer to determine what the excess head-space amounts to, and if more than .002" to .003" it is too much. In fact, several brands of ammunition should be tried until one is found which shows no excess head- space and, if other things about the ammunition are equal, it should show better accuracy than a brand which shows excess head-space in that rifle. The single-shot falling breech-block and the bolt-action types should have no excess head-space, as these actions have ample power to close the breech on tight cartridges, but don't overdo this tightness so that the case head is crushed, or the priming mixture may be displaced and poor ignition will result. An ammunition that shows no excess head-space for one lot number may show it in another lot number, due to change of dies or different dies being used to turn out ammunition carrying different lot numbers, so after finding one lot number of ammunition that does well in the rifle, buy a quantity of it, and when in need again, buy single boxes of different lot numbers, to again try out the ammunition before buying a further supply.

As .22 rim-fire rifles are used more than all other calibers combined and, since the introduction of high- velocity rim-fire .22 cartridges, maintaining proper head-space has become important from a safety stand- point, simple and low-cost ways of taking care of wear in breech-block locking mechanisms are necessary.

Some of the popular slide-action .22 rim-fire rifles lock the breech-block into a notch in the receiver top, either on the inside of the top of the receiver or cut clear through the top of the receiver. The breech- blocks themselves are often hardened, but the receivers are nearly always soft, and there is where the wear occurs. This low-cost repair is done in the same way as that to repair wear in cheap single and double shotguns, by peen-ing the metal behind the locking- notch. As the inside of a .22 rim-fire receiver is too small to get a hammer into it, a heavy punch with a rounded end is placed on the metal of the receiver be- hind the notch into which the breech-block locks and, with the receiver lying upon a heavy piece of brass, this punch is struck with a hammer. Move the punch slightly and strike it again, repeating this process evenly across the receiver behind the notch, being care- ful not to do the peening too close to the locking notch or you may burr its edge.

This peening will swell forward the metal of the receiver, thus moving the rear face of the locking notch slightly forward, locking the breech-block closer against the rear end of the barrel. If, in this operation, the breech-block is caused to lock-up too tightly, a very fine file is used to cut back the edge of the notch slightly and, after using the file, the face of the notch is stoned with a hard Arkansas stone, to remove all file marks and leave the locking face smooth and polished.

In the bolt-action .22 rim-fires, the breech-bolt is often locked by the bolt handle turning down into a notch cut in the receiver wall. The inside of the receiver wall, just back of this locking notch, can some- times be reached with a rather slender, rounded-end punch by bending the punch slightly and putting it into the receiver through the top slot through which the bolt-handle travels, or up through the bottom opening in the receiver. The important point is near the bottom of this locking notch, usually the last quarter-inch. If it is impossible to get any punch in place to peen this receiver wall to stretch the metal forward into the notch, the rear face of this notch may be built forward with an electric welder, at small cost. After this is done, the notch must be dressed back with fine files arid then polished with the hard Arkansas stone until the bolt just closes nicely on a cartridge in the chamber.

If the bolt-action rifle has a lug upon the bolt, opposite to the bolt handle, which turns into a notch in the left receiver wall, this notch must also be peened forward, or welded, and both notches dressed so that the bolt handle and lug bear equally. A little prussian-blue or lamp-black mixed in oil and applied to the locking lugs in a very thin coat will show when both bear equally.

Badly enlarged chambers will usually show poor accuracy, due to the cartridge lying at the bottom of the chamber so that the bullet strikes the rifling on an angle when leaving the case, but usually before a cham- ber is enough oversize to give trouble from an accuracy standpoint, extraction troubles will have forced the purchase of a new barrel or at least the cutting of a new chamber.

Noncorrosive priming mixtures in use today do not all have the same chemical content and while, from a standpoint of danger of rust forming in the barrel if only one brand of ammunition is used without cleaning the barrel, cleaning is unnecessary, yet it is better to do this cleaning, for it may be forgotten in case another brand of ammunition is used and the mixture of the two different priming formulae may promote rust in the bore. Also, cleaning a bore through which lead bullets are fired will prevent any accumulation of lead from the bullets, for some barrels are slightly rough and will pick up lead readily. A brass brush is the best method to use to remove this lead fouling and if the brass brush is dipped in water or in some good barrel cleaning mixture, or protective grease such as Rig, it will take care of any primer fouling. If water is used as a cleaning medium, the barrel should be thoroughly dried by running dry patches through it afterwards and should then be oiled with an acid- free oil or gun grease.

If rust does gather in the bore to such an extent that it cannot be removed with a brass brush and gun oil, a mild abrasive, such as fine optical emery or crocus- powder on tight patches dipped in oil, should be used to remove it. If it is a bad enough case to require a coarser emery powder at first, followed by the fine grade mentioned, then the surface of the bore will be minutely pitted and thereafter the bore will have to be cleaned with a good brass brush each time much firing is done through it, for these pits will rapidly pick up lead and the rifle will be inaccurate. For a bad case of leading, a cork is placed in one end of the barrel, mercury is then poured in the opposite end and that end corked, and the barrel turned about by the hands for an hour or more until the liquid mercury reaches every part of the bore, so that it can amalgamate with the lead. The mixture is then poured out, the barrel cleaned with a brass brush and examined to see if the cleaning was complete, and if it is not then the mercury treatment must be repeated until the barrel is clean.

Dry (meaning unlubricated) ammunition should never be used, for this not only leads a barrel badly but also wears it very rapidly. One company manufacturing ammunition made a test of accurate barrel life for unlubricated ammunition and the decrease was about 90% compared to accurate barrel life with lubricated ammunition.

Bullets lodged in the barrel of a .22 rifle can usually be removed with a square (flat) ended rod of almost full-bore dimensions, provided the bullet has not remained in the barrel too long. A length of #3 drill- rod makes a good rod to remove bullets of .22 short, long or long-rifle size, and a length of #2 drill-rod works best in .22 Special and .22 W.R.F. barrels. The rod should be cut flat and smooth on one end in a lathe and this flat end placed against the base of the bullet, preferably, unless the bullet is lodged in the barrel much closer to the breech than to the muzzle, in which case the rod is placed against the point of the bullet. Before trying to drive the bullet out, oil the barrel well from each end with a thin oil, allowing it to stand above the bullet at one end for an hour, then reversing the barrel and pouring the oil in the opposite end to allow it to stand for another hour. After this, place the flat end of the rod against one end of the bullet and strike it a sharp blow with a good sized hammer, whereupon it will usually drive on out with repeated blows. If it moves a short distance and then sticks, drive it from the opposite end. If the bullet has been lodged in the barrel for some time and will not drive out, machine a point on one end of the drill-rod with a 60-degree included angle, like a center-punch, and center-punch the bullet at one end with the rod. A #4 wire-gauge drill is then brazed onto a piece of drill-rod, either #3 or #2, whichever one fits the barrel in question, and after the rod is straightened so that the drill runs true the bullet is drilled out from the end which was center punched. The remainder of the bullet is removed from the bore with stiff brass or bronze brushes of the Parker type and if necessary use the mercury treatment to get it all out. Never heat a barrel to try to melt a lead bullet from it, as the barrel will be ruined by this treatment.

Never leave rags or antirust ropes in the barrel, for they will almost surely rust tight if left there very long, they are the very devil to remove and usually arc not worth removing, for the barrel will nearly always be ruined. Rags or antirust ropes that are stuck in the barrel can be removed by picking them into pieces with a sharp- threaded wood-screw brazed to the end of a piece of steel rod. The screw is screwed a short distance into the cloth and then is yanked out by a straight pull on the rod. Pieces of the cloth dislodged are then shaken from the barrel and the process is repeated until all the cloth is removed. This method is faster and also safer than burning the rags out with a red-hot rod.

If a wooden rod is broken off in the barrel, the bore is oil-soaked, as directed for the removal of a bullet, and the square-ended piece of drill-rod is used to drive it from the barrel. If this fails, then the wood rod must be drilled out as was the bullet.

The .22 rifles sometimes refuse to feed cartridges from the magazine. This happens more often in the tubular magazine type than in the box magazine type. First, check the magazine spring to see that it is not broken, or cramped, or too weak. Next, make sure there is no dirt or pieces of metal in the magazine tube, then examine the outlet end through the frame to see that it is smooth. Also examine the magazine tube for dents. If these points are all in good condition the trouble is in the cartridge stop or carrier. Sec that the cartridge stop clears the tube opening perfectly when the action is operated and if it does not do so examine it for dirt, roughness and straightness. One of these things will be found wrong with it, if it fails to operate. If the cartridge stop is all right, examine the slot in the carrier into which the cartridge slides from the magazine. These are usually rough enough anyway at the edges, and a small additional nick that is not readily noticed can easily prevent the cartridge moving back fully into the slot. These nicks can be smoothed out with a fine file and if they are in a position where they can be reached with a small abrasive stone the final finishing can be done with this, if the stone will not .reach the spot, carborundum cloth may be used.

Consistent ignition is a deciding factor in developing the accuracy of any .22 rim-fire rifle and it is necessary that both gunsmith and rifle owner give close attention tn the profile of the firing-pin point, its protrusion from the face of the breech-block, the percussion developed by hammer impact and the fit of the firing-pin in the breech- block. Also, the point of impact on the case rim is of vital importance.

These figures on Plate XIV are intended to represent certain faults and virtues of different firing-pin arrangements and types.

"A" is the .22 rim-fire case head, unfixed. The entire circumference of the inside of the rim is filled with the priming mixture, spread as evenly as possible around the recess with some inadvertently getting smeared across the head of the case. To secure proper ignition, some segment of this primed rim must be crushed between the firing-pin and the "anvil" of the rifle barrel — and this crushing must be done suddenly and evenly from shot to shot, with the cartridge held solidly against the "anvil" with no cushioning or movement.

"B" illustrates a dangerous condition through the use of a firing-pin having too sharp a profile. This is a quite common type of emergency firing-pin, made up in a hurry by the use of an 8d or 10d round wire nail. It is extremely dangerous, especially with the new hi-power type 22 cartridge, as pierced heads, with their accompanying gas-spurt, are certain to occur.

"C" shows wrong point of impact. Too far inside case head, rim cannot be smashed and misfires certain to predominate.

"D" is also a poor arrangement. Protrusion is too great and hammer-blow too heavy, tending to burst the rim of the case upon firing. Point of impact is a bit too far inside case head.

"E" is about right for round-end firing-pin — but this is not an especially good profile to use.

"F" is a poor arrangement — chisel-pointed pin with sharp edges which cause many split rims with accompanying gas-spurts.

"G" illustrates insufficient protrusion or percussion. Impact is too weak to crush case rim together and detonate priming.

"H" is correct for round-end firing-pin, better point of impact than "E."

"I" is correct impact for narrow, flat-end firing-pin — and this is about the best type of all.

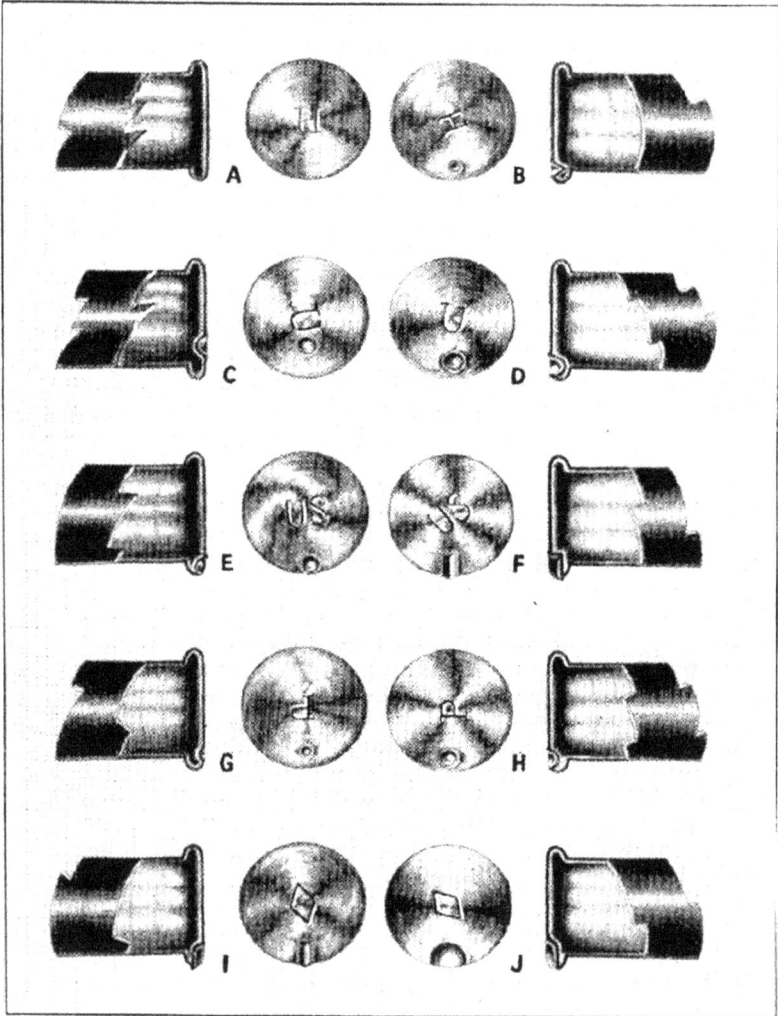

Plate XIV

(Descriptions given on opposite page.)

If the carrier has been bent so that the cartridge slot is partially closed, remove the carrier from the rifle, place in a vise with padded jaws, then insert a round, straight punch or a piece of steel rod in the cartridge slot and straighten it up.

If the carrier fails to rise when the action is worked, it is probably broken and must be replaced with a new one.

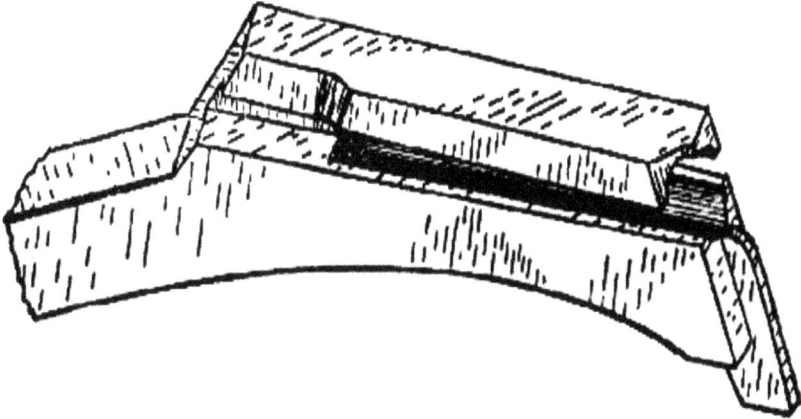

Bent carrier of a repeating action. The hole is closed so that the cartridge cannot enter from the magazine.

When cartridges fail to feed from a box magazine, if the spring is all right, see that the cartridge plat- form does not cramp in the magazine and see that the magazine walls are free of dents. If all these points are all right the trouble is probably in the lips of the magazine. They are either bent, or a cartridge has been forced into the magazine from the wrong point, in loading, and has perhaps made a burr on one of the edges. If no burr is found, the lips of the magazine are bent and must be straightened. If the bend is a short one it can usually be easily detected but if it is a rather long gradual one it is sometimes hard to find. If a second magazine in good condition is avail- able, a steel scale may be laid along the sides of the bent magazine, at different points, and then laid on the good magazine at the same points and the bend located in this manner. If no other magazine is avail- able, the steel scale may be laid along first one side and then the other of the faulty magazine and the defect sometimes is shown up by this method. In straightening the lips of a magazine, pliers with smooth jaws should be used but if none are at hand, pieces of thin copper may be bent over the jaws of grooved- jaw pliers, so that the magazine's lips will not be scored.

These box magazines are often held in place in the rifle with a catch that engages a notch cut in the magazine and both the catch and the notch sometimes wear, allowing the magazine to drop too low for the bolt to pick off the top cartridge. To remedy this, the catch may be replaced by a slightly longer one, cut from a piece of steel or the old catch may be heated to a low- red heat, near the end, and drawn out a little longer with a hammer, after which it can be filed to the proper length. Sometimes a new magazine is necessary, as all the wear may be on the cut for the catch in the magazine.

Trigger-pulls on our .22 rifles, especially those not strictly designed for target shooting, leave something to be desired. Usually the pull is entirely too long and is seldom smooth enough for good off-hand work, which requires a very much better trigger-pull than rest or prone shooting. The set-trigger is really the ideal one for off-hand work, not necessarily the ultra light double-set pull, but a good single-set with adjustable pull.

If the trigger-pull is not satisfactory in the .22 rifle, examine the trigger parts to sec if the hammer or the firing-pin, if it is a bolt-action rifle, is cammed back by pulling the trigger. If this is the case, carefully grind the sear nose, or cocking notch, or both if necessary, until there is no movement whatever to the hammer or firing-pin when the trigger is slowly drawn back. Once this is accomplished, examine the contact surfaces of the sear nose and cocking notch with a good magnifying glass, to locate all rough spots. The faces of the sear and cocking notch, besides being of mirror smoothness, should be absolutely flat and straight, so that the bearing of one upon the other is full, clear across them. One of the surfaces may be coated with prussian-blue and the parts assembled to check for high spots, the blue showing up these spots clearly.

Clamp the part showing high spots between two rectangular pieces of steel in the bench vise, so that the surface to be trued-up is just slightly above the surfaces of the two pieces of steel. These steel pieces will prevent a rounded surface being developed on the sear nose or hammer notch being stoned. A small carborundum stone is used to dress down the surface of the part, until it is as flat as possible. The white Arkansas stone is then used to give the surface a high polish. Here again, use that magnifying glass, to make sure that you have missed none of the surface in the polishing process. If the surface is perfect, then use the white Arkansas stone to just round the edge which contacts the other part, so that the extreme sharpness of the edge is removed. Now, coat this surface with the prussian-blue, assemble the trigger mechanism again and cock the gun, after which disassemble the parts again, and the high spots will show' up on the second part, then they may be stoned off and the surface polished and the edge rounded, as w-as done with the first part. The frontispiece show's this operation.

Usually in the hammer, or so-called hammerless actions with the inside hammer, the engagement of the sear nose in the hammer notch is not too deep, but if the trigger-pull is entirely too long from the fact that this notch is too deep, a hole can be drilled into the body of the hammer at the back of the notch, a pin is then driven tightly into this hole and the outer end filed off to shorten the pin enough so that the sear nose is just allowed to engage the hammer notch a short distance. The shorter this engagement of the sear in the hammer notch, the shorter the trigger-pull will be, but try it carefully , with the gun empty, by cocking the hammer and striking the butt sharply on a wood door or heavy piece of wood if the rifle has a steel butt-plate. If the butt-plate is of hard rubber, hold the rifle in one hand and strike the side of the butt stock sharply several times with the heel of the other hand, to make sure that the sear will not be jarred from its seat in the hammer notch. If the rifle is a repeating type, operate the action rapidly, a number of times, with the gun empty, trying it each time the action is operated, to make sure that the sear catches properly in the hammer notch. If it jars off or fails to catch a single time file the pin a little shorter, to give the sear a deeper hold in the hammer notch, for one accident is all that is necessary and death is so final.

The bolt-actions very often have a far deeper engagement of the sear nose in the cocking notch than is necessary and the best remedy on these is to grind down the top of the sear, to shorten its depth in the cocking notch. The speed-actions generally do not have too deep an engagement of the sear in the cocking notch, and usually trueing up the engaging surfaces and bringing them to a high polish is all that is necessary to give them a good trigger-pull.

Shortening the sear or trigger spring slightly, or replacing it with a lighter one, will very often improve the trigger-pull greatly, but be sure that the spring remains strong enough to return the sear fully to its seat in the cocking notch each time when it is only partially withdrawn and the trigger is again released with- out completing the pull. Try this a number of times without completing the pull any time, for this is a vital point of safety and that sear must return to its full depth of seat each time.

If the trigger and scar are two separate parts, so that the trigger has a fulcrum point that rests against the receiver or some other part to get the necessary leverage to draw down the sear, polish this fulcrum of the trigger and the part on which it rests to a very high polish, so that as little friction as possible is developed at this point. The .22 Springfield rifle is a good example of this type of trigger-pull. Coating the trigger, sear and cocking-notch surfaces with Gunslick, made by the Outer's Laboratories, Onalaska, Wisconsin, working the parts against each other for several minutes and then wiping off the excess grease will smooth up the working surfaces quite a bit.

Iron sights supplied on .22 rifles today arc far superior to those that were standard equipment a few years ago but they still do not always answer the purpose of the shooter. All types of special sights can be purchased from Lyman, Marble, Wittek, Pacific and Redfield gun sight companies and the Merit Gun Sight Co. of 3764 Ruby St., Oakland, California, sells an iris shutter peep-sight disc for $2.25 by which the size of aperture can be changed instantly. Special designs of front sights that are easily made are often desirable for special purposes. The cross-wire mounted in a short section of tube for use in small game shooting is one example of this. A short section of steel tube can be made by drilling a hole through a short length of $4" to Yi" steel rod and fine wire such as that obtain- able from an old Ford coil can be stretched across the tube to form a cross, passing the wire through four small holes drilled through the wall at equidistant points and the wires soldered to the outside of the tube. Instead of running one wire horizontally and one vertically they may be crossed at 4 5 -degrees from the vertical and horizontal points. Also a dot may be placed on the intersection of the wires, by dipping the end of a fine wire into Dupont cement and placing a small dot of it on the intersection of the wires. A single horizontal cross-wire with a dot of cement upon it at the center may be used instead of the cross-wires. These wire-type iron sights are only practical where the shooting is to be done in good light against a back- ground on which the sight will show up well, but under these conditions they are very accurate.

The flat-topped, small, half-round notch, open sight such as the Savage Company used to supply on some of the model '99 rifles is an excellent type of open rear sight to use in connection with a bead front sight. Any open-type rear sight can be converted to this type by drilling a small hole through a piece of light black sheet-steel, then filing down one edge until half the hole is filed away, leaving a semicircular notch. The piece is then put in nitric-acid and left there until it turns a dull gray-black color, after which one side is polished and the rear face of the regular rear sight is polished, both are tinned with solder and they are then sweated together.

Avoid the vee-shaped notch rear open sight, as they are useless for anything except the very coarsest work at close range, due to the shooter's inability to hold the front sight at the same elevation each time in this type of notch. The Palridge type sights are very poor for any shooting except paper target work, unless the light is very good, due to the trouble of holding the proper elevation against varying backgrounds. This can be corrected by setting in a piece of white celluloid on the rear face of the front sight at the top. See the chapter on making sights for directions on how to do this.

Special apertures for rear sights are easily made in the lathe from pieces of steel rod. The rod should be about the diameter you wish the eye-cup to be. The shank, to be threaded 7/32" x 40 threads per inch, is turned and threaded, with the lathe, upon one end. This end is then drilled out. while still in the lathe, to a larger size than the aperture, to within of the face of the eye-cup. A small drill, of the size the aperture is desired, is then used to drill the hole on through the face of the eye-cup. The piece is cut off and then held in the lathe chuck by the threaded shank while the eye-cup end is machined out. These aperture cups can be placed in nitric-acid and left there until the surface' is a gray-black, after which they arc re- moved from the acid, rinsed in running water and boiled for a few minutes in clean water to stop further action by the acid. If a deeper blue color is desired on them, they may then be heated to just under a red-heat, so that their color is a deep black. Hold them at this heat for a minute or more, then dip them in a light oil, such as gun oil, for about one second, lift them from the oil and hold them in the air for eight or ten seconds, then return them to the oil and allow them to cool in it.

The low-power telescope of three to five power makes an ideal sight for the small game .22 rifle and, thanks to a few of our progressive tele-scope sight makers, these scopes may be bought for less money than a high grade set of iron sights. If most of the small game shooting is to be open field work on chucks, prairie dogs or picket pins, the five power sight with medium fine cross-wires of .001" or a little less in diameter, will be the best choice. For squirrel shooting in tall hard- wood trees, the three power scope with a narrow flat-top post will be the best. The higher power scopes are only adapted to prone or rest shooting for target work or long distance work on small game in the open. Colonel Whelen s "Telescopic Rifle Sights" is an excellent guide in choosing the telescope and it should be well studied before making your first purchase.

The scope manufacturers supply directions for attaching the scopes to the rifle with each scope, but the directions sent with side-mounted scopes are not quite as complete as they could be. In the directions sent with scopes of internal adjustment for windage or elevation, or both, these directions tell you how to center the internal adjustments and state that with adjustments centered, as they are supposed to be when shipped from the factory, the mount with the scope in it is clamped on the side of the ride and the rifle is then bore-sighted upon some object 50 to 100 yards away. The rifle must be held in a vise or clamp of some kind while it is bore-sighted and then, without moving the position of the rifle, the mount is moved around on the rifle until the scope's aiming point coin- cides with the point upon which the rifle is bore-sighted. The clamps holding the mount upon the rifle are then drawn tight and the position of the screw-holes on the rifle are marked through the holes for these screws in the mount.

Finding something to bore-sight the rifle on while it is held in a vise or clamp is not always easy to do at a distance of 50 or more yards. Also the bore of the rifle is somewhat too large to do this bore-sighting with much accuracy. This work can be done better in the shop, at a distance of a few yards or feet.

If a smooth wall is not available a short distance from the bench vise, set up a smooth board, vertically, a few feet from the vise, and at about the height of the vise, tack a sheet of paper on the board and mark a cross, about 1" in length each way, upon the paper. Clamp the rifle in the vise, with padded jaws, train it upon the cross marked on the paper and level the rifle both ways with a small level. Make a cap that will just push over the muzzle of the rifle by hand, with no shake when it is in place. Make this cap with a hole in the outer end larger than the bore of the rifle. If you have a piece of tubing that will just push onto the muzzle end of the barrel, this will do as well as a made-up cap, as it doesn't matter how much larger than the bore of the rifle the hole in the cap is made. Across this hole in the cap stretch cross-wires and solder them in place. These wires can be any diameter up to about .005". Set the cap so that one wire is vertical and the other is horizontal, to match the cross on the paper. Adjust the rifle in the vise until the cross-wires on the cap coincide with those on the paper and keep the rifle leveled in the vise, both ways. When this adjustment is complete tighten the vise to hold the rifle in place.

The scope, within its mount, is now clamped on the side of the rifle and adjusted until it is apparently central over the bore. Measure the distance the center of the scope is above the center of the rifle bore and make a dot or a cross upon the paper this same distance above the first cross on the paper, keeping the two marks in line vertically. Then screw the elevation adjustment of the scope as far down as it will go and now look through the scope and move the mount the necessary distance to make the aiming point of the scope coincide with the second aiming point on the paper, after which the clamps holding the scope mount on the rifle are tightened up, both aiming points are again checked, and the position of the screw-holes for the mount arc marked on the rifle, according to the manufacturer's directions of how to mount the scope.

This same method is used to mount scopes on larger center-fire rifles but in this case it is best to drill the primer pocket out of an empty cartridge case and insert this case in the breech of the rifle to act as a rear aperture while bore-sighting the rifle.

The mounting of target scopes in target mounts with base blocks on the .22 rifles is a simple matter, as the mount manufacturer will supply base of the proper height for the rifle and it is only necessary to level up the rifle in a vise, or in vee-blocks upon a surface plate or sheet of plate-glass, and set the blocks on the barrel at the proper place so that the scope can be drawn back to the eye, and the proper distance apart. The blocks are then leveled and clamped to the barrel with machinist's parallel clamps so that they act as guides for the drill and tap, to tap the screw holes into the barrel for the base blocks. A #27 wire-gauge drill is first used to spot the holes, as this drill fits the holes in the blocks closely. The #31 wire-gauge drill is then used to drill the holes to depth to be tapped out for the screws. The main point where great care is necessary in this job is not to drill too deeply into the barrel.

Chapter 10 REVOLVER AND AUTO-MATIC PISTOL JOBS

Our American made pistols and revolvers usually do nut require much repair work if they are given any kind of intelligent care at all, but when a part does break a new part should be obtained from the factory, except in the case of minor parts easily filed out of tool-steel when the time element is important in making the repair.

New hand-guns often require adjustments, either to cure minor faults or to satisfy the owner as to shape of grips or trigger-pull. Revolver and pistol trigger- pulls are treated in the same manner as described for rifle or shotgun pulls. The exception is that hand-gun hammer or firing-pin notches are seldom, if ever, too deep so that they require pinning. Some owners foolishly grind down the front edge of the hammer above the full-cock notch in an effort to lighten or shorten the trigger-pull. This usually results in broken half- cock and safety notches and perhaps a broken sear point.

If the hammer cams back upon pulling the trigger when the hammer is in the full-cock notch, the shape of the notch, or sear point, or both, should be changed so that the hammer does not move while the trigger is being pulled. The only other trigger-pull adjustment necessary is the thorough polishing of contact surfaces of the full-cock notch and of the sear. This is done with the line carborundum and the white Arkansas hand stones. If the double-action pull of a revolver is too hard, examine all parts, including the cylinder ratchet and the hand which engages it, for burrs. These, when found, are polished off with the white Arkansas stone.

A dragging cylinder lock will also cause a heavy double-action pull. This is easily discovered by examining the surface of the cylinder between the locking notches, as scratches will show here if the lock drags. The remedy is to dress enough off the top of the lock with a small hand stone, so that it clears the cylinder.

The .22 revolvers sometimes tighten-up in the cylinder so that it becomes almost impossible to turn it. This may be caused by a high spot on the front end of the cylinder, so that a little fouling on this end of the cylinder and the rear end of the barrel will make the cylinder drag and sometimes stick completely. This is remedied by locating the high spot and filing it off with a fine flat pillar file. A second cause may be lead flakes from the bullets piling up between the top of the barrel extension and the top strap of the frame, until they build out far enough to press against the top edge of the cylinder. Remove the lead, point it out to the owner and tell him to keep that place clean. I also had one case, in a medium-priced .22 revolver, where the case heads of fired cartridges dragged on one spot on the breech face. Filing this high spot down corrected the trouble. In center-fire revolvers the recoil plate, through which the firing-pin strikes, sometimes becomes loose and dirt gets behind it and holds it forward, so that it drags on the head of the cases. To correct this, remove the plate and clean the hole and the plate itself thoroughly, after which either get a new plate or tin the edge of the old plate with solder and press or drive it back into place with a brass rod passed down the barrel from the muzzle.

Misfires in revolvers are often caused by the owner's misdirected efforts to lighten the trigger-pull by filing the main-spring thinner. A new main-spring will correct the fault. A badly worn firing-pin, shortened by much use, will cause misfires, so check its length. Where the firing-pin is separate from the hammer and is located in the frame, both the hole in the frame and the pin may become so worn that misfires occur. Fit a new pin, made oversize in the body so that it fits the enlarged hole more closely. Be careful not to fit it too closely, or a trifle of dirt may cause it to bind in the hole and make the gun misfire. In hammerless autoloading pistols where the firing-pin is driven for- ward with a coil-spring, misfires may occur from the weakening of this spring, caused by the gun being left at full-cock for long periods of time. The correction for this is a new spring or the stretching and retempering of the old spring.

Misfires may also be caused by shortening the hammer-fall too much in speeding-up the action, or by lightening the hammer too much. A new hammer is the best correction in either case.

If, when a revolver is slowly brought to full-cock by drawing back the hammer by hand, the cylinder can then be turned slightly by hand and you hear the cylinder lock click into place, it denotes wear on the cylinder ratchet or on the hand which turns the cylinder. This is not serious, unless it still occurs when the hammer is drawn back rapidly, as in natural use, in which case the hand must either be heated and drawn out slightly longer with a hammer and then re- hardened or it must be replaced with a new' one, so that the cylinder lines up properly with the barrel. A replacement hand is left a little longer than is necessary so that it will take up wear in the ratchet on the cylinder, so it usually has to be ground slightly to make it fit.

If, when the hammer is at full-cock and the cylinder lock is in place in its notch in the cylinder, the cylinder can be rotated a little back and forth by hand, either the lock or the notches in the cylinder are worn. A new lock will usually fit up closely and remedy the trouble. The notches for the lock, in the cylinder, should be cleaned out, as dirt in those notches will prevent the lock seating fully, so that it sometimes appears to be worn badly when it is not in bad enough shape to require replacement.

Some revolvers have too great a trigger movement to the rear after the hammer is released in firing. This is liable to allow the sights to wobble off the target. It may be corrected by tapping a hole through the rear of the guard for a small headless screw, that is screwed in flush and is long enough so that its point stops further travel of the trigger after the hammer is re- leased. A #3 x 56 thread screw is a good size to use at this point.

Owners of the single-action Colt revolver often want the hammer spur lowered, or both lowered and widened. To lower the spur, remove the hammer from the action and place it between vise jaws sheathed with copper, then draw the vise up tightly on the hammer with only the spur showing above the jaws of the vise. Heat the spur with the acetylene torch until it is red-hot, then place a brass or copper rod upon the spur and bend it down. If necessary, tap the rod with a hammer to bend it. After the spur has cooled, the checking may be repaired with a three-square needle file if it has been damaged, and if the hammer has bulged a little where the spur joins the body dress this off with a file.

If the owner of the single-action wants a Bisley-type hammer spur, remove the firing-pin from the hammer, heat the spur to soften it and then cut it off, or else grind it off while still hardened. A piece of steel for the new, wide, low* spur is then welded onto the hammer and ground and filed to shape. The spur is checked with a three-square needle file and the hammer is then case-hardened.

The type of sights for a target revolver or pistol do not matter, just so they suit the owner but sights on the ordinary hand-gun are sometimes a poor type for use in hunting, either due to poor visibility against certain backgrounds or due to the fact that they are not well adapted for holster use. As a usual thing, the gold bead sights are better adapted for hand-guns carried in a holster than are the ivory bead type, be- cause of the greater strength of the gold bead and also due to the fact that it does not absorb oil. The shape of the gold bead sights however, is no better than that of the ivories when it comes to getting a gun out of a holster quickly. The fully-rounded steel front sights supplied on revolvers and pistols other than the target guns comes out of a holster the easiest but they soon wear shiny so that there is a glare when the light strikes them. The Lyman Gunsight Corp. makes a rifle sight with dovetail base, called a semi-jack sight, which is rounded like a steel revolver sight mentioned but on the rear side there is a notch cut and in this notch a hole is drilled from the top down toward the bottom but sloping back at an angle to the vertical. In this hole they set a small shaft of ivory, so that the rounded side of the shaft is to the rear and the ivory stands up above the bottom of the notch to the top of the rounded blade. While this sight itself is not adapted to revolvers or pistols, the principle used can be applied and the same type of sight made out of the rounded steel sight supplied on revolvers and pistols. To the man who prefers ivory sights this shows up well, although red may be used in place of white, and the sight is well protected from breakage and the rounded top prevents it' from catching on the holster.

A rather long, high ramp, with just the bead of the sight appearing above the top of the ramp, is better than the type of sights usually furnished, which stick up like a lighthouse on a rock, to be caught in the holster when the gun is drawn. Ribs for revolvers and pistols are becoming popular of late years and these are even better looking than ramps, but have the rib run-up in height to just below the sight bead, to prevent that bead digging its way in the holster and catching there.

The wide steel front sights may be slotted with a y$ 2 " thick slitting saw, filed down in height, and fitted with any standard blade-type bead sight by thinning down the blade below the bead, setting it in the slot and using a flush pin through both the old sight and the blade of the head to hold it in place.

It is hard to do much with rear sights except to keep them as low as possible, so that the front sight may be low on the barrel. The shape of the notch may be changed by cutting out a vee-notch to a round or square shape or sweating a thin piece of steel to the back of a square-notch type to change it to the round-notch type, to match a bead front sight. The sharp vee-notch is almost worthless under most light conditions. Peep sights on hand-guns are not much good in calibers larger than .22, as to be of any use the peep must be held fairly close to the eye and this may result in a bruised eye with large-caliber guns.

Most of the troubles of autoloading pistols, such as jams or failure to load while firing, are caused by the ammunition lacking power, with the exception that jams are sometimes caused by the weakening of the magazine spring, brought about by leaving the magazine fully loaded and thereby compressing the magazine spring over long periods of time. A new magazine spring will remedy the trouble.

Autoloading pistols have extraction troubles at times caused, in the .22 caliber, by wear of the extractor hook or by an excessive amount of grease or dirt on the breech face. A new extractor corrects the wear and cleaning the breech face regularly prevents the dirt and grease accumulating there. Barrels should be cleaned regularly or the chamber may corrode, causing cases to stick so that the extractor pulls over the rim.

The larger autoloading hand-guns sometimes get to throwing the fired cases back in the shooter's face. A new extractor is the best way to correct this trouble, but stoning the hook on a slight bevel at the end will sometimes fix it, as this will cause the case to release quicker at the top, but it may be overdone so that the hook releases the case too quickly, so be careful.

The Luger autoloading pistol is a hand-gun that seems to be misunderstood in this country from the way it has been panned by various writers in sporting magazines. The truth of the matter is that it is a very superior type of pistol, with the best designed grip that has ever been placed on any hand-gun. You may think this matter of grip-shape is my own opinion, if so you are correct, it is, but this opinion has been confirmed for the past twenty years by seeing any number of men who have never fired one before pick up these Lugers and have no trouble hitting an object at a reasonable distance. Out here, these Lugers are a favorite gun with men in the hills and they use them to kill deer, elk, sheep, goat and antelope with. The 7.65 m/m or .30 caliber is the preferred size.

There is only one brand of ammunition loaded in this country that has been consistently successful in the Luger pistol and that is the Winchester ammunition. The only reason for this is that it is loaded to sufficient breech pressure, which for the Luger is a minimum of 25,000 pounds per square inch. Nearly all malfunctions with the Luger can be traced to am- munition of insufficient power.

The Luger carbine, which is the standard Luger pistol action with a weaker action spring and a 12" barrel, handles regularly the German black cartridge which, according to Kings Powder Company of Kings Mills, Ohio, gives a velocity of 2,030 foot seconds in the 12" barrel and a breech pressure of 40,000 to 50,- 000 pounds per square inch. This test was run for R. W. Goodman of Boise, Idaho, who has used this load in these carbines since 1923 to kill big game. Mr. Goodman holds his Luger in both hands but does not use a shoulder stock.

These Luger actions of the best type which perform so well are the

DWM actions with the coil action spring. The initials DWM appear in a monogram on top of the action. These actions made since the war are well fitted and are of excellent material, well hardened. Trust no other Luger actions than these or those put out lately by the Mauser works and stamped Mauser on top of the action. Mauser bought the Luger outfit a few years ago.

These DWM actions were sometimes sold to other manufacturers who made up the barrels for them, so examine Lugers to be used with high-power loads to see that the extractor cut in the top of the barrel does not extend forward of the end of the extractor farther than is necessary to give it clearance, or a case may blow out at this point, either breaking the extractor or breaking it out of the top of the breech-block which makes a new' breech-block necessary.

Various ammunition manufacturers seem to use different head- space standards in making Luger ammunition, caused, I expect, by getting hold of barrels chambered by various companies, but I have seen Lugers handle ammunition giving excessive head-space measurements up to .015" which apparently caused no trouble, still it is better to find one ammunition for your Luger that fits it well and use only that.

The Luger is not a blow-back action in which the breech-block is held against the breech of the barrel only by a recoil spring. When the Luger action is closed, the pins in the links are in a straight line, locking the breech to the barrel. Upon firing, the barrel and receiver complete with the breech-block and links all recoil together, still locked, until the finger pieces, by which you open the action by hand, strike against the slope of the ramp at the rear of the frame, which breaks the straight line of the link joints. At the same time the lug on the under side of the receiver strikes its stop in the frame at the front end, stopping further movement to the rear of the barrel and receiver. After the straight line of the link joints is broken and the receiver slopped, the breech-block continues its movement to the rear, due to the energy stored in it by its first travel to the rear with the receiver, opening the breech and extracting the fired cartridge. There is no remaining pressure in the barrel at all when the breech opens. You may prove this by firing the gun with the extractor removed from it. When the breech opens the fired case remains in the chamber, although it may be picked out easily with the finger nail or shaken out of the chamber. The recoil spring, running down inside the butt behind the magazine, returns the breech-block to its forward position, picking up a new cartridge from the magazine on the way forward.

These recoil springs are balanced with the barrel weight, the long heavy barrels having the lightest spring and the short light barrels the heaviest spring. In changing to barrels of different length, the action should be carefully checked for correct working after- wards. as the long spring in connection with a long heavy barrel does not work well, often failing to allow the action to open far enough to pick a new cartridge from the magazine. If the short spring designed for the long barrels is used with a short barrel, the recoil of the action will be too violent, often picking a new cartridge from the magazine and throwing it entirely out of the gun, or the violent recoil action may cause the link between the rear action link and the recoil spring to unhook from the recoil spring.

The Luger action is easily dismounted for cleaning, or for barrel inspection, with the fingers only. These actions should be kept very well oiled with a good light- bodied gun oil, except in the coldest weather, when Gunslick or some like lubricant should be well worked into the slides of the action and then all excess thoroughly wiped off.

Lugers are easily made into single-shot .22 rim-fire pistols by substi- tuting a .22 barrel, chambered for the short or long-rifle cartridge, for the regular Luger barrel. The center-fire firing-pin can be cut off flush with the face of the breech-block and the body of the pin drilled at one side for the insertion of a new firing-pin nose and the breech-block drilled for the new nose. Both the firing-pin and the breech-block are hardened and must be annealed by bringing them to a red-heat and burying them in slaked lime to cool, which will leave them soft so that they can be drilled. They are afterwards rehardened and the breech-block reblued. An extension is welded onto the nose of the extractor, so that the fired .22 case may be extracted.

I have had a hunch for some time that the Luger could be made to operate on the autoloading principle with the .22 long-rifle cartridge of the high-speed variety, using a recoil spring balanced to handle it, but I have never had the time to experiment with it. The magazine could be narrowed inside with pieces soldered in at each side and the cartridge platform narrowed down. A new magazine spring might have to be made.

Some time ago I made up a special .22 Hi-Power Luger for Mr. Good- man of Boise. I obtained a .22 six-groove target barrel from W. A. Sukalle, barrel maker of Phoenix, Arizona, and made from this an 8" barrel, chambered with a special chambering reamer for the Luger cartridge necked down to .22 caliber. I used the Remington 45 grain Hornet bullet and put in the cartridge case 9. grains of #1204 Dupont powder, all the case would hold and allow the bullet to be seated to a 'depth so that the cartridges would work through the magazine. The magazine spring was cut off a very little at a time until it balanced the action. This gun has a rather sharp report but excellent ac- curacy, giving 1J4" ten-shot groups at 50 yards, when fired by Mr. Goodman, holding the gun in both hands but without rest. We have never tested this load on a chronograph for velocity yet it shows much higher speed than the heaviest pistol load of 7.65 m/m caliber in an 8" barrel but less speed than the black, carbine cartridge gives in a 12" barrel, so we estimated it at between 1700 and 1800 foot-seconds velocity. Mr. Goodman has made many excellent kills on our small chucks at over 100 yards with this .22 Luger.

The Luger is subject to the same troubles as other autoloading hand- guns in regard to damaged lips on the magazine causing the gun to fail to load, so examine these periodically to see that they do not become bent or broken. Also from time to time, if the gun is left with the magazine loaded for long periods, a new magazine spring will be necessary, as this weakens the spring. The recoil springs will stand a great deal of use but will weaken in time and will need to be re- placed. This Luger action will not handle as much dirt as some of the looser-fitted actions, so keep it well cleaned and above all do not fail to keep it well lubri cated, for the closely fitting parts will develop a roughness, causing the action to bind if you do not keep it well oiled. Another point is to be careful about getting the receiver arms bent while the gun is taken apart, for if these arms are too close together they will bind on the breech-block, and if too far apart they will bind on the inside of the frame at the rear.

I have heard many complaints about the trigger-pull of the Luger pistol, but a Luger trigger-pull can be made very smooth, with a sharp let-off. This is merely a case of stoning the notch in the side of the firing-pin and the end of the sear until the proper smoothness is obtained. In some Lugers the engagement of the sear is too deep in its notch and this may be corrected by grinding down the back of the notch, as it would be done in any gun. There is a take-up in the Luger trigger action that is objected to by many shooters but this may be largely eliminated by a screw through the frame bearing against the front extension of the trigger, so that much of this take-up is taken out of the trigger action. Mr. Goodman (who, by the way, has more than twenty Lugers) welded Haynes Stellite into the notch in the firing-pins of some of his favorite long- barreled Lugers and then cut the trigger-pull down very fine, so that it is as good as any high-grade target pistol with plain trigger. This Stellite is obtained from the Haynes Stellite Co. of Kokomo, Indiana.

The 6" and 8" barrels are the best length to use on the Luger .30 pistol, the 8" barrels giving almost 1500 foot seconds velocity with the latest-type pistol am- munition. Paul Jaeger of 4655 Fernhill Road,

Philadelphia, Pennsylvania, supplies good 8" Luger barrels at a price of about $15.00 each.

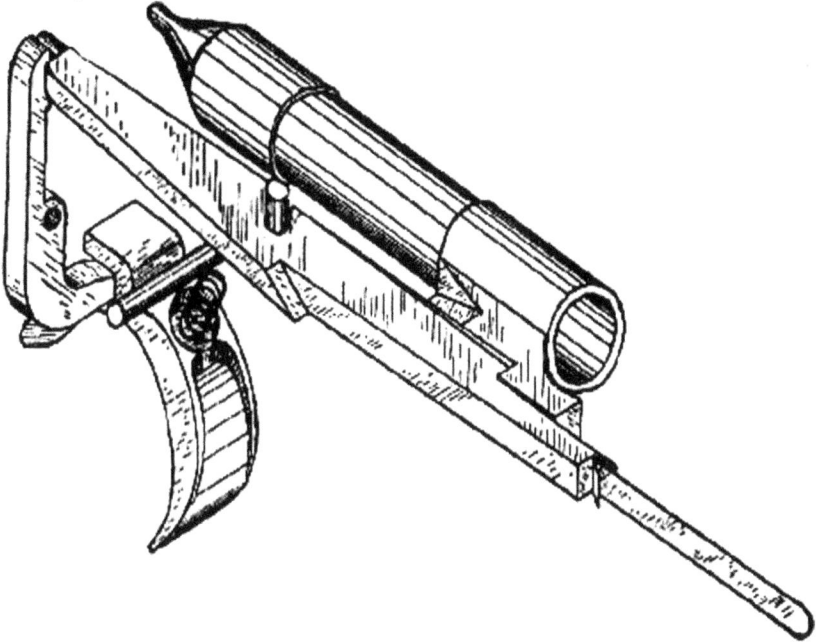

Luger trigger mechanism, with sear and firing-pin.

The Colt .22 Woodsman pistol is also in a class by itself and deserves some special mention. The accuracy of its barrel is very good, the only complaint being their light weight, which has been somewhat corrected in the new model released in August, 1938. This how- ever does not help the older models as the new barrel, due to its shape at the rear, does not fit up to the older frames. For the older models a heavy barrel, slabbed off slightly on the sides to frame width, as has been done with the new Hi-Standard heavy-barrel pistols, will give the necessary weight, as the barrel can be made as heavy as the width of the frame, at the front, from top to bottom. King of San Francisco makes ventilated ribs for the Woodsman barrel which will also increase the barrel weight.

The trigger-pull on the Woodsman may be stoned down to a low-weight pull with safety, provided the shape of the notch in the hammer and of the sear nose is not changed. This means the use of a good mag-nifying glass to align the hammer and the sear between two pieces of square-edged steel, in the vise, with the surfaces of the steel pieces. Use a straight edge and the magnifying glass in making this set-up and be sure the surface of the notch or sear nose being stoned is parallel to the top surfaces of the steel pieces and not inclined at an angle. Usually these hammer and sear nose contact surfaces are good enough as they come from the factory, so that a hard white Arkansas stone is all that need be used, but if one is out of square or extremely rough the work may be started with a fine carborundum stone, then completed with the white Arkansas stone.

The older model Woodsman has one serious fault in the trigger-pull and that is the excessive travel of the trigger to the rear after the sear is withdrawn from the hammer notch. This can be corrected with a small screw set into the trigger guard, or rather into the frame, in the rear of the trigger and so adjusted for length that it stops all travel of the trigger after the sear is released from the hammer notch. This one thing will make a great improvement in the scores you can make with the Woodsman.

Watch the face of the breech-block and the rear end of the barrel for grease and dirt in the Woodsman, as they may cause misfires or hang-fires, due to cushioning the firing-pin blow.

Also keep dirt cleaned from the extractor, for while the Woodsman is a blow-back action and will usually extract fired cases, even with no extractor on the gun, the fired case may be dropped into the action instead of clearing the gun entirely ii too much dirt gets under the hook of the extractor. Extractor points will wear with use and while they may be sharpened slightly and given more hook as they wear, by using a fine Swiss type three-square file, yet these extractors will need replacement from time to time as they are not always good for the life of the pistol.

Greased or wax-coated ammunition, never the dry type, is what should be used in these pistols and regard- less of what the manufacturer may say, clean your barrels, for lead will accumulate in the barrel and dirt in the chamber. This dirt in the chamber can very easily absorb moisture and cause a light rusting of the chamber which, while not always visible to the eye, will lead to extraction troubles.

The Woodsman, just as other autoloading pistols, is prone to magazine troubles caused by bending of the thin lips at the top of the magazine. Cartridges should never be forced into the magazine. If they do not enter easily you are either trying to force the head of the cartridge into the magazine at the wrong point or else the lips of the magazine are bent out of shape.

While this Colt .22 autoloading pistol is called "The Woodsman" its sighting equipment does not live up to its name. Worse sights with which to equip a woods- man's hand-gun do not exist than those which are usually found on these pistols in the average dealer's stock. It is true that bead sights are optional, but most of the pistols are equipped with the Patridge sight, which is an excellent target sight, as has been proven many times. The bead sights supplied however are not much better than the Patridge sights for the average plinker's and woodsman's use. A colored-bead front sight should be chosen for these purposes, either a gold, ivory or red bead. King makes an excellent set of sights for the outdoorsman's use, a rear sight with U-notch outlined in white and a red-bead front sight. He also supplies these sets of sights with the square rear-notch outlined in white and a square post-type front sight, in various widths, in red, white or gold to match it, a-la-Patridge style, which will suit the target shooter, who is used to this shape sights, for outdoors use against various backgrounds where the Patridgc- type iron sights in the black fail to register well.

One other complaint against the old-model Woods- man pistol is the short grip, which climbs badly in a large hand. There are several different custom made stocks available for this pistol, Walter Roper's being the most noteworthy, as they are fitted individually to the user's hand. Anyone can make grips for himself, fitted to his hand, by dipping the present oiled walnut grips, after removing them from the pistol, into boiling lye-water for a few minutes to remove the oil, then drying them out thoroughly, after which they are re- placed on the pistol and coated with plastic wood. While this plastic wood is still in the plastic shape, grip the gun naturally and squeeze it hard in the hand to impress your finger imprints into the plastic wood. Before gripping the plastic wood in your hand, give the hand a coating of light machine oil to prevent the plastic wood from sticking to your skin. The plastic wood may be made more plastic, and also tougher and more crack-proof, if some duPont cement is worked into it before it is placed upon the grips. After it has dried the excess plastic wood may be carved off with a sharp knife or cut away with a file and made a slightly better fit to the hand at all points.

If you wish to lengthen the grip on one side or the other, depending upon whether you are right or left- handed, the wood grip on that side may be replaccd by a longer slab of wood, extending below the bottom of the grip, before the plastic wood is put onto the grips.

Some people do not like the looks of plastic wood and in this case a new set of grips may be carved out of wood, using the plastic wood-coated grips for a model. If you like metal grips, the plastic wood grips may be shellacked and, after they arc dry, can be pressed into a plaster of Faris mold, then this mold can be used to cast metal grips of aluminum, or bronze.

Another hand-gun deserving special mention is the Colt Single-Action Army, more commonly known as the Colt .45 Single-Action, as this is the caliber in which it has been most widely used. In the West it is best known of any revolver or pistol that has ever been made. This action has its weaknesses, yet it has survived many actions designed and built since its inception that are now almost forgotten. While it could never be called a thing of beauty, it has a hang and fit that has always found favor with men who use it for an everyday tool. One reason for this is the shape and placement of its grip for holster use, for it is almost the only gun that can be rapidly drawn from the holster with the hand on the grip at the proper place.

The grips themselves, of hard rubber, are one of the poorest types to use on a gun but they may be easily replaced with wooden grips, carved from walnut or other woods to suit the user's fancy. Due to the construction of the frame where the grips are attached, the grips may be carved from one piece of wood and held in place by the frame parts themselves, doing away with the screw from side-to-side through the grips. Colt supplies fancy grips of carved ivory or pearl and other firms supply grips of so-called stag, which is horn with grooves burned into it to roughen and beautify it.

In the large calibers, this gun gives some trouble from the loosening of the frame screws. These screws may be locked so that they cannot loosen by using a small lock-screw engaging a groove cut on an arc in the head of each frame screw, as has been done to lock some of the screws in the Remington autoloading shotgun. Another method that will keep these frame screws tight is to heat them to a low red-heat and then put them in place, screwing them up tightly, while still hot. When the screws cool they will shrink and draw very tightly on the threads. It will often be necessary to heat screws to remove them if they have been put in by this method; the heating for removal being done with a fine torch flame.

Action parts in the single-action are not of the best design for long life, and the breakage runs high. The sear and bolt spring is the worst offender, it is closely followed in this tendency to break by the bolt itself which has two thin, spring-tempered legs. The hand spring breaks fairly often and the hand itself is subject to a good deal of wear, due to the deep notches of the cylinder ratchet. The sear nose, which is part of the trigger, is pretty light and often breaks, especially if someone grinds down the front of the full-cock notch in the hammer to shorten the trigger-pull, as this often results in the half-cock notch landing on the sear nose with a crash when the trigger is pulled.

The hammer is quite heavy and has a long fall, which is not the best combination for accuracy, but little can be done about it as the hammer is of such shape that it is not safe to alter it by weight removal in the upper part, for fear of weakening it. Due to the fact that the hand which turns the cylinder is attached to the hammer, the hammer travel cannot be shortened except for slow-fire use. To do this the full- cock notch is ground entirely out and a new notch cut between its location and the half-cock notch and a heavier main-spring is fitted, although this is not al- ways necessary. When cocking a gun altered in this manner, the hammer must be drawn fully to the rear to revolve the cylinder and is then allowed to go for- ward to the new full-cock notch after drawing it clear to the rear to turn the cylinder. Due to the fact that the hammer operates the hand which turns the cylinder, this is the only revolver which can be fanned by holding the trigger back and striking the hammer spur with the other hand than that in which the gun is held, thus driving the hammer back, turning the cylinder and al- lowing the hand to slip on back past the hammer, which allows the hammer to go forward and fire the cartridge. All the other revolvers have the hand for turning the cylinder attached to the trigger, so if the trigger is held back the cylinder will not turn and the gun cannot be fanned except for one shot.

The base pin and the base pin bushing should be re- moved from time to time and thoroughly cleaned and oiled, as should the seat tor the base pin bushing in the cylinder, for these parts have a tendency to rust tight if this is not done.

The solid frame of this single-action gives it slightly greater strength than the frames of revolvers with a swing-out cylinder, so there is less chance of springing it in removing or inserting barrels, but as the strength of a revolver in regard to the loads it will handle lies in the cylinder, rather than in the frame, this solid- frame does not mean that it can handle cartridges with a heavier load than can the New Service model.

The sights are non-adjustable, but this matters little as it is not a target gun. However, adjustable sights can be fitted, as the rear of the frame where the top strap joins it is heavy enough to be slotted for a rear sight, adjustable from side to side for windage. The slot and the dovetail base of the sight should have parallel sides, so that the sight can he moved and a headless set-screw, set into the base of the sight, so that it bears on the. bottom of the slot, can be used to lock the sight in position. The front sight can be removed and a band with a slotted block on top can be fitted to the barrel at the muzzle and the Colt Woodsman elevating front sight can be fitted into the slotted block to give elevation.

Due to the travel of the trigger to the rear, after the hammer is released from the sear, the gun is liable to wobble off of the target, but a small screw fitted into the rear of the trigger guard can be adjusted to stop this excessive travel.

This is the easiest revolver to alter to .22 caliber, rim-fire, by fitting a .22 caliber barrel and bushing the cylinder chambers, for ejection is handled individually for each chamber by the ejector rod beneath the barrel instead of simultaneous ejection by lifting out a section of the cylinder, as is done in other revolvers. The bushings to reduce the cylinder chambers to .22 rim- fire caliber should be of tool-steel, hardened and temper-drawn at purple color. They should be a press fit into the cylinder chambers, allowing .001" for this press fit. They need not be soldered in place if this is properly done. If they ever loosen up in use, a small hole can be drilled through the side of the cylinder, beyond the chamber, at right-angles to the bushing and a threaded pin screwed tightly in and finished off flush on the outside.

A new recoil plate with the firing-pin hole in a different location to line up with the rim of the .22 rim- fire cartridge must be made. Make this plate of tool- steel and harden it and draw the temper at purple color. A new firing-pin, with the nose in the proper location to line-up with the hole in the recoil plate, must be made and fitted to the hammer. This firing- pin should be of tool-steel, hardened, and tempered at deep blue color. Make the nose of this pin the correct shape for use on the rim-fire case, not the shape of the old center-fire pin for this single-action.

The cylinder is unduly long for the .22 rim-fire cartridge, so if you wish it, this cylinder may be cut off at the front end just long enough to handle the .22 rim- fire cartridge that you use, either short or long-rifle. The cutting off of the cylinder makes a new base pin bushing necessary, one with a longer shoulder on it, to bear against the new front of the cut-off cylinder. The barrel is carried back through the frame far enough to meet the front of the shortened cylinder, with .002" to .003" clearance between the end of the barrel and the cylinder. Examine the rear end of a factory .22 revolver barrel and taper the edge of the lands at the rear of your barrel in the same manner. You will note that this taper is rather short, and tapers out to just slightly greater diameter than the groove diameter of the barrel. The finish of this taper should be very smooth, or the barrel will lead badly and accuracy will suffer.

Chapter 11   CLEANING , CLEARING AND LAPPING BARRELS

A neglected barrel will often rust, due to climatic conditions or rust will sometimes appear in a barrel in which rustless primers of various makes have been used, as different chemicals are often used by different companies making primers and the combination of some of these chemicals allow rusting to start.

The first treatment for rust is to use a good bronze brush, such as the Parker type, and if the rust has not been in the barrel for a very long time this will remove it. After using the brush, no matter how good the barrel looks, a good rust remover such as the Win- chester Rust Remover should be used on a tight patch and the barrel given a good polishing. Be sure to use a full-size steel rod so there is no danger of the rod buckling and rubbing the bore. Clean the bore well with dry patches, then follow these with a few dipped in white gasoline and then another dry one. After this apply a good antirust oil to the bore, wipe it out again the following day with dry patches and apply another coat of antirust oil or grease.

If the rust is too heavy to be removed with a bronze brush, use one of the one-way steel barrel-scourer brushes, being careful not to let it run out of the muzzle, and scour the barrel forward and back until this removes all the rust it will take out. This should be followed by the rust remover or opticians' polishing rouge on tight patches. The rouge is a dry powder and should be mixed with a light oil to form a paste. A leather or heavy felt lap may be used instead of the tight patch if the rust appears stubborn.

A last resort to remove rust is to dip a patch in muriatic acid and swab the bore with this. This is only to be used in extreme cases and the barrel must afterwards be cleaned with boiling water and then lapped with the polishing compound on a leather or hard felt lap until the bore is well polished.

If the barrel is pitted, there is nothing that can be done with the pits. Their effect can be somewhat minimized by lapping the bore with a leather lap dipped in #90 emery mixed with a light oil.

As bullets jacketed with cupro-nickel are no longer in use in this country, you do not often encounter this type of fouling in a barrel, but as copper-jacketed bullets driven at extreme velocities will often deposit lumpy metal-fouling in the bore and this fouling can be removed with the same solution as that used to remove cupro-nickel fouling, the formula is given here with instructions for use.

Ammonium Persulphate 1/2 ounce

Ammonium carbonate 100 grains

Stronger ammonia (28%) 3 ounces

Distilled water 2 ounces

The first two ingredients are powdered together in a mortar, as they are dry, and the second two are added and all stirred together until the powder is dissolved. The same solution should not be used more than once and it is not practical to keep it more than a few days at a time, as it loses strength.

To use this solution in a barrel to remove lumpy metal-fouling, push a rubber cork tightly into the breech, put a piece of rubber tubing a few inches long over the muzzle and, with the rifle standing upright, place a funnel in the upper end of the rubber tube and pour the solution into the barrel, pouring in enough so that it rises half an inch or more above the muzzle in the rubber tube, for steel surfaces wet with this solution and exposed to the air will rust rapidly.

Plate XV

Removing a cartridge case with head blown off from rifle chamber, using a broken-screw extractor.

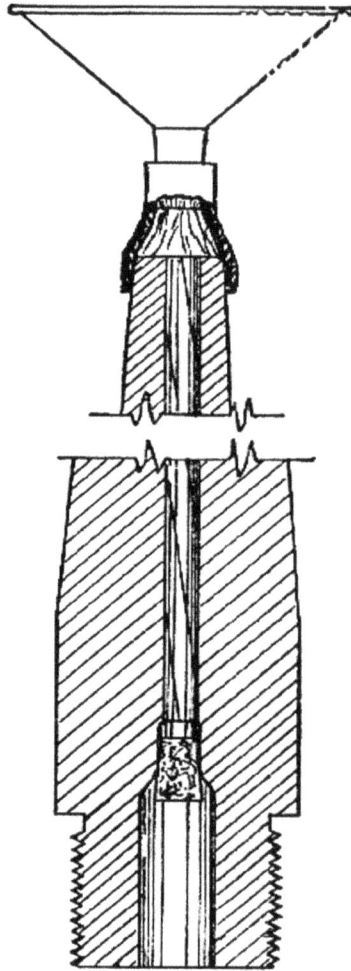

Method of plugging breech of rifle with rubber cork and connecting funnel to muzzle with rubber tube, in order to use the chemical solution for removing metal fouling from a barrel.

Allow the solution to remain in the barrel from twenty to thirty minutes, no longer, then turn the rifle muzzle-down and allow the solution to run out. Keep the rifle in the muzzle-down position , remove the rubber tube and insert a steel rod in the barrel from the muzzle end, which is still in the inverted position, and push out the rubber cork from the breech. Have some boiling water at hand and a clean funnel with a short piece of clean rubber tube upon it and, inserting the rubber tube in the breech of the rifle, run a gallon or more of hot water through the bore to wash out the solution. Dry the bore with clean patches and inspect it to see that all fouling has been removed. If any fouling remains, cork up the breech again and, using the rubber tube and funnel on the muzzle, put another dose of the solution into the bore and clean as before.

The modern jacketed bullet with copper or gilding- metal jacket leaves a copper wash, quite thin, in the rifle bore. If it is desired to clean this out, swab the bore with patches dipped in 28% ammonia or put the ammonia in a small can and, placing the muzzle of the rifle in the ammonia, use a tight patch on a steel rod run into the bore from the breech to pump the ammonia up and down in the barrel. In doing this, don't let the patch come out into the chamber or some of the ammonia may get into the action of the rifle and cause some rust. Follow this ammonia cleaning with hot water to wash the bore thoroughly, then dry it well and apply a good grease or gun oil.

Modern powders and primers do not leave any foul- ing in the bore that cannot be removed with plain boiling water, but a brass or good stiff bristle brush will hasten the cleaning process. Where hot water is not available a good nitro-solvent oil can be used.

Lead can be removed from a rifle barrel by corking up one end and pouring liquid mercury into the barrel, after which the opposite end is corked and the barrel tilted back and forth by hand until the mercury and lead amalgamate, when it can be poured from the barrel. This can be hastened if the barrel is first well scrubbed with a heavy bronze brush, to remove an)' lead that can be loosened this way. After the mercury has removed the visible lead fouling from the barrel, the barrel can be swabbed with patches well greased with mercurial ointment (blue ointment) readily obtained at any drug store. Follow this with patches or bristle brush dipped in gun oil. If liquid mercury cannot be obtained easily, the job can be done with the mercurial ointment and a good bronze or mild steel brush, although it takes plenty of scrubbing.

Mercurial ointment on a good brass shotgun brush is very effective for removing lead from cone and choke of shotgun barrels.

If a bullet core separates from the jacket and leaves the jacket in the bore, it can usually be removed with a square-ended, steel rod that is a very close fit to the bore. The rod should not be more than .005" below bore diameter. If this fails to remove the jacket, due to the jacket being welded into the grooves, the barrel must be plugged with a rubber cork at the breech, the rubber tube and funnel placed over the muzzle and the solution for the removal of lumpy metal-fouling used to dissolve the jacket.

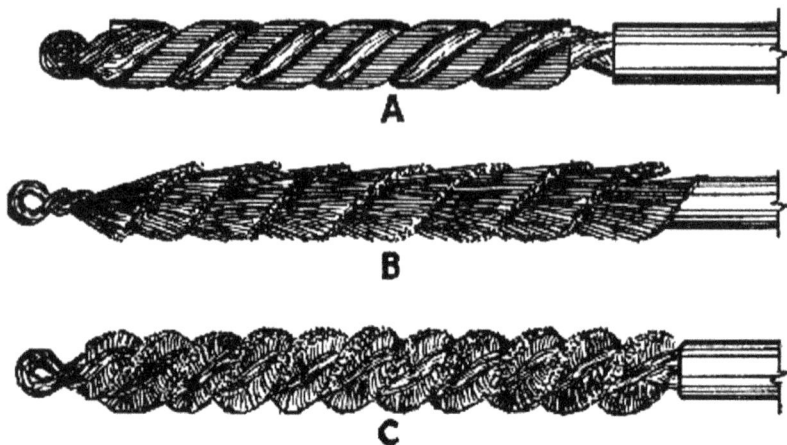

The Parker brushes for rifle barrels. A is the leather buffing brush for polishing of barrels. B is the drooped steel wire barrel scourer necessary for a thorough cleaning or a mild case of leading and C is the generally-used bronze or steel wire brush.

Sticks will sometimes be found lodged pretty tightly in a rifle barrel and these can be driven out with the flat-ended steel rod of close to bore-size dimensions.

Sometimes a bullet becomes stuck in the bore and such can be removed with a rod of steel that fits the bore closely. Never use a rod of much smaller diameter than the bore , as it will drive into the bullet, spreading it and giving a wedging effect. The bore should be oiled with a thin oil in end out of which the bullet is to be driven. Always drive the bullet out of the end of the barrel to which it is closest. When the rod is to be placed against the base of the bullet to drive it out, use a flat-ended rod. Use a rod with a flat end also when the rod is to be placed against the nose of a round-nose bullet to be driven out base first, but I have found that when a pointed-nose bullet is to be driven out base first, a hole drilled in the end of the rod about 1/8" in diameter prevents slugging the point of the bullet and adding to the friction. A fairly heavy hammer should be used in driving bullets out of the bore, for a light hammer, or light taps with a heavy one, will wedge the bullet tighter instead of starting it down the bore, so use a hammer of two pounds' weight or more and strike a good blow on the driving- rod to start the bullet.

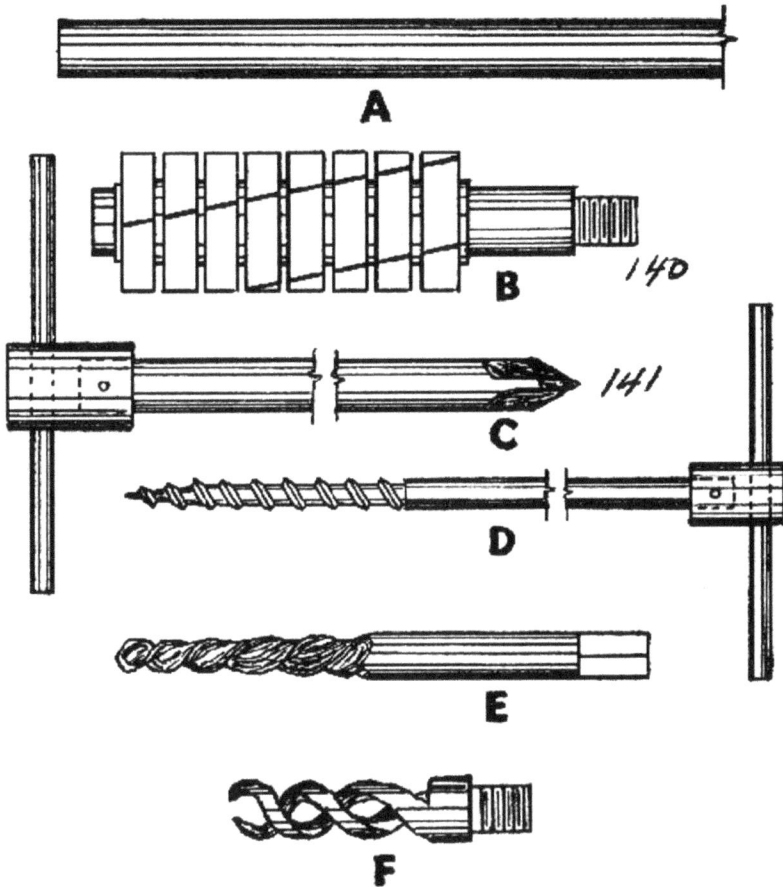

Barrel clearing appliances. A is the type of heavy, flat-ended rod necessary to drive an obstruction from a rifle bore. B is a Parker type
shotgun bore polisher, made of leather washers with spacers between.
This same type may be made up for use in rifle bores. C is a special
type of short flute, three fluted drill for drilling lead bullets from a
barrel. Its shaft should be practically full bore size. D is a wood
screw, brazed to a steel shank, with cross handle on end so it can be
screwed into pieces of cloth patches, etc., which may be lodged in the
bore. E is the Cleveland broken screw extractor, a splendid item to
use in removing cartridge cases which become stuck in rifle chambers
or sizing dies. F is the conventional shotgun worm, made of steel,
for use in picking out stuck cloth patches, etc.

If a cloth patch or a twist of cotton or tow is stuck in the barrel, oil
the bore well from both ends with a good penetrating oil and allow it
to stand for an hour or more. Using a steel rod with a flat end of nearly
bore size, try to drive the obstruction in one direction with a heavy blow
on the rod, using a heavy hammer. If it fails to move, try driving it from

the opposite end. If it still will not move after two or three attempts in each direction, braze or weld a sharp, long-pointed wood-screw onto a steel rod, making sure that the screw is true and central with the rod, and pick the obstruction out, a piece at a time, by twisting the screw into the material and then pulling on the rod, repeating until the obstruction is all picked out.

If a rag or cloth patch is stuck in a shotgun bore, oil it well with penetrating oil, allowing it to soak two or three hours, then heat the barrel slightly at the point where the obstruction is located, but do not heat it enough to make it change color if it is a single- barrel without rib. If the gun is a double-barrel or a single-barrel with rib, pour boiling water upon it w-here the rag is located. When the barrel is well warmed, use a wooden dowel-rod, close to bore size, and try to push the obstruction out. If it will not push, try tapping it a few light blows to start it. Do not use heavy blow's on an obstruction in a shotgun bore or you may bulge the barrel. If the dowel-rod will not push the obstruction out, it must be picked to pieces with a wood-screw on a rod or with a regular barrel-wormer. Never try to shoot an obstruction out of any gun barrel, either rifle, pistol, revolver or shotgun barrel or you may have a burst barrel.

If the neck breaks off of a cartridge case and lodges part-way up a rifle barrel, it can be removed with the square-ended steel rod of very nearly bore diameter.

A cartridge case lodged in the chamber of a rifle with the head broken from the case can usually be easily removed with a Cleveland broken-screw ex- tractor. Numbers 4 and 5 will cover all cartridge sizes up to the Magnum .300. They are more effective than the regular broken shell extractors, as the twist you can give a broken case with these tools will nearly always loosen it readily. I have removed .30'06 cases, with the heads broken off, from a full-length resizing die by placing the die in a vise and giving a twist and a pull on the #5 broken-screw extractor, using only a 6" pair of combination pliers as a handle.

If the broken -screw extractor fails to remove a broken case from the chamber, clean the inside of the case so it is bright, then push a small cork up to the neck of the case from the rear end and run some very hot solder into the case. Have a well-tinned, steel rod ready and place this in the solder inside the case before the solder can cool, after it is cool the case can either be pulled from the chamber or a heavy steel rod placed in the bore from the muzzle will drive the broken case out.

Scored, grooved or badly-rusted rifle chambers will sometimes defy all types of pullers in attempting to remove a broken case and when this happens the only thing to do is to remove the barrel from the action and, using small chisels, cut the broken case out of the chamber. On a job of this kind a strong steel scriber can often be driven between the case and the chamber wall without scratching the chamber. After the case has been started away from the chamber wall at one point, small chisels made from needle files or dental chisels (with the point used next to the chamber wall slightly rounded to prevent scratching the chamber) can be used to cut the broken case so that it can be removed.

Chapter 12 WORKING WITH HAND TOOLS

A great many of the ordinary gunsmithing jobs can be done with hand tools almost as well as with machine tools, the great difference between the two methods being the amount of time consumed by the hand tool method over the machine tool method. Even to this day many good target barrels are bored and rifled by hand.

You have seen in the earlier chapters of this book that many of the operations, such as adjusting trigger- pulls, speeding up actions by lightening hammers, making small parts, filing extractors to shape or increasing the hook effect of them to make better extraction, can easily be and usually are done by hand work.

One of the most common jobs of gunsmithing, that can readily be done by hand, is remodeling the military rifle. Taking the model 1917 rifle for example, removing the rear sight protective wings from the receiver is easily done with high-speed steel hack-saw blades and files. I have found the high-speed steel blades made by the Simonds Saw & Steel Co., of Fitchburg, Mass., to be excellent. For sawing these receiver wings and other like jobs on tough steel, the 24 teeth-per-inch blade is best.

For a strictly hunting sight the regular peep on the model 1917 rifle is hard to beat. A sufficiently high front sight may be used with this rear peep so that the rifle shoots center at about 100 yards, then the regular elevating slide may be used for longer shots. The wings can be sawed and filed off of the receiver, leaving two small ears to hold the sight in place. After the wings are sawed off roughly, a coarse file is used to bring the receiver close to the final size and shape. A common 10" or 12" half-round file is very good for this. After using the coarse file, a fine file of the Swiss type, such as the various size pillar files, as made by the American Swiss File Co., of Elizabeth, New Jersey, is used to remove the coarse file marks and give the receiver its final shaping. As the job nears completion with the fine file, keep rubbing chalk on the file, to prevent small particles of steel sticking in the file teeth and scratching the work.

Removing the file marks left by the fine file is done with carborundum cloth, starting with #120 and using gradually finer grades until the desired polish is reached.

If you do not desire to use the regular rear sight of the model 1917 rifle, it may be entirely cut off and the receiver rounded up to the measurements of the Remington model 30, after which any receiver sight made for the Remington may be mounted upon the receiver.

The sharp angles can be filed off the receiver at the left rear of the bridge and the clip slots cut and filed off at the front end, bringing these places down in gradual, graceful curves and streamlining the receiver.

The front sight protecting wings are of soft steel and can easily be sawed off and the block filed up to a graceful shape. Standard bead sights can be pur- chased from Pacific Gun Sight Co., of San Francisco or D. W. King Sight Co., of San Francisco to replace the military blade sight.

If you wish to shorten the barrel saw off the de- sired amount and, with the barrel held upright in the padded jaws of the bench vise with the new muzzle three or four inches above the jaws, select a medium- coarse flat file of ten or twelve inch length, put a good file handle on it and file the muzzle flat and square, using a small machinist's square such as made by L. S. Starrett Co., or Brown & Sharpe to check the squareness of the muzzle. As the barrel has a taper, the muzzle will not be at right-angles to the sides when it is square with the bore, the angle will be slightly greater than a right-angle, but by filing the muzzle until the variation is alike from all four directions the muzzle will be square with the bore.

After the muzzle is squared, take a fine flat pillar file, chalk it and remove the coarser file marks, then using this fine file, round the sharp corner where sides and muzzle meet, finishing it smoothly with a fine grade of carborundum cloth.

Use a sharp countersink with six or eight cutting edges to round the mouth of the bore. Hold this in your hand, holding it as nearly vertical as you can, and turn it slowly, without too great a pressure upon it, until the edge of the bore is Vie" or more lower than the end of the barrel.

Now clean the bore thoroughly from the breech and then drive a wood plug into the bore, just to the lower edge of the countersink cut, from the muzzle end. Get several ball-bearings of sizes from to Y/' and tear some coarse carborundum cloth into nar- row strips, about the width of these balls. Starting with the smaller ball, place a strip of the carborundum cloth around it and grip it tightly between the thumb and forefinger of one hand, then proceed to polish out the countersink cut in the muzzle by pressing the carborundum cloth around the ball into the end of the muzzle and twisting it back and forth. Keep moving the ball to new positions along the strip of carborundum cloth, so that the cloth cuts freely. After the countersink cut is polished out clear to the bottom with the small ball, use the next larger size and so on until you have the muzzle of the bore shaped to suit you, then start over again with the small ball using a very fine grade of carborundum and, going up the line of balls again, give the muzzle a good polish. Re- move the wooden plug from the muzzle by pushing it out with a rod inserted in the barrel from the breech end. The purpose of the plug is to keep carborundum particles out of the bore.

If you desire to use the same front sight band that came upon the barrel, it may be refitted to the barrel if the latter hasn't been shortened more than three or four inches. To do this use a pillar file to file the bar- rel down in diameter for about from the muzzle until the sight band can be tapped upon the barrel for almost its length. Then, holding the barrel in one hand, just back of the sight band, use a small hammer to tap the band smartly all over. Use the flat face of the hammer for this work, as you don't want to mar the band any more than is necessary. This hammer- ing will stretch the band so that it can be driven farther onto the barrel. Continue the hammering and driving the band farther onto the barrel until you get it to the place you wish.

Now set the barrel and action on a surface plate or a piece of plate- glass, with a square piece of steel be- neath the bottom of the receiver and a vee-block be- neath the barrel a few inches back of the muzzle and, using a machinist's square set upright on the plate be- side the muzzle, first on one side and then on the other, measure the distance from the edge of the square blade to the edge of the front sight mount block, tapping the block and band one way or the other until it is properly centered on the barrel.

If you have no surface plate or sheet of plate-glass, a good dining table top will answer the purpose pretty well, but you had better pick an afternoon when the boss of the family is at her bridge club and then cover the table top with a single thickness of newspaper, unless you have a dog or tom-cat to blame the scratches upon when the Mrs. asks questions.

After the sight band is in place, place a small drill in the hand or electric drill and drill the hole for the cross-pin, to lock the band onto the barrel. In some cases you will find that this cross-pin bites only into the original lug on top of the barrel and not into the top surface of the barrel proper. If this is the case, you will have to drill a slightly larger hole and use a larger cross-pin to make it bite into the barrel surface, as you have no lug on top of the barrel with the sight band in its new' position on the shortened barrel.

Start this cross-pin hole from each side, and at the start of the drilling hold the drill at a 45 degree angle downward instead of horizontally, for if you don't the drill will ride up and go through at an upward angle. After the hole is just started with the drill in the angle position, the drill can then be dropped to the horizontal position and you can drill pretty straight through, but drill the hole only halfway from each side, after which the drill or a small round needle file can be used to re- move any high spot that may remain in the center.

In using standard length drills of small size in a hand or an electric drill, it is very hard to drill holes true to size or to prevent the drill bending, due to the pressure put upon it. This can be avoided by building center-drills, which are 1" to 1 1/2" in length, and considerable pressure may be put upon them without any trouble, as these short drills bend very little. These center-drills can be purchased from Greenfield Tap & Die Corp. of Greenfield, Mass., Morse Twist Drill & Machine Co., of New Bedford, Mass., Cleveland

Twist Drill Co. of Cleveland, Ohio, or any other drill manufacturer. This is the type of drill supplied by the Lyman Sight Co. to drill holes to tap out for screws holding telescope sight base blocks.

Instead of using the standard military front sight band, you may wish to make a ramp upon which to mount the front sight. This can be done by getting a piece of thin walled steel tubing of the right diameter to drive tightly upon the barrel, and welding a straight piece of rectangular steel lengthwise of it. This tubing can be had from the National Tube Co., of Pittsburgh, Pennsylvania.

The piece of rectangular steel is filed to a chisel edge along one side. The tubing is laid upon its side and the steel piece to form the top of the ramp is laid lengthwise of it, upon short pieces of round or flat steel of sufficient thickness to bring it up to the center of the tubing with its chisel edge against the side of the tubing. Welding of this light type can be done by the low priced electric welders upon the market, an example of which is the Electric Torch, made by the Electro Torch Co., of 2613 Michigan Ave., Chicago. This torch sells for $6.95 and plugs into any 110 volt electric socket.

After welding the steel piece to the tubing, or rather dotting it at three or four places along one side, turn it over and make a full weld along the opposite side, then reverse it and make a full weld along the first side.

If you cannot do the welding yourself, a welding shop will do this small job for 35c to 50c.

The top part of the ramp may now be sawed off and filed to shape to make the tail, then the tubing is filed away beneath, at the rear, leaving a band to wide at the front to encircle the barrel. A cross-pin hole is drilled, to anchor this to the barrel as the regular sight band was anchored, or a screw hole can be drilled and tapped through the part of the ramp in which the sight is mounted, running down through this part to the top of the barrel, where a shallow spot is drilled into which to set the point of the screw. If the top of the screw is left flush with the bottom of the dovetail slot, in case a dovetail base front sight is used, the screw cannot loosen. If a blade front sight is used, thread a piece of steel rod of about 1/4" diameter to make the screw and, before cutting it off the rod, screw' it tightly into the hole and mark the north and south sides of it, so that the slot in the head can be cut lengthwise of the ramp. Remove the threaded rod, cut off the screw and slot it at the marks with a slot the width of the sight blade. Now screw it back into the hole, setting the slot lengthwise and file the top down flush with the top of the ramp. When the ramp is slotted with hack-saw and thin Swiss type files for the sight blade, the blade will set into the slot in the screw also and when the blade is pinned in place with a pin through the ramp top, from side to side, the screw is locked so that it cannot move.

The tail of the ramp may be cross-ribbed upon the top surface to break up light reflection, or it may be matted to achieve the same purpose. To look right, the cross-ribs should be laid out evenly and while this can be done fairly well by eye, it can be done more surely by using a checking file. These files are flat and have teeth set in rows, so that the file plows grooves on a steel surface. These files are supplied by the American Swiss File Co. in 6" and 8" lengths in cuts from 00, the coarsest, to #2, the finest, the cuts of the 6" file being finer, number for number, than those of the 8" file. After the grooves are marked out with the checking file, they can be deepened with a knife file and then brought up to an edge with a three-square file, both of these Swiss type needle files being made by the American Swiss File Co.

Matting can be done upon the ramp tail or upon the receiver ring and barrel of a rifle with a fine-pointed prick-punch and a light hammer, or with an automatic center punch of the small size as made by the L. S. Starrett Co. or Brown & Sharpe. To operate these punches, you simply place the point upon the work and press down upon the back end of the punch and as the blow is struck by a spring mechanism within the punch it will be the same weight each time.

Another way of doing matting is to use an electric door-bell which has a ball -type clapper. A small hole is drilled into the ball and a steel phonograph needle is driven tightly into the hole so that the point projects out of the side some distance. The point of these needles is pretty fine, so if you desire, it may be blunted by grinding it to a steeper taper on a grinding wheel, or it may be blunted with a hand stone. The door-bell is connected up to a storage battery or four dry cells or, by using a door-bell transformer, it can be connected to the 110 volt lighting circuit. You had better cover the binding post connections on the bell with some tape to prevent getting a shock. The bell may be held in the hand and, after some practice, you can turn out a pretty even job of matting with it. A light steel frame may be made for it, so that, it is held the same distance above the work for each stroke, then each blow has the same intensity.

If a ramp without a band is desired, take a piece of rectangular steel of the right size and, using a round or half-round file, shape the bottom so that it fits the barrel contour closely. Saw and file the tail slope to shape and groove or matt it as previously described, then drill a hole down through the part in which the sight mounts, so that a fillister-head screw can be passed through it and screwed into a hole drilled and tapped into the barrel for a fine-thread screw'. A #6 x 48- thread telescope base block screw r makes a good one for this purpose if you can get one long enough. If this cannot be obtained, get a #6x40-thread screw and use it. Drill the hole through the ramp as nearly vertical as you can, then mount the ramp on the barrel, squaring it up as before so that it stands vertical, and clamp it in place with two machinist's parallel clamps which can he purchased from the L. S. Starrett Co., Brown & Sharpe, or any ten-cent store. Take a #27 wire-gauge drill and, putting this down through the hole drilled in the ramp, spot the barrel with it, then substitute a #31 drill if you are using a #6 x 48-screw or a #30 drill if you are using the #6 x 40-screw, and drill a hole halfway through the top side of the barrel, being sure that you stop at this point and do not drill into the bore or you will have to cut the barrel off again. After this hole is drilled, grind the point off the drill so that the end is flat, and drill out the hole again so that it is flat-bottomed. Still leaving the ramp clamped in place, tap the hole with the proper tap, starting it with a plug tap and finishing with a bottoming tap. If you have only a plug lap, after tapping the hole with this, grind the end of it flat back to where the full size threads start and use this as a bottoming tap. Be sure to use a good thread-cutting oil on the tap each time, either lard-oil or black sulphur oil compound. Hardware stores or plumbing shops can supply these thread-cutting oils.

After the hole is tapped, cut the screw to length so that its head is flush with the bottom of the dovetail slot if a dovetail-base sight is to be used, or flush with the top of the ramp as previously described if a blade sight is to be used. The slot in the screw' can be widened out to accept the sight blade, which will act as a lock for it.

Mark around the ramp on the barrel with a scriber, then remove the ramp from the barrel and, using a small scraper or file, remove the blue-ing from the barrel within the scribed lines and tin this place upon the barrel with solder. Tin the bottom of the ramp and replace it upon the barrel, putting the screw in place and drawing it up tightly. Place a piece of copper upon the tail of the ramp near the rear end and use a parallel clamp to draw the tail down tightly upon the barrel. Use a blow-torch or gas torch to heat the barrel and ramp, and when the solder begins to run at the edges of the ramp, draw the screw up tightly until the slot in the head lines up properly, then tighten the parallel clamp on the tail and let the job cool.

Front sights can be made with hand tools ; the dove- tail base type by sawing the form roughly out of a small block of steel and then filing it to size and shape ; the blade-type by using steel of the right thickness and filing it to shape. Standard commercial sights may also be changed, in case of dovetail base types, to narrower base types and in case of blade sights to lower heights to meet special conditions.

If the front sight being made is to have a composition bead of white, red or green, it is often better to drill the hole for the insertion of the bead before the portion holding the bead is filed to final size, as in drilling these small holes by hand the hole may be a trifle to one side which will make the sight look slightly unbalanced. This applies to the Call-type head also, where a gold bead is set in flush with the surface. The hole should be drilled before the bead is made, because the shank of the bead of the composition type should fit the hole pretty closely and the bead itself of the Call-type should be a close fit in the hole.

Plate XVI

Buffing a rifle chamber with a crocus cloth buff in the chuck of the DeLuxe "Handee" grinder. The buff is cut in circular form, then partially clipped into sections as you would cut a pie and mounted on a long spindle. This method will finish the chamber to a high polish.

an electric motor with a chuck on it. The material is held in the chuck and a small dental chisel or a narrow wood chisel may be used to cut the shank to size, by nailing a piece of wood on the bench top to act as a tool rest to rest the blade of the chisel upon. Files may be used instead of a chisel to size this bead shank, or in case no electric drill or motor is available, the material for the bead may be held in a pin-vise of the round-handle type such as those made by the L. S. Starrett Co. and revolved with one hand, with the pin-vise against the partly opened jaws of the bench vise, while the shank is filed to size. After the bead is cemented in place in the front sight with Du-Pont cement, the face of the bead can then be filed to shape with small files and finished with sandpaper.

A front sight of the composition bead type should be blued before the bead is cemented in place, as heat from the blueing process or some of the chemicals used may loosen the cement. This does not apply to gold bead sights either of the Sheard or Call pattern unless heat and oil blueing or some other type requiring high temperatures is used, as the Call bead is soldered in place and the temperature of boiling water used in many blueing processes, or even that of the immersion type blueing which is under 300 degrees, does not loosen the solder. The Sheard-type gold bead is or should be brazed to its steel shank, so any heat used for blueing purposes will not affect it.

Shotgun sights are easily mounted with hand tools, as all that is required usually is one hole drilled for the rear sight, the front one can usually be mounted in the hole left by the removal of the standard front sight. Small reamers and directions as to what size holes to drill come with the shotgun sights.

The receiver sight is easy to mount with hand tools, as the base is clamped to the receiver with parallel clamps and squared up by setting the gun on a surface- plate or good flat surface with a rectangular piece of cold-rolled steel under a flat portion of the receiver and a vee-block beneath the barrel, while a machinist's square is set upright on the plate with its blade against the sight base and the base is moved upon the receiver until it is parallel to the square blade. In the case of rifles not having a flat on the underside of the receiver, two vee-blocks are used beneath the barrel and the rifle is squared up with the surface of the plate and then clamped in the vee-blocks with the clamp supplied for this purpose.

After the sight base is square, it is tightened against the receiver with the parallel clamps and a drill that fits the screw-holes of the base closely is used to spot the screw-holes on the receiver. Still leaving the base clamped to the receiver, lay the gun upon its side with the sight base uppermost, put the proper size tap-drill in the hand drill and, being careful to keep the drill vertical, drill the two screw-holes through the receiver. Leave the base clamped to the rifle and tap the holes, using the base as a guide for the tap.

If the receiver is case-hardened, the spots to be drilled may be softened either with the sun lamp carbon attached by a heavy wire to an automobile storage battery, as elsewhere described, or an electric welder will soften the spots in the same manner. If you have a small hand electric grinder of a type like the "Handee" grinder, a small, mounted grinding point may lie used to grind through the case-hardening at the points to be drilled for the screws.

Telescope sights are easily mounted with hand tools by clamping the base blocks or side mounts in their proper position and using these as guides for the drill and taps in drilling and tapping the screw-holes. Some of the thin side mounts, like the Weaver, are of no use in acting as a guide, so follow the manufacturer's directions carefully in mounting these scopes. In drilling holes by hand, the smaller the drill is, the easier it drills, so after spotting the holes with a drill that fits the holes in the blocks or mounts closely, use a drill smaller than the proper tap-drill to drill the holes with first, then enlarge them with the tap-drill. Another reason for doing this is that all the hand drills I ever saw do not run true, and this causes the twist-drill used to drill a larger hole than its true diameter, but if a small hole is drilled first, this causes the second drill, used to enlarge the hole, to run on a true center and the final hole will be very close to size.

A barrel that is rough on the outside, or that shows tool marks, can be smoothed up by using a 12" pillar file, held crosswise of the barrel in both hands, one on each end of the file on each side of the barrel, and drawing and pushing the file back and forth length- wise of the barrel, working around the barrel. This will leave small flats upon the barrel and these are removed by using strips of coarse carborundum cloth, used in a circular direction around the barrel, moving them rapidly back and forth across the barrel as a shoe- shiner uses his cloth upon your shoes. Follow this coarse carborundum cloth with fine grades used in the same direction, then use fine grades to polish the barrel lengthwise to cut out the cross polishing marks, using crocus cloth for the final polish.

Dovetail slots, if necessary in a barrel, may be cut roughly with a hacksaw and then finished up with a three-square file with one side ground smooth, as was previously described in an earlier chapter.

Barrel bands made from heavy clock spring or phonograph spring that has been annealed by heating red-hot and being allowed to cool in the air, are fastened to a steel block beneath the barrel within the forearm by four small screws with countersunk-type heads. A #4 x 40-screw is a good size to use and the holes for these screws can easily be drilled with a hand drill. A hole is drilled and tapped into the underside of the block for a screw or sling-swivel through the forearm.

The bending of sling-swivel loops by hand was de- scribed in an earlier chapter, so we shall pass it here and take up the making of the balance of the swivel.

Front swivels of the type which pass through the forearm and are screwed into a nut within the fore- arm or into a barrel-band base can be made from standard thread cap-screws. These screws have a hexagon head and these heads may be filed to a round shape and drilled for the sling loop. It is better to drill the hole for the sling loop before filing the head round, as the drill will start easier on the flat surface of one of the sides than it will on the round surface after the head has been filed.

These cap-screws have rather a shallow head and if you wish a swivel fixture with a deeper head, it may he made from two pieces of round cold-rolled steel. You can use a piece of 3/16 " diameter round rod for the threaded shank and cut a piece of 7/16" or 1/2 " diameter round rod for the head. This larger piece is drilled lengthwise with a 3/16" hole, but do not drill the hole clear through it. Insert the 3/16 " rod in the hole in the larger piece and, with the two parts clamped together, drill the hole through the head and upper end of the shank for the sling loop, which will hold the two parts together.

For the butt swivel and swivels attached to the out- side of the forearm by screws, the plate type with two mounting screws such as those used on our Springfield military rifle are the best type. These are easily filed to shape from steel plate and the holes drilled with a hand drill.

Triggers may be grooved or checked without having to be annealed or straightened by using a fine-grain knife edge wheel in a small electric hand grinder such as the "Haiidee" grinder. If nothing of this type is available, the trigger, if hardened, should have its upper parts set in water or wrapped in wet cloths, while a torch is used to anneal the lower part which is contacted by the finger. If the trigger is deeply curved it had better be straightened while red-hot and, after it is allowed to cool, it may be grooved or checked with a small file. A good type of file for this job is the die- sinker's riffler with curved knife-edge ends. These are listed by

American Swiss File Co., and by Frank Mittermeier of 3577 E. Tremont Ave., New York City. If the trigger has been straightened to make it easier to work on, it is again heated red-hot and bent to its original shape after the grooves or checking have been cut.

Checking of other steel parts or matting them has been described earlier in this chapter in the making of ramps. Matting will look better after being finished if, for a finishing touch, it is rubbed a little with fine carborundum cloth or with a fine hand stone.

To get back again to our remodeling work on the 1917 rifle, it is often desirable to shorten the magazine and straighten the lower guard of this rifle. The magazine is easily shortened by sawing off the lower end of the magazine box at the point desired, but if we merely straighten out the guard the distance between the guard-screw holes will be lengthened and they will not match the screw holes for the guard-screws in the receiver, so this lower guard must be shortened when it is straightened.

There are two methods of shortening this lower guard, one of which is to cut the front extension off with a horizontal hack-saw cut, run straight back just beneath the head of the front guard-screw. The top of this cut-off piece is then filed on an angle to match the angle on the under side of the rest of the guard just beneath where the saw-cut was made. The two parts are then lap-welded together to bring the guard- screw holes the proper distance apart.

The second method of straightening this lower guard at the front end is to make a forging die out of a piece of cold-rolled flat steel, fairly thick, by cutting out a portion of one side of it with drills and files so that the front end of the guard will lie snugly within it. The front end of the guard is then heated red-hot and straightened and, while being kept red-hot by repeated heatings, is forged back to proper length, using the forging die to preserve the shape and set it back. The guard-screw hole will be more or less closed up during this process but may be easily drilled out again.

New barrels that do not quite screw up to place may be fitted by hand by filing a little off the front end of the receiver with a 12" pillar file, being careful to file an even amount off all sides.

In cases where the rear end of the barrel screws up against a shoulder within the receiver, a small amount is filed from the rear end of the barrel to seat it to its proper position.

If the barrel screws in a little too far, a thin steel shim is used between the barrel shoulder and the receiver to make it tight when in the proper position.

As noted in an earlier chapter, revolver barrels seldom, if ever, screw up to the proper place and in fitting these by hand a pillar file may be used to take enough off the front end of the frame which the barrel screws up against to bring the barrel to its proper place. The rear end of revolver barrels can be shortened by filing so that they clear the cylinder the proper amount, .003" to .004" and this work is best done with the barrel screwed up to place in the frame. Be sure to keep the rear end of the barrel square, for this is important in revolver barrels. After the barrel is filed to proper length it is removed from the frame and, using a sharp six or eight-blade countersink turned in the fingers, the rear end of the barrel is slightly countersunk. After this countersinking use a fine-grain tapered hand stone to smooth up this countersink cut.

Barrel blanks may be had from barrel-makers, threaded to fit any certain action, although it is best to send the action to the barrel-maker at the time the blank is ordered and let him fit the blank to the action. The barrel-maker will also supply these blanks turned to shape on the outside. With hand tools you may then cut the muzzle end off, finish up the muzzle and polish the outside of the barrel and chamber the barrel for any cartridge you desire that the action will handle. Chambering reamers of the finishing type may be bought from A. F. Stoeger Inc., at 507 Fifth Ave., New York City, in a few sizes, and many different reamers may be bought from Paul Jaeger, 4655 Fernhill Road, Philadelphia, Pennsylvania. These reamers may be honed down with hand stones to cut a minimum chamber and most of the lead for the bullet stoned off of the reamer, as the Germans seem to believe that a lead should be cut about half-way to the muzzle to give the bullet a good running jump for a start. When these reamers are stoned to proper size and smooth- ness, you may then cut your chamber by hand in the barrel blank obtained from the barrel-maker. Cham- bering reamers can usually be purchased from any of the American barrel-makers also, and (for some car- tridges) from the Winchester Repeating Arms Co. These reamers will be much closer to the correct size than the ones mentioned above, but they will be much more expensive.

The lapping of barrels as described in an earlier chapter is best done by hand, with a lead lap cast on a rod within the barrel, or with the leather washer type of lap described.

Chambers sometimes become rust-spotted or very dirty and these can be polished out with discs of crocus cloth mounted on a long arbor and held in the chuck of the small hand- type electric grinder such as the "Handee." Lacking one of these grinders, a very fair job can be done by substituting a hand drill for the electric grinder. In doing this polishing of chambers with crocus cloth discs, the polishing discs should be moved slowly and steadily back and forth in the chamber while revolving. This job can also be done with a felt mop about as long as the chamber, using a thin paste of very fine-grain carborundum mixed with a light oil. White rubbing felt is the proper felt to use.

The magazine follower of military rifles is left square-edged at the rear so that when, with magazine empty, the rifle bolt is drawn to the rear, this follower rises up in front of the bolt face and prevents the closing of the bolt until the follower is pressed down. This feature is not desirable in a sporting rifle, so these followers in commercial sporting rifles are dressed off at the top rear with a backward slope so that the bolt rides over them and closes on an empty magazine. Try examining one of these commercial sporting rifles you can see the angle at which the follower is dressed off at the rear and can dress off the follower of the military rifle at a like angle by using files and carborundum cloth to give it a polished finish, for if it is left rough the lower edge of the bolt will gradually dig into it and increase the roughness until the bolt will hang up at that point. Some of these followers are soft enough to cut with a file, while others are so hard that they must first be annealed at the rear end. Remove the Z-shaped magazine spring from its groove in the bottom of the follower before heating the fol- lower to anneal it.

Shotgun barrels and chambers can be polished out with hand tools, a tight polisher of white rubbing felt on a stiff rod being best to use. Dip this in a paste of carborundum grains and light oil, using grains of vari- ous coarseness as required by the job at first, then following this with the finer grains for finishing. Use this polisher with a back-and-forth stroke in the barrel while at the same time giving it a twist. Finish with the straight back-and-forth stroke.

Gun actions that work roughly can be smoothed up by coating parts, except locking lugs, with fine grinding compound and oil and working the action until it smooths up. Wash all parts thoroughly with gasoline and then coat them with Gunslick, made by the Outers Laboratories of Onalaska, Wisconsin, and work the action for a while again, then wipe off the excess Gun- slick.

Many of the old-type lever-action rifles with a full-length tubular magazine under the barrel have been cut off to carbine-length, to increase their handiness for hunting. This job is done with hand tools by cutting off the barrel and finishing up the muzzle as de- scribed earlier in this chapter. The magazine is re- moved and sawed off with a fine-tooth hack-saw to the desired length. A piece of dowel-rod that fits the magazine tube closely will make a smoother job of cutting off the tube, if it is placed inside the tube be- fore the saw-cut is made. New holes for the screw holding the magazine cap in place in the tube are drilled with the hand drill, with the dowel-rod inside the tube, and sometimes these magazine cap screws, if only one is used, extend into a shallow hole drilled in the underside of the barrel which hole can easily be drilled with the hand drill. A pair of cutting pliers will cut the required amount off of the magazine spring and the job is complete with the exception of cutting a new dovetail slot in the barrel for the front sight, or if the rifle is a round barrel type a ramp may be bought or made and mounted on the barrel to hold the front sight.

TAPS AND DIES AND THEIR PROPER USE

Thread-cutting dies are not often broken in use until they get very dull so that the chips, instead of cutting clean, tear off and roll up, which usually results in breaking some teeth out of the die. The remedy for this, of course, is to keep the cutting edge (which is the leading edge) of the die teeth sharp. In a die of the Little Giant type made by the Greenfield Tap & Die Corp. of Greenfield, Mass., the dies are readily removable from the holder so that the cutting edges can be ground on an emery wheel. Other manufacturers make dies of this type also, in fact they are the best type of thread-cutting die because a tap will tap a hole just a certain size and the ordinary button die has not always a large enough adjustment to produce a thread cut large enough to be a tight fit in the tapped hole, whereas the die of the Little Giant type has a very wide range of adjust- ment and will produce a screw-thread large enough to fit tightly in the tapped threads of the hole.

An important point in cutting threads with a die is to keep the die, also the screw' being threaded, well flooded with a good cutting oil such as lard-oil or black sulphur oil compound, as the oil will keep the die cool, prevent it from dulling so rapidly in use, and will turn out cleaner threads as the oil will wash chips from the die while the thread is being cut.

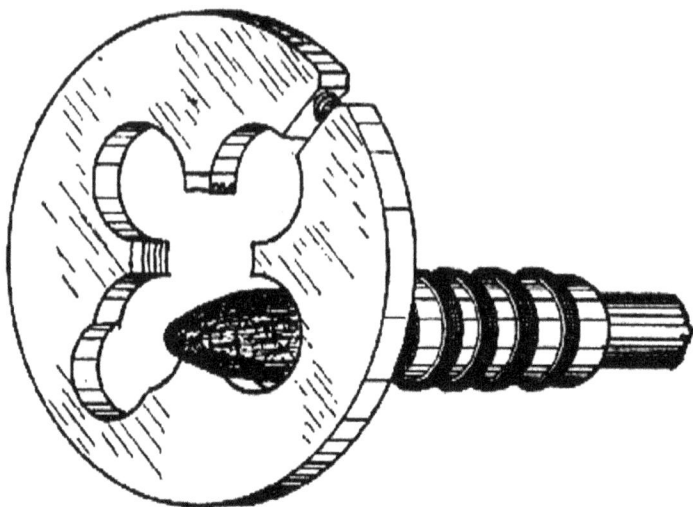

Using a mounted carborundum point to sharpen a button die by grinding the leading edge of the die teeth in the chip clearance hole.

The button-type die can be resharpened by using an emery pencil of small enough diameter to enter the round holes in the die. This emery pencil is held in a chuck mounted on a flexible shaft or upon the shaft of an electric motor. The button die is more often broken by over-expanding it with the screw put in the die for expansion purposes. The die is cut open, in manufacture, at the side in which this expansion screw is placed and the opposite side is left closed but is very thin, with a spring temper, so that the die can be sprung open to cut a larger thread. If the die breaks at this point while it is in use and another die is not at hand, the broken die can be used to cut the thread if the parts are carefully lined up and the die then well tightened in the holder.

One side of the die is funneled-out slightly by grinding the threads off on a slope into the die and this is the side to start the thread with, so that the screw being threaded centers in the die, this also prevents all the work being put upon the first thread of the die.

This side of the button die should be on the open side of the die-holder, if a guide is not used on the holder, so that the opposite side of the die is backed by the solid rim of the die-holder. When a guide is used, this funneled-out side of the die is placed toward the guide.

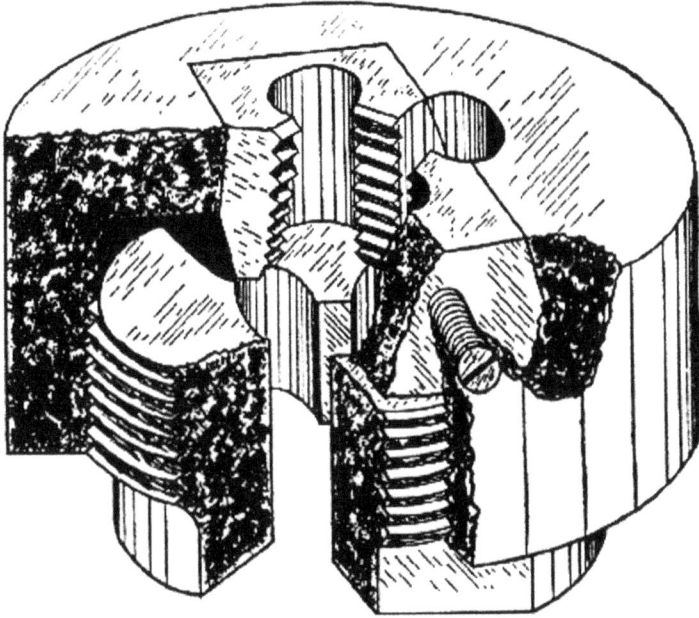

An enlarged, sectional view of the "Little Giant" type of die, showing the two adjustable parts of the die, the collet and the guide.

Taps are much more liable to be broken than a die, and this breakage is more liable to happen while tap- ping threads in a blind hole than in a hole open clear through, for the chips cannot well get out of a blind hole, so while tapping this type of hole the tap should be frequently removed and both it and the hole cleared of chips. Taps should be oiled with a good thread- cutting oil, just as dies are oiled.

Never attempt to use a small tap in a large tap- wrench, as too much pressure is put upon the tap. clue to the greater leverage of the large tap-wrench. If the tap-wrench being used has a horizontal handle, or is a tee-handle type, do not use it with one hand, put equal pressure on both handles of the wrench or the tap will be easily broken. Be careful to start a tap straight, not leaning to one side, as this will put un- equal pressure on the tap and lead to breakage. If possible, I place the work to be tapped in a smooth- bottomed machine vise and place it on the drill press table, then put the tap in the drill chuck and hold the lever down with my arm or with my one hand while I turn the drill spindle by hand to start the tap straight in the hole. After it is well started I loosen the drill chuck from the tap, leaving the tap in the work, and then use a tap-wrench to complete the tapping job by hand. I only do this in cases where I do not use a guide, with a hole in it for the tap, clamped to the work. The guide will assure the straight starting of the tap.

Tap and drill manufacturers supply a table of the size holes to drill to be tapped out with all standard taps. These holes are large enough so that the tap does not cut a full-depth thread, the depth cut being a 75% thread. This relieves the work of the tap greatly and supplies enough depth of thread so that the screw being screwed into the hole will twist off before the threads will strip, so it is wise to follow these tap-drill size- tables in drilling holes to be tapped.

Taps can be resharpened by grinding them in the flutes. This can be done with a narrow grinding wheel with its face shaped to fit the grooves of the tap or, in the case of taps with semicircular grooves, it can be done with a small mounted grinding point in the chuck of a small electric

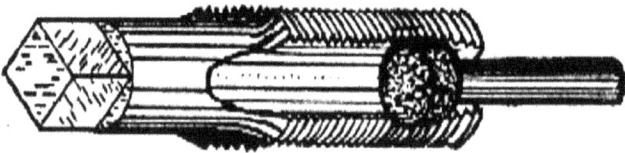

Using a mounted carborundum point to sharpen a tap by grinding it in the flutes.

or air-driven hand grinder or flexible shaft. In grinding carbon-steel taps and dies to re- sharpen them, be careful not to heat them enough to make them change color, or it will be necessary to reharden and retemper them.

A hole to be tapped should always be threaded first with a taper tap of the correct size and lead. If it is a blind hole, the plug tap is next run into it and the tapping is then finished to the bottom of the hole with the bottoming tap. If the blind hole is too shallow for the taper tap to start the thread in, the plug tap is used to start the thread and the threading is then finished with the bottoming tap.

If, in use, the tap sticks do not try to force it, back it up two or three turns then turn it forward again, repeating this performance until the tapping is com- pleted. Holes drilled in work in the lathe chuck or work clamped to the face plate can be tapped while still in place in the lathe. For tapping small holes, put the tap in a small drill chuck with a center hole in the end of the shank and place this center hole of the shank over the tail stock center of the lathe. The chuck holding the tap is turned by hand while the tail stock center is kept closely in the center hole of the chuck shank by feeding it forward with the tail stock wheel or feed handle. This will result in a straight tapped hole. If the tap being used is a medium to large size, place a clamp dog on the flat of the drill chuck shank holding the tap and let the clamp rest on top of the lathe tool rest while the tail stock feed is worked with one hand and the lathe belt pulled with the other hand. If the tap is a very large size the clamp may be put directly on the shank of the tap and the back gear of the lathe used for added power.

If a small tap breaks off above the surface of the work, the tap can be grasped with a pair of pliers if the portion above the surface of the work is too short to get hold of with the tap-wrench, and by working the tap back and forth the chips can be freed in the hole so that the tap can be unscrewed from the hole.

If the tap breaks off flush with the surface or below the surface but is not yet against the bottom of the hole, it may often be broken up by tapping it with a hammer and small punch, as the tap is quite brittle. It may sometimes be backed out of the hole by placing a fine-pointed punch or a heavy scriber against the side of a flute of the tap and driving against it with a light hammer. Tf these methods do not work, and heat applied to the tap will not injure the work, it can be heated red-hot with a torch and buried in slaked lime to cool. This will soften the tap so that it can he drilled out. The drill used should be smaller than the tap so that the threads in the hole will not be injured. After the center is drilled from the tap, so that the flutes are no longer connected to each other, a scriber will pick out the remaining parts of the tap.

If the work in which the tap is broken off cannot be heated for fear of injury, a small mounted grinding point of straight-cylindrical or slightly-tapered shape, or even a small ball-shape may be used in a high-speed electric or air-driven hand grinder or dental engine to grind the still-hardened tap as the softened tap was drilled, so that the flutes are disconnected, after which the remains of the tap can be picked from the hole.

If no grinder for these small grinding points is at hand, fill the hole around the tap with either nitric acid or hydrochloric acid and let it stand, keeping the hole full of acid, for an hour or more and the acid will eat away enough of the steel so that the tap is loosened in the hole and can be gently tapped around in a left-hand direction, with a small punch or scriber and a small hammer, until it is unscrewed from the hole.

A tool called The Broken Tap Extractor is made by the Walton Co., of 311 Pearl St., Hartford, Conn., for removing taps of 3/16 " to 1 1/4" diameter that have been broken off in holes. These cost from about $1.50 each on up, according to size, and are made for both three and four-flute taps. The tool consists of a steel shank of the diameter of the tap-drill used to bore the hole

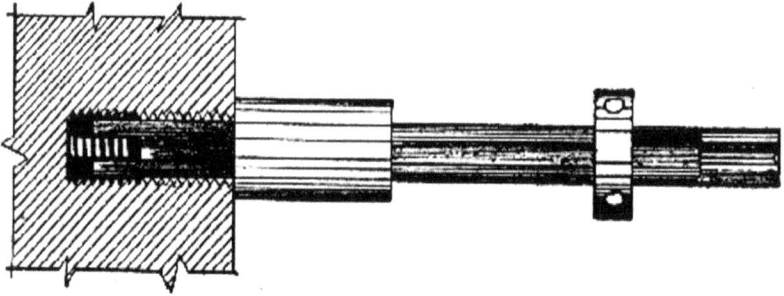

The "Walton" broken tap extractor.

for tapping out. This body has three or four grooves milled lengthwise of it spaced to match the tap grooves. In these grooves are crucible-steel fingers attached at the top to a heavy ring. The body of the tool is set on top of the broken tap with its grooves in line with the grooves in the tap and the ring is then tapped down on the body and carries the fingers with it into the flutes of the tap. Around the body of the tool, against the surface of the work in which the broken tap lies, is a steel cylinder which fits the body of the tool closely to prevent the fingers from springing out of their grooves. After the fingers are tapped down into the flutes of the broken tap, a tap-wrench is placed on the squared end of the body of the tool and the tap is unscrewed from the hole. A tool of this type may be improvised by milling or filing grooves in a piece of round steel rod and laying in these grooves pieces of spring-steel wire, commonly called music wire and obtainable from or through any hardware store. A steel cylinder can be slipped over the wires and body of the tool to hold the wires in place after they have been driven into the tap flutes.

Plate XVII

Method of starting a tap straight in a hole, using the drill press and turning it by hand. The article is held in a vise upon the drill press table and after being drilled with the proper tap drill is left undisturbed in the vise. The tap is then placed in the drill chuck and, while putting some pressure on the feed lever by an arm hooked over it, the drill spindle is turned by hand to start the tap straight in the hole.

Chapter 13 NOTES ON FIRING-PINS

Firing-pin size, shape and protrusion have been referred to at several places throughout this book in speaking of center-fire and rim-fire actions, but I now wish to again impress the reader with the extreme importance of proper firing-pins, both from a safety and from an efficiency standpoint, so I will discuss the principles of firing-pin construction of both rim and center-fire types as a separate chapter.

What T have to say as regards safety may be of interest to some lad who has been in the habit of making his new firing-pins from some convenient wire- nail. The factors affecting efficiency which I speak of should, I am sure, prove of value to many expert small-bore riflemen ; even though they will not have the slightest interest in the practice of gun-smithing these notes may help explain those unaccountable scores which creep into our shooting now and then, and which often, unfortunately, stay with us longer than we care to have hanging around.

There is only one correct shape for the center-fire firing-pin nose and that is the hemispherical, or ball- shaped point. Furthermore, this point should be highly polished and free of scratches, to prevent any abrasion of the soft cup, which would increase the liability of puncturing the primer. The diameter of the firing-pin nose, for center-fire cartridges, should be .073" to .075". This diameter is taken just at the rear edge of the hemisphere that forms the actual point of the center-fire pin. The protrusion of the center-fire pin beyond the face of the breech, with the pin in the fired position, should be .055" These dimensions and shape of point apply to all center-fire firing-pins, whether for rifle, revolver, pistol or shotgun and, furthermore, they are highly important from a standpoint of both safety and efficiency.

The three items — protrusion, diameter and shape — go hand-in-hand, because with the dimensions given, the entire hemisphere of the point is sunken within the primer at the instant the pressure of the fired charge comes back against the inside of the primer. This allows the firing-pin hole in the breech to practically be completely filled and sealed by the full diameter of the firing-pin behind the hemispherical point, preventing any pieces of brass, or gas under high pressure, coming back through the firing-pin hole in case a primer does rupture.

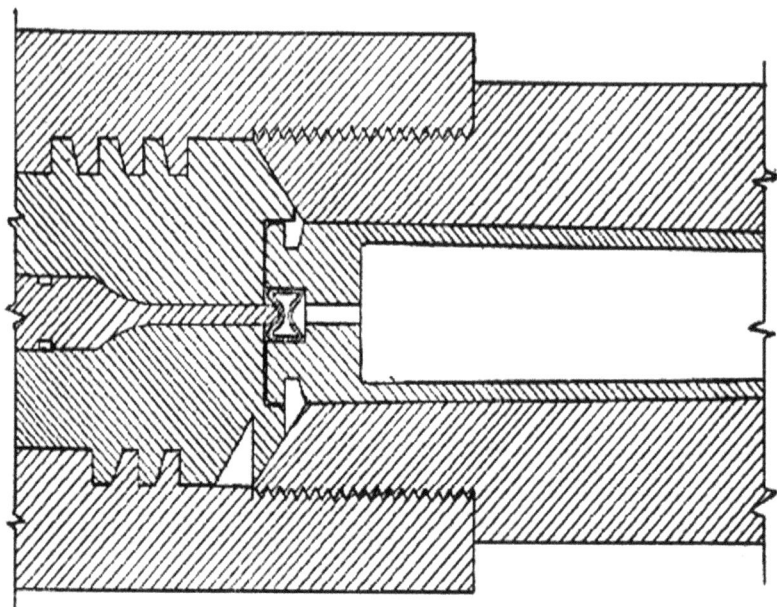

A properly proportioned and shaped center-fire firing-pin after impact
on the primer.

When the firing-pin nose is a larger diameter than the dimension given above, the hemispherical point is proportionally longer and in this case may easily be long enough so that in firing the firing-pin does not move far enough forward through the breech face to completely seal the hole through the breech face with the shank of the firing-pin back of the point and, in case of a ruptured primer, this allows pieces of brass or gas under high pressure to escape to the rear through the breech-block, which may easily cost the shooter the sight of an eye.

Another point to realize, if a firing-pin of over-large diameter is used, is that as the diameter of the firing- pin nose approaches the diameter of the primer there is a greater possibility of puncturing the primer by cutting the center of it out against the side walls, as the flexibility of the rear face of the primer is decreased as you approach its side walls.

A sharp-pointed firing-pin will, of course, puncture a primer every time, so never make a firing-pin from a nail, using the point of the nail as a nose for the firing- pin. To illustrate this, let me tell you the experience of a friend of mine who was visiting a farmer acquaintance. This man saw a number of wild ducks on a pond in the farmer's pasture, so called the latter's attention to them. The farmer handed my friend a double-barrel shotgun, telling him to go ahead and shoot some of the ducks, which he started out to do. When within range, he took a shot with the right, modified-barrel at the ducks. As the gun fired he felt something strike his right hand, upon looking down saw some slivers of wood sticking in his hand and further saw a hole with splintered edges out through the grip of the stock. He immediately forgot all about the ducks and returned to the house with the shotgun, asked the farmer for a screw-driver and, taking the stock from the shotgun, removed the screw holding the left-hand firing-pin in place and took out the firing-pin. This firing-pin turned out to be a wire nail, with its original point being used as the nose of the firing-pin. The right-hand firing-pin was missing, having stripped the end off its stop-screw, passed out through the hole it broke through the grip of the stock and disappeared, luckily leaving my friend with nothing worse than a few splinters from the stock in his right hand. Had he been a left-handed shooter, or had he fired the left barrel first, he would have undoubtedly have lost an eye and perhaps his life. The farmer told him he had made those firing-pins himself, from wire nails, as the original firing-pins had both been broken.

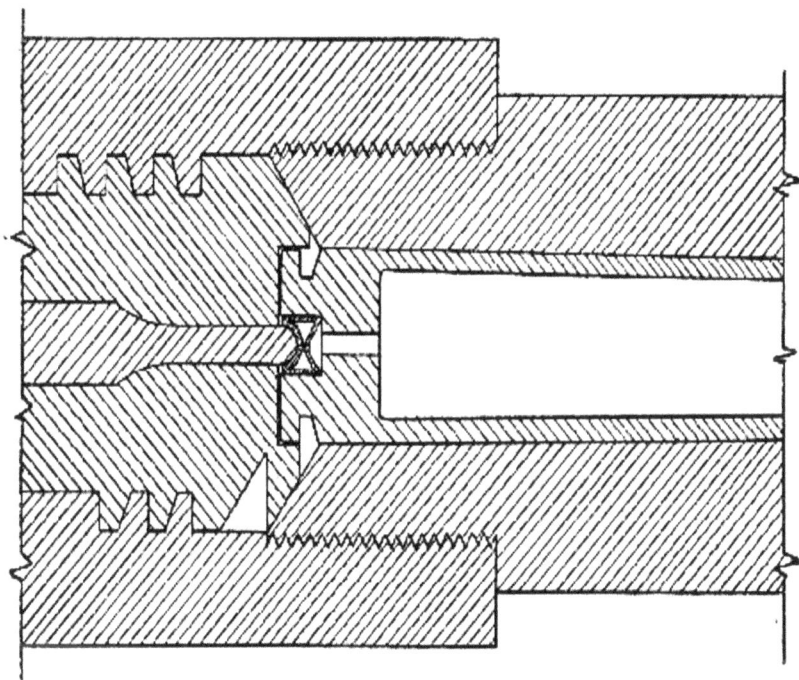

Too large a center-fire firing-pin after impact. The rear face of the primer may cut out against the side walls.

In the rim-fire firing-pins, in regard to shape of point, we have a different proposition. There are a number of different shapes of firing-pin noses that have been used, more or less successfully, for rim-fire work. These have, however, narrowed down to three shapes ; the rectangular shape, at present far in lead of the other two in favor; the round, flat-end type, second in favor; and the rounded-end type, with few sup- porters. This last type is divided into two divisions, one using the rounded-end of a hemispherical shape, resembling the center-fire pin nose-shape but much larger in diameter, and the other a rectangular-shaped firing-pin nose with the end rounded like the side of a cylinder instead of being flat-ended, as is the rectangular-shaped nose most highly in favor.

The flat-ended firing-pin for rim-fires, with the edges very slightly rounded to remove the sharp edge, which might easily cut a rim-fire case, is by far the most successful. The reason for this is that the end of the pin covers a greater portion of the rim than does the hemispherical point or the point rounded like the side of a cylinder, and this is important in good ignition, as the priming is not always distributed evenly around the rim in spite of all the manufacturer's efforts to do so.

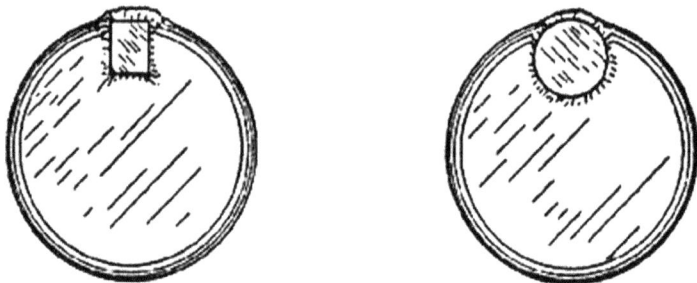

Left is impression made by the rectangular shape, flat-pointed rim-fire firing-pin on a .22 rim-fire case. Right illustrates impression made upon same case by the round, flat-pointed, rim-fire firing-pin.

Therefore, the less effective striking-width the nose of the firing-pin has, the more liable it is to strike a portion of the rim without a full quota of priming, which results in a hang-fire or a misfire. This also applies to a flat-ended pin of rectangular shape if it is made too narrow, with the added danger in this case of cutting or splitting the rim of the cartridge. On the other hand, if we increase the width of the firing- pin nose too much we reduce the effective power of the firing-pin blow, as we have only so much spring pressure available behind the firing-pin and must drive the firing-pin deeply enough into the case-rim to insure properly crushing the priming mixture to get good ignition. This is another point where the rounded-end firing-pin fails, as part of its power is consumed in what amounts to pushing the case-rim aside in the rounded sides of a semi-circular of hemispherically-shaped depression made in the rim by this shape of firing-pin nose, and there is little or no crushing action at these points.

The depth of the depression made in the rim of a rim-fire case by the firing-pin should not be less than .015", and .020" minimum depth is a better assurance of even ignition from shot to shot. As mentioned above, we have only so much spring pressure available for power in driving the firing-pin, so to get this depth of depression in the case rim our firing-pin nose can be only so wide. This has to be determined for each make of action, as they differ considerably in weight of firing-pin, length of its travel and strength of spring. A firing-pin nose-width for the rectangular-shaped flat- nose pin, that will insure good ignition when driven to a proper depth in the case-rim, is .050" to .060". A proper diameter for the round, flat-nosed firing-pin, to give good ignition, is .075". The reason for the in- creased size of this nose over the rectangular one is that the entire diameter of the end of the pin must strike within the rim, not out over the edge, and as the impression in the case from this pin is a flat, circular depression, its full diameter is not available on that part of the rim which contains the priming mixture.

Speed-actions introduce another difficulty, for it is seldom possible to get as much power behind the firing- pin in this type of action as in the slower type with the longer firing-pin travel. For this reason, these actions are only successful when using the rectangular- shaped firing-pin nose with the flat end, and are not too successful at that, because they have a narrow margin of power and some heavy oil or dirt causes them to fail completely, as does too stiff a cartridge case. These actions are at their best in high-grade target models, that are not subject to so much dirt as the guns used in the field and are usually given better care in regard to cleaning and proper oiling of the action.

In these speed-actions, the width of the firing-nose is often reduced to give a deeper impression, a width of about . 040 " being used. This is permissible from a safety standpoint, as these speed-actions do not have sufficient drive to cause this narrowed firing-pin nose to puncture the case rim. These speed-actions work best on the target-type cartridge with its lower velocity and slightly softer case, rather than upon the high- speed cartridge with its very stiff case.

The second type of firing-pin nose mentioned, the round type with a flat-end, requires a little more power than the rectangular type, as a greater portion of the end of this pin, due to its circular form, strikes on the head of the cartridge entirely inside the rim, where there is no priming mixture nor any way to crush it if there were any. This tends to have a cushioning effect on the firing-pin blow and while this shape is a good one, because it has small tendency to puncture a case unless it has very sharp edges or the end is very rough, it requires considerably more power than the rectangular shape to make as deep an indentation in the case-rim. For this reason it falls short of the rectangular shape in favor with the manufacturers.

The rounded or hemispherically-shaped firing-pin end for rim-fire work must be quite large in diameter to be either safe or effective, and yet this very matter of large size defeats both of these objectives. If its diameter is small, its point of greatest impression, its center, is then too small to cover enough of the rim to be sure of not striking a point in the rim where the priming mixture is thin or entirely missing, thus causing hang-fires or misfires. The smaller this hemisphere end is, the greater would be its liability to puncture the case rim, causing a blowout at that point. There- fore, by making this type of firing-pin nose quite large in diameter, we supposedly get away from danger of striking a point in the rim where priming mixtures are thin, by reason of the point covering more territory and we supposedly get away from the danger of a punc- tured and blown case that might be caused by the small-diameter nose. Both of these suppositions are, however, a fallacy, the first one because the center of the hemisphere on the end of the pin must strike on the rim of the case to be able to crush the priming mixture, but on account of the large diameter of this nose, part of it is extended clear over the edge of the rim, making it necessary for this shape firing-pin to crush down the very stiffest part of the case rim, where it is supported by the side wall of the rim. This results in a heavy cushioning effect on the blow of the firing-pin, thus defeating its object of better ignition.

Now as to the second supposition of superior safety over the small-diameter pin. The head-space for a .22 rim-fire case is .050", so to give deep enough penetration and yet allow the firing-pin to be snapped down on an empty chamber without striking the chamber rim, the protrusion of the firing-pin beyond the breech face when the pin is in the fired position cannot be more than .035". A hemispherically-pointed firing-pin with a point short enough so that when in the fired position the shaft of the pin behind the point would seal the firing-pin hole in the breech face, could there- fore only be .0175" in diameter, a much smaller diameter than any firing-pin used. Therefore, our large- diameter firing-pin with a rounded or hemispherically- shaped point would fail to fill the firing-pin hole in the breech face, and would therefore fail to support the head of the car- tridge, thus increasing the liability of a blowout and defeating our second supposition of greater safety from the liability of a blown case head.

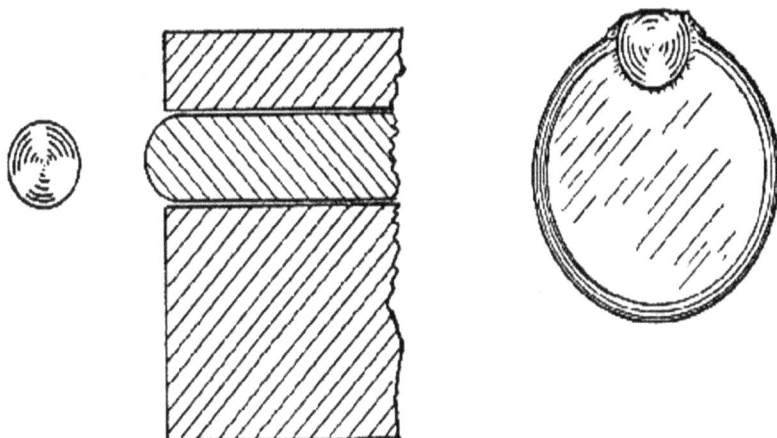

The round-bodied, rim-fire firing-pin with a hemispherically-shaped end, showing end view, poor sealing of firing-pin hole in breech block and impression made by this shape pin on .22 rim-fire case.

The fourth type of firing-pin nose-shape referred to ; the rectangular shape with the face rounded like the side of a cylinder, is safe enough as far as puncturing the case head and causing blowouts is concerned, but its narrower point of impact increases the liability of hang-fires or misfires from imperfectly primed cases, and as it offers no great advantages of any kind there is no reason for its use.

A rim-fire case of .22 caliber is made of thin material, less than .010" in thickness. They are holding pressures of 20,000 pounds or more per square inch. They are made of brass and we all know that brass of that thickness has no real strength, yet these cases hold such pressures. They hold them because they are well supported by surrounding steel of the gun barrel and breech. Yet this steel cannot support them closely enough, because there must be some clearance to allow insertion and extraction with ease, to prevent movement and stretching of these cases under the pressure of firing. Yet these cases are being held rather tightly, at the one point, by the firing-pin. Therefore, the face or point of these firing-pins must be made as smooth as it is possible to make them, for any sharp edges or roughness of the firing-pin at this point will easily tear the thin case as it stretches and attempts to move under the pressure of the firing charge. This is an important point and do not neglect it.

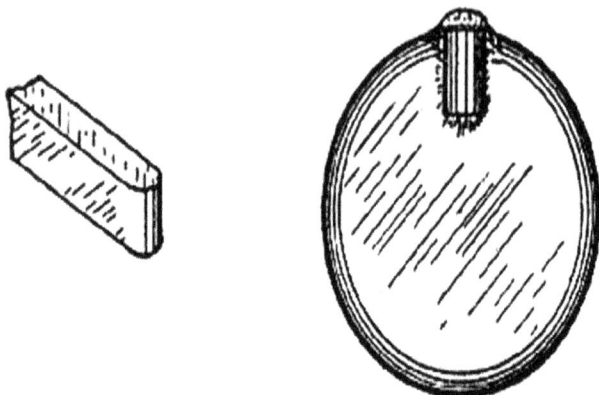

Rectangular bodied, rim-fire firing-pin having end or point shaped like the side of a cylinder and impression made by such pin in a .22 rim-fire case. This is a poor shape to use.

If a firing-pin end becomes rough, and they often do, through small particles of foreign matter in the metal of which the cases are made, and from a burst case now and then, resulting in a gas-cut on the pin, the pin should lie replaced with a new one, because dressing the end of a rough pin to a new smooth surface results in shortening the pin and as the pin protrudes only .035" when new, a few stonings necessary to dress it up soon shortens it so that it becomes too short for good ignition. The type of pin made for the Colt Ace pistol is, of course, a different type that is too short to reach through the breech-block with the hammer down, made this way as a safety measure. It is a "free" or "floating" pin and drives forward under impact of the hammer, but its length of travel is limited just the same as pins of other type, so a few stonings will make it too short to function well also.

Dirt, in connection with extractors and other parts, has been spoken of before but I wish to impress you with the fact that dirt in connection with firing-pins is just as bad, or worse. Heavy oil or grease will also have the same bad effect on ignition. The reason for this is that priming mixtures are made to be fired by percussion. The dictionary defines percussion as "the act of striking smartly on or against. The effect of violent collision." Dirt on any part of the firing-pin has the tendency of slowing down the speed of travel of the pin, whether the pin is struck by a hammer or driven by a spring. When we slow down the speed of travel we lose that "smartly" part of the definition, turning the firing-pin blow almost into a pressure, and pressure very seldom fires a priming mixture. I have crushed good center-fire primers in an arbor press to prove this without ever having one fire, although you notice I do not say that pressure will not fire a primer, for it may happen, but it happens very seldom.

Firing-pins fit rather closely in the breech-block or bolt, and a little dirt on the sides or end of the body of the pin behind the breech face slows down the pin travel, until it loses that speed which makes of it a percussion instrument. When dirt is removed from the sides of the pin, or the hole in the breech-block in which the pin travels, examine these surfaces to see that no grit in the dirt has caused a roughness of these surfaces. If roughness is found, dress it off with fine polishing cloth, then wash the parts well in gasoline and re-oil with a thin oil which will not gum.

Beware of too much oil, or too heavy an oil, in the hole in which the firing-pin travels, or you may make an oil-seal that will trap air in the hole and badly slow down the speed of firing-pin travel, resulting in a misfire. In very cold weather, all oil should be re- moved from the firing-pin and the hole in the breech- block or bolt. Very fine, dry graphite, such as col- loidal graphite, should be rubbed well over the dry pin, using the fingers to rub it into the surface. This will supply plenty of lubrication and will not thicken up in any temperature. This same advice of cleanliness and very light oils, or dry graphite, applies to the coil-spring back of the firing-pin in a bolt-action, to the sides of the hammer in a hammer-type action and to the spring behind the hammer. Speed-actions, of course, need special attention with thorough cleanings quite often, to keep up that speed necessary to develop percussion.

Chapter 14 SOLDERING AND BRAZING

Soldering is a method of joining two pieces of metal together with an alloy of lead and tin, sometimes with bismuth added if a solder with a low melting point is desired. As lead has the highest melting point of the three, solders containing a high percentage of lead and a lower percentage of tin, or a high percentage of lead and a low percentage of tin and of bismuth have the highest melting point. Lead has a melting point of 620 degrees Fahrenheit, tin a melting point of 445 degrees Fahrenheit. The solder most commonly used, called half-and-half, composed of 50% lead and 50% tin has a melting point of 428 degrees Fahrenheit. A solder composed of 32% lead. 15.5% tin and 52.5% bismuth has a melting point of 205 degrees Fahrenheit, which is below the boiling point (212 degrees Fahrenheit) of water at sea level.

The gunsmith does not have much use for solder except in sweating ramps, barrel bands, scope base blocks or rear sights to the gun. He also uses this process at times in making tools, such as when he sweats two pieces of steel together temporarily for machining in lathe, drill, grinder or milling machine.

Sweating is a slightly different process than ordinary soldering and approaches brazing in its strength when it is properly done. In sweating two pieces of steel together, each piece is tinned, (giving a thin coating of solder) then the pieces are placed face-to-face with the tinned surfaces in contact, are clamped tightly in this position and are then heated with a torch so that the pores of the steel are well opened by the applied heat, whereupon the solder enters these pores making a good joint between the two pieces. The pieces are left clamped together while cooling. This last is a point to be remembered in either soldering or sweating, keep parts stationary and together while a soldered or sweated joint is cooling , for any movement of one piece independent of the other being joined to it causes the solder to crystallize in the joint and when this happens its holding power becomes negligible.

In sweating parts together the two surfaces that are to be joined should make as perfect a contact with each other as possible, so contours of the two surfaces must match to produce a good joint. These surfaces must also be clean and not too highly burnished . They may be scraped with a knife or scraper, filed, or a medium coarse carborundum cloth may be used to free the surfaces of any corrosion. They must be free of any grease also.

After the surfaces are cleaned they are coated with a flux to prevent oxidation. For steel, either one of two fluxes will answer the purpose. One of these is rosin, usually used in powdered form. It is spread upon the surface to be tinned and the heat of the iron used in tinning the surface melts the rosin and flows it completely over the surface. Rosin is the flux to be used where all danger of rust forming must be avoided.

The second flux for steel is zinc chloride, made by dissolving zinc chips or cuttings in hydrochloric acid. To prepare it, put all the zinc the acid will dissolve into the acid. This flux is applied with a stiff brush such as supplied with small bottles of glue. This flux will cause corrosion and rust on surfaces adjacent to the sweated or soldered joint, so these surfaces should be well washed with water or ammonia after the parts have cooled, which prevents this.

The soldering copper, or "iron," used in tinning surfaces should be a large size, such as the two pound iron, for the solder should be well rubbed into the surface of the steel by the iron and to do this the iron should retain its heat for quite a period of time, which a small iron will not do.

The soldering copper should come to a point and the sides of this point should be square and flat. The iron should be well tinned upon these sides at the point. This tinning is a coating of the iron with solder and is best done with a block of salammoniac. The iron is filed until the point and surfaces back of it are clean and smooth. It is then heated, hot enough so that when applied to the salammoniac the latter fumes and smokes, melting under the temperature of the iron. Small pieces of solder are dropped onto the block of salammoniac and the hot iron is rubbed upon these so that the iron has a coating of solder upon it.

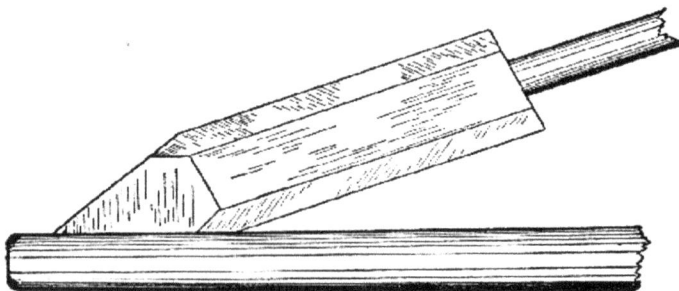

Position of soldering iron for tinning a barrel surface, preparatory to fitting a ramp sight.

In heating the soldering iron avoid overheating it, as this will burn and roughen the surface of the iron, forming a scale upon it through which the heat does not pass very well to the surface being soldered. If overheating occurs, the iron must be filed clean again and retinned. After heating an iron, just before applying it to the solder, it should be dipped into a liquid flux such as the zinc-chloride as this brightens it and enables it to hold more solder upon its surface.

In sweating two pieces of steel together, such as sweating a ramp or barrel band onto a barrel, all blueing must be removed from the barrel surface and from the inner surface of the ramp or band if it is already blued. Put the ramp or band in place on the barrel and mark around its surface with a very sharp scriber, such as a phonograph needle. Remove the ramp or band and, using a small scraper or file, remove all blueing from the barrel within the scribed lines. If the ramp or band is blued on its inner surface, also scrape all blueing off of this surface that comes in contact with the barrel.

Have the soldering iron good and hot and, applying the flux to the cleaned surface of the barrel, dip the soldering iron into the zinc-chloride flux, then touch it to the solder and apply it to the fluxed surface of the barrel, holding it in one place until the barrel surface heats up, then rubbing it around at that point so that the solder is well rubbed into the surface. Gradually extend the rubbing process as the barrel continues to heat, until the barrel is well tinned with solder within the scribed lines.

The barrel band, or the ramp if it is equipped with a band that encircles the barrel, may be too small to be tinned on the inside with the large iron, although the point of the large iron should reach all parts inside the band. If this large iron is too big a smaller one should be used.

After both parts have been tinned, heat them with a torch and use a cloth to wipe off the excess solder when the torch flame has softened it sufficiently. Place the ramp or band upon the barrel in proper position and, if the item is a ramp, place a piece of sheet-copper on the tail and put a clamp upon it, to draw the tail down tight to the barrel. If the item is a tightly-fitted barrel band and was properly fitted before being tinned, this will probably not drive quite up to place until it is heated, so the contraction of the band itself will make a clamp unnecessary upon it. Apply the heat with a torch to the item being sweated on the barrel and heat it as evenly as possible until the solder begins to run at the edges, then if a clamp is used tighten up the clamp a little more and hold the heat on the job a moment longer, then shut it off and let the job cool without moving it.

Plate XVIII

Using a jeweler's lathe, set vertically, as a sensitive drill press for very small drills. A lever action, tail stock spindle is fitted up as shown and a small Jacobs drill chuck of 0 to 1/8" capacity is used.

A method of tinning small parts, as the inside of a ring too small to get into with any soldering iron at hand, is to heat the piece in a torch flame, after applying flux, and then apply wire solder to the surface to be tinned, turning the piece so that the solder coats the entire surface in good shape. Either acid-core or rosin-core wire solder will work the best for this job. An acetylene torch, using the gas acetylene only and no oxygen, is very good for these soldering and sweating jobs as the acetylene combines with oxygen in the air and burns it, preventing oxidation of the surface to be soldered.

Brazing is a method of joining two metals with molten brass. It requires a much higher heat than soldering, as the metals to be joined must be hed-hot, so its use is limited to parts which will not be injured by the high heat required. The joint made by brazing will stand a pretty heavy strain, so long as it is not a bending strain at the point of joining.

Silver soldering or hard soldering is often confused with brazing but there is a difference between them, because while brazing uses molten brass, which brass will become molten at about 1660 degrees Fahrenheit if it is the standard type spelter (which is really half copper and half zinc), silver-solders may be had in mixtures requiring heats of from 700 or 800 degrees Fahrenheit to 2000 degrees Fahrenheit to become molten.

Brazing requires the heat of the acetylene torch to accomplish a good joint, as the steel or iron parts to be joined must be brought to a good red-heat at the joint. The parts to be joined must be thoroughly clean and as they are brought up to red-heat, borax in powdered form is sprinkled upon them to act as a flux. This will melt and cover the surfaces and the brazing spelter, in the form of fine filings or melted from the rod by the torch, is applied to the joint, where it will run into the smallest crevices. In doing the work the job should be turned so that the molten spelter can be run in from all sides. The borax used as flux will form a hard scale and may be ground- off if there is excess material to be removed from the finished joint, or it may be removed by placing the piece in an acid pickle of one part sulphuric acid to twenty parts of water.

Neither brazing or hard soldering are processes suitable for attaching parts to barrels or receivers, for even if the bore of the barrel is protected by file- hardening compound or something else to prevent oxidation under the high heat, the heat may cause the barrel to develop a kink in it. Heat treatment will be removed from receivers by the necessary heat for brazing or hard soldering, and the part will have to be reheat-treated. Brazing or hard soldering are suit- able however for making or repairing parts removed from the gun if the joint is not visible when the part is in place, as the brass in the joint will show and can- not be blued successfully.

Brazing a block to a barrel band.

An example of a brazed joint in gun work is the brazing of a block of steel onto the bottom of a barrel band, so that a screw or swivel passed through the forearm will screw into the block, as in this case the joint is entirely concealed by the forearm. Another example is the brazing of the barrel lugs onto the bottom of shotgun barrels. Box magazines made of sheet-steel and entirely concealed within the stock may be made by brazing the sheets together or a bar may be brazed between the tangs of a gun into which a bolt passed through the butt may be screwed.

Silver soldering or hard soldering is done with a silver-brass alloy, usually supplied in fine granular or thin ribbon form. As mentioned above this may be obtained in alloys with various melting points. The ribbon form is usually the best to use, as a piece of the ribbon is placed between the two parts to be joined, after they have been thoroughly cleaned and then coated with a paste made of borax mixed with water.

The parts are then clamped tightly together and the heat is applied until the silver solder melts. The parts are left clamped together until thoroughly cool, after which the borax scale is removed by placing the parts in the acid pickle mentioned above. Very little, if any, of the white silver solder will show at the edge of the joint if the pieces are well filled and, as this is less objectionable than the brass color of a brazed joint, the silver soldering is preferred for joining parts in gun work where the joint remains in sight. This method can be used to repair broken tangs, such as shotgun tangs, although if a good welder is available the job had better be welded. Brazing or hard soldering requires less skill and knowledge of metals than welding requires, so in some localities where good welding shops arc not available the brazing or silver soldering may be used. Jewelers are usually very good at brazing anything within the capacities of their equipment, and pointers may be picked up from them.

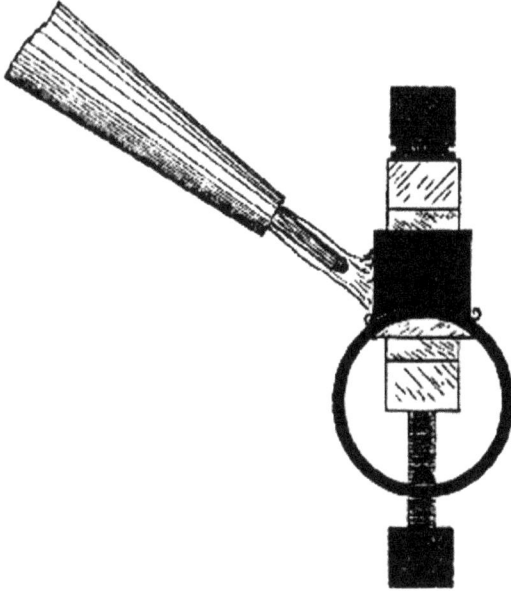

Silver soldering a block to a barrel band.

Chapter 15 FORGING AND WELDING

T he gunsmith of today does not have much use for forging processes hut sometimes a job turns up, such as making a vee-type flat-spring or the straightening and setting back of the front end of the model 1917 guard. Both of these jobs have been described previously in this text, so we won't go into them again beyond stressing, at this point, the proper heat for these jobs.

In forging high-carbon steel, such as spring-steel, a lower heat is used than with common low-carbon steels. A good cherry- red is as high as should be used in forging carbon-steels, for a high heat on these steels will easily decarbonize them for some distance below the surface and in spring making this will cause a slow, sluggish action in the finished spring, instead of the snappy action desired. This proper heat lies between 1350 and 1400 degrees, Fahrenheit. Too low a heat is to be avoided, for carbon-steel may crack while being hammer forged at too low a temperature.

In forging the low-carbon steels, a heat just at the lower edge of the welding heat is the proper temperature. The welding heat is that at which the surface of the steel has a glassy appearance and just begins to throw off sparks, so in heating low-carbon steels for forging watch the surface of the steel and, just as the glassy appearance starts to show, take the steel from the fire and forge it as desired.

Charcoal or coke makes the best fire in an ordinary forge, as these fuels are sulphur-free and lack most of the gases common to bituminous coal. Bituminous coal, ground fine, is the next best fuel in the forge. It should be piled two or more inches deep around the fire and well wet-down with water, which causes it to coke, making a better fuel of it.

Either the gas or the electric furnace may be used in forging instead of the open forge. Their positive temperature control makes them ideal for the purpose.

Lighter hammer blows should he used in forging thin sections of high-carbon steel, such as gun springs, than in forging the low-carbon steels, for this carbon-steel spring-stock is forged at the lower tempera-ture, as mentioned above, is a more brittle steel and will de- velop surface checks or cracks more easily than the low-carbon steels. In fact, this brings out another point in forging, that of surface hardening by the hammer method. Hammering a piece of steel, either hot or cold, changes the surface structure of it, making the grain finer and more dense, which in turn makes the surface harder, which is the cause of the surface checks or cracks. This is quite pronounced in forging steel cold and quickly develops. Before the introduction of case-hardening, this method was used by the smiths to give surface hardness to steels to cut down wear. The low-carbon steel is heated almost to welding temperature and, while kept as close to this temperature as possible, it is hammered with fairly heavy blows with a heavy, flat-faced hammer, which treatment gives the steel the dense surface mentioned.

Forge or hammer welding is done at the higher temperatures just below the burning heat for the steel. The pieces to be welded are scarfed (cut off or heated and pounded-out on a taper) then heated in the forge until the surface is quite glassy-looking and almost at white-heat. Just as the steel reaches this heat the flux, of powdered borax, or ground-glass and powdered clay, is sprinkled on the heated surfaces and allowed to melt, as the heating is continued for a minute longer. The pieces are then taken from the forge to the anvil and laid upon each other at the point the weld is to be made and, while holding the upper one in a pair of tongs, it is hammered into the lower piece with heavy, rapid, hammer blows. The pieces, if properly pre- pared and heated, stick to each other at once and as the steel cools to cherry-red they are returned to the fire, more flux added and reheated to the white welding-heat, again withdrawn and hammered together again, with the performance repeated until the weld is perfect and no dividing line shows between the pieces.

The above weld is what is called a lap-weld, from the fact that one piece is lapped upon the other in making the weld. A second type of weld is the fork- weld, in which one piece is split for a short distance and the two sides opened up in a vee-shape. The piece to be welded to this is then scarfed or cut off on both sides to a chisel edge at the end and is placed inside the vee or fork, when both are heated to welding temperature and the sides of the vee are then hammered down upon the inserted, chisel-shaped end of the second piece. Thin pieces, to be welded together end to end, are often split for a short distance and the split ends of each piece are then bent in opposite directions, just as you take a sheet of paper in your hands and pull one hand toward you and push the other hand away from you to tear the paper. This is done with each piece at one end, then in making the weld the two pieces are placed together so that the bent split- ends lap upon each other and are then hammered down, one into the other. In making a tee-weld, a spot on one side of the top or bar of the tee is scarfed-off and the end of the other piece, which is to be laid in at this point, is also scarfed-off and when being welded is laid into place and hammered down. This is the tee- weld used in welding flat stock. The tee-weld made in round stock is called a jump- weld, the top or bar is notched in a vee-shape at the point of the weld and the second piece is ground or cut off in a very blunt chisel shape, then set into the vee-notch.

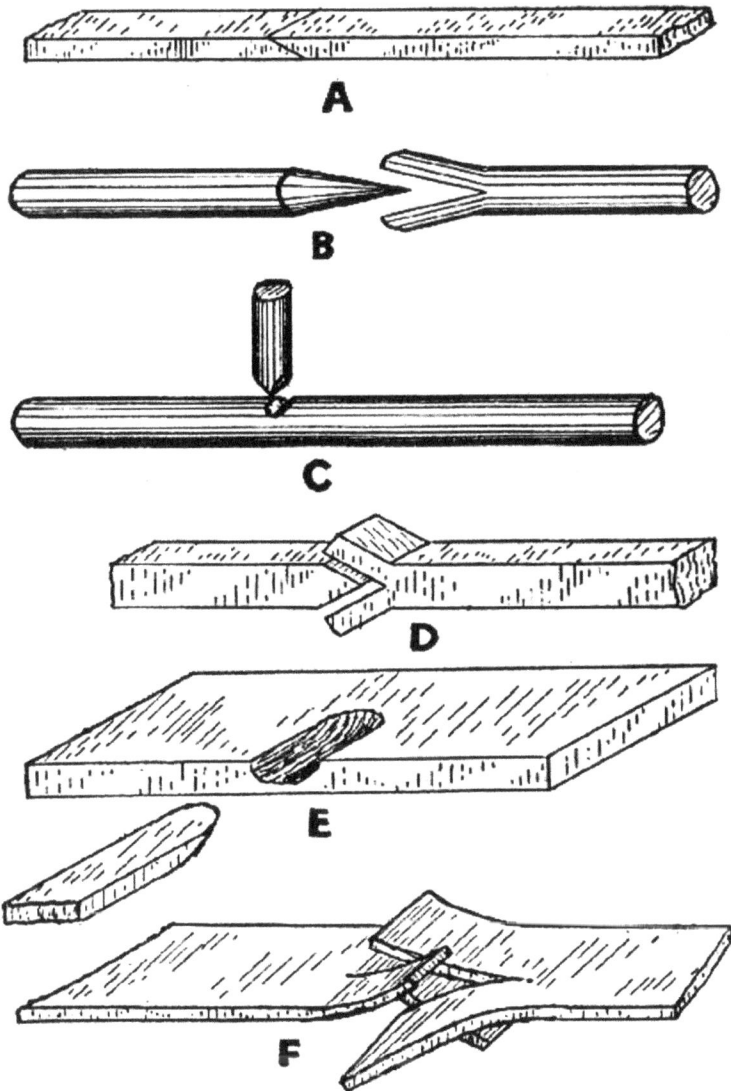

Various types of welding, made at the forge. A is lap weld, B is forked weld of round stock. C is jump weld. D is forked weld. E is a Tee weld and F is a double lap weld of thin stock.

clean, properly fluxed surfaces and plenty of heat. Hammering a weld after it has cooled too much is very liable to open it right up, if done on the first heat before the weld is completed.

Welding with the oxy-acetylene torch is much faster and more satisfactory than the forge and hammer weld. It is also applicable to much larger pieces. Its draw- back for the gunshop is the cost of the equipment, which may run anywhere from $50.00 to $200.00. If only a small amount of welding is done the oxygen may be bought in the small tanks, under the name of medical oxygen, from a physicians and surgeons supply house, and the acetylene bought in Prest-O-Lite tanks. This will make both the oxygen and acetylene a little more expensive, but the investment is less than the large tanks and you get away from the monthly rental charge they assess you on the large tanks.

A large torch does not work well on small parts, so two torches are necessary, one large one for heavy work and quick heating for bolt-bending jobs, with a small torch of the airplane type for small work such as on extractors, front sights and barrel band work.

Parts to be welded are scarfed or cut off at the ends on a much shorter and steeper taper than for forge welding and the ends are butted together, the scarfed portions thus forming a vee. The ends are heated to the melting point and the welding rod is brought to the point of the weld and melted into the vee, building it up above the surface of the surrounding metal. In welding steel, and usually in welding cast-iron, no flux is required but in welding aluminum or in brazing or welding brass a flux is required. The prepared flux for each of these metals is the one that should be used, although borax does a very good job on the brass.

Thin or medium-thick parts to be welded need only be scarfed on one side and the weld made completely from this side. Thick, heavy pieces should be scarfed on each side, or in the case of round stock, all around, leaving the two ends to be welded in a point, and the weld made from both sides or all around.

Very large pieces should be preheated before being welded. If the pieces are very thick, this is best done in a furnace or large forge, but if not too thick it may be done with a large heating torch, such as the large kerosene-burning torches. This preheating assures a good weld by even expansion and contraction of the work and avoids expense by saving on oxygen and acetylene gas.

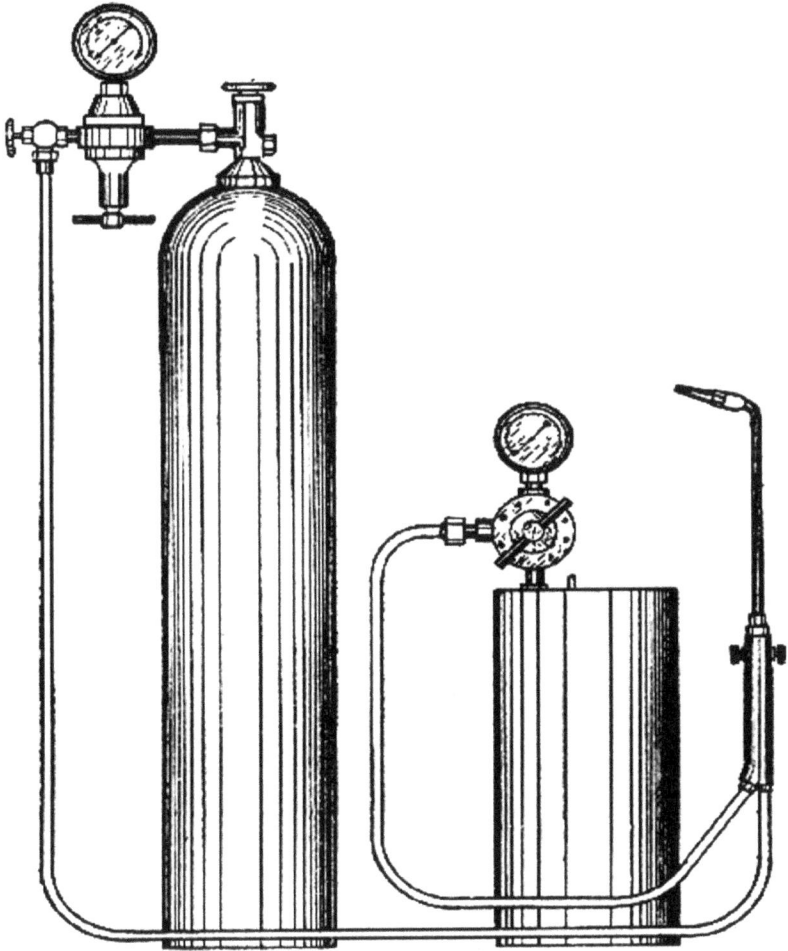

The acetylene welding torch, with tanks and gauges.

A neutral flame is used in welding, as too much oxygen oxidizes the weld and too much acetylene carbonizes it. Oxidation causes the metal to scale on the surface while carbonizing it makes it very hard, so that it may be too brittle and cannot be machined without annealing. A manual and full instructions accompanies a welding outfit, which covers all the necessary points of torch adjustment and many others.

The electric welding outfits have some advantages over the gas welding outfits for gun work, for one of the big drawbacks of the gas welding torch is the large amount of metal surrounding the weld which is also heated. While this may be an advantage in assuring a perfect union of the two pieces, it has its disadvantages by often annealing a hard part close to the weld, which must then be rehardened. The gas torch is more to be desired in heating work to be bent, as while the electric arc-welder is supplied with a carbon point for heating, it is more difficult for instance to heat a bolt-handle for bending with the arc- welder than with the gas torch. On the other hand for a build-up job, such as lengthening an extractor or a job of welding a bolt-handle back onto a bolt at a different angle, the electric arc-welder spreads its heat so little beyond the weld that it is to he preferred to the gas torch. Electric welding is much faster than gas welding, for it takes quite a little while to heat up the parts to welding temperature with the gas torch but with the arc- welder as soon as the arc is struck the metal is at welding heat. The arc-welder, A.C., will cost practically the same as the gas welder of the same capacity, but the cost of operation is less for the arc-welder than for the gas welder. In using the gas welding torch, dark-glass goggles are used to protect the eyes from the glare but in using the arc-welder gloves and a face mask are used to protect the skin from the rays of the arc. This mask has dark glass set in it to protect the eyes from the glare as well as from the rays of the arc.

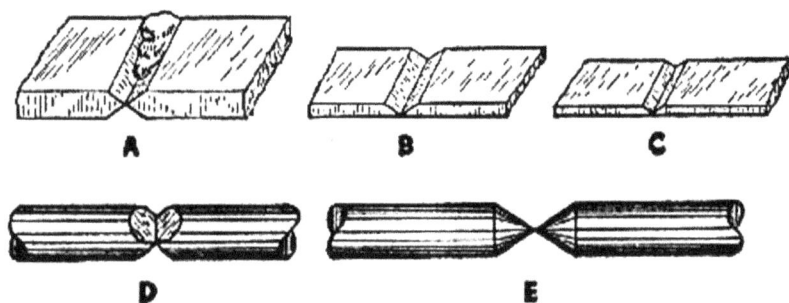

Various methods of arc welding. A shows the scarfing of thick stock in preparation for acetylene or electric arc welding. B and C are methods of scarfing medium and thin stock. D and E are methods for scarfing round stock.

The weld itself is prepared by scarfing in the same way for the electric arc-weld as for the gas torch weld. One terminal wire of the arc-welder is fastened to the work or to a steel plate upon which the work is placed and the other terminal wire goes to the torch or hand clamp in which the welding rod is held. This rod is different from the welding rod used for gas welding and is usually coated or shielded.

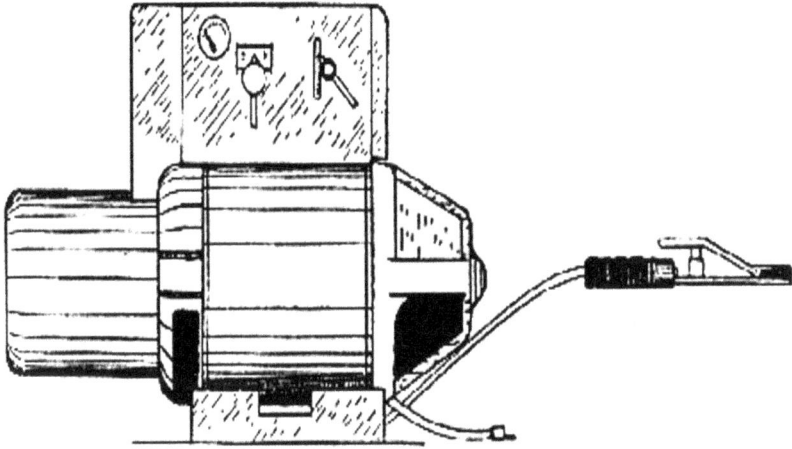

The motor-generator type of D. C. electric arc welding outfit.

In making the weld the welding rod, held in the electrode clamp, is touched to the weld and withdrawn slightly, which strikes an arc of very high temperature. The welding rod is held steadily at about this same distance from the work to maintain the arc while the rod melts and runs into the weld, where it is built up above the surrounding metal just as was done in making a weld with the gas torch. The proper welding heat for different thicknesses of work is controlled by different current taps on the welding machine.

In brazing or in heating or cutting with the electric arc-welder, a carbon rod is used in the electrode clamp in place of welding rod. The regular brass rod for brazing, such as is used with the gas torch, is used in brazing. With this carbon tip, soldering and spot- annealing, such as softening receivers at points where holes are to be drilled and tapped, is easily and quickly done. In spot-annealing, the heat is so high and so instantaneous that the desired spot is annealed and the heating carbon removed from the surface before the heat has time to spread any distance from the spot annealed. Electric arc-welding is somewhat simpler and easier to learn than gas welding, due to the much wider range or torch control on the gas torch to regulate heat, along with the several different size tips for the gas torch.

The D.C. type electric arc-welder of the motor- generator type is much more expensive than the A.C. type. These D.C. types have been in the field for many years and have proven satisfactory, although they are so expensive that unless a shop has enough work of other types than gun work, so that the arc-welder can be kept busy from one-third to one-half of the time, they will hardly pay for themselves.

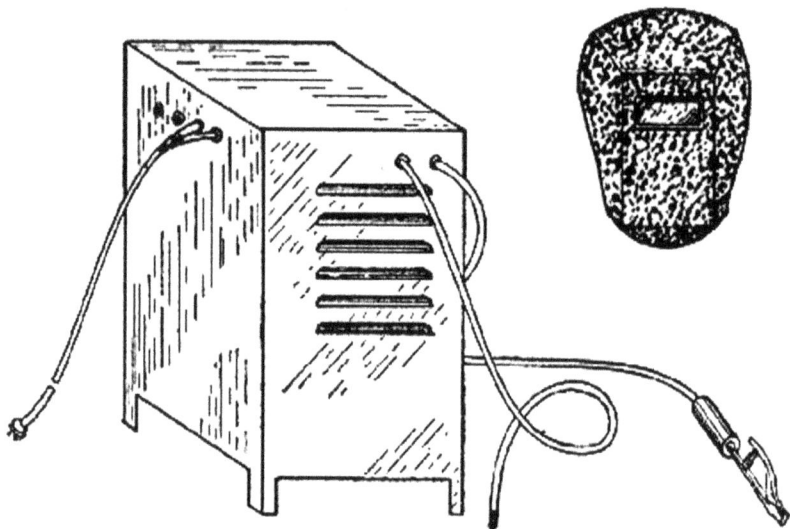

The A. C. type of electric arc welder. The mask shown is used with both types of electric arc welders.

The A.C. type will cost about the same as the gas torch and is a late-comer to the field. Power companies sometimes have a high installation charge for this type that will increase its cost.

Chapter 16 HEAT TREATMENT OF STEEL

Heat treatment of steel causes a rearrangement of its grain structure, resulting in a harder, tougher product. To accomplish any change in the grain structure, the steel must be heated to what is known as its critical point or range, whereupon a change will occur in the metal at the lower edge of this critical range and again at its upper edge. The desired change to refine the grain structure occurs within this range, be- tween the low point and the high point in temperature. This critical range varies somewhat for different types of steel, the higher the carbon content is the lower is the temperature of the critical range for that steel.

As this critical range is rather narrow, 50 to 75 degrees, the heat must be closely controlled, as upon entering this range from its lower point the steel assumes the finest grain structure possible for it, but upon passing through it to a higher temperature the grain changes to a coarser struc- ture and a little more heat burns the steel. If the steel is heated above its critical point, but is not burned, it may be restored by allowing it to cool slowly and then reheating to its critical range again, upon which the fine grain structure is restored.

The pyrometer is used to check these high tempera- tures, as they are above the range of a thermometer. The element of the pyrometer which is subjected to the heat of the furnace is protected by a metal or ceramic case. For average use, the nichrome tube is regarded as the best protection for the element. With continued use the metal of the clement gradually disintegrates, causing a change in accuracy of the pyrometer. For this reason, all large shops have a master pyrometer to check the pyrometers in use in the furnaces but the small shop which does not use the pyrometer every day can return it to the manufacturer periodically to be checked and repaired if necessary.

There are three general types of heat treatment furnaces in use, the gas-fired, the oil-fired and the electric, the last being the most expensive of the three to purchase but probably being the easiest to operate.

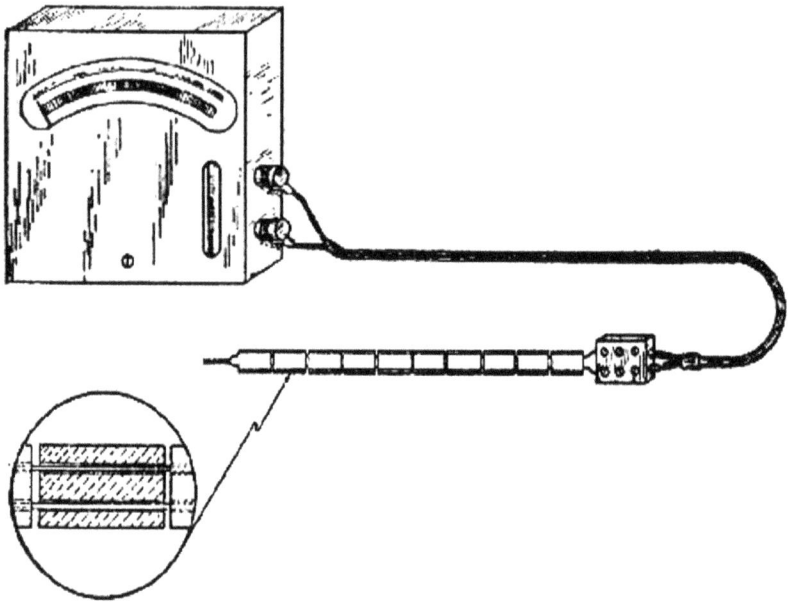

Non-recording, non-controlling type pyrometer for high temperatures.

The flame-type furnace, either gas or oil-fired, has an arched roof and the flames of the burners are directed against this arch and are not turned directly upon the work, for this direct flame would ruin the steel, due to uneven heating.

The electric furnace, of course, does not require an arched roof, as no flame is present and is the type best adapted for the actual hardening and tempering of steel.

These furnaces can be built within the shop in the small sizes necessary to the gunsmith. They are built upon a substantial base of concrete and the walls are made of fire brick, usually three thicknesses of brick being used. The roof is of arched type for the flame- type furnace and the door is made the full width of the furnace. Doors are of steel, lined with fire brick and the inside of the furnace and the door is plastered with fire clay. A shelf is made outside the door so that pots or boxes used when case-hardening may be drawn out upon this shelf and then picked up with hooks or tongs.

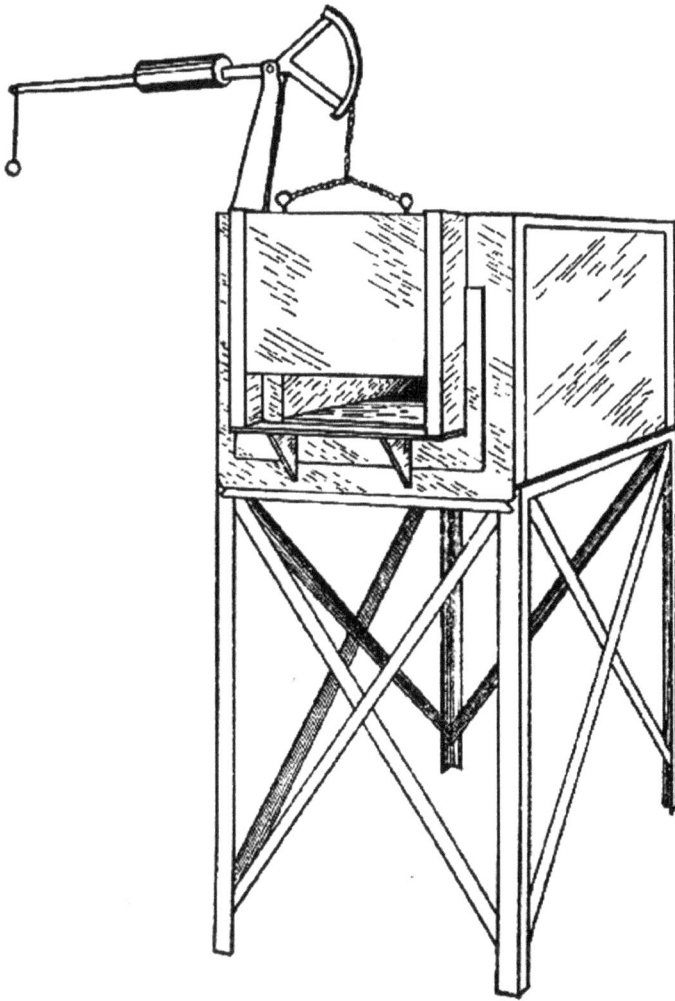

Commercial-type electric hardening and tempering furnace which may be simplified and easily built in any small shop.

Bolts are set in the concrete base around the sides of the furnace so that steel hands can be drawn over the brick work to hold the furnace together, which is necessary due to the expansion and contraction caused by heating and cooling. The flame-type furnaces must be connected to a flue and have dampers in the pipe so that the rate of cooling may be controlled. Burners are let into ports along both sides and so set that their flame enters at a tangent to the roof arch.

In using this flame-type furnace for hardening, the flame should be neutral or slightly rich in gas to prevent surface decarbonization of the steel. This also applies while annealing steel but does not matter in case-hardening. Also in using the furnace as a muffle furnace in hardening or annealing, the steel is protected by the muffle and the type of flame does not much matter.

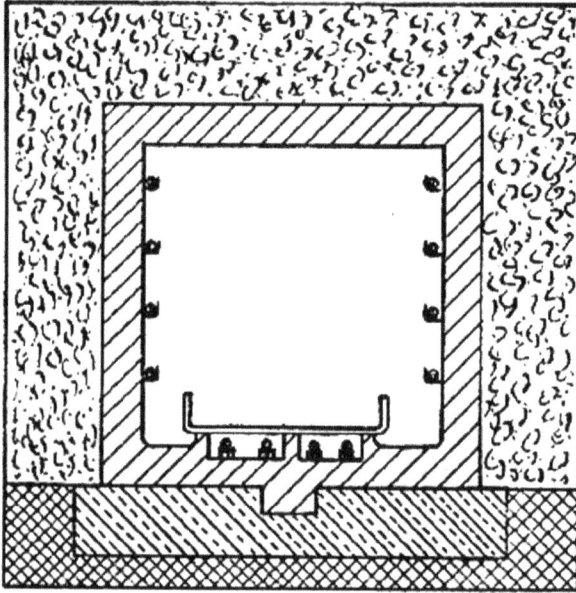

Construction detail of commercial-type electric furnace, showing "Cal-rod" type heating elements in place on sides and bottom.

The electric furnace is built in the same way as the flame- type in regard to construction of base, walls and door but it does not require an arched roof, a flue connection, (although it does require a vent with damper) nor are there ports along the sides for burners, as the enclosed type of burner can be used, such as the "Calrod" element and these are fastened to roof and sides, inside the furnace.

Pyrometer connections into the furnace should be arranged at the farthest distance from the flame or heating element and should be loose enough so that in case the tube surrounding the element breaks, the element can be immediately withdrawn from the furnace, to prevent damage by the heat.

The high-speed steels require higher temperatures for treatment than the carbon-steels need. Temperatures for high-speed steel range from 2100 degrees Fahrenheit upward, while those for carbon-steel range from

1350 to 1650 degrees Fahrenheit for annealing, normalizing and hardening and 1500 to 1700 degrees Fahrenheit for case-hardening.

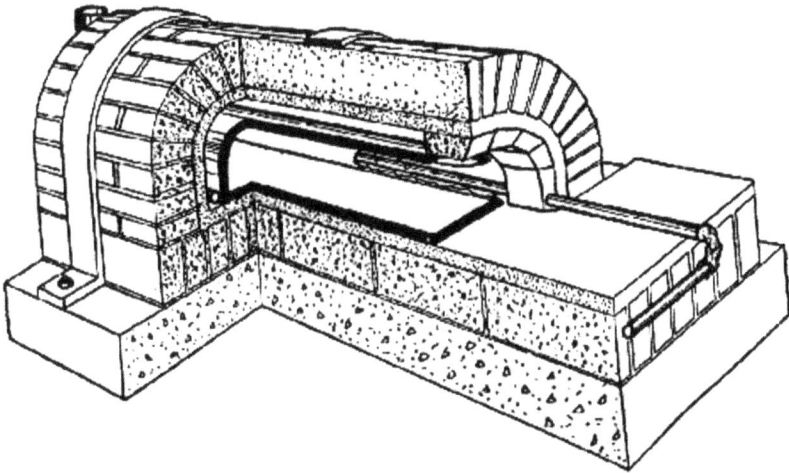

Shop built, gas furnace of fire brick lined with fire clay, set upon a concrete base. A steel muffle, removable through the door opening, is shown in place with a cut-away section showing ports in gas burner, two of which are used.

For hardening and tempering the carbon-steels, heating in a lead or salt bath, usually barium-chloride, or a bath of cyanide-of-potassium has proved very satisfactory. Lead is usually used where the temperature tolerance is narrow. The lead should be chemically pure and especially free from sulphur, as this injures the steel. The surface of the lead is usually covered with a dusting of charcoal to prevent oxidation and when it is necessary to clean the bath add dry, common salt and stir in with the melted lead. All dirt and foreign matter will rise to the surface and can then be skimmed off. To prevent lead from sticking to the steel, the steel to be heated should be dipped into a solution of one pound of powdered cyanide-of-potassium crystals to one gallon of boiling water and thoroughly dried before being placed in the melted lead. As lead gives off poisonous fumes when heated to 1200 degrees or more, the lead bath should be covered with a hooded safety flue to lead these fumes to the outer air.

The barium-chloride bath has proved very satisfactory, as it is suitable to the high temperatures necessary in the hardening of high-speed steel as well as to those used for carbon-steel.

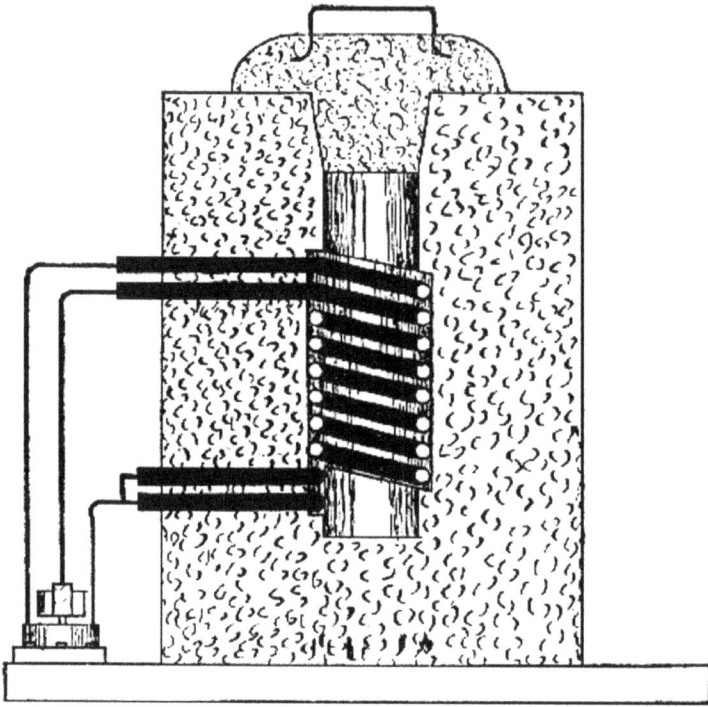

A small, shop-built, electric hardening and tempering furnace for reamers, cutters, firing-pins and small parts. Two "Calrod" elements of 750 or 900 watts are spirally wound to a two inch internal diameter and set in asbestos cement inside a stovepipe casing, 8″ × 12″, set upon an asbestos-board base. A three-point range switch is used to connect it to 220 volt, three-wire circuit and a rheostat should be used to control the current and keep the heat from running higher than necessary. Total cost about $15.00.

The salt forms a film on the steel that adheres to it and cuts down its rate of cooling while being transferred to the quenching bath ; in which this film readily leaves the steel. Parts heated in this bath always come out cleaner from the quenching bath y especially high-speed steel. After being used for some time this heating bath shows a tendency to pit the steel and must then be renewed.

The cyanide-of-potassium bath has some advantages for carbon-steels in that it prevents scaling and soft spots and also adds an additional percentage of carbon to the surface of the steel, which makes this surface harder. It is however highly poisonous and should be covered with a hood connected to a flue for the fumes are deadly in very small amounts.

Steel used for the making of gun parts, or of tools to be subsequently hardened, should be heated to its critical temperature for purposes of annealing and normalizing, so that all strains set up in the steel are relieved before it is machined. This heating to the critical point for normalizing should also be repeated after the part is partly machined, so as to relieve strains set up by the machining process. In the case of tools such as reamers, drills or other cutters that are to cut exact sizes, this is done just before grinding to rough finish.

The temperatures used for annealing, normalizing or hardening carbon-steels are as follows:

Up to .20% carbon 1600 to 1650 degrees Fahrenheit

From .20 to .35% carbon 1550 to 1600 degrees Fahrenheit

From .35 to .50% carbon 1500 to 1550 degrees Fahrenheit

From .50 to .70% carbon 1450 to 1500 degrees Fahrenheit

From .70 to .90% carbon 1400 to 1450 degrees Fahrenheit

With .90% carbon or over 1350 to 1400 degrees Fahrenheit

Carbon or high-speed steels should be brought up to heat slowly and when annealing or normalizing should be cooled very slowly, either by being buried in slaked lime to cool, or better yet by being packed in a cast- iron box or pipe in charcoal, sand or slaked lime, sealed with fire clay and heated in the furnace while so packed ; after which the furnace is shut off, all dampers closed and the parts allowed to cool slowly in the furnace, usually over night.

As stated before, steel heated to its critical point assumes the finest grain structure possible for it for strength and hardness, and to enable it to retain this strength and hardness it must be quenched at this temperature. For this purpose the quenching bath is used. Water saturated with salt, making a brine, gives the greatest hardness but also the greatest brittleness. Plain soft water of low temperatures, just above freezing, comes next in line, giving slightly less hardness and brittleness. This hardness decreases as the temperature of the water is raised, until it reaches a temperature of about 120 degrees, when the steel quenched in water of this temperature remains comparatively soft. Oil is usually considered the best quenching bath when both hardness and toughness are desired. Lin- seed and cottonseed oils give very good results on high- speed steel,

while sperm or lard-oil is preferred for springs. Good results in hardening carbon-steel are obtained by using a water bath of 60 to 70 degrees
temperature with an inch or two of cottonseed oil on top of the water. An
air blast is often used to harden high-speed steel. Mercury is sometimes
used to harden a carbon drill for use on very hard steel, but it makes the
drill very brittle.

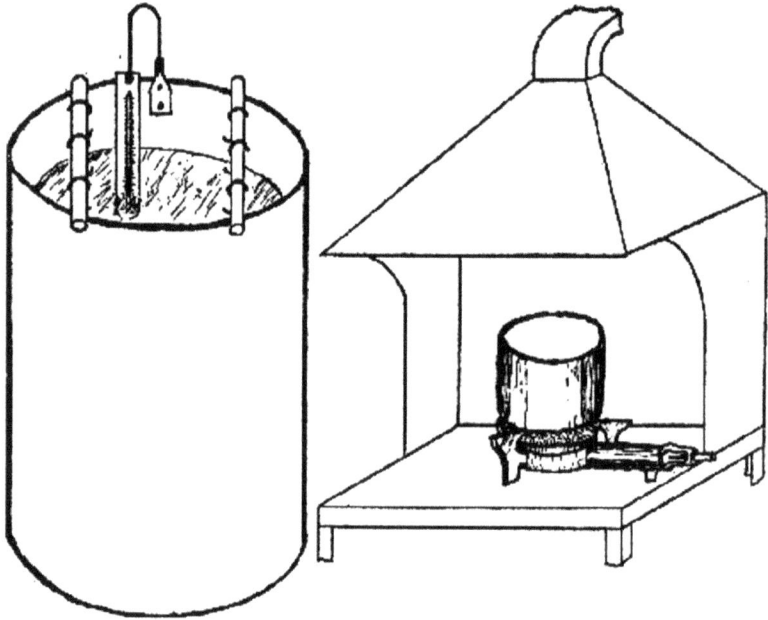

**Left shows oil tempering bath, with high-temperature mercury ther-
mometer hanging in the bath. Right shows set up of lead bath or
potassium cyanide bath for hardening, showing hood arrangement to
carry off the poisonous fumes.**

The quenching bath should be of large enough size so that the part
being quenched does not heat the bath. Slender parts of such shapes as
drills and reamers should be inserted in the bath endwise and disc shapes
edgewise. The parts should be agitated in the bath or the bath agitated
by an air jet. Parts which are considerably heavier at one point than at
another should always be quenched heavy-part first. Parts should never
be dropped to the bottom of the bath or they will have soft spots on the
under side.

High-speed steels are heated to 1470 or 1500 degrees for annealing
or normalizing while packed in cast-iron box or pipe with slaked lime for
a period of two hours for small tools and a longer time for large pieces

and allowed to cool slowly in the furnace, with the heat shut off. A higher temperature than this is required for hardening high-speed tool-steel. It is usually heated slowly to about 1800 degrees and then heated rapidly to 2200 degrees and quenched in linseed or cottonseed oil, although a dry air blast is sometimes used as a quenching medium.

The surface of finished dies or tools must be protected from contact with the air while the steel is heated or the surface of the steel will become oxidized, forming scale. To prevent this, the steel is painted on all ex- posed surfaces with a mixture of bone-black and sperm- oil if it is to be heated in furnace or forge without being packed in an iron box of slaked lime or charcoal. This mixture will easily wash off in the quenching bath, provided the steel has been heated in a furnace and not exposed to the direct action of the flame. If it is so coated and then heated in a forge with- out being encased in a box, this coating will protect the surface fairly well but it must be polished off with fine emery cloth after- wards. Finished steel parts or tools may be heated in an open forge provided the articles are packed in a cast-iron box or pipe with slaked lime or charcoal. Use a deep fire and cover the box completely with the live coals. This works very well for annealing or normalizing where the temperature need not run quite as high or be quite so closely controlled as in heating for the hardening process.

After carbon-steel tools or parts have been hardened, the temper must be drawn to give them the proper toughness, for in the hardened state they are usually too brittle for use.

Drawing the temper, or tempering, is done at a much lower tempera- ture than the hardening process and is much easier to control. It is not necessary to use a pyrometer for this process, as the high temperature, mercury thermometers used for deep-fat frying run up high enough for temperatures used in the tempering process. These thermometers are not expensive, costing from one to two dollars usually.

While tempering can be done in an open fire, by watching the colors produced on the polished steel by the rising heat and then quenching the article when the proper color has appeared, this is the poorest method to use in tempering, as colors produced on steel by heat vary with the carbon content of the steel, the more carbon the steel contains the quicker the high temperature colors appear.

For this reason it is much better to heat the articles in a bath of some liquid that can be held to exactly the proper temperature. The articles to be tempered are hung in the liquid so that they do not touch either sides or bottom of the container and are left in it long enough to be heated to the same temperature as the bath. The thermometer should be hung in the bath in the same way, clear of sides and bottom, so that the temperature of the bath can be read and the heat properly regulated.

Oil is one of the best tempering baths, but this can- not be heated over an open flame or it will catch fire, so if a flame burner of any type is used the flame must be fully covered so that it cannot rise around the pot containing the oil. The modern high-speed electric element used on modem-type electric ranges with its several point control makes an excellent heat for tempering baths. In case an oil bath is used, the pot should be large enough to cover the burner completely, so that fumes from the oil bath will not be ignited.

Various alloys of lead may be used for tempering baths. Lead alone melts at too high a temperature for tempering, but lead alloyed with varying amounts of tin will melt at temperatures low enough for tempering. The greater the amount of tin in the lead the lower the melting point will be. Experiments can be made with these alloys and the proper alloy found for the temperature desired by checking the melting points with the thermometer.

A sand bath is sometimes used for tempering. The sand should be very clean of course and it may be heated over any type of fire, which is one of its ad- vantages. One of its disadvantages is that it is not as easy to obtain an even temperature in a sand bath as in a liquid bath, so temperatures should be taken at a number of different points throughout the sand bath.

If it is necessary to temper parts or tools without a bath of some type, an iron plate should be heated to a low red-heat and the polished parts placed thereon. They must be turned constantly, so that the heating is as even as possible on all sides, and the article is then quenched in oil when the proper color appears.

Parts heated in a bath of course require no quenching, as they can become no hotter than the bath. Tempering must be done on the rising heat and not on descending heat. If a part is heated above the proper temperature, it must be put through the hardening process again and then retempered. Cold parts or tools should not be placed in a hot bath, either the article should he preheated before being placed in the tempering bath or else the article should be placed in a cool bath and the heat brought up.

When using a lead bath for either tempering or hardening, the steel will not sink in it, as lead is heavier than steel, so attach parts or tools to stiff wires fastened to a heavy piece laid across the top of the bath or bend the wires at right-angles and put them in holes drilled through the side of the pot above the liquid line.

Case-hardening is accomplished by impregnating the surface of steel with carbon, by heating it at high temperatures while packed in an iron or steel box with proper carburizing materials, or by heating the steel in potassium-cyanide in an iron pot.

These carburizing boxes may be made of malleable iron, cast-steel or nichrome steel. The steel pots arc rather expensive but the ones made of malleable iron are moderate in cost and give a service of from 450 to 500 hours. Nichrome boxes or pots have given several thousand hours of service. Cast-iron boxes are the cheapest and give the shortest service. The boxes should be at least one-half inch thick, with a removable lid of the same thickness. Boxes must be large enough so that at least one-half inch of carburizing material surrounds the parts on sides and bottom and one inch on top, to allow for shrinkage. Parts should be separated from each other by at least one-quarter inch of carburizing material.

Case-hardening by heating the articles in liquid potassium-cyanide to a temperature of 1562 degrees Fahrenheit gives a quick and very even case, but it is superficial and won't stand any further finishing after being case-hardened as the hardening will be cut through. As the cyanide gives off deadly poisonous fumes, this type of case-hardening should be done in an open pot, under a hood attached to a flue with a good draft, and the operator should stand back from the pot.

The best case-hardening is done by the pack-harden- ing method, that is, packing the articles to be hardened in iron boxes in which the article is surrounded by powdered charcoal, coke, leather or bone and heated at a rather low heat over a long period of time. This method gives a deeper hardening and the temperature is more easily controlled. The time required varies with the size of the pieces. Temperatures may be held at 1550 degrees Fahrenheit. Green bonc should never be used as a carburizing material, as it contains phosphorus. The carburizing material must also be free from sulphur and be perfectly dry.

The lid of the box is sealed with fire clay and the thermocouple of the pyrometer is inserted through a hole in the lid, which is also sealed with fire clay.

The high-carbon steels do not accept case-hardening as readily and therefore as deeply as do the low- carbon steels classed as machinery steel, of which cold- rolled steel is a good example. However, there are times when a high-carbon steel is required for a part and it is desired to give the part a very high surface hardness and for this purpose the high-carbon steel is used and is tempered after being case-hardened, the case-hardening giving an additional carbon content to the surface only.

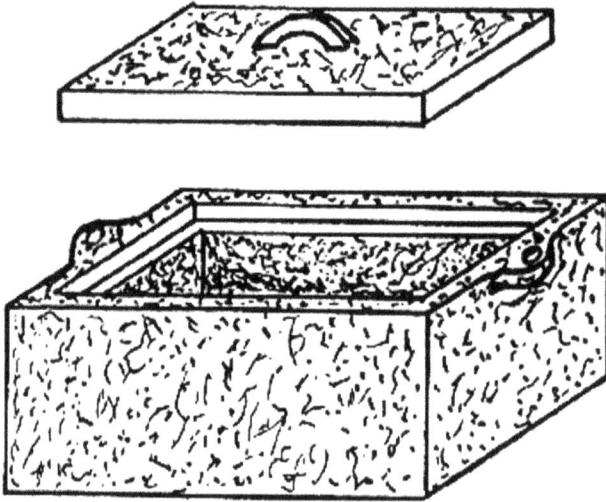

Cast iron box, in which articles are packed for case-hardening.

To harden the carbon placed in the steel, regardless of the type of steel used, by the case-hardening process it is necessary to quench the work while it is at the hardening heat. The poorest way to do this is to quench the work directly from the carburizing box, although it is the quickest method. This does not give the maximum strength and toughness. The best method is to allow the work to cool slowly in the box, remove it from the box when it is cold, place it in the furnace and reheat to the hardening temperature (1550 to 1600 degrees Fahrenheit) and then quench. This will give a good case-hardening and a tough core, but if the maximum is desired, quench it in oil after the reheating and then reheat the work a second time and quench it in water. This will give the toughest possible core and the finest crystalline case, with a graduation of case into core.

As stated above, if a high-carbon steel of .90% to 1.25% is used for a case-hardened part, the temper may be drawn after hardening by heating to the correct tempering heat and quenching.

Here are the tempering colors and temperatures.

420° F., very faint yellow

Drawing dies and punches and gun parts subject to friction but no shock 430° F., very pale yellow

Wood gravers, checking tools 440° F., light yellow

Chambering reamers 450° F., pale straw yellow

Hand reamers, rifle action-pins 460° F., deep straw yellow

Milling cutters, machine reamers, points of triggers and sears 500° F., yellow brown

Twist-drills, firing-pin body only 550° F., dark purple

Gun hammers, flat springs, extractors, screw- drivers, cold-chisels 570° F., dark blue

Firing-pin noses, light flat springs, small screw- drivers

The proper heat treatment of a rifle or shotgun ac- tion requires quite a bit of equipment and considerable experience, so that in case the reader has only an action or two which he wishes to reheat-treat — either to re- harden worn spots, such as action-pin holes after reaming them to larger size and fitting new pins, or to re- color an action from which the finish has been worn — it would undoubtedly be best to send this work to a shop which can do it properly, without danger of warp- age or improper treatment.

A centrally-located firm which can do this work properly and at a reasonable price is the Twin City Steel Treating Company, 1114 S. Third Street, Minneapolis, Minnesota. They can do either cyanide or pack hardening — either plain, to be blued, or in rich colors. The cost of this in the plain will run from 80f to $1.00, depending upon the size of the action, while in colors the cost will be $1.00 to $1.50 per action.

Plate XIX

Lathe setup with steady rest supporting the rifle barrel while turning down
some of its outside diameter. A straight portion is turned upon the barrel, long
enough for the jaws of the steady rest to bear, about 8" from the tail center end
of a barrel being machined upon centers in the lathe. The portion of the
barrel from the tail center end to the jaws of the steady rest is then turned to
size, after which another straight portion is machined upon the barrel 8"
closer to the live spindle end and the steady rest is moved to the new position
and this second section turned to size. This operation is repeated until the full
length of the barrel is turned to size.

Chapter 17 THE BLUEING OF FIREARMS

In this chapter we shall mainly take up shop practice and the various little handling kinks useful in the polishing and blueing of gun barrels or small parts, and will refer you to Angier's "Firearm Blueing and Browning" — a companion book to this one, gotten out by the same publisher — for the necessary formulae of various solutions to use or to experiment with. Angier's book is a most complete one in this respect, containing be- tween two hundred and three hundred different blueing solutions, some of which are certain to be well adapted for use in your locality and by your method of handling.

It must be kept in mind that a definite formula and system of application cannot be followed identically, nor be expected to give the same result in one section of the country that it does in another place some hundred of miles away, where the climate, humidity, altitude, water and other considerations may differ greatly. The blueing of guns by the application of these various solutions is actually a complex chemical process, one very apt to be radically affected by small but important variations in the basic ingredients employed in the different operations, if not in the solution itself. A solution and a method of application which gives perfect results here in Boise may not work well at all along the coastal section of Louisiana, so be prepared to try something different if the results at first do not turn out as you would have them.

For convenience and speed in blueing guns, three tanks are necessary. These three tanks can be made of 24 to 26-gauge black sheet-steel or iron, such as can be obtained from any sheet-metal shop or stove and furnace installation outfit. They are best made by being bent to shape from a single sheet for each tank, with no soldered joints and therefore no chance to develop leaks. There is however, no objection to making these tanks with the end pieces separate if these ends are welded in place, but this is not necessary.

Blueing tanks should be at least 40 inches long, 6 inches wide and 6 inches deep. A sheet of metal 18 inches wide by 52 inches long will make a tank of about this size. Clamp a piece of 2" x 4" timber as long as the sheet on the metal 6 inches from one edge and bend this edge up at a right-angle. Repeat this on the opposite edge and you have an open ended trough 52 inches long and 6 inches wide by 6 inches deep. Clamp a 6 inch piece of 2" x 4" timber across the bottom of this trough 6 inches from one end and bend that end up at a right-angle. Bend the triangular-shaped pieces developed at each side of this end back along the outside of the sides, hammering them down tightly, then put a rivet through each point and through the side of the tank near the top. Bend the other end up in this same manner, and one tank is made. Make the other two by this same method — or a better one if you can think of it.

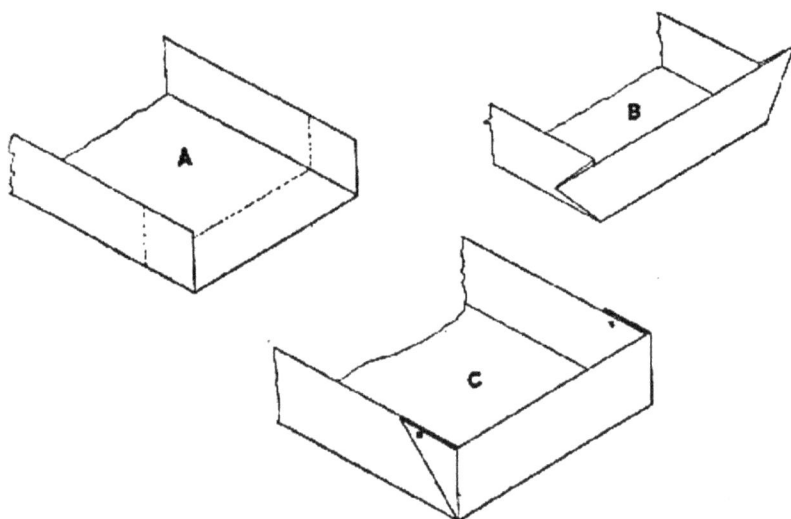

Various bending steps in the making of sheet-iron blueing tanks.

The purpose of three tanks is; one for boiling of parts in the de-greasing solution, a second for hot water to rinse the parts afterwards, and the third to hold the clean water used for heating the parts, so that the blueing solution will take. You can get along with two tanks by letting the parts lie in the rinsing tank while you clean the first tank thoroughly and fill it up with water to heat the parts in while doing the swabbing on of the blueing solution.

The method used to heat the tanks will vary according to the cost and suitability of heating elements in various locations. Where electricity is available at a low rate it is the best method of heating, as it makes no fumes and heats up the shop less than most of the other methods used. This electric heat may be applied by hot plates of 750 watts capacity, four of them being used, with the steel tank bottom set directly on the plates, or two 1000 watt hairpin- type heaters may be used in each tank, one inserted from each end through boiler flanges riveted and welded on each end of the tank as close to the bottom as will allow the heaters to be screwed into the tank. For this type of heater the tank should be covered on sides and bottom with half- inch thickness of cane board insulation and a top, covered likewise, should be kept on the tank. Hard- ware cloth (coarse-mesh heavy wire screen) of mesh is placed in the tank over the hairpin-type heaters to prevent parts getting caught beneath the heaters. The edges of this screen are turned down at each side to support the screen above the heaters and the heaters themselves will support the screen.

If the four hot plate type heaters are used, it will not be necessary to insulate the tank, but a cover should be used. This can be merely a sheet of the black iron a little larger than the tank, and will speed up the heating of the water no matter what kind of heat is applied to the tanks.

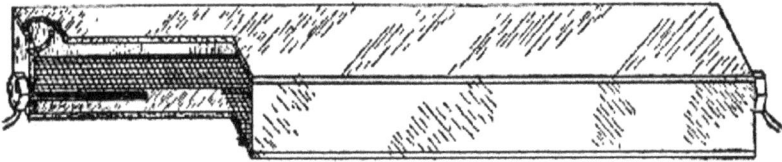

The electrically heated tank, covered with ½″ insulation, showing hairpin type heaters, ¼″ mesh hardware cloth screen and strap across one corner to hold jar of blueing solution in place. Parts go from the rinsing tank to this tank for the actual blueing operation.

Next to electricity in convenience for heat is gas. This will give a very even, high heat, its only objection being that it heats the shop considerably. A three or four-burner gasoline or kerosene stove will give equally good heat but usually requires more attention than gas or electric heat.

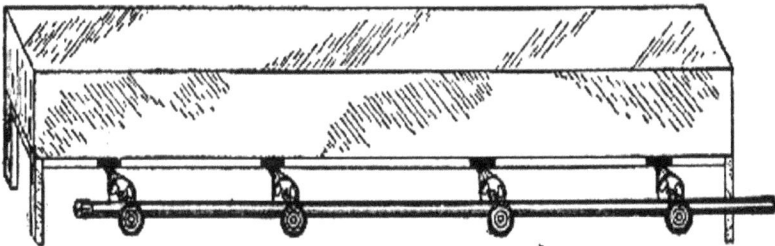

The gas heated blueing tank, here shown ready for washing the gun parts free of oil in a lye or caustic soda solution.

While we are speaking about heat is a good time to mention that as altitude increases water boils at a lower temperature., and as its sea-level boiling temperature of 212 degrees is none to high a heat for good results in blueing, when you are working at altitudes of 3000 feet and more the water temperature is hardly sufficient for a good job of blueing. Small parts and thin parts that cool off rapidly when removed from the water should be held in the flame of an alcohol torch, or a gas torch with a neutral flame, to have their temperature raised a little. Don't overdo this superheating or you will have trouble with excessive rusting, which will leave a dark brown coating on the steel. The temperature only needs to be raised a few degrees in the torch flame to do a good job of blueing.

Guns must be entirely taken apart to do a good job of blueing as when a gun is left partly assembled, water remains in crevices and after the blueing solution has been applied this water will run out over the surface as you turn the gun in your hands and will either wash away the blueing solution or will "watermark" it.

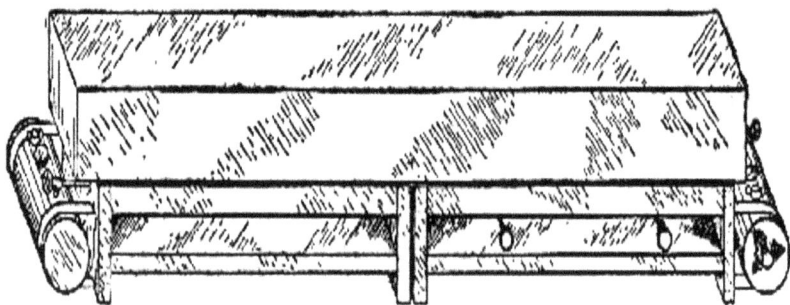

The gasoline or kerosene heated tank, here ready for rinsing the parts as they come from the degreasing tank.

After the gun has been completely taken apart, wash all parts in high-test gasoline, using a stiff brush to get into all corners and if necessary use a small screw-driver to scrape away heavy grease and dirt. You can now see all scratches and cuts, which* must be polished out before the blueing is applied if the gun is to look well afterwards.

Use fine files to remove scratches and cuts, then polish the file marks out with carborundum cloth, starting with coarse and finishing with fine grades, polishing lengthwise of the barrel and action, as cross- polishing shows up badly after the blueing is finished.

Examine carefully for rust all surfaces to be blued and if this rust is anything beyond a very thin surface coating, apply hydrochloric acid to these places. Wear rubber gloves to keep the acid off your hands and apply fresh acid continually for several minutes with wads of cotton. If the acid is not used to kill the deeply rusted spots, no matter how well you polish it there will be times when this rust will show spots on the steel after it has been chemically cleaned with lye or caustic-soda solution.

All parts to be blued should now be buffed to a good polish on muslin buffing wheels, using emery paste in stick or brick form on the buff. These buffing wheels can be obtained from William Dixon Inc., 32-36 E. Kinney St., Newark, New Jersey. A diameter of 8" is about right for these buffing wheels when run at a speed of 1750 R.P.M., or a 6" wheel at 3600 R.P.M. These wheels can be bought in sections of 18-ply and upward and about 100-ply will make a wide enough buff. They can be mounted on any ordinary 1 /\ -horse motor with a standard arbor attachment, which Dixon can supply or which can be bought from any of the home shop equipment manufacturers such as Walker- Turner of Plainfield, New Jersey; Delta Mfg. Co. of Milwaukee, Wisconsin ; Sears-Roebuck or Montgomery Ward & Co.

The emery cake used can be bought of William Dixon Inc. in grades from 180, the coarse, to F, the fine. To apply it to the wheel, turn on the motor, starting the buffing wheel, and hold the emery cake against the revolving wheel until it is well coated. Always polish the barrel, receiver and other parts in a lengthwise direction, never crosswise, except where necessary next to a shoulder, and then remove these cross polish marks with a piece of crocus cloth. It will be necessary to renew the emery paste upon the buffing wheel from time to time as the polishing proceeds. Gloves should be worn during the polishing operation, as the parts will get quite hot and if you take hold of a hot spot bare- handed you may drop a barrel and receiver on the floor, if the floor happens to be concrete it will not improve the appearance of the gun.

If you desire a wider range of polishing grit than you can buy in the regular emery stick or cake, you can buy carborundum powders in a wide range of sizes from the Carborundum Co. at Niagara Falls, New York. The buffing wheels can be coated with stick- type belt dressing by holding a stick of it against the wheel and after the wheel is well coated you can stop it and rub the carborundum powder into the surface of the buffing wheel.

Sometimes a gun is quite scaly with rust which has eaten slightly into the surface and in these cases it is best to get a circular wire buffer that can be mounted on the arbor on the motor. The wire of this buffer should be of the crinkly type and be of a diameter of .008" to .010". These may be purchased of William Dixon Inc., Sears Roebuck & Co., or Montgomery Ward & Co. A 6" wire wheel will be large enough and in using it, the parts should be buffed lengthwise and do not bury the parts in the wire buff while using it but let the ends of the wires impinge upon the sur- face being buffed, for it works faster used this way.

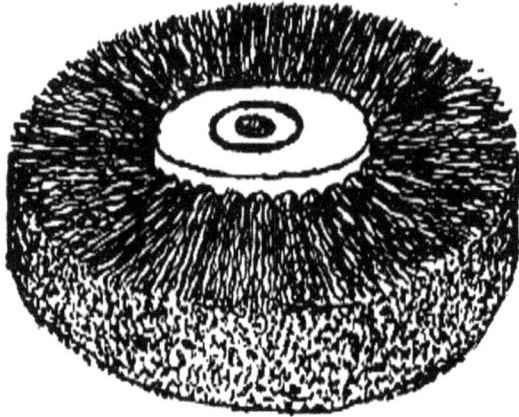

The wire buffing wheel, used to buff off the rust coating deposited by the blueing solution, leaving the blue film formed beneath the rust.

After this wire buffing has removed all the loose rust you can get off with it, use a leather buffing wheel coated with the carborundum grains, glued onto it. William Dixon Inc. can supply the leather wheels, called "Bullneck" polishing wheels, and they can also supply the glue, in flake form, which is used to coat these wheels. If you desire you can make a very good substitute for these bullneck wheels by getting rather thin sole leather from a shoe maker, laying enough sheets together to make a wheel 1" thick, and riveting these sheets together about 1" from the edge. A wheel of 6" diameter is large enough. After the center hole is made, it is mounted upon the motor shaft and, with an improvised tool rest to steady a wood chisel upon, use the chisel to true up the edge of the wheel.

Spread the carborundum powder, of #100 grit or finer, upon a newspaper laid upon a flat surface, spread- ing the grains out evenly, then coat the edge of the wheel with glue and, putting a short piece of shaft through the center to act as a handle on each side, roll the glued edge of the wheel upon the carborundum grains, rolling it back and forth until it has a good coating. After the glue has dried, mount the wheel on the motor arbor, stand out of line with it as you start the motor and let it run a few minutes to throw off any grains that did not adhere to the glued surface.

After the scaly spots are cut down with this leather wheel, buff the parts to a polish with the muslin buff described above.

After all parts are polished, they are ready for the chemical cleaning bath of lye or caustic-soda. Put sufficient water in one tank to cover the parts by an inch or more and add to it a heaping tablespoon of lye or caustic-soda for each gallon of water. Start your heat and be sure that all the lye or soda is dissolved, before you put in the parts to be blued.

Small parts should have wires, about #15 gauge iron wire, attached to them so that the free end of the wire can be bent in a hook over the edge of the tank, allowing the parts to hang beneath the surface of the water.

Thin parts, such as magazine tubes and shotgun barrels, are too thin to retain the heat long enough when the blueing solution is applied to them, so they should have iron rods inserted inside of them to act as heat holders and this has to be done before these parts are placed in the lye cleaning solution. The rods can be longer than the tubes or barrels and just beyond the ends of the tubes or barrels drill a hole through the rods at each end, so that iron wire can be placed through the hole and wound around the rods, to pre- vent them from slipping out of place. The rods should be of a size to fit the tubes or barrels closely.

Showing a bar of solid steel passed through the thin magazine tube of a shotgun and held in place with wire wrapped around the bar at each end of the tube. The purpose of this is to keep thin barrels or tubes hot while applying the blueing solution to them.

Many directions that you read for blueing gun barrels tell you to grease the inside of the barrel and insert tightly in each end a hardwood plug, several inches long, that has previously been boiled in lye or caustic soda solution and thoroughly dried. This plug, or rather these plugs, are to keep the water from entering the bore and are also to act as handles. This may be all right on a light-weight rifle barrel of .30 caliber or more, or for a shotgun barrel, but for a heavy-weight barrel of .22 or .25 caliber such plugs are too light and after being in the boiling water for a while they will become rubbery, bend very easily and often work out of the barrel, then, as the inside of the barrel is greased, the water in the blueing tank becomes greasy so that you are obliged to empty it out, reclean the barrel with the de-greasing solution, wash out the tank and start all over again. If you wish to plug the barrel in these smaller calibers, grease it inside and drive in wood plugs, flush with the ends and don't try to leave the plugs long enough to use as handles. These plugs may swell and give you some trouble in removing them but, if this happens, drill a hole through the one in the chamber end, just large enough to admit passing a small rod through it and then push out the muzzle plug. The breech plug may then be removed from the muzzle end by inserting a full-sized rod.

In using any solution that docs not contain a high percentage of acid there is no necessity for plugging the barrel, as boiling water never hurt the interior of any barrel and the barrel may be wiped out after the blueing is completed and then polished with a tight patch dipped in any good solvent such as Fiendoil. Some slight discoloration may remain in the barrel but this is quickly removed by the shooting and cleaning. If you are using a "swab-on" blueing solution that is very highly acid, the water in the tank may be neutralized by the addition of a small quantity of caustic potash (30 to 45 grains per quart) a 5 recommended in Angiers book. This is for the water in which you boil the guns to heat them while applying the blueing solution, not the cleaning bath of lye and water.

After the parts are boiled for fifteen or twenty min- utes in the cleaning solution, lift them out, taking hold of the wires only on the small parts and handling the large parts with two iron wire hooks of about #10 wire, for from now on the metal must not touch your skin or it will absorb oil from it and the cleaning bath will then have to be repeated. After lifting the parts from the cleaning bath, immediately place them in a second tank of clean boiling water for about ten min- utes, agitating them in the water to hasten the removal of any lye or caustic-soda. If you have a large sink with plenty of running hot water they can be thoroughly rinsed beneath the faucet and the second tank can be dispensed with. Do not let the parts touch the sink or faucet while rinsing them.

The parts are now ready to be placed in the tank of clean, pure, boiling water, to be heated so that the blueing solution can be applied. Fill this tank fairly full, so that you will not have to add more water than absolutely necessary while the blueing progresses and the water boils away, for cold water, or even ordinary hot water added, will cool off the boiling water in the tank and delay you.

This last tank should have a 1/2"-wide strip of sheet- steel fastened across one corner, inside the tank, so that a glass jar to hold the blueing solution can be pushed down rather tightly in that corner, behind the strap. This strap can be soldered in place, but it will hold better if a small rivet is placed through each end and through the side of the tank.

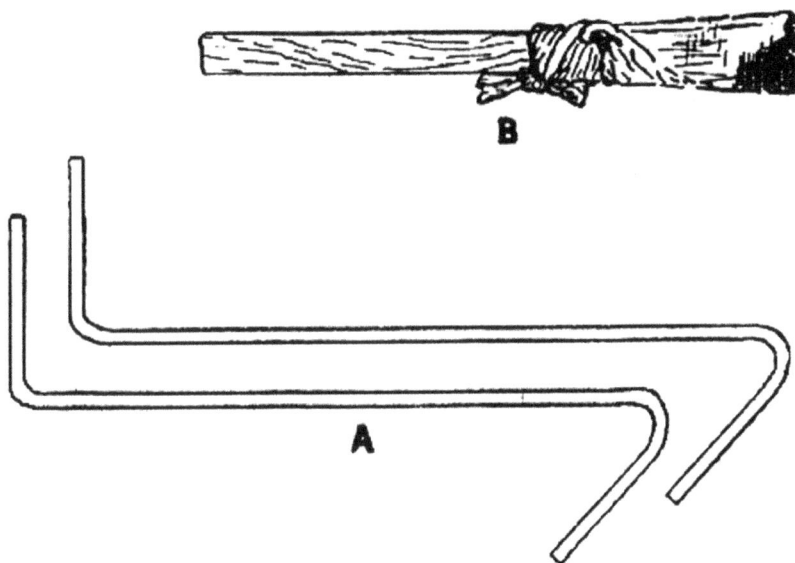

A illustrates heavy hooks of iron wire, necessary for handling large parts and gun barrels in the blueing, rinsing and degreasing tanks. B shows swabbing stick, prepared with a swab of surgical dressing fastened upon it, ready for applying the blueing solution.

The small *4 -pint salad-dressing jars are the best thing I have ever found to hold the blueing solution, as they seldom break. This jar should be put in place and a small amount of blueing solution placed in it, when the tank is filled with water and the heat turned on to boil the water. A depth of ^ 2 " in the jar will be enough of the blueing solution and if more is needed it can be added later.

Distilled water is the best for this final tank, it is not absolutely necessary but water containing a lot of chemicals may cause trouble. Some city water is very pure, containing only a small percentage of chloride-of-lime put in to kill bacteria, and this water is all right to use. If your city water or well water contains various chemicals, which so-called hard water always does, it is safer not to use it but use rain water instead, if it is free of acid and alkalies. This can be determined by getting some litmus paper from your druggist with directions on how to use it.

The best type of jar to use for blueing solution.

After the parts have boiled in this clean water for a few minutes, lift them out and, in case of large pieces, stand them on end on a table or bench covered with a couple of thicknesses of clean newspapers and apply the etching solution of nitric-acid and water, 1 to 10, or 1 to 13, or the salammoniac priming solution as directed in Angier's book. In the case of gun parts that are case-hardened or are of some special anti-rust steel, use Spencer acid, the formula for which is given in Angier's book.

These etchants, or primers, open up the pores of the metal so that the blueing solution will take hold readily. They are applied with a cotton pad dipped in the etchant, which is used with long even strokes on the parts and the parts are returned to the boiling water as quickly as possible afterwards.

As to the blueing solution, Angier's book gives numbers of them, some of which I have used. His salammoniac blueing solution has always intrigued me but I never have tried it. The solution with which I have had the best success, among the swab-on solutions that I have tried, is the Clyde Baker formula. This is given both in Angier's book and in Baker's book "Modern Gunsmithing." As Baker says, it is a basic solution (this is his #1) and you will make slight changes in it perhaps, to meet varying conditions to get the best results. If a red or burnt-orange color appears after the parts are buffed, the solution is too strong for the steel in question, and a small amount of distilled water should be added to the solution in the jar in the blueing tank. If you add too much water and get it too weak, in which case the. blue buffs off, leaving the steel bright, more of the solution from the bottle can be added to that in the jar to strengthen it again.

A piece of 3/8" dowel -rod which has been boiled in lye-water, well rinsed in clean hot water and then dried, is sawed for a distance of 1", lengthwise. Using 1 1/2"-wide surgical gauze, insert one end into the sawed slot and wind twelve or fifteen thicknesses of the gauze around the end of the dowel-rod, leaving a few inches more hanging at the end so that this part can be split lengthwise and wound around the dowel in opposite directions at the rear end of the swab and tied, to hold the swab in place. This swab is placed in the solution in the jar and allowed to heat up with the solution, while the parts to he blued are getting hot in the boiling water.

Clean cotton gloves should be worn, so that parts will not be spotted by being touched with bare hands. These gloves will also protect you from the heat of the parts, in fact it is advisable to wear a close-fitting, double-silk or finely knit glove beneath the cotton glove on the hand with will hold the parts while the other hand applies the blueing solution, for these parts are plenty hot. These cotton gloves should be put through a washing and be dried before being used, to remove any oil that might be in the fabric.

A part is removed from the boiling water by its attached wire, or in the case of large parts, by one or both of the hooks and the excess water that lies in crevices is blown out, for if you wish a smooth looking job of blueing the parts must be dry, and they must dry instantly from their own heat when removed from the water. Take the swab from the blueing solution, pressing out all excess solution from the swab against the mouth of the jar, for if the solution runs from the swab over the surface of the work when the swab is applied, the work will be streaked. Cover the surface to be blued as rapidly as possible, using long, even strokes, going over the smaller surfaces, such as receivers, a couple of times. The parts should be hot enough to dry the solution instantly and if they are not this hot, blow on the solution to dry it, or if the heat of the boiling water is not sufficient, hold the part in a torch flame for an instant to raise the temperature, then reapply the solution. Get the part back in the water as quickly as possible and take out a second part. In the meantime, the swab is returned to the solution in the jar as soon as the first part is well coated, so that it can be getting a new load of hot solution. Get the water off the second part and, using the swab as before, coat this part and repeat until all parts have been given a coating of the solution.

Some directions for blueing tell you to buff the parts or rub them with steel -wool after the first coating of the blueing solution has been applied to them, but I have always found that two or even three coatings of the parts with the solution between buffing seems to give a more even coat of blueing, with less trouble from streaks. The parts are returned to the boiling water each time between coatings with the solution, so that they will be good and hot for the next coating.

If you are going to remove the rust coat formed by the solution by hand, you will use a fine grade of steel- wool, which you have first boiled in lye- water to make oil and grease free. A second pair of cotton gloves should be used in handling the parts while buffing off the rust coat, for the first pair that you use while applying the solution may be wet or have some solution on them and this may cause a spot on the blued surface, so keep the second pair of gloves dry and change gloves before the buff-ing operation.

Remove a part from the water, blow all water from crevices and allow it to dry. You can take your time for this operation, so don't hurry. Take a wad of the clean steel-wool, rub the rusty-gray coating formed by the blueing solution from the surface of the steel, rubbing gently with strokes lengthwise of the piece. Do not rub the steel bright but rub it until a uni-form blue or gray-black surface appears. You will need some wire scratch brushes of fine wire to get right up to shoulders and into sharp angles. These should be made of wire of .004" to .005" diameter and they can be purchased of William Dixon Inc. Sometimes brushes like this can be bought at hardware stores or jewelry supply- houses in any large city. The shape of the brush doesn't matter much, hut it should not be too wide. If the steel bristles are too long and tend to matt badly in use, a pair of heavy shears or tin-snips can be used to cut them off shorter.

After the piece has been rubbed down on all blued surfaces, return it to the water and start in on another piece and work on through them all, returning each piece to the boiling water to get hot again so that you can give them the next coating of the blueing solution. Repeat this performance on each piece until they are all the color you wish. If a dull red sheen appears upon them, that does not rub off easily, this must all be rubbed off even if you have to rub until the steel is bright again, then add a little distilled water to the blueing solution in the jar as was directed above and re-apply the solution to the steel until you get the proper color.

Sometimes bright spots appear which will not take the solution. These are sometimes very small round spots or they may be streaks where a barrel has been rubbed until the surface is burnished and very dense. This will sometimes show up on shotgun barrels of the repeating type, either pump or autoloading, where the forearm rubs the barrel. The cure for these spots is a little rubbing with clean, fine, carborundum cloth, 180 grain or finer, and then some of the etchant solution applied to the spot or streak. The barrel is then re- turned to the boiling water and, when hot, the blueing solution is again applied and the blueing continued.

If, for removing the rust coating between swabbings, a power buff is used, a buff of six-inch diameter of crinkled wire of .004" to .005" diameter is correct. It should run at about 1750 R.P.M. These buffing wheels of wire can be purchased from William Dixon Inc. or from almost any large hardware supply house such as H. Channon & Co. of Wacker Drive and Randolph St., Chicago, Illinois. In using these wire buffing wheels, the part, being buffed should not be buried in the wheel but should be so held that the ends of the wires just contact the surface nicely. If a very high polish is de- sired, a finer wire can be specified for the buffing wheel, wire of .0025" or .003" diameter. These wire buffing wheels should be of steel or iron wire, never of brass, and they should be given a good bath in the lye solution and then rinsed before being used. They should be run for a while after the water is drained out of them before being used, so that they will be dry. They should not be handled with bare hands after being chemically cleaned, and after use they can be wrapped in clean paper until used again, so that they need not be put through the lye solution each time, the once being sufficient if they are kept wrapped as directed.

It is often a good plan to empty out the solution that remains in the jar when you are ready to buff off the rust coating, then rinse the jar in clean hot water, put in new solution and put a new swab of gauze on the dowel-stick, before again applying the solution to the buffed surface. Small parts that will easily go into the jar can often be coated by dipping in the solution in- stead of having it applied to them with a swab. In this way they do not cool off so much and they there- fore take the blueing better. As soon as they are lifted from the jar after being dipped, blow- all excess solution from them so that they are dry before returning them to the boiling water.

After the proper color has been attained on all parts, boil them for a few minutes, then lift them from the water and blow off all water to dry them rapidly, and immediately coat them with boiled linseed oil, using a piece of canton flannel or a brush, but do not rub them hard.

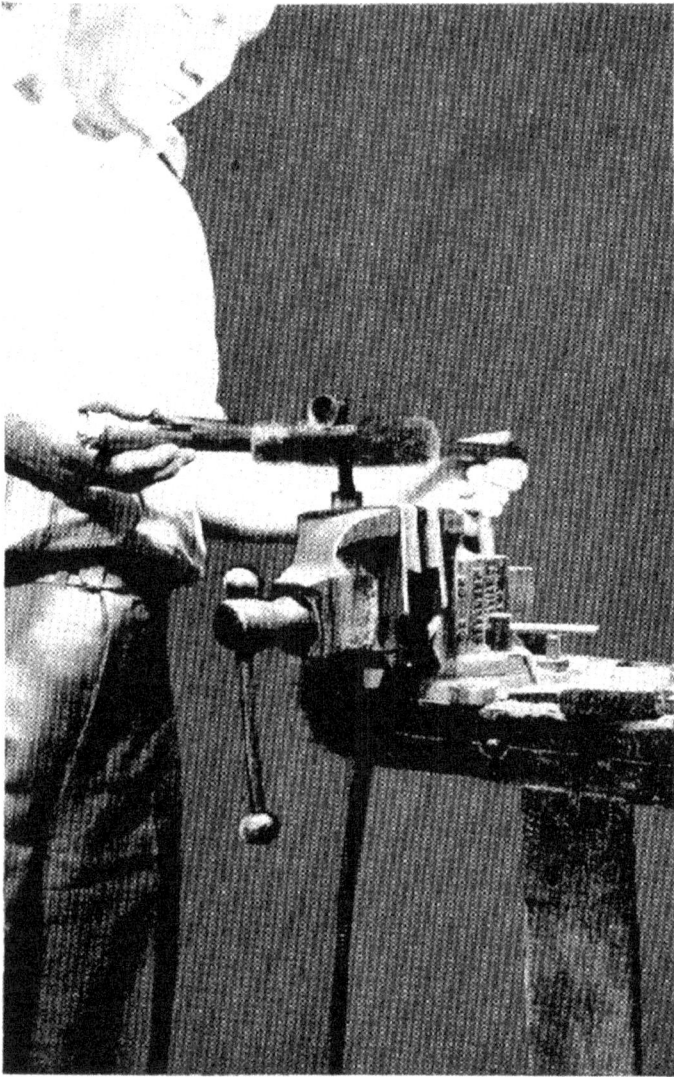

Plate XX

Using a fine wire buff, mounted on flexible shaft, for buffing a shotgun barrel in the blueing process. By running the buff in a horizontal plane, as shown, it is easier to watch the work at the point being buffed. It also prevents wires, which may be thrown from the buff, striking the face or eyes which will happen if the wire buff is operated in a vertical plane.

Hang them up and when the oil begins to gum on them in three or four hours, rub it off with another piece of canton flannel and then apply gun oil to all surfaces. Allow all parts to hang until the following day, when the gun oil may be wiped off and the gun assembled. The interior of receivers and other parts where surfaces were not buffed will show a rust- like coating but this can be removed with a stiff brush, like a tooth-brush, dipped in gun oil. The best time to do this is after the linseed oil is rubbed off and while you are applying the gun oil. Allow the gun oil to re- main on these unbuffed surfaces until the following day when wiping off the oil applied to the blued surfaces, at which time this oil on the unbuffed surfaces may also be wiped off.

The jar used to hold the blueing solution gradually accumulates a rust-like coating on the inside, which may be removed by placing in the jar a couple of tea- spoonfuls of ordinary liquid bleach, such as Clorox, which can be purchased at any grocery store, then fill- ing the jar to the top with water and allowing it to stand for a few days, after which a cotton cloth is used to rub the coating off and the jar is then well rinsed.

Nickel-plated arms can be blued. Formulas for re- moving the nickel will be found in Angier's book on Firearm Blueing, but very often the surface of the steel beneath the nickel plating has been left rough, to give the nickel a good grip on the steel, and the work involved in bringing this surface to a polish is so great that the expense is high, except on a gun of your own where time is of no object.

A few years ago a new type of blueing was introduced by the A. F. Stoeger Co. of 507 Fifth Ave., New York City, called "Stoeger's Black Diamond Lightning Bluer." This is a heavy-salt solution, the salts being supplied dry, ready mixed, by Stocger. For pistols and revolvers the five-pound can is recommended, for rifles and shotguns the twenty-pound can. These salts are placed in the tank dry and it is necessary to wear rub-ber gloves and goggles when doing this, as the dust that rises from the salts will blister your hands and injure your eyes if they are not protected. These salts in a dry state do not harm clothing or shoes but after water has been added to them, at the rate of 1/3 gallon for each five pounds of dry salt to make a solution of working strength, any of the solution that splashes on your clothes or shoes will eat its way through the material, so be careful. Of course after the salts have been made up into a solu-tion, no further danger re- mains from the dust. After being used, the salts may be left in the tank where they will solidify after cooling. Each time they are used some more water must be added to replace any that has boiled away, but it is added a little at a time to bring the solution up to about the same height in the tank that it occupied when first made up. When, after continued use, the solution looses strength, Stoeger can supply rejuvenation salts, which can be added, a little at a time, to bring the solution back to proper strength. The blueing salts and the rejuvenation salts both sell at $3.75 for five pounds, $12.00 for twenty pounds and $20.00 for forty pounds.

The parts to be blued should be cleaned and polished beforehand, just as they were for the swab-on solution blueing, chemically clean, and should not, thereafter, be touched with the bare hands. Stoeger says that a fair job can be done if the parts are only thoroughly washed in gasoline to remove all grease, oil and dirt but that the results will not be quite as uniform as they will be if the parts are boiled in the regular lye or caustic-soda degreasing solution. Stoeger also states that the old finish need not be all removed if it is in fairly smooth condition.

After the water has been added to the salts (evenly distributed along the tank) the heat is started and, as the temperature of the blueing bath should be as uniform as possible, four burners should be used be- neath a rifle or shotgun length t3nk, one being enough of course for the pistol or revolver size tanks. As the temperature of the blueing bath rises, it should be stirred from time to time with a wooden paddle and a thermometer should be used to check the temperature at different points in the bath. Use a deep-fat frying thermometer such as is sold by Sears Roebuck or Montgomery Ward for about 904, or by the Taylor Instrument Co. through all local hardware stores for about $1.50. This thermometer is supplied with a metal clip on the back, so that it can be clipped to the side of the tank with the mercury bulb in the solution, in order that the parts to be blued can be placed in the solution when it reaches the proper temperature. This temperature varies between 250 degrees and 275 degrees.

The chemically clean parts have wires attached to them, so that they can be placed in and be removed easily from the solution. As barrels do not have to be plugged, a long wire may be run through them and turned up at the ends above the surface of the solution so that the ends of the wire may be grasped to lift the barrels into and out of the solution. When the bath reaches the proper temperature the heat is turned off to prevent the temperature rising too high and the parts to be blued are placed in the bath and allowed to re- main there for ten minutes. I find that the finish is improved if the parts are slightly agitated while in the bath by taking hold of the wires attached to parts and moving the parts gently back and forth beneath the surface of the bath. If you have many parts to blue at one time, only a few of them should be put in at once, so that you can take care of them better, and for this reason watch the temperature of the bath closely, if it begins to cool oft* much start the heat again to keep it close to the 275 degree mark, to keep the color even on all parts.

After a part has been in the bath for ten minutes, lift it out and move it rapidly about in a cold bath of clean water, which will loosen the greenish scum on the surface. Follow this by placing the part in boiling water, which is done merely to raise its temperature again so that it will dry rapidly when it is removed.

If, when the part is lifted out of the hot water bath, it has a gray color, the blueing solution is too weak and needs to have rejuvenation salts added to it. If the part has a light reddish coating, it should be all right and as soon as it is dry it is rubbed with a piece of wool cloth dipped in any acid-free oil and the reddish coating should rub off, leaving a deep blue color. If the reddish color will not rub off, or if the part is speckled, it indicates that the solution is too strong. If this happens, add a little water to the blueing solution, wipe all oil off the part and wash it with gasoline and as soon as it is dry, place it back in the solution for two or three minutes and then try it again.

As steels vary somewhat, the light gray color may be caused by too low a heat, so check your temperature carefully if this happens and even try the part again, before oiling it, at a higher temperature. You might also try leaving the part in the solution for a longer period than the ten minutes. Conversely, too high a temperature may be responsible for the reddish color not rubbing off. or for the spotted finish mentioned, so if these occur try lowering the temperature if you are sure the solution is not too strong.

Case-hardened steels will take the blue better if they are first dipped into a 15% by weight solution of potassium-cyanide in water. Be sure that all parts are perfectly dry before placing them in the blueing solution, for water on them will cause the blueing solution to explode and fly. If any of the blueing solution spatters on bare skin apply cold water in quantities at once, for the salt will stick to the skin and burn into it if not washed off.

The parts need no further attention after having the rust-like coat rubbed off with the acid-free oil, they arc then finished. Stoeger can supply his Black Diamond Finishing Oil at $1.00 a pint, $1.75 a quart, $6.00 a gallon. I find that sperm-oil answers the purpose very well. This can be purchased at drug stores and they can also supply litmus paper with which to test the oil to make sure that it is acid free.

An article in Field & Stream of February, 1938, gave a formula for an immersion process of blueing for which the directions for handling are about the same as the Stoeger process. This formula is as follows:

3 pounds, 1 ounce sodium hydroxide (caustic-soda flakes) 1 pound trisodium phosphate (trisodium)

3 pounds sodium chloride 5 pounds, 1 ounce sodium nitrate

10 pounds of water.

The dry chemicals are mixed together and placed in the tank and the water is then added. The author states that the solution is brought to a boil and the cleaned parts immersed in it for ten minutes, then placed in boiling water for a few minutes and then rubbed with gun oil when dry. Water should be added each time to keep the solution at the proper level in the tank, also to control the strength of it. The author states that only gasoline washing is required, not boil- ing in a degreasing solution, to remove heavy oil and grease as all the caustic-soda necessary to kill light oils is in the solution itself.

Baker's #1 Basic Hot Blueing solution has given me the best results in gun blueing. If the etching and Spencer acids are used, I have found this to work very well on case-hardened parts. I have thought at times that the addition of 50% more spirits-of-nitre made an improvement in this solution but at other times I was not so sure. This difference may have been caused by a variation in the strength of the nitre, as it loses strength after a sealed bottle of it has once been opened.

I use straight hydrant water but the water here is quite soft, being 99.99% pure. The local water company chlorinates this water before it is put into the mains. Water is what makes the greatest differences in how blueing solutions work, so wherever possible, distilled water should be used. Rain water will be all right provided you test it with litmus paper to make sure that it is free of acids and alkalies, although if it contains any oil, which will not be shown by the litmus paper, it will be useless.

In stating that Baker's #1 blueing solution gave me the best results in gun blueing, I was referring to "swab-on" solutions. The color given by this is no better, except on case-hardened parts, than the color I got with Stoeger's Lightning Black Diamond Bluer, and this Black Diamond bluer is easier to use than the "swab-on" solution although it is more expensive.

The success of any blueing job depends a great deal on the proper attention to all details, for if you slight them the job will show it every time. No universal formula can be given to cover all steels as they vary greatly, so experiments and changes will have to be made as demanded by the job. In the swab-on solution process chemical cleanliness is paramount and must not be slighted.

Chapter 18 CARTRIDGE CASE AND BULLET DIES

As special cartridge cases are usually made by necking-down an existing case of larger caliber, a full- length die to neck the case down is required.

This can be made in two different ways, the first of which is to turn up a reamer blank in the lathe to the form desired for the special cartridge. This reamer blank, instead of being fluted as a regular chambering reamer is made, is usually cut away between the pilot and the shank, to one-half its diameter. This is done either in the milling machine or is rough-ground to approximately half its diameter and is then filed with a fine flat file to just over half-diameter. The reamer is made of carbon steel and, after being hardened and then tempered at light straw color, is honed down with a hand stone to exactly half its original diameter.

A piece of drill-rod one inch in diameter is chucked to run truly in the lathe and a hole is bored and then reamed through it slightly longer than the case to be formed. The reamed hole should be .001" larger than the diameter of the pilot on the reamer. The compound rest of the lathe is set at the angle of the body- taper of the case to be necked-down and a taper hole a little smaller and a little shorter than the body length of the case is bored in the die blank. The die is then reamed with the reamer and is polished inside to a very smooth finish.

A case is now necked-down by pressing it into the die with the arbor press or a heavy vise. The case should be very lightly oiled with a thin oil before being placed in the die. After being pushed out of the die with a rod inserted from the muzzle, the case is carefully examined and measured to make sure it is correctly formed and if it is not, then any changes necessary in the die can be made while it is still soft.

After the die is correct, it is coated inside and out with bone-black mixed with sperm-oil and is hardened and very slightly drawn at very light straw color. In hardening the die, it is best to have a small stream of water rising through the quenching bath from a tube in the bottom of the bath, so that the opening in the die can be placed over this stream of water in quenching the die, for otherwise enough steam may form in the hole of the die to prevent it hardening properly on the inside.

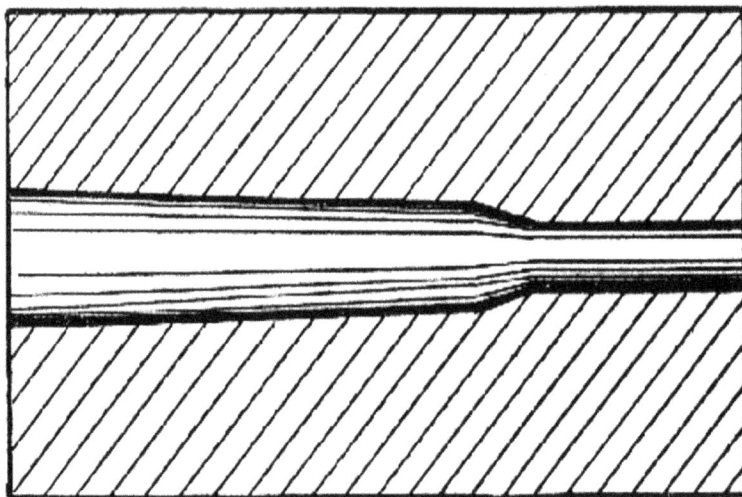

The one-piece forming or full length case sizing die.

If the water tap has a hose thread upon it, a piece of copper tubing can be inserted in a hose nut by soldering it to a heavy piece of galvanized iron, cut to fit inside the hose nut. A rubber hose washer is inserted and the hose nut screwed onto the water tap. The lower end of the copper tubing can be bent in a curve so that the end points upward and when the quenching bath is placed under the tap with the curve of this tubing on the bottom, inside the bath, a small stream of water will rise through the water in the quenching bath.

Difficulty may be encountered in necking-down a 7 m/m or .30 caliber case to .22 caliber in one operation, as this amount of reduction may cause the case to buckle. For that reason two dies may be necessary, the first necking to .25 caliber and the second necking from .25 caliber to .22 caliber. As this would require two reamers to be made, it adds to the expense of producing the special cartridge case. This may be over- come by adopting the alternate method of making the necking-down die.

This second method is to make the die entirely in the lathe, by boring it with a small boring tool instead of making a reamer and reaming it. This type of die is made in two pieces. A piece of drill-rod one inch in diameter, just long enough to form the body of the case to where the shoulder starts to drop from the body to the neck, is chucked to run true in the lathe and a hole is drilled through it, from end to end, smaller than the smallest diameter of the cartridge case body. The compound rest is set at the proper angle to bore this out to the taper of the body of the case, but is so angled that the shoulder end, or smallest diameter of the hole, is at the outer end, where the boring tool enters, the hole tapering out to larger size at the inner end of the die.

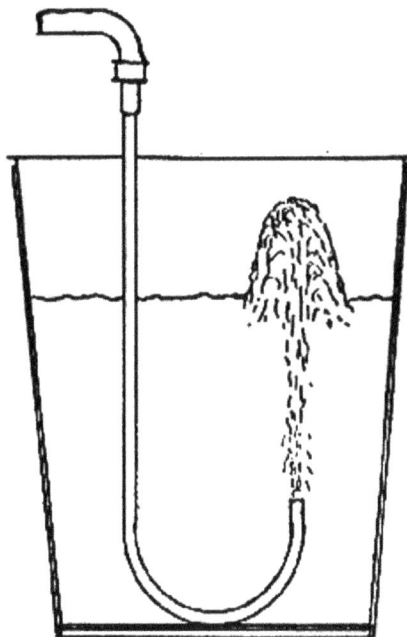

Arrangement of quenching bath used in hardening sizing dies.

After this body taper hole is bored out as smoothly as possible, turn down the outer end of the die, for a distance of to an outer diameter of Remove the piece from the chuck and reverse it with the larger end of the hole outward, replace it in the chuck and polish the hole, rounding the edges of the outer end of the hole slightly, but not the edge of the inner end.

Place in the lathe chuck a shorter piece of one inch drill-rod, a little longer than the length of the cartridge case from the upper end of the shoulder to the outer end of the neck, plus 1/8". Drill a hole through this, smaller than you wish the outer diameter of the neck of the necked-down case to be. Machine a recess in the outer end of this piece 3/32 " deep and just large enough so that the turned-down end of the body portion of the die will enter it to the bottom without any shake. Pore out the drilled hole to neck size.

Now set the compound rest of the lathe to the proper angle to bore the shoulder taper and bore this in the outer end to about .005" greater diameter at its outer end than the small end of the hole in the body portion of the die. Where this shoulder taper joins the straight neck portion, round off the edge on a radius of 1/16" to 1/8". Polish the shoulder taper and neck portion.

Test the die after assembling it by necking-down a cartridge in it before hardening, so that any corrections necessary may be made. Harden it as directed for the previous described die, coating it inside and out with the bone-black and sperm-oil before heating it.

With this type of die. if it is necessary to put a cartridge case through two necking operations to bring it clown to the required size it is only necessary to make two neck portions of the die, interchangeable upon the body portion, instead of making two complete dies to accomplish the result.

It is sometimes desired to produce a special cart- ridge case with a shorter neck and a more abrupt shoulder slope than the original case has, from which the special case is being made. This type of die is made in one piece in the lathe by drilling a hole slightly below neck size through a piece of drill-rod and reaming and polishing the hole to correct diameter for the outer diameter of the neck of the finished cartridge. The outer end of the hole is then bored out to the same taper as the body of the case used for a slightly longer distance than the length from the head of the case to be necked-down to the beginning of the neck of the case. After the chamber desired is cut in the barrel of the rifle, the cases are necked-down in the die, then loaded with a charge a few grains lighter than the load to be used and are fired in the rifle chamber to shape them to the new shoulder and shorter neck. It may be necessary to load and fire each case two or three times to bring it out to a close fit in the chamber, but once is usually enough to accomplish it.

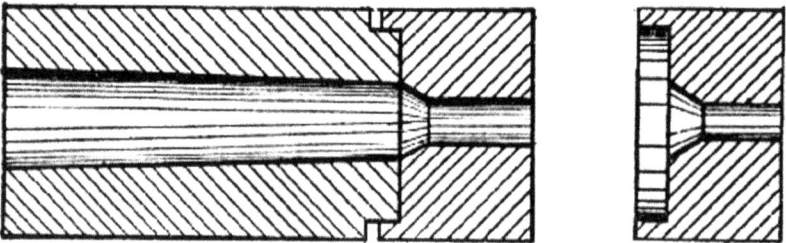

The two-piece cartridge case forming or necking die, showing the two different size necking parts interchangeable upon the body.

The chambering reamer for these special or experimental cases is usually made from carbon-steel and is made without flutes, as was described for cutting the one-piece die for necking down cases. As this type of reamer has but one cutting edge, it cuts slower than the fluted type and during the cutting operation it will often be necessary to hone the reamer to keep the cutting edge sharp and smooth, to prevent scratches. The barrel is chucked in the lathe and the body portion of the chamber is bored out undersize, to reduce the amount of metal to be removed by the reamer, or some- times a smaller reamer that you have on hand with the proper size pilot is used to rough-ream the chamber first.

Usually for these special jobs only one reamer, the finishing-size reamer, is made, for you may never be called upon for another chamber of the same type. The chamber is polished out after this finishing reamer is used, either with a high-speed hand-type electric grinder using fine carborundum cloth discs followed by crocus cloth discs on a long man-drel, or a hardwood dummy cartridge is turned up in the lathe and a fine grained carborundum powder is mixed with light oil to form a paste and the chamber is given its final polish with this.

It may be necessary to make special, jacketed bullets in developing an experimental cartridge, to get the weight or shape bullet to give the best performance. If commercial bullets of the desired weight can be obtained, it will be best to buy these where it is necessary only to change the shape of the bullet point, as open- point bullets can readily be changed to sharp-pointed soft-point ones in a simple die with an arbor press.

A reamer blank is first turned up from drill-rod to the shape and size desired for the bullet. This blank is highly polished and is then ground or filed and honed down to just over one-half its diameter. It is then hardened by heating to cherry-red, after being coated with bone-black and sperm-oil, and quenching in oil. The temper js then drawn at straw color and the reamer is honed down to exactly one-half diameter with a hand stone.

The die is made in two pieces, from tool -steel, the body having a straight hole at least twice as long as the bullet and having one end recessed to a depth of half-an-inch or a little less. The base is turned for a distance a trifle longer than the depth of the body recess to a size which allows it to fit tightly into the recess without shake. The die should have an outer diameter of at least one inch. While the body portion is in the lathe to be recessed, drill a hole lengthwise of it smaller than the body diameter of the bullet and while the base portion is in the lathe to be turned to fit the recess step, drill this for the point of the bullet. To do this, carefully center this base with a center- drill smaller than the bullet, then drill a short distance with a drill smaller than the bullet point near where it joins the straight body of the bullet. Drill the hole a little deeper with a smaller drill, then deeper again with a still smaller drill, etc., until the hole is drilled almost as deep as the length of the bullet point. Clamp the two parts of the die together and, using the reamer made for the purpose, ream the bullet die. Use plenty of good cutting oil and remove the reamer frequently to clean it and the hole of chips. Also inspect the edge of the reamer and hone it, if it is necessary.

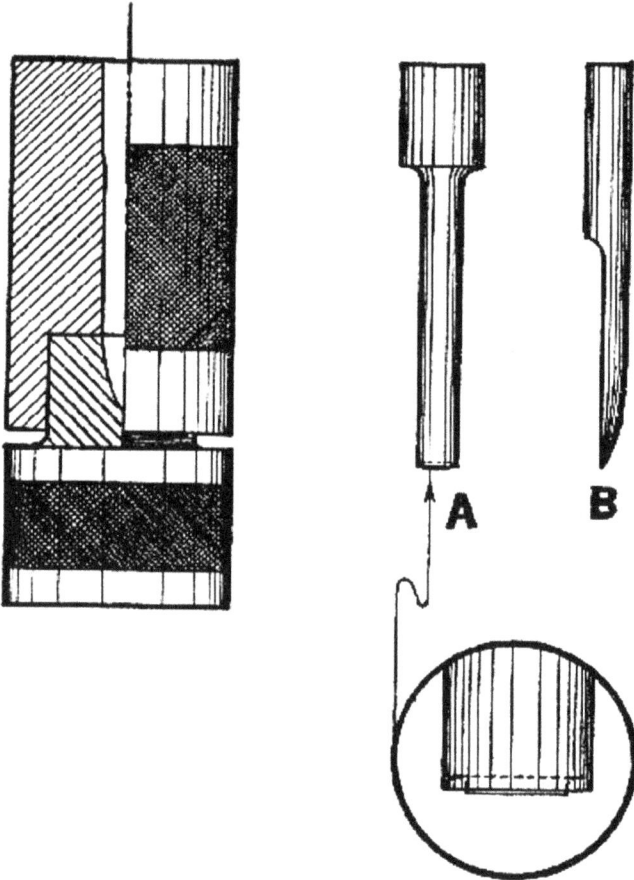

Details of swaging die for making jacketed bullets. A is the punch and B is the type of reamer used to cut the die.

After the die is completed, make a plunger of drill- rod .0005" smaller in diameter than the hole in the die and a little longer than the body portion of the die. Leave a larger portion on the upper end of this plunger about one inch long to act as the head. The lower end of the plunger, which rests against the bullet when in use, should he turned to a diameter about Yui" less than the bullet for a distance of . 012 " to .015" back from the end, leaving the central portion of this end longer than the edges. This puts a little more pressure, or rather a quicker pressure, on the central portion of the bullet than upon the edges and seems to reduce any tendency to raise burrs at the edge of the base of the bullet.

The die is coated inside and out with hone-black and sperm-oil and the plunger is also coated with it. They are then heated to a cherry-red and quenched in oil to harden them, after which they are tempered at very light straw color.

In use, the two parts of the die are placed together and a bullet is placed in the die, point down. The plunger is put in on top of the base of the bullet and the die is placed on the arbor press or in a heavy vise and pressure is applied to the outer end of the plunger. When movement of the plunger stops, the two parts of the die are separated with a twisting pull and the bullet remains in the body portion of the die, which is replaced on the arbor press, or in the vise with a brass ring between the lower edge of the die body and the vise jaw, and pressure is again applied to the outer end of the plunger to push the bullet from the die.

This die will usually leave a slightly raised ring around the bullet, where point and body meet. This ring is very narrow and, if the die is well fitted, not more than .001" greater in diameter than the body of the bullet so it will not matter if it is left upon the bullet, but it can be easily removed by pressing the bullet through the body portion of the die once more.

If no commercial bullets can be had in the weight desired, jackets of gilding-metal drawn in the form of straight cups of the right size can be made for you by any company specializing in the deep drawing of sheet-metal, or if the bullets wanted are of .22 caliber and the velocity is not to be more than 3200 foot seconds, the copper cups from which .22 caliber rim-fire cartridge cases are made can be purchased from am- munition companies. These .22 rim-fire cases are first drawn as a straight copper cup and are trimmed to length. The cup is then held in a machine while the closed end of it is bumped or pressed out to form the rim, so order them as straight cups before the rim is formed upon them. Fired .22 rim-fire cases can be used for jackets by pressing them through a taper-mouthed die, base first, which will remove the rim, drawing them again into a straight cup. This operation is best performed on an arbor press or it can be done in a fairly heavy drill press.

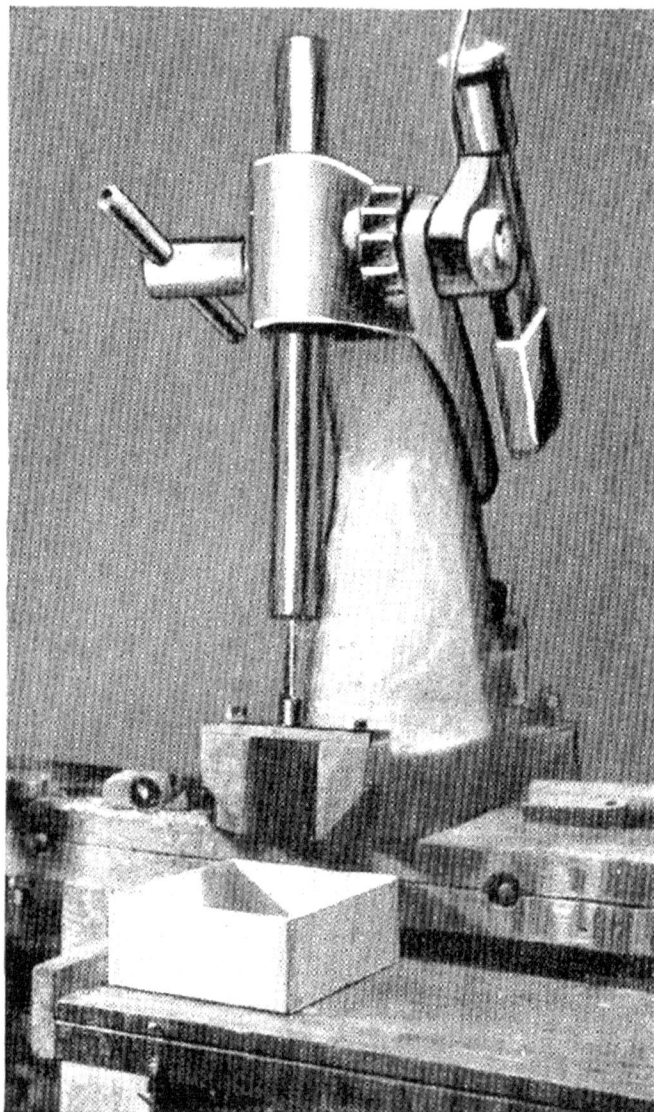

Plate XXI

Pressing .22 rim-fire fired cases through a die held in the arbor press. The die has a tapered mouth and is fastened to the bed of the press while a shaft small enough to enter the mouth of the case is screwed into a tapped hole in the end of the press ram. The fired case is put through head first in order to remove the rim, leaving a cup suitable for jacketing bullets.

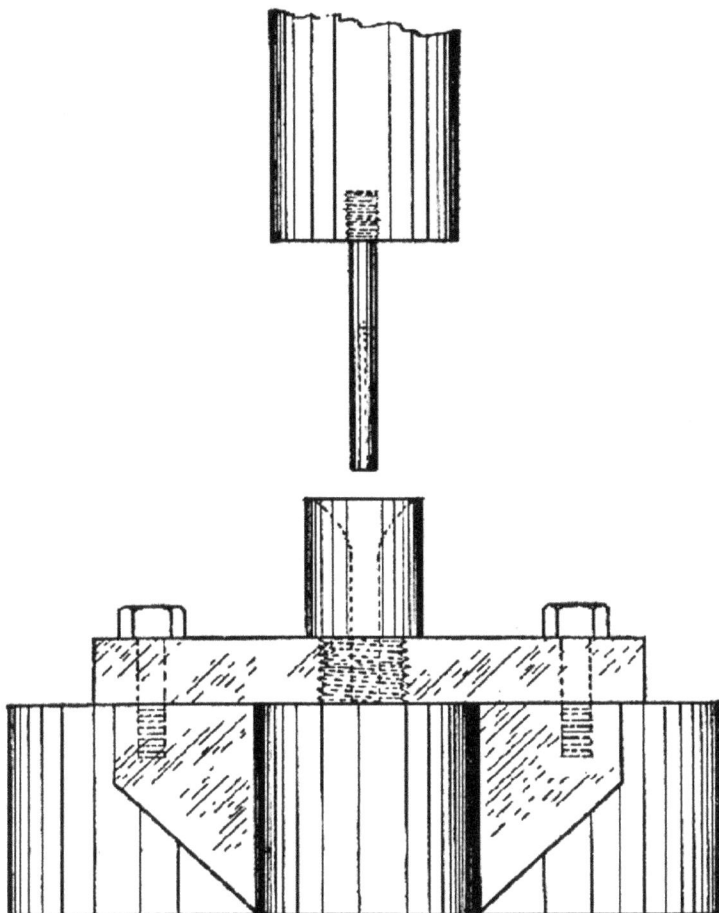

The special die and punch, together with their setup on the arbor press for removing the rim from .22 rim-fire fired cases, preliminary to using them as jackets for metal-cased bullets.

First, make a short die, with a hole through it of the diameter you wish the outside of the jacket to be. A diameter of .221" is about right for .22 caliber jackets. This hole in the die is tapered out larger than the rim diameter of the case, at the end where the fired cases are to enter, and this taper is blended into the central hole in the die with a sweeping curve and the taper and the hole are highly polished. The die is threaded at the bottom end on the outside so that it can be screwed into a plate which is clamped down upon the arbor press base or upon the table of the drill press. Be careful not to taper the hole in the die at the lower end and leave this lower edge of the hole sharp.

A punch that will just slip easily into the inside of the fired case is made and the lower edge of it is rounded off, so that it will not cut the head out of the fired case. A small hole is drilled lengthwise into this punch, from the bottom end, longer than the length of the case and at some point above the length of the case a hole is drilled into this first hole at right angles. This is to break the air lock in the case around the punch, so that the case will strip off the punch easily after it passes through the die. If the punch and die are to be used in the arbor press, the upper end of the punch should be threaded and the punch screwed into a drilled and tapped hole in the end of the press ram. If the punch and die are to be used in a drill press, the punch can be left unthreaded and can be held in the drill-chuck.

The fired cases are rolled on a felt pad oiled with a light oil and a case is picked up, set head down in the tapered opening of the die, the punch is brought down into the open mouth of the fired case and the case is pressed through the die. A box is set beneath the die and as the punch is drawn back up through the die, the lower edge of the die strips the case off of the punch. Sometimes a case sticks upon the punch and that case is usually ruined in getting it off, but this does not hap- pen often if the punch is well polished and the lower edge of the die is square and a close fit is made around the case by the die.

Now that we have the jackets made, the next thing is the core. This is lead wire, bought on spools from any of the large lead companies. It usually is supplied on 5-pound and 50-pound spools and should be purchased in a diameter that is not more than .005" smaller than the internal diameter of the jackets or the jacket may wrinkle in the forming die. This wire is cut to the proper length to make the correct bullet weight with the jacket. It may be cut in the lathe by making a fly- type cutter and mounting it on an arbor in the lathe chuck. This cutter is ground perfectly flat on the side toward the tail stock of the lathe and is tapered down to an edge on the side toward the chuck. A piece of steel with a smoothly ground face toward the chuck and a hole through it, lengthwise of the lathe, just large enough to take the lead wire is clamped down upon the tool rest, with the ground face carefully squared to the fly cutter and a close fit against the cutter. A second piece of steel is clamped on the tool rest between the first piece and the lathe chuck just far enough away from the first piece, with the hole through it to act as a length gauge for the cutting of the wire. The lathe is operated at a low speed and the wire is pushed through the piece of steel with the hole in it until it comes against the second piece, which stops it. The slowly revolving cutter cuts a piece off the wire and the wire is pushed forward against the stop again while the cutter is revolving to make a sec- ond cut.

This wire can be cut in a simpler way by using ordinary cutting pliers if you arc careful. A length gauge is made by drilling a hole lengthwise into a piece of round rod a little larger in diameter than the lead wire. This hole is the proper depth, so that when the gauge is placed over the end of the wire so that the wire touches the bottom of the hole, a pair of cutting pliers placed against the open end of the gauge will cut the wire the correct length to make the weight desired. Be careful, in using this method, to press the gauge against the end of the wire with the same pressure each time, as the cutting pliers leave a chisel edge on the wire and if the gauge is pressed very hard against this edge the edge is turned back, causing a longer and thereby heavier slug to be cut from the wire. This method is quite fast and is very simple as far as equipment needed. . ... .

Instead of using lead wire, a mold may be made and slugs may be cast of junk lead, just the right diameter and length for bullet cores. By this method longer bullets may be made by alloying some light metal with the lead, thus getting a longer bullet to obtain the weight wanted, or cores of tempered lead of any temper desired may be made by alloying tin and antimony with the lead.

After the cores are prepared they are inserted into the jackets, placed in the bullet die and pressure applied on the punch, either by the arbor press or a heavy vise as was done when changing the shape of factory bullets.

In making pointed, soft-point bullets with just a small amount of lead exposed at the tip the jacket should be 1/8" or more longer than the core. If a larger soft-point is desired, the jackets themselves may be used as length gauges in cutting lead wire cores. To do this each jacket is placed over the end of the lead wire and the wire is cut off against the mouth of the jacket with cutting pliers, leaving the lead core in the jacket. This type of bullet is suitable for muzzle velocities of about 2400 foot seconds or less.

Making jacketed bullets in this type of a die is necessarily a slow process, as the die must be taken apart and reassembled for each bullet, so where bullets are required in numbers of an hundred or more it is better to make a bullet press which will turn them out faster.

This press is not difficult to make and will handle bullets of various weights, shapes and calibers by merely making up different sets of dies or parts of dies.

The back bone of the press is a piece of flat steel, l"x 2"x 6 1 / 2 " long. Measure off 1 3/8" from one edge, on the center line of each end. Using these marks as centers, drill and ream a hole lengthwise of the piece. Next

measure off l 3/8" from each end on the edge of the side on which the
hole was drilled and reamed. From these points cut a square notch, 1"
deep and 1 " long, extending from the marks toward the center of length
of the piece. This leaves the back- bone shaped like the letter E. Now
drill and ream a 3/8" hole through the flat side of the piece, 3 1/2" from
the top edge and 1/2" from the back edge. Drill and ream another 3/8"
hole through the flat side 1 1/2" from the bottom edge and 1/2 " from
the back edge. Make two steel straps 6 1/4" long, 3/4" wide and 5/16"
thick. Drill and ream 3/8" holes at. each end of these straps, 5 1/2 " apart
on centers. Make two more straps 4" long 3/4" wide and thick and drill
and ream 3/8" at each end of these, 3/4" apart on centers. Take a piece
of 1"-square steel and bend it at a square right- angle, leaving the ends
2" long measured on the in- side of the bend. Drill and ream a 3/8" hole
near one end, from side to side. Bend a piece of 3/4" x 5/16 " strap-steel
into a square-U, 3/4" between the legs and braze this on top of the leg
of the bent 1"-square steel, open side up, on the leg in which the 3/8"
hole is drilled and reamed, its center 13/8" from the center of the hole
in the leg. Drill and ream a 3/8" hole from side to side through the legs
of this U, near the top ends. Take a piece of 1"-square steel 30" to 36"
long and drill and ream a 3/8" hole through it from side to side, near one
end. Make a second square-bent U of 3/4" x 5/16 " strap-steel and braze
it on one edge of the 30" long piece, parallel to the hole drilled with the
center of the U 1 3/8" from the center of the hole. Center the ends of a
piece of 3/4 "-square cold-rolled steel. 3 1/2" long and turn down 2 7/8"
of its length to round, leaving a 3/4 "-square head 5/8" long. Through
this head, from side to side, drill and ream a 3/8" hole and in the end of
the part turned to round, drill and tap a hole, lengthwise into the end,
threaded with a 3/8"x 24 thread, 1/2" deep. Make a second piece just like
this but only 2 1/2" long.

Set the square head of this shorter plunger into the square-U brazed
onto the l"-square steel piece bent at right-angles and slide the 1/2" round
part of the plunger into the bottom of the *4" reamed hole of the back-
bone piece, using a 3/8" hardened steel pin through the sides of the U and
through the square head of the plunger. This pin should be a free-turning
fit in these holes. Using the short pair of 4" long steel straps, connect the
T'-square bent piece to the hole drilled through the back-bone piece from
side to side, 1 1/2" from the bottom edge. Use 3/8" hardened steel pins
in each end of the straps.

Place the square head of the longer plunger in the U of the 1"-square
piece 30" long, which is the handle of the press, using a 3/8" hardened
steel pin to connect the plunger to the U. Now slide this plunger into the
top end of the 1/2 " hole reamed in the back-bone piece and, using the

long pair of 6 1/4" long steel straps connect this handle, by the hole in its end, to the hole drilled from side to side through the back-bone piece 3 1/2 " from the top edge, using 3/8" hardened steel pins through each end of the straps. These pins may have holes drilled in the ends, through the diameter, for cotter-pins to keep them in place, or they may be threaded on each end and fitted with nuts.

The press is now complete except for the dies and plunger. The press is set upright in a heavy vise by clamping the down-bent 2" long end of the 1 "-square bent piece in the jaws of the vise. You will note that when you apply pressure on the handle the two plungers are forced toward each other through the hole lengthwise of the back-bone piece.

This size press will handle .22 and .25 caliber bullets. For .30 caliber bullets a larger size would be required.

The body part of the bullet die is made of 5/8" diameter round drill rod, 1" long. Of this 1" length 15/16" is turned to a diameter of leaving a flange 1/16" thick and 5/8" in diameter. This body part is drilled and reamed lengthwise with a hole of the proper size for the bullet. The opposite end from the flange is then recessed, by being bored in the lathe, with a recess 1/8" deep and 3/8" in diameter. This body die is now placed in the hole in the central portion of the back-bone piece, between the ends of the two plungers, with its recessed end down. It should be a close fit in this hole. With this die clamped in place, drill a small hole through the central portion of the back-bone piece, from side to side, near the top of the die, with half the diameter of this small hole in the back-bone piece and half its diameter in the side of the die. Ream this hole with a small taper-pin reamer so that a taper-pin can be driven in here to lock the die in the back-bone piece.

Chuck a 1"-long piece of round drill-rod so that it runs true in the lathe and step-drill the end of it and ream it out for the point of the bullet, using a flat bullet-die reamer of whatever shape point you wish. Reduce the diameter of this end of the point die to 3/8" so that the recessed end of the body die will just push over it with no shake whatever. Round the outer edge of this end of the point die so that it bottoms perfectly in the body die around the center hole. The reduced diameter portion of this point die need not be longer than necessary to clear the end of the body die.

Reverse this point die in the lathe chuck, making sure it runs true, and turn the opposite end to 3/8" diameter for a distance of leaving a square shoulder, and thread it with a 3/8" x 24-thread die so that it will screw into the top of the bottom plunger of the press.

The bullet plunger is also made of 1/2 " diameter round drill rod, about 1 5/8" long. Turn down one end of it to 3/8" for a distance of 3/8" and thread it, against a square shoulder with a 3/8" x 24-thread die so that it will screw into the bottom end of the upper plunger of the press. The other end of this bullet plunger is turned to a diameter .0005" less than the hole in the body die and it should be about .010" longer than the hole through the body of the die. The end of the bullet plunger is reduced in diameter about 1/16 " for a distance of .010" as was done on the plunger for the type of bullet die used in the arbor press or vise previously described, leaving the center of the plunger longer than the edge.

Both parts of the die and the plunger are coated with bone-black and sperm-oil, heated to cherry-red and quenched in oil. They are then polished, heated to straw-yellow and again quenched. Now assemble the two-part die and the plunger in the press and we shall make a bullet.

Lift the handle of the press, which will withdraw the plunger from the bullet die, and drop a bullet or a jacket with the lead core in it into the body portion of the die, the hole of which is slightly relieved at the top so that the bullet will enter. If a soft-point bullet is desired, place the bullet in the die point-down or in the case of the jacket and core, open-end down. If a so called full-jacketed bullet is desired, reverse the bullet in putting it or the jacket and core into the die.

Pull down on the handle which will cause the bullet plunger to force the bullet into the die. When all movement of the plunger ceases, do not lift the press handle but push straight back on it, which will cause the back-bone of the press to swing back on the lower strap pins, which in turn withdraws the lower plunger taking with it the bullet-point part of the die. Now continue the down pressure on the press handle and the plunger on top will continue its downward travel and push the finished bullet out of the body part of the die. The bullet will drop loosely into the point section of the die, from which it can easily be picked up.

This die, just as the previously described one for use in an arbor press or vice, will leave a narrow ring around the jacket at the junction of the point and body of the bullet. After all bullets have been formed in the press, the point section of the bullet die may be removed and the bullets pushed straight through the body portion of the die with the bullet plunger, which will remove this slightly-raised ring from the bullet.

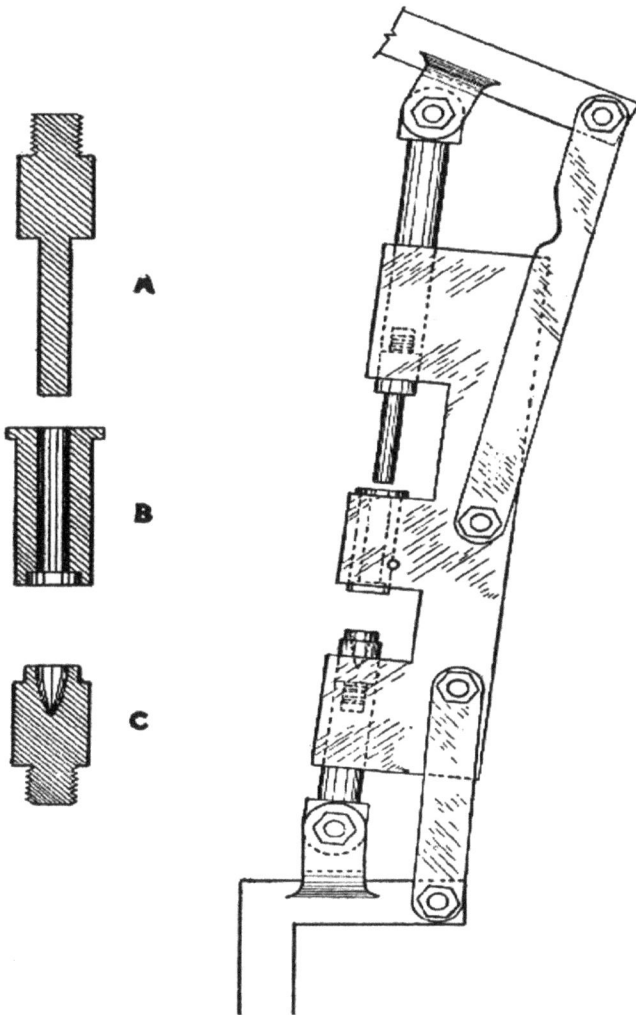

Special bench press for making jacketed bullets, together with interchangeable dies and punches. A is top punch. B the body die and
C is the point die.

The operation of this press is fairly fast, enabling one with a little
practice to turn out 300 or more bullets per hour.

To make bullets of different shape points, it is only necessary to make
a new point section for the die. The body section is long enough to make
bullets of different weights simply by using longer jackets and cores. Tf
bullets of extreme sharp-point shape are desired, it is necessary either to
vent the die with a small hole drilled in from the point and connected

with a side hole to the open air, which will allow the bullet to be formed with one pressure, or to put the bullet through the press twice, with a light pressure each time. The reason for this is that air is trapped in the die beneath the bullet, and the extreme pressure necessary to force this air out and form an extremely sharp point on the bullet, with one pressure in an unvented die, may cause fins around the edge of the base of the bullet.

In putting open-end jackets, with a core inside them, open-end down into a die, the core may slide downward and partly out of the jacket unless it fits quite tightly within the jacket. When the core slips downward, it makes a larger soft-point than when it is retained against the base of the jacket. If cores fit too loosely in the jackets, a punch can be set upon the core and tapped once with a light hammer while the core is in position, to upset it tightly in the jacket.

MAKING CARTRIDGE CASES

Cartridge cases, in obsolete types that may no longer be purchased, can be made in the lathe from yellow brass rod by boring them out with a small boring tool and turning the outside to size and shape. The straight-type cases are the easiest to make, of course. The inside is bored out in a straight hole but the outside is turned on a slight taper, being thicker in the wall at the rear end and thinning down toward the mouth of the case. The brass should be turned at the highest speed of the average engine lathe, around 600 R.P.M., to give the case a good finish.

If a sample case is at hand, or can be obtained, it is simple to take measurements from it, but if none can be found a sulphur cast can be made of the gun chamber and the outside dimensions for the cartridge case obtained in this manner. As you know what the diameter of the bullet is, the internal dimensions can easily be figured from this. The internal size of the neck should be .003" to .0035" smaller than the bullet, in order to give a good friction grip. In taking the outside dimensions from a sulphur cast of the chamber, remember to make the case small enough outside so that it will easily enter and extract from the chamber. About .002" is enough clearance to allow all over, except on the outside of the neck where the bullet will raise the diameter of the neck .003" to .0035", so .005" clearance should be allowed for on the outer diameter of the case neck.

To make a sulphur cast of the chamber, get a cork that is a good tight fit in the bore and run a wire through this from the small end of the cork, making a knot on the end of the wire at this small end of the cork. The wire should be eight or ten inches long, so that when you insert the cork into the chamber and push it forward about an inch into the rifling, the wire will extend well back of the action. Melt the sulphur in a small container with a cover on it and do not use an open flame to melt it either, as the sulphur will catch on fire. If you use a gas burner or an electric hot plate to melt the sulphur, place a piece of sheet-iron over the burner and set the covered container with the sulphur in it on top of this. Add a small amount of lamp-black, 3 grains to 2 ounces of sulphur, and dissolve some gum-camphor in alcohol and add 3 drops of this to the mixture. This formula will make an almost shrink-proof cast. Heat the mixture slowly with a low heat and stir it gently, so that the lamp-black mixes evenly. As soon as the ingredients are well mixed, pour the composition into the rear end of the chamber, with the gun in a muzzle-down position. After allowing to cool, place a rod in the barrel from the muzzle and gently push the cast out of the breech. Handle it carefully, as it is brittle, and measure it as soon as possible so as to give it little chance to shrink.

Straight-bodied cartridge cases are not the only ones that can be turned out of brass rod on the lathe. Bottle-necked cases, from .25 caliber up, can be bored out with a small boring tool. Drill a hole first with a twist-drill, smaller than the internal neck diameter, then rough-bore the body from about the body-shoulder location on back. You can then take a small boring tool and, setting the compound rest of the lathe on the proper angle for the shoulder taper, bore the inside shoulder taper, after which the body back of the shoulder can be finish-bored. The outside, of course, is easily turned to shape by setting the compound rest to the proper angle. You may spoil one or two bottle-neck cases before learning how to do it, but it can be done. Be very careful about all internal dimensions in making cartridge cases so that all your cases will have the same capacity, for if they are of different capacities the pressures will vary with the same load and your accuracy will suffer.

Brass is not the only material from which cartridge cases can be made in the lathe. It is very little more labor to turn these cases out of mild steel, commonly called cold-rolled steel, and their tensile strength will be much higher, or if made from car bon-tool steel their strength will be still greater. Cases for some of the high-velocity foreign rifles have, I understand, been made from nickel-steel.

The steel cannot be turned at as high a speed with ordinary lathe bits as the brass, so the time involved in making steel cases will be greater than in making cases of brass rod.

Chapter 19 LOADING TOOL ACCESSORIES AND APPLIANCES

A ll of the late-model loading tools and some of the earlier ones are readily adapted to various cartridges by changing the dies. A majority of these loading tools have the dies attached to the tools by threaded ends. This makes a somewhat slow method of changing dies but on the other hand has two advantages: first, that of security of fastening; second, that of adjustment, for the threaded ends allow the dies to be moved in or out of the body of the tool to adjust them to the proper length for cartridge cases fired in different guns with slightly varying chambers.

Very often it is inconvenient to wait for a new die, for some other cartridge than the one the loading tool is equipped for, to come from the factory, or perhaps a special cartridge is to be loaded for which no factory dies are available. In cases like these the new dies must be made-up on the lathe, for the threads on the die are never a standard thread so these must be lathe- cut. If reamers are available for the cartridge in question, the dies are rough-bored or drilled while in the lathe and then finish-reamed. If no reamers are avail- able the dies may be completely bored in the lathe, then polished, to remove tool marks, with carborundum cloth and crocus cloth. If a small high-speed electric grinder such as the Handee is available, the polishing may be done with this. Resizing dies should be cut to reduce the internal neck diameter of the cartridge case .005" to .006" below bullet diameter if a neck expander plug is to be used. If this neck expander plug is not to be used the resizing dies should reduce the internal diameter of the case neck .003" to .0035" below bullet diameter. A very useful measuring gauge in making these dies is the #829 Starrett small-hole gauge. These gauges come singly or in a set of four.

The Starrett small-hole gauge, adjustable for size.

The smallest gauge covers internal diameters from to 1/8 " to 2/10", the second from 2/1 0 " to 3/10 ", the third from 3/10" to 4/10 " and the fourth from 4/10 " to 1/2 ". These gauges vary from about 2 3/8" to 3" in length. The handles are well knurled, as is also the operating nut on the rear end of the handle. The measuring end is a split ball on the end of a split shank, upon the other end of which is the handle and operating nut. A rod with a tapered head, between the split halves of the ball, runs through the gauge from the ball end to the operating nut on the rear of the handle. Tightening the nut on the rear end of this rod draws the tapered head between the split halves of the ball and expands the ball. After the gauge has been placed within the hole to be measured it is expanded until it fits the hole closely, then withdrawn and the diameter of the ball is measured with outside micrometers. These gauges sell for $1.80 each, or $8.20 for the set of four in a red leatherette case.

You may wish to enlarge a sizing die to resize cases for use with lead bullets, instead of jacketed bullets for which the die was made, or later batches of cases may be made of heavier brass and the die will have to be enlarged to handle them. If the enlargement is only to be a few thousandths of an inch, it can be lapped out without annealing the die. If a small, high-speed, hand-type electric grinder like the Handee is available, the die may be mounted to run true in the lathe chuck, and the grinder mounted with a clamp in the tool post and used as a tool post grinder, with a small mounted stone in the chuck of the grinder to grind out the hole in the die. Without a lathe, discs of carborundum cloth can be mounted on an arbor for the Handee grinder and the hole in the die cut out a few thousandths of an inch by this method. If a high-speed drill-press or motor be available, with a chuck upon it, either the die or an arbor with carborundum discs may be mounted in the chuck and the die lapped out by this method. If no power is avail- able, cut strips of carborundum cloth just the right width so that they will wrap around a reamer or twist-drill, carborundum side out, with the edges just meeting, the reamer or drill being the right size so that when wrapped it will be a tight fit in the die. The reamer or drill is gripped in the bench vise and the die is forced over it with a twisting motion and turned around and worked back and forth until the hole is lapped out enough. It may be necessary to use new strips of carborundum cloth on the reamer or drill from time to time.

If a die needs considerable enlarging and is case-hardened so that grinding it out with a tool post grinder will cut through the hardening of the die, the die is heated red-hot and buried in slaked lime to anneal it. After cooling, the hole in the die may be enlarged by reaming or by boring it out larger in the lathe, after which the die is rehardened by case-hardening as directed in the chapter on heat treatment of steel.

Plate XXII

Showing method of use of the bullet forming press—a jacketed bullet is just coming out of the die. After the bullet jacket, with the lead core inside it, is dropped into the bullet forming die the handle of the bullet press is pulled down until it stops. The handle is then pushed straight back, raising the body part of the die from the point portion. A downward pull on the handle then ejects the finished bullet from the die.

Dies should be made of tool-steel, hardened clear through and in this case the die is heated and buried in slaked lime to anneal it, as is the case-hardened die before being cut out larger. To reharden it, heat it to cherry-red and quench it in water, then polish it and heat it slowly to straw color and quench it again in water.

Neck expander plugs may be reduced in size, if necessary, by mounting them in a lathe or drill-chuck and revolving them at high speed, while bolding a piece of carborundum cloth against them to cut them down. They may also be ground down smaller while in the lathe chuck by using a tool post grinder, if the desired reduction is very great. If these are case-hardened instead of being tool-steel hardened all the way through, they will afterwards have to be re-hardened by the regular case-hardening method.

On many reloading tools, depriming, or removal of the fired primer, is a separate operation, which is an inexcusable waste of time. Tools of this type which can be drilled with a hole for the outlet of the fired primer through the case bead holder, can readily be changed over to deprime the case while they are being resized. If the tool uses an expander plug for case necks, a new plug is made-up with an extension below the expander plug which carries a depriming punch on the end of it, so that as the case is forced into the resizing die the decapping pin goes through the flash- hole and pushes the fired primer out of the case, where- upon it drops from the tool through the hole you drill down through the case head holder. If the case head holder is on top and the die for case resizing is below, a hole longer than the depth of the primer is drilled into the case head holder and a slot is cut from this hole to the outside of the case head holder, large enough to allow the primer to pass. When the decapping punch raises the fired primer out of the case being resized, it remains resting upon the top of the case and may set back into the case far enough to prevent the case being withdrawn from the case head holder, unless the slot mentioned above is cut through the side of the case head holder so that the case, with the fired primer resting on top of it, can be drawn out of the head holder.

If no expander plug is used, a straight shaft with a decapping pin upon the end of it can be set into the die, or into the end of the operating plunger of the tool to which the die is fastened.

The decapping pin may be made as part of the shaft, in which case the shaft had better be made of drill-rod or other high-carbon steel, or it may be made as a separate pin with a head upon it and be held to the shaft with a threaded cap. This threaded cap should be about half an inch long so that the pin has good support through the outer, unthreaded portion of the cap. Pins should be of drill-rod or other high-carbon steel but need not be hardened, as the thrust is all on the ends of the pin. If the pin does become bent it may be straightened if it is not hardened, whereas a hardened pin that is bent always means a broken pin. The end of the pin should be well rounded and the last 1/8" of it tapered so that it will easily enter the flash- hole. The rest of the body of the pin should be the full size of the flash-hole, so that it will clear it of any caked fouling or turned-in brass from a burred edge on the hole.

Bench-type tools that are strong enough for full- length resizing are strong enough to neck-down cases to a smaller caliber, such as necking-down the .25-20 single-shot case to the .22-3000 Lovell or necking-down a .250-3000 Savage case to .22 caliber. The loading tool is merely used as a press, the necking-down die, with the case to be nccked-down already in the die, is placed between the plunger and the die holder of the tool and the tool is used to force the case into the die. For removing the case from the die, a pin a little longer than the die is placed inside of the case and, with the die against a wide ring placed in the tool or against the frame of the tool with the regular dies removed, the plunger is used against the pin to force the formed case out of the necking-down die. The necking-down die may be made for regular attachment to the tool and the case to be necked-down may be held in the case head holder and pushed into the die and then withdrawn, just as in resizing any case in the tool.

In changing over a case head holder of a reloading tool to handle a larger head case or in making a new case head holder to hold a smaller case, the groove in the holder for the case rim is cut with a milling cutter of flat circular form, a trifle larger than the case head, which is very nice if you have the milling cutter or the time and equipment to make it. It may be made in a lathe, the cutting head and shank being turned out in one piece from carbon or high-speed tool-steel, the shape being like a woodruff key-seat cutter which is illustrated in any catalog of milling cutters such as Brown & Sharpe or Morse Twist Drill & Machine Co. The head, on which the cutting teeth are made around the edge, should be slightly thicker out at the edge than any where else, so that the cutter will have clearance and not bind in the slot. After the blank is turned to size and shape, the teeth may be cut in the edge with a three-square file and the clearance filed upon them, after which the cutter is hardened and then tempered at medium to light straw color.

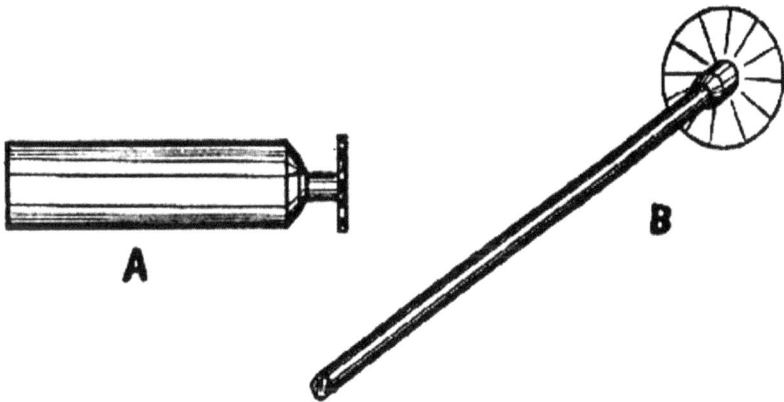

A is special milling cutter used to cut rim recess in the cartridge case head holder. **B** is a long-shanked buffer, used with carborundum discs cut so that they bend back over the shank to enter small holes.

For cartridges such as the .30'06 or cases of like head size, or for a rimmed case that has the same head diameter as the .30'06, a regular woodruff key-seat cutter of 1/2' diameter by 1/16 " thick may be used, although if it is ground to a thickness of 3/64 " it will make a better fit.

The steel on which the head holding slot is to be cut is first cut with an end mill of the same diameter as the cannelure in the case, near the head of a rimless case or the same size as the body of a rimmed case just ahead of the rim, whichever case the head holder is for. This end mill is started at the edge of the case head holder and mills a groove across the end from this one side to the position in which the case is to set in the holder, the depth of the groove being the thickness of the case head plus about Yi$". The cutter of woodruff key-seat type is then started cutting at the same place the end mill was started, but with the end of this cutter right on the bottom of the slot cut by the end mill. This cutter is run-in the width of the case rim farther than the end mill was run-in, to give clearance for the rim, which completes the milling cuts for the case head holder.

Now, if we have no milling machine or milling attachment available, this case head holder can be machined on the lathe and finished by hand. The steel for the head holder is mounted in the lathe chuck and the end is faced off square and drilled with a drill the same diameter as a rimless case in the cannelure or extractor groove or the diameter of the body of a rimmed case just ahead of the rim, whichever is to be held in the case head holder. A high-speed steel lathe bit is then notched, with a thin grinding wheel, at one side, near the end, the notch being as deep, plus a little clearance, as the groove for holding the case rim. The end of the bit, beyond the notch is then ground to the thickness of the case rim and the sides and front, below the cutting edge, are ground back to give the cutting edge clearance. This bit is then used like a boring tool to cut a groove a little larger than the diameter of the case rim, starting about y 1Q " from the end of the case holder. We now have a hole in the end of the case holder the diameter of the extractor groove or body of the case, depending upon whether it is for a rimless or a rimmed case, and Yiq" below the outer end of this hole we have a groove cut, slightly greater in diameter and depth than the rim of the case. The next operation is to cut a side outlet to this groove and hole so that cases may be inserted and withdrawn.

This operation may be done in two ways, either by making a saw cut, with a hack-saw. across the end of the case head holder, at the edge of the circular hole for the case body and then making another hack-saw cut at right-angles to this, from the closest edge of the case head holder to the first saw cut, just the distance from the end of the steel that the bottom of the groove below the circular body hole for the case is. This side outlet is then cut out straight with files, so that the case may be slid into place in the case head holder. This method gives all the metal necessary to hold the case head while the case is being resized.

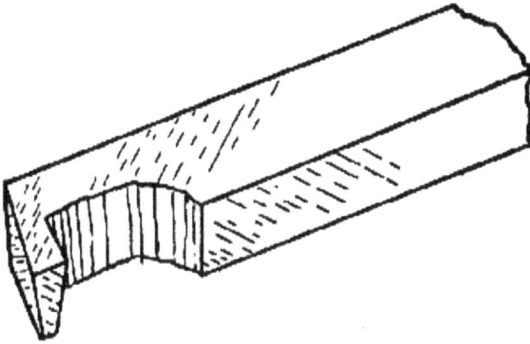

Special lathe tool, of high speed steel, ground to cut the rim recess in the cartridge case head holder.

The second method is to carry the groove for the case rim and the body hole clear out to the edge of the case head holder. To do this the body hole is first carried out in a straight slot the full width of the hole to the edge of the steel with files. A thin flat file is then used to carry out the slot for the case rim, at each side, clear to the edge of the steel. This leaves more metal on the end of the case head holder than the first method but is slower and adds very little to the strength of the case head holder. The end of the case head holder which holds the case should be case-hardened, so that the edges of the groove will not round off with use and allow the case head to slip out. As the rim left above the groove for the case rim is thin, too deep a case-hardening will make it brittle so that it will easily crack off, so for this case-hardening job the cyanide method will be the best to use.

Bullet-seating plungers are easily changed, to handle bullets of differently shaped points than they were de- signed for, by making a flat reamer the shape of the bullet, as was described as the type of reamer used to cut bullet swaging dies. These bullet plungers are usually of soft steel, if not they can be heated to a red-heat and buried in slaked lime to anneal. Mount the bullet-seating plunger in the lathe chuck so that it runs true, then place the reamer in a drill chuck in the tail stock of the lathe. Loosen the clamp that locks the tail stock to the lathe bed and loosen the clamp that locks the tail stock spindle and run it out of the tail stock as far as it will go and still remain on the screw. Run the lathe at low speed and, putting plenty of lard-oil or black sulphur-oil on the reamer, push the entire tail stock along the bed of the lathe until the reamer enters the hole in the bullet-seating plunger and feed it in, while it cuts, by pressure of your hand against the entire tail stock, so that it slides forward on the bed of the lathe as the reamer cuts. This makes the reamer cut a smoother hole, truer to size than if you locked the tail stock to the bed of the lathe and fed the reamer with the hand wheel of the tail stock spindle. During the cutting, withdraw the reamer from the hole from time to time, clean it and the hole and give it a new supply of cutting oil. Each time you withdraw it examine the cutting edge and if it is roughened or dulled, stone it on the flat top with a hand-stone of fine grain. After the hole is fitted to the bullet you are going to use, relieve the edges of the hole at the end with a tapered, round hand-stone or a taper reamer, followed by carborundum cloth to smooth the edge up. If you do not do this, the edge of the hole will probably leave a mark around the bullet or may even seat on the bullet tightly enough to cause an air lock. The pressure applied to seat the bullet should be applied about half-way down the cavity or farther, not at the lower edge.

The reamer for recutting the bullet-seating plunger may be made without a lathe, if the right diameter tool-steel or drill-rod can be obtained. It may be held in a chuck on the end of the shaft of an electric motor and filed to shape with a fine flat file, then polished with carborundum cloth to remove file marks. Keep the file well coated with chalk, which will prevent it pinning and scratching the work.

After the blank is filed to bullet shape and polished. it is removed from the chuck and the shaped end is filed down to just half its thickness, plus about .002" left for stoning. The reamer is then hardened by heating to cherry-red and quenching in water, after which it is polished and then heated slowly to a dark straw color and is then quenched again in wafer. Take a fine hand-stone with a good flat surface and stone the flat of the reamer until that part is just half the original thickness of the blank.

By using the reamer in a tee-handled tap- wrench of medium size, the bullet seating plunger may be recut to the reamer shape by hand. This type of reamer is not easy to use by hand, so go carefully and do not crowd it too much. Use plenty of cutting oil and clean the reamer and the hole of chips quite often.

Primer magazine tubes and feeding plates may be added to many of the bench tools but as these tools differ considerably, no detailed directions can be given unless a completely detailed description is given for each tool which would take up too much space. One general type can be applied to many of the tools and with modifications can be fitted to most of them, so I shall describe this type.

It consists of a body longer than the cartridge and somewhat larger in diameter. This body is drilled with a hole, lengthwise, of a diameter that will let the cartridge case go into it. A shaft is set into this body part, extending up through the hole previously drilled, of a diameter that the case will easily slide over. This shaft is drilled for a distance down from the top with a drill of any diameter that will leave a fairly heavy side wall. A coil-spring is placed in this hole in the shaft and a second shaft with a head the diameter of the first shaft and a shank a diameter to be an easy slide fit in the hole in the first shaft is put into the first shaft on top of the coil-spring. These parts should be regulated for length, so that a cartridge case placed mouth-down over the spring-backed shaft can be pressed down so that when the head on the second shaft is tightly against the top of the first shaft, within which it slides, the top surface of the cartridge case will be 1/8" below the top of the body part. When the finger pressure is released from the top of the cartridge case the spring-backed plunger should raise the case high enough so that it is easily withdrawn from the body part with the fingers.

The top of the body part is slotted, from side to side, across the center, with a slot 1/2" wide and 1/8" deep. In this slot is fitted a piece of flat steel, 1/2 " wide and 1/8" thick and as long as the distance across the top of the body part, or longer. At the center of this, at one end, a narrow piece, about wide, of the same material is left, an inch or more long. At one edge of this body part, at one end or the other of the slot cut across the top, a thick piece of steel is attached, to the side of the body part. This piece has a slot cut through it so that the 1/2 * 1/8" flat steel slide can pass through it. On the outer end of this slot a stop is attached which may be a steel plate or only a screw with the edge extending over the end of the slot so that the 3/16" wide part of the slide can pass but the 1/2" wide part is stopped when it reaches the end of the slot through the heavy piece. This heavy piece is drilled through from the top into the groove in which the flat slide operates for the primer magazine tube, which is a brass or copper tube. Directly below this hole for the primer tube a hole large enough to admit a primer is drilled through the slide plate while the slide is clear out against its stop. A coil-spring is put around the 3/16" wide part of the slide plate so that one end of it is against the outside of the heavy part carrying the primer tube. A washer is placed over the shank of the slide plate against the other end of the spring and the shank is drilled for a small pin outside or beyond the washer, to hold the spring in place.

When the outer end of this narrow shank of the slide plate is pressed, the slide plate moves over the head of a cartridge case in place in the body part and carries with it, in its hole below the primer tube, a primer, open side down.

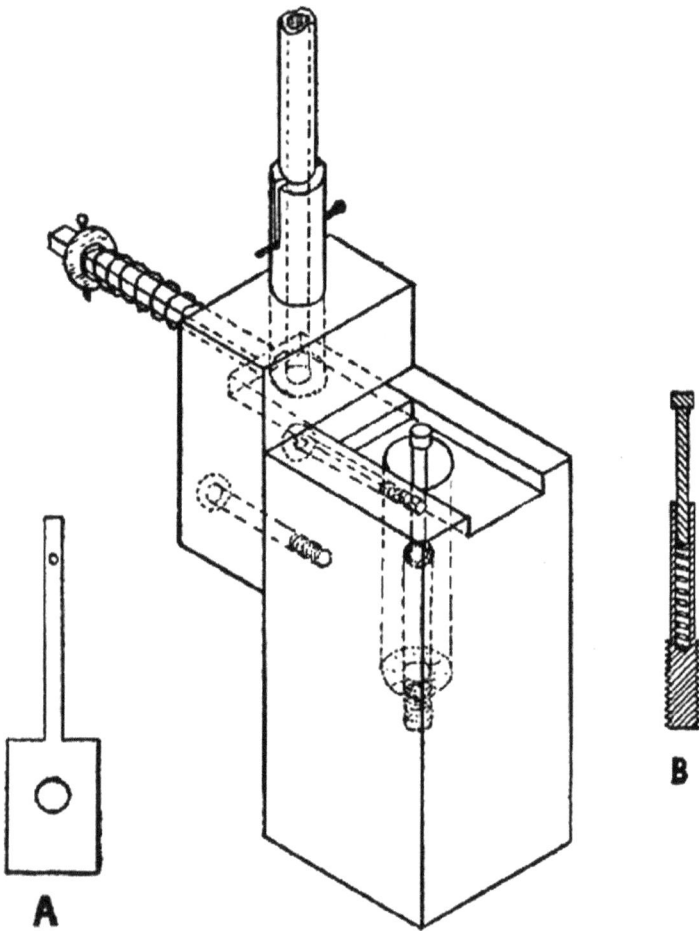

Home-made automatic priming device. A is primer slide plate.
B shows detail of the spring plunger upon which the case rests while
being primed.

The spring around the shank of the slide plate may be cut the right
length to act as a stop when the hole in the slide plate is directly over
the primer pocket of the cartridge case, or another type of stop may be
arranged, such as a tube over the coil-spring, so that the washer behind
the spring pushes this tube against the heavy part carrying the primer
tube and stops the slide with its hole directly over the primer pocket of
the case. The cartridge case may be depressed in the body part of the
primer mechanism with the thumb, while one of the fingers of the same
hand pushes the primer slide plate across the top of the cartridge case.
The spring around the shank of the primer slide plate should be stiffer

than the spring on the plunger which lifts the cartridge case out of the body part. This is so that as soon as the primer seating plunger starts the primer into the primer pocket in the cartridge case, the pressure can be re- moved from the end of the shank of the primer slide plate and when the primer is fully seated and the seating plunger withdrawn from the slide plate, the stiffer spring on the shank of the slide plate will snap the slide plate back off the top of the case head and beneath the primer tube to receive a new primer. The primer magazine tube may be set solidly into the heavy part on the body of the tool, or a socket may be set into this heavy part with a slot sawed lengthwise of the socket part- way down from the top, so that the magazine tube can be drilled crosswise, near the bottom end, for a small cotter pin or cross pin of any type in order that the tube can be lifted from the socket, the cross pin inserted, the tube filled with primers and turned upright and placed back into the socket, after which the cross pin is withdrawn, allowing the primers to pass out of the bottom of the tube as they are used. The slot in the socket is to allow the primer tube to be placed back into the socket full depth, with the cross pin holding the primers in place still in the tube. The upper end of the tube for the primers can be slotted with a thin saw blade and the sides of the tube sprung slightly together at the ends so that the primers may be picked up by pressing the end of the tube over them. The primers can be dumped out in a box top and all primers turned the correct side up are picked up in the tube, after which the box top is shaken so that more primers are turned over, and so on until the tube is filled.

The plunger that seats the primers in the cartridge case is mounted in the opposite part of the tool than that to which the body part of the primer mechanism is attached, so that when the handle of the tool is operated the body-part carrying the case to be reprimed and the primer seating punch meet, so that the repriming is completed.

On some tools it will be possible to have the shank of the slide plate operated by the movement of the tool, an inclined surface coming against the end of the slide plate shank to move the slide plate across the top of the cartridge case. If this principle is used, it will operate better if a small roller is fitted on the end of the primer slide plate shank, or instead of the roller a hardened ball may be used.

Loading tools having sufficient leverage can be equipped with a bullet-pulling device. It is usually desirable to make this so that it can readily be adapted to various calibers that you may reload for as time goes on, so a rather heavy body with a clamp device should be made to attach to the opposite part of the reloading tool from the case head holder. This heavy body part is bored out at the end to take dies of a diameter of J4" or more to clamp onto the bullet. These dies are all made with the same outside diameter but are drilled and reamed with an internal diameter to fit different caliber bullets that are to be pulled. These dies are of high-carbon steel and are split, lengthwise of the hole for the bullet, so that pressure applied to the sides will close the split sides together upon the bullet.

The clamping part of the device is attached to the heavy body part and may be made in either the screw-clamp type or the eccentric-lever type, which is the fastest. In the screw-type, the heavy bod}' part is split lengthwise, at one side, for a distance up from the lower edge and a coarse-thread screw with a tee- handle

is passed through the two sides, clear of the central hole however, so that tightening up the screw will draw' the slot together and cause the sides to exert pressure upon the split bullet die, closing this down tightly upon the bullet. If it is not possible to hold the bullet die in place in the heavy body part with a screw from the end of the heavy part threaded into the upper end of the bullet die, a screw may be run in from the side through the body part and into the die near the upper end.

The eccentric-lever clamp-type uses a lever with a rounded end, set in a slot cut in one side of the body part, and swung on a pin through the body at right- angles to the slot. The pin hole in the rounded end of the lever is not in the center of the rounded end but is slightly off-center, or eccentric, so that when the lever is swung down or up, as the case may be, the rounded end is forced farther into the center hole where the bullet die is placed. The bullet die is so placed that one of its solid sides is presented to the rounded end of the lever, so that pressure upon the die by the rounded end of the lever forces one side of the split bullet die toward the opposite side and clamps down upon the bullet.

This bullet die is not split for its full length but only for about 3/4" and the saw slot ends in a drilled hole drilled through both sides of the die, at right- angles to the hole for the bullet. This hole may be 3/16" or 1/4" in diameter. After this hole is drilled and the slot is sawed, following the drilling and reaming of the hole for the bullet, both of these holes are plugged with mild steel rod and the die is heated red- hot and quenched in a thin oil. It is then polished and heated slowly to a deep blue and again quenched in the thin oil. This will give it a spring temper. The mild steel plugs are withdrawn and the die is ready for use. The die is, of course, tapped for the screw holding it in place in the body part before being hardened and tempered.

If the eccentric-lever clamp is used, this lever should be made of tool-steel. To harden and temper this, heat it to a red-heat and quench it in water, after which polish it and carefully draw the temper to deep blue all over, except the side from the hole for the pin to the rounded edge that bears against the bullet die. This portion must be drawn as little as possible, so start your tempering heat at the other end of the lever and work down toward the eccentric end and as soon as the portion beyond the pin hole turns to a straw- yellow quench the lever in water. This lever may be made of flat tool-steel 1/8" or 3/16" thick and it is set edgewise into the body of the bullet-puller. The handle part may have two pieces of wood or of rounded mild- steel riveted upon its sides to make it easier on your hand in operating it.

If the bullet pulling is to be done usually in a shop where a lathe equipped with draw-in collet chucks is available, this will beat any loading tool for pulling bullets. A head holder for the cartridge cases is made up on the end of a piece of round stock and the shank of this is gripped in a chuck set tightly into the tail stock spindle. A collet chuck of the size to fit the bullet is placed in the head spindle, the tail stock spindle is then run out an inch or two and a loaded case is placed in the head holder. The tail stock spindle is then run forward far enough so that the bullet enters the collet up to the case mouth. The collet is then tightened upon the bullet and the tail stock spindle is drawn away from the head stock by turning the hand wheel or crank on the tail stock, thus drawing the case off of the bullet.

RECUTTING BULLET MOULDS

After a barrel for lead bullets has been recut to a larger size, ("freshened" as it is often called) to re- move pits or wear, a larger bullet must be cast to fit the new groove diameter of the barrel. To cast this larger bullet the old mould must be recut to a larger size, which means the making of a reamer or bullet cherry. This cherry is made in the same form as the old bullet, but its outside diameter is made .002" to .003" larger than the new groove diameter of the barrel.

A templet should be cut from thin sheet-steel, following the contour of the old bullet so that the nose shape of the new cherry can be checked and made the same shape as the old bullet while it is being turned and filed to shape in the lathe. This blank for the cherry is made from high-carbon tool-steel or drill-rod. After the blank is the proper shape, polish it thoroughly to remove all tool and file marks, bringing it to the proper size.

A parting or cut-off tool is then ground to the exact width of the grease grooves, these are cut into the blank at their proper places and to the correct depth, after which the cutting grooves are milled lengthwise of the blank, six grooves being made. Just as in cutting grooves in other reamers, the cutting edge is located .010" ahead of the center of the blank. A milling cutter of 60-degree angle is used to cut these grooves and the grooves must, of course, run clear to the point of the blank.

If no milling machine is available these grooves may be cut with a three-square needle file if you work care- fully. It may be easier to start them, in this case, with a needle file of the knife or slitting type and then finish them with the three-square file.

After the grooves are completed, use a very fine needle file to remove the burrs left at the edges of the grooves by the milling cutter and use this file also to file clearance on the sides of the grease grooves from the cutting edge back to the milled groove behind it. Be sure and keep the bottom corners of these grease grooves sharp and square.

Clearance is now ground, filed or stoned on top of the flutes back of the cutting edge, after which the cherry is heated to red-heat and plunged endwise into cool water, in which it is moved rapidly in circles to prevent steam forming at its surface, which would prevent proper hardening. The cherry is now polished and then reheated with a low heat to a straw-yellow, then quenched again in the water. The cutting edges of the flutes are now stoned with a fine stone to remove tool marks on the face of the cutting edges and the top of the edge is touched lightly with the stone to remove any scale at that point. A stone should also be ground to small size and used to stone the sides of the grease grooves at the cutting edges.

In use, the cherry is placed in the mould and well oiled with a good cutting-oil compound or lard-oil. The mould is then closed upon the cherry with a light pressure and the cherry is turned with a tee-handled tap-wrench to cut the mould to the larger size. As the cutting proceeds the cherry is removed often from the mould and both it and the mould are carefully cleaned of chips.

An entirely new mould may be cut with the cherry by first drilling a pair of blank mould blocks with a twist-drill a little smaller in diameter than the body of the cherry in the grease grooves. The hole is drilled to slightly less depth in the blocks than the length of the bullet, but the difference is very slight so that the cherry will just clean up the end of the drilled hole when it is in full length. In cutting a new mould the cherry is usually held in the chuck of a drill press and is driven by power at the lowest speed.

Plate XXIII

Finishing the crown of a rifle muzzle by hand, using a strip of
carborundum cloth wrapped around a ball bearing. After a countersink
is first used to slightly crown the muzzle, the bore is plugged with a
wooden plug to the bottom of the countersunk portion and the barrel
end is then finished by hand as shown above.

If the mould blocks are equipped with handles, the blocks are allowed to lie upon the drill press table to keep the mould square with the cutter and the mould handles are held in one hand and gradually squeezed together. The mould blocks may be held in a drill press vise, the jaws of the vise being gradually tightened to bring the blocks together as the cutting proceeds. In this case the vise is not clamped to the table of the drill press, for if it is the tightening of the jaws will throw the halves of the mould out of line with the cutter.

After a barrel has been recut to a slightly larger size and a mould made to cast a bullet to fit the larger groove diameter, the necks of the cartridge cases must be increased in internal diameter to accept the new bullet. To do this, make a new inside neck sizing plug to fit the reloading tool being used. A correspondingly larger outside neck sizing die is also made ror the tool by grinding out the old neck sizing die.

Increasing the external diameter of the cartridge case neck by seating a larger bullet in it makes it necessary to enlarge the neck of the chamber in the barrel to accept this loaded cartridge. The amount of increase in size of the neck of the chamber should be exactly the same as the differ-ence between the out- side neck diameter of the old cartridge and of the new cartridge. This can usually be done by grinding a commercial hand reamer of slightly larger size to the correct size, grinding it on a slight taper and beveling the end at 45-degrees with clearance ground or stoned on the end of the flutes at the cutting edges. A commercial reamer of the correct size can sometimes be obtained and it is then only necessary to bevel the end and grind or stone the clearance on the ends of the flutes. These straight reamers have a slight taper at the end but it is more than is necessary so part of it should be stoned off. This taper at the end of the commercial straight reamers makes them smaller than their body size at this point so a reamer marked y. T for instance will not cut a J4" hole at the end so take this into consideration when picking a reamer to enlarge the neck of a chamber, as this end portion is the part of the reamer that will do the cutting in the neck of the chamber.

Chapter 20 POSTMORTEM

After careful consideration, we have decided that it will very likely be better to hold our own postmortem here and now, rather than have an autopsy surgeon do it for us later on.

The first thing to realize is that no one becomes an expert by reading a book. For instance, the dictionary contains all the words with full instructions for their use, yet few people would consider that study of the dictionary would make orators of them. Any art re- quires practice — which gives experience. I well remember that one of my early experiments resulted in the burying of a #6 1/2 primer three inches beneath the point of my collar-bone, where it still reposes, in peace, I hope. At any rate, the surgeon doubted his ability to follow with a scalpel the track of that primer past those large veins and arteries without touching them as the primer luckily had done, so he advised that it be left there. It gave me a chill to think what might have happened if that primer had chosen my eye for a path, rather than my chest.

Of late years there has been a revival of that urge to experiment with high velocities that so agitated Charles Newton in the early days of this century. As we have the advantage of better powders than New- ton had, we have been able to reach some undreamed-of velocities. These higher velocities have generally been reached by decreasing the bore and increasing the powder space. Both of these practices result in increased breech pressures which, if handled with care and proper steels, need have no bad results, but therein, for the experimenter, lies the catch, for very often he has neither the ability nor equipment himself to build a proper action of the correct steel to give him a margin of safety in his experiments. The result is that he fits a barrel chambered for some large cartridge, necked-down to his special caliber, to some existing action which someone gave him or which he picked up for a few dollars, and the results are often disastrous. I read of one case where a supposedly adult citizen rechambered his Stevens Favorite .22 rim-fire rifle for the Savage .22 Hi-power cartridge. Luckily he was able to display to a friend, who had more knowledge of rifles than he had, the pieces of the former Favorite and receive a well-earned lecture about monkeying with the buzz-saw.

There are several existing actions for rifles that, with a full knowledge on the experimenter's part of the forces he is handling, are safe for experimental use for high-power cartridges. The outstanding one of these is the model 1917 U. S. Army rifle, commonly known as the Enfield, or its counterpart, the Remington model 30 bolt-action. These actions are made of nickel-steel and have a very heavy receiver ring. This receiver ring is the weak spot of a bolt-action and for this reason I condemn, for experimental purposes, an action with any holes drilled through the receiver-ring, such as is often done for mounting telescopes, for this weak- ens the ring and the screws inserted in these holes do not replace the lost strength to the ring.

Yes, I know that the Winchester model 70 action has this receiver ring drilled and tapped at the factory for scope mounts, but Winchester does not sell this receiver for experimental purposes, they sell it, attached to a barrel of their own make, for cartridges loaded to standard pressures — for which it has ample strength and a wide safety-margin.

Some of the heavy-type single-shot actions are suit- able for experimental purposes with a rim-type cartridge case where pressures do not exceed 50,000 pounds per square inch. The outstanding action of this type is the Winchester heavy-type, high side wall, # 3 action, blued, not case-hardened. The latest actions of this make were of nickel-steel, and are marked (NS) on the receiver ring. The English Farquahrson action is a second one that is strong enough for this work and a third is the Stevens #44 action, but not the Stevens #044 1/2 , which is the light-weight English model and too light for the larger-bodied cartridges for use in experimental work. The fourth suitable single-shot action is the Sharps Borchardt and the last is the Remington Hepburn.

Some of these actions, in fact all of them except the nickel-steel, blued Winchester action, are case-hardened, a type of heat treatment we have been taught is unsafe. This is true to a certain extent, in that extremely deep case-hardening will make a piece of steel too brittle to withstand continued shock. The design of these single-shot actions listed, however, leaves no part of them thin enough for the case-hardening, of the type used on them, to penetrate completely through the steel, leaving them safe enough, as stated before, for pressures up to 50,000 pounds per square inch, provided proper head-space is maintained. Usually, in experimental work, there is no excess head-space, as the experimenter is dealing with cartridge cases he forms himself and they can, and should, be formed to fit the chamber exactly. Using a commercially-made cartridge in case-hardened actions comes under a different head, as these are made by various factories, or in different dies in the same factor}' quite often, and you will find a variation in their head-space measurements. A cartridge that fits the chamber exactly, gives the action one type of shock, and the cartridge with excessive head-space that allows it to take a running jump at the breech-block transmits a totally different type of shock to the action, besides allowing the cartridge case to stretch and sometimes reach the bursting point, and never forget that an action is only as strong as the cartridge case. When a cartridge case bursts and lets the pressure back into the action, no action we have will withstand it. These rimmed cases, which arc adapted to these single-shot actions, are all of more or less ancient design and do not have the strength of the modern cases such as the .220 Swift case.

The reason that the case-hardened Springfield actions have been condemned by most authorities for use with pressures of 50,000 pounds and more is that the receiver ring, where it is cut out for the bolt lug space, is very thin, and on many of these actions the case- hardening has penetrated entirely through the receiver ring at this point, making it glass-hard and very brittle. A case of excessive head-space on a rifle with a receiver ring as brittle as that will quickly result in a burst action. Drilling these receiver rings, for telescope sight mounts, further increases the danger of a burst action.

When the .220 Swift cartridge was introduced, a new set of complications was handed to the reloader. Old reloaders of many years' experience found their pressures running unaccountably high, often reaching 66,000 and 68,000 pounds per square inch. Careful checks showed that lengthening of the cartridge cases, by the brass flowing forward under high pressures, was sometimes crimping the mouth of the case upon the bullet, thus causing extreme pressures. These checks further showed that when the brass flowed forward it thickened the neck of the case, cutting down neck clearance in the chamber, another cause of rapid rise in pressure. It was further discovered that a change in the length and shape of the bullet nose made a difference in pressure. None of these troubles had appeared in larger cartridges using pressures approaching the .220 Swift standard pressures, at least to no appreciable extent. Reloaders found that these .220 Swift cartridges and others of later appearance of the same type, had to be checked for overall length from time to time, and be shortened at the mouth as they stretched, also to have the inside of their necks reamed to standard size as the brass in the necks thickened.

These examples show you that in experimental work involving high pressures, the cartridge case must be examined carefully after being fired, before being re- loaded. It should be carefully checked with a good micrometer caliper and the measurements checked against those of the unfired case. Heads of the fired cases should be thoroughly examined, both inside and out, in a good light with a high-power magnifying glass for cracks, for these will often be found, especially on the inside of the head, near the side wall of the case.

Actions used in firing this class of cartridge should also be taken apart and very carefully examined with a good glass from time to time to check them for cracks, especially the bolt lugs, and for signs of battering. Several of the Krag actions, in which the .22- 3000 cartridge has been used, have developed cracked bolt lugs and as the Krag has only one bolt lug to crack it is evident that this action should not be used for high-pressure work. Don't think that because a cartridge is small in size it cannot develop high pressures, for it can and usually does when a fine-grained powder is used in large charges.

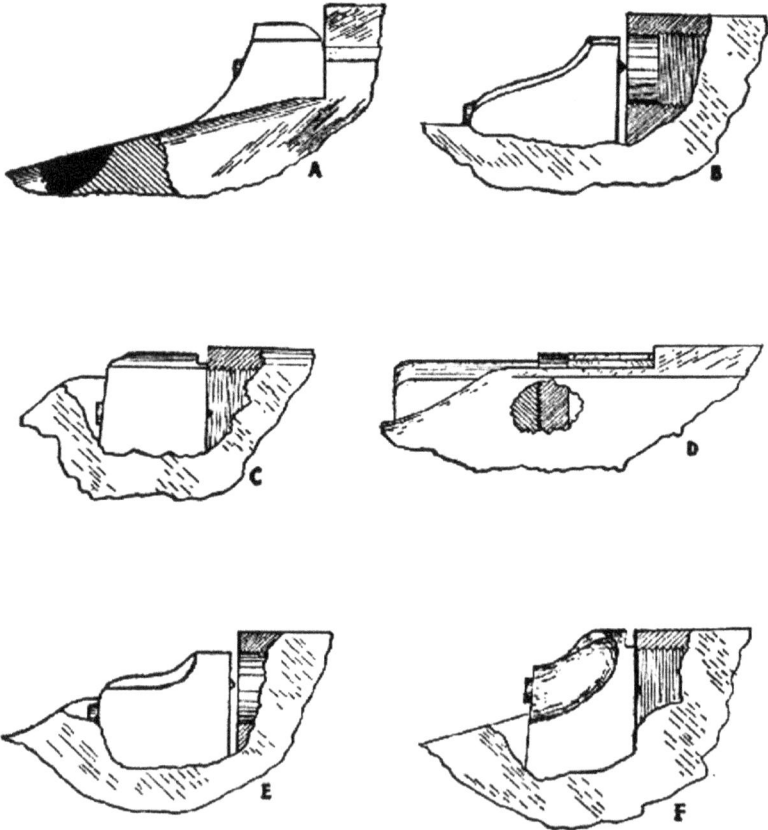

A Study of American Single-Shot Actions.

The amateur gunsmith should exercise considerable caution and study as to just what model and type of rifle action he utilizes, or modifies, to adapt for use with some more modem barrel or cartridge. Not every action readily procurable may be suitable for the purpose in mind — and a mistaken choice in this vital part of the arm can prove extremely serious, if not fatal. Above are shown sketches of the various single- shot actions available to American riflemen for remodeling into modern target and varmint rifles.

A is the old Ballard action, which has a vertically-split breech-block, pivoted at the front and swinging up in an arc to lock. Breech-block is supported 1 3/4 " behind end of barrel and 7/8" below barrel top when locked. The Ballard action has a forward camming movement as it locks and is thereby much liked by small-bore shooters for conversion into a 22 L R match rifle, for which cartridge it is well adapted, but it should never be used with modem cartridges of power greater than the 22 Hornet.

B is the old Stevens #44 action with a solid breech-block, pivoted at front and swinging up in an arc to lock. It is supported 1 1/8" be hind end of the barrel and at bottom edge of barrel when locked — and is not a very "tight" action. This model has been obsolete for more than a generation and is not a suitable action to convert for use with modern cartridges.

C is the Winchester high side wall #3 heavy action. Its solid breech-block slides vertically in grooves in the frame and when locked is supported 3/4" behind end of barrel, clear to the top of the chamber. This is the safest of all American single-shot actions to convert for use with modern, high-pressure cartridges.

D shows the Sharps Borcliardt, with its solid breech-block sliding vertically in grooves cut in the frame sides. It is a strictly hammerless action, using a firing-pin of the bolt type, surrounded by a coil spring. The block, when locked, is supported 1" behind the end of the barrel, clear to the top of die chamber. This is a powerful and safe action, much liked for conversion, but it is rather hard to obtain and is not often seen amongst shooters.

E. is the popular Stevens #44 1/2 action, having a solid breech-block sliding vertically in grooves cut in the sides of a very heavy frame. When locked, this block is supported 7/8" behind end of the barrel and 1/2" below its top. The hammer is set very low. at the bottom edge of the barrel, and the firing-pin passes through the breech-block at an upward angle - broken firing-pin noses are common with this action. When converted, it makes a handy, neat-looking job, hut it Is not as strong an action as the ti Winchester nor the Sharps Borchardt.

F. The Winchester light action has a solid breech-block sliding vertically in grooves cut in the frame sides. This block is supported 3/4" behind the end of the barrel and 1/2 " below its top, when locked. This is a handy-loading action, neat and well-liked for conversion to lightweight hunting rifles — but it should not be used with any but cartridges of moderate power.

The Remington Hepburn action is not shown — but it is one of the strongest of all. It is a solid block, vertically sliding action, operating in grooves cut into the sides of the frame. The breech-block, when locked, is supported v /i n behind end of barrel and clear to the top of die frame. The hammer is set low in the frame and firing-pin passes upward at an angle. However, this is a rebounding hammer, which does not support the firing-pin — thus making it unfit for very high pressure work unless the action is altered, removing this rebounding feature from the hammer. Another desirable alteration to make is to fit the action with an operating lever working underneath the trigger guard, because it is troublesome to extract stuck cases with the standard side-mounted, thumb-operated lever — and plenty of cases are apt to stick in this action use with high pressures or for use with any of our modern-type cartridges beyond the Hornet or the .25-20 single-shot Super Speed. The fact that the .22-3000 has cracked lugs off of Krag bolts shows that this cartridge is not safe for use in a Ballard action. There are two reasons for this, one of which is the two-part breech-block of the Ballard and the fact that it is not supported on the sides nor at the rear directly behind the barrel, as the Winchester high side wall action supports its breech-block. A pierced primer or a spread case head with high-pressure loads will allow gas to enter between the two sides of the breech-block, which may result in blowing the firing-pin entirely out of the breech-block and into the shooter's face. The second reason for condemning the Ballard action for high-pressure work is that many of these actions are made of Norway iron, which is much softer and lacks the strength of steel.

I consider the model 44 Stevens action unsafe with any cartridge of modern type, beyond the Hornet, as the breech-block is not well supported and the hammer fails to completely cover the rear end of the firing-pin, making possible the escape of gas to the shooter's face in case a primer is pierced in a high-pressure load.

In trying out new charges, or newly-formed cartridges, the rifle should not be used from the shoulder until a number of cases have been fired and carefully examined for signs of pressure and improper chambering. Glasses, of the type known as "Armor Plate" glass, should be worn in testing out various charges for accuracy in a new-type cartridge, so that in the event of gas or primer pieces flying to the rear the eyes are well protected.

Some years ago T had an experience with reduced charges in the .256 Newton rifle. The bullet used was an 87 grain and the powder charge was 18 grains of #80 duPont. When I first loaded these cartridges they shot very well and gave no trouble, but one box of these had remained unfired and had been moved around and shaken up considerably. I decided to fire them one day and upon firing the first one received a blast of oil in my eye, from around the firing-pin. I examined the fired case and found that the primer had been pierced. I was sure that there were no overloads in this box, the fired case showed no signs of pressure and as I had been firing high-power loads with the rifle steadily I knew the tiring-pin was all right. Well, to make a long story short, I fired five more of these loads, holding the rifle in my hands but not at my shoulder. This resulted in five more pierced primers, so I stopped shooting and came home with the balance of the loads unfired and proceeded to tear them down and investigate. I found nothing wrong at first, except that the loads ran a consistent amount light in powder charge, according to the weight marked on the box. As the amount they were short was very small, I thought nothing of it at first until I examined the powder more closely and found that it contained a rather large amount of fine stuff in it. As #80 is a soft-grained powder it breaks-down rather easily and it had done so in these loads because they had been moved about and shaken up considerably since being loaded. I still couldn't see that this would make high pressures in this large .256 Newton case in the small amount of 18 grains of powder and neither did the fired cases show signs of high pressure. A thought suddenly came to me, so I carefully pressed out an unfired primer from one of the emptied cases and found my answer to the pierced primers — each primer pocket, beneath the primer, was packed with dust-like #80 powder, setting up an extreme pressure directly against the primer when the cartridge was fired. Just a small thing, but it again taught me that nothing is too small to be neglected in connection with a firearm. The modern primers are very stiff and heavy, especially the Remington primer, and for this reason do not rely upon the appearance of the fired primer to judge pressures. This does not mean that you can neglect the appearance of the fired primer, for a study of it will show you a great deal. There are certain appearances of the fired primer that indicate high pressures; such as a sharp, square, or an overflowed edge, where the rear face of the primer meets the primer side wall; a raised rough ring around the firing-pin indentation, although this may only indicate an enlarged firing-pin hole in the breech face; or black streaks on the head of the case, radiating from the primer, although this may be caused by cartridge cases with too soft a head-anneal, allowing the head to spread slightly, enlarging the primer pocket. A primer partly raised above the level of the case head, after being fired, indicates excess head-space. Commercial primers vary quite a bit in weight, indicating uneven charges of priming mixtures, as the metal parts of the primer will vary practically nothing in weight. The Frankford Arsenal primers run very even in weight, giving very consistent ignition from shot to shot. They are, however, softer than the latest-type commercial primers, although the material out of which they are made is very tough.

Brass cartridge cases vary widely, between different makes, in thickness of brass, anneal and grain structure of the brass. The ideal brass case is one made of heavy, very fine-grained brass with a tough, springy anneal. The life of this type of case, under ordinary use, is almost unlimited and it is the ideal case for experimental work. All our commercial cartridge factories turn out very good cases and Frankford Arsenal does so at times, but none of them consistently give us the ideal case described above, so examine fired cases carefully in experimental work. Cases may be cut to determine brass thickness but should be broken to see the grain structure. Discard at once all cases of any certain make that show a coarse grain structure, for they are dangerous. If they are annealed to a point to leave them springy, they are very liable to break after very few reloadings. If they are annealed soft enough so there is little danger of breakage, they will stick badly in the chamber at pressures of 50,000 pounds or more per square inch and have the added danger of spreading heads, that will allow bad gas escapes around the primer besides dropping the primer from the case into the rifle action. There is always the chance of a few cases sticking in the annealing drum and going through the annealing process twice, which will leave them quite soft, but this does not often happen, so a soft case turning up now' and then is not reason enough to discard all cases of that make.

Beware of very tight chambers. They show no improvement in accuracy over the chambers used in the model 54 and model 70 Winchesters (which in my opinion are ideal) and they run up pressures very fast. A standard load used in them usually results in primer pockets spread enough to drop the primers and they give practically no increase in velocity. A fired case should show at least .002" expansion all over, above the size of the unfired case. On the other hand look out for the over-large chamber. A fired case that shows an expansion of .008" to .010" at the rear of the body, just where it joins the solid head, indicates a chamber far too large, although in isolated cases this may be due to an undersized cartridge case, which is liable to happen once in a while in a caliber that is not universally made, of which there are several, such as some of the 6.5 m/m calibers.

Be very careful in using Newton rifles with which you are not familiar, as many of these have been carelessly fitted-up by inferior mechanics and often have a great deal of excess head-space in the chamber. I have seen a .256 Newton with .027" excess head-space and only recently repaired a .30 Newton having .025" excess head-space.

Before using one of the many models of Newton rifles, either examine a fired cartridge case from the rifle or place a new cartridge within the chamber and then cut shims of brass or thin steel and place these upon the head of the cartridge within the chamber until the bolt closes with some effort upon the cartridge and the shims. You may then remove the shims, measure their thickness with a micrometer caliper and thus determine the excess head-space, if any. If it exceeds .008" do not fire the rifle.

If a cartridge case is available that has been fired in the rifle, carefully compare it with a new, unfired cartridge. If excess head-space is present in the cham- ber the distance from the head of the fired case to the shoulder will considerably exceed that same distance on the new, unfired cartridge, also the body of the fired case will be greatly expanded near the rear end, just ahead of the solid head. This is caused by the car- tridge backing up in the chamber upon being fired and as the chamber is tapered, being larger toward the rear, the farther to the rear the case moves in firing the larger the body will expand. This body expansion may occur from a large-diameter chamber which has no excess head-space, but this condition is almost as bad as excess head-space.

Recently I was asked to remove excess head-space from a .30 Newton rifle which has .025" excess. As no .30 Newton chambering reamer was available, the shoulder of the barrel which butts against the front of the receiver was cut back .022". The barrel was then screwed tightly into the receiver and the new position for the extractor slot was marked on the rear of the barrel. The barrel was then removed and the new extractor slot cut. The sights had previously been removed from the barrel, the rear one being an open sight set in a dovetail slot and the front one being a blade sight set in a band encircling the barrel at the muzzle, but separate from it. The old dovetail slot in the barrel for the rear sight was filled with a tight steel block which was filed and polished down to the barrel contour, then a slot was cut for the sight in its new position. The band for the front sight was re- placed on the barrel in the new position, fastened there and the barrel was reblued and replaced in the receiver.

The shape of the cartridge case has a great deal to do with what breech pressure a load develops. A case with very slightly tapering sides, such as our .30'06, with a sharp, short taper at the shoulder from body to neck, causes turbulence of the gases, upon firing, on account of the gases striking this sharply- tapered shoulder and turning back upon themselves. This turbulence increases the speed of burning and thereby increases the breech pressures. When a case of this type is necked-down, following the original sharp shoulder taper, to a smaller caliber, without changing the body taper, we have a very rapid rise in breech pressure, for the turbulence is increased. When Donaldson necked-down the Krag case to .22 caliber, to produce the .220 Donaldson Krag, he increased the taper of the body of the case, decreased the diameter of the case at the shoulder and decreased the taper of the shoulder from the body to the neck, thus easing the passage of the gases to the neck. This resulted in .220 Swift velocities with decreased pressure, because the turbulence was reduced.

The .280 Ross case has a large powder capacity and you will note that it has quite a steep body taper. This had two objects, it decreased turbulence of powder gases, and thereby reduced breech pressure, and it also gave easier extraction than with a straighter case. The .257 Roberts cases, as custom made, had a long, easy shoulder taper which was replaced with a shorter, more steeply tapered shoulder by Remington when they began manufacture of this cartridge. While making this shoulder steeper in taper raised breech pressures somewhat, it corrected one fault the original cartridge had. This long, easy-tapered shoulder on the original cases directed the powder gases against the throat of the rifle bore, beyond the neck of the cases, whereas the steeper tapered shoulder directed these powder gases against the inside of the cartridge case neck. This probably reduced throat erosion somewhat. The second result of shortening this shoulder and making its taper steeper, was to give much longer life to the dies which produced the cartridge case, which would be an important point in manufacture.

When a large-bodied cartridge case, or any cartridge case for that matter, is necked-down to a smaller caliber, the powder must be changed from that previously used in the case, to get the best results. The change should always be to a coarser, slower-burning powder, for turbulence will be increased by the decreased neck diameter of the case, raising the burning speed of the powder. This condition calls for a slower burning powder, which in turn allows us to use a heavier charge, resulting in increased velocity. If a cartridge case using a more or less modern type of powder is necked- down to a smaller caliber, it is unsafe to use the same powder in the same weight charge that was previously used, for pressures would run dangerously high.

Primer flash-holes, in cases that have been fired and reloaded a number of times, become enlarged by the primer flash. This has two results, it raises breech pressure by igniting the charge faster, causing faster burning within the case, and it allows more pressure from the charge to

Plate XXIV

Method of taking measurements of a rifle cartridge for body taper, by use of a protractor. The blade of the protractor is held upright in a smooth jaw vise, with the base of the protractor head on the upper side and the head clamped to the blade. The angular adjustment of the head is left loose and the cartridge to be measured for body taper is set head down upon the base of the protractor head. The protractor head is then angled until the edge of the blade contacts the full length of the body portion of the case being measured for taper. This taper, in degrees, is then read off of the protractor scale. This will be the angle with the center line or one-half the included angle made by the tapered sides of the cartridge body.

A sensitive balance has many more uses to the experimenter and target shot, doing his own reloading, than merely to weigh powder charges. In critical work, bullets should be weighed and separated into groups having the same weight, cases should also be weighed and separated into groups of like weight as variation in case weight means variation in capacity, which results in erratic pressures and velocities. An important point often overlooked is the weighing of primers. As stated earlier in this chapter, commercial primers vary quite a bit in weight and this is due to differing amounts of priming charge, which causes a difference in the length and size of the primer flash, which in turn gives a variation in ignition. '

Bullets, besides being weighed, should be measured for diameter and separated into like groups, and for target purposes should be, tested for concentricity, all nonconcentric bullets being discarded.

Cases should be measured for thickness of brass in the necks all around, as case necks that are thick on one side and thin on the other results in bullets being seated out of line with the body of the case, which may result in poor accuracy.

A careful study of a good book on reloading, such as Naramore's "Handloaders Manual," should be made in preparing loads for cartridges, especially cartridges of the "home brew" type made by re-forming some existing cartridge. This volume of Naramore's is the best book of this type for the beginner that I have ever seen, for it teaches him fundamentals, but the old handloader can learn considerable from it also.

We have cautioned you in this chapter about handling high-powers, suggesting the proper actions, etc., and these actions arc the ones to be used, but they must be in good condition , don't forget that point. A badly-battered, old action, with loose-fitting pins should be shunned, for it may have enough looseness so that it cannot hold proper head-space. No 22 or 25 rim- fire action should ever be used for any kind of a high-power cartridge.

The .22 rim-fire high-speed cartridges should also be handled cautiously, in regard to rifles in which they are used. The older type of .22 rim-fire cartridge gave only half as much pressure as the high- speed variety and there are many old .22 rifles floating around that were not strong enough when they were new to handle the .22 high-speed cartridge. Makers were more careless about length and shape of firing-pins years ago, when making rifles for the .22 rim-fire cartridges, and while the brass cases used on most .22 high-speed cartridges today are stiffer and stronger than the old copper cases were, these brass cases are more brittle so that when not properly supported by a close-fitting chamber and breech-block they are liable to split, or when struck by some of those old firing-pins mentioned the rim may break, letting gas of 20,000 pounds or more pressure back into the action, which may blow an extractor, firing-pin or hammer into the shooter's face, endangering his eye- sight and even his life. Hence, I am warning you again, be careful of these old klucks and how you graft new barrels on them for higher-power cartridges than they were designed for, because it will usually result in grief to someone

The End